Media and Awards

"A bundle of ideas." —*Wall Street Journal*

"A sharp-elbowed New Yorker." —*NBC News*

"Hilarious and candid." —*BookBub*

"Gloria puts into words what's in our heads at 4 a.m." —*Reader review*

Amazon #1 Bestseller

Indie Book Cover Award —*TopShelf*

C'mon Funk, Move Your Ass

THE C'MON FUNK SERIES

Book 2

C'mon Funk, Move Your Ass:
How a Demure Little Wife
Made Her Husband a Big City Mayor

C'MON FUNK, MOVE YOUR ASS

How a Demure Little Wife
Made Her Husband a Big City Mayor

GLORIA SQUITIRO

GSP
BOOKS

Also by Gloria Squitiro

THE C'MON FUNK SERIES
Book 1

May Cause Drowsiness and Blurred Vision:
The Side Effects of Bravery

and

How to Become Unintentionally
Published in Harper's

ISBNs: 978-1-7327216-7-8 (print), 978-1-7327216-6-1 (ebook)

This book is a memoir. It reflects the author's present recollection of experiences over time. Some events have been compressed and some dialogue has been recreated. All dates are approximate.

The views expressed are solely those of the author. In "speaking her truth," she frankly describes her unique perspectives and experiences. She respects and honors all the individuals presented in the narrative. If any of them perceive her insights or revelations as hurtful, she apologizes. The author intends no malice or unkindness.

Print page design by Greta Sibley (gretasibley.com)
Editing by Jean Zimmer and Andy Reed
Cover art, interior sparkles, and e-book page design by Ian Koviak (bookdesigners.com)

Some photos are reprinted courtesy of Sabrina Staires. Other photos were provided by photographers whose identities are unknown to me. I regret that I am unable to provide credits for them.

Gloria Squitiro Publishing, LLC

Library of Congress Control Number: 2022914710

Publisher's Cataloging-in-Publication Data
Names: Squitiro, Gloria, author.
Title: C'mon Funk, move your ass : how a demure little wife made her husband a big city mayor / Gloria Squitiro.
Description: Washington, DC : Gloria Squitiro Publishing, 2023. | Series: C'mon Funk, bk. 2.
Identifiers: ISBN 978-1-7327216-7-8 (paperback) | ISBN 978-1-7327216-6-1 (ebook)
Subjects: LCSH: Wives--Biography. | Women--Biography. | Feminism. | Mayors--Election. | Kansas City (Mo.)--Biography. | United States--Politics and government. | Autobiography. | BISAC: BIOGRAPHY & AUTOBIOGRAPHY / Women. | BIOGRAPHY & AUTOBIOGRAPHY / Personal Memoirs. | BIOGRAPHY & AUTOBIOGRAPHY / Political. Classification: LCC HQ1123 .S78 2022 (print) | LCC HQ1123 (ebook) | DDC 920.72--dc23.

For information about this title or to order other books or electronic media, please contact the publisher: Gloria Squitiro Publishing, LLC (gloriasquitiro.com) at info@gloriasquitiro.com

Printed in the United States of America

DEDICATION

In memory of my brother Robert. When I was little and afraid, it was your bed that I crawled into at night. Thank you for always lifting the covers.

And as ever, to my beautiful sister, Jane. I miss you more than words can tell.

CONTENTS

PROLOGUE

I GREW UP IN A REALLY WEIRD HOUSE.

I came into this world knowing things. I don't know how I knew, only that I did. This didn't go over so well in my New York Italian home. Girls in my family didn't get to have a voice, and they certainly didn't *know* things. Only special people knew things. Special, meaning males.

It has taken me a lifetime of therapy to untangle my childhood. To overcome my superstitions. To release my anxiety born from not being heard. To cope with insecurities from unmet emotional needs. To free myself of self-doubt.

My earliest memory of rejecting intuition dated back to when I was two years old. Our family doctor came to the house to remove my newborn brother's shriveled-up umbilical cord. I had been so scared of that thing. When the doctor left, something told me I shouldn't look in the trash can. Yet, already doubting my gut, I looked. And there was the cord, back to frighten me.

When I was around four or five, I began sensing spirits hanging about. The only way I can describe what that felt like is to say that it's just like the sensation you get when you know someone is staring at you.

My parents believed ghosts could control people. On the one hand, the idea of ghosts terrified them, but on the other, they revered people who could see them. My Uncle Carl was one of those people. Not me. Because what little girl could be powerful or special? It was clear to me from an early age that my questions and my fears scared my mother, so I never brought up that I could sense presences. So it was that I suffered the spirits alone.

Returning from the bathroom one night, I saw a man standing against the back wall of my bedroom. I was so terrified I couldn't scream. When my voice finally returned, the sound was so bloodcurdling that my father was instantly at my side, searching for the intruder. No one was there. And he didn't get mad, which was strange, because he usually popped off in a rage whenever disturbed.

Seeing that spirit was one of the biggest reasons I was afraid every moment of every day. I was terrified of going to sleep and even more terrified of waking in the dark. When I roused, I'd implore myself to keep my eyes closed. But sensing someone there, I couldn't resist. Making a deal with myself, I promised I'd crack an eye and only look at my mattress. Which didn't help, for there on my bed were all sorts of creepy things — like dried-up animal bones — scattered about me.

That's when the story of the cherry man came to life. My little brother San and I shared a bedroom for ten years. Just outside our window stood a cherry tree. Every time the wind blew, the branches would scratch at our window and scare the shit out of us. Using this to my advantage, I told San that as soon as he fell asleep, a cherry man jumped down from the tree and danced a little jig on our windowsill. I even outfitted the guy with a top hat and cane, hoping the show would be exciting enough that San would stay up waiting for it to begin. Because if he was awake, then I could go to sleep, knowing there was a sentry on duty, unknowingly on the lookout for ghosts. That didn't work either. I was only five, which means he was only three, and what three-year-old could stay up all night?

I remember thinking when I turned ten, I wouldn't be afraid anymore. I was. To soothe myself, I started planning my escape from the house of torture. I imagined being Cinderella, married to Prince Charming. But instead of Prince Charming, God gave me Funk, a six-foot-eight hick from West Vagina. He was nine years older than me, a professor at the college I attended. After he deciphered one of my dreams, I was taken with him. Once he snagged me, we moved to Nashville, Tennessee. Soon after, my childhood girlfriend died. Laurie was nineteen and her death sent me into a debilitating, four-year bout of anxiety. I ran through six different therapists before finding one who knew how to help. Ed said I had to find my voice. Let out all the things I wasn't allowed to express as a child. Poor Funk suffered through my unleashing of twenty-four years' worth of pent-up thoughts.

Now I was still anxious, but not like before. To learn how to resolve arguments, Funk and I returned to therapy for couples counseling. Before long, I was solid enough in myself, and Funk and I were solid enough in our marriage, and we felt it was safe to bring children into the world. I gave birth to Tara and Andrew via unnecessary cesarean sections.

My C-sections motivated me to start my business, BirthWays, which focused on stopping the medical establishment from slicing women open for no good reason other than to add another trinket to some doctor's already-swollen pocket. The business was a success. At a time when the cesarean rate had risen past 20 percent, the rate for my students was what you'd expect from nature, around 5 percent.

THE NEW AND BETTER ME

I HAD ANOTHER BOUT OF ANXIETY in 2004, not as debilitating as the first one but not so good either. It came at the start of my "empty nest" phase, probably because raising my children had been the most fun time in my life.

Since we now were living in Kansas City, I had to find a different therapist. Shelley helped get me back on my feet. I decided to stick with counseling and continue evolving. I wanted to overcome the rest of my fears. Find my strength, my power, my purpose. A connection. To reach for my dreams and live the bigger, more carefree life I knew I was meant to live. I told Shells about visions I have whenever things get rough, in which I unwillingly zoom off to a place that looks like a horrible sea of black muck. Whenever I disassociate from myself, I find myself standing in this place of fear.

I was still afraid to fly in a plane, and I felt safer at home than anywhere else, but eventually I grew tired of living a condensed life. In 2006 I decided to "reach for brave" and go after my dream of living in Europe for a summer. The problems that brought on were threefold. One: I was a homebody. Two: how would I get there? And three: where would the money come from?

Not one to let logistics get in my way, I tackled the money issue first. Which meant I had to fulfill yet another one of Funk's dreams so I could achieve mine. My husband was yearning to write a book that required researching audit shops around the world. Good wife that I am, I helped him win a grant to fund that desire. And good mother that I am, I told him the kids and I would accompany him and that we'd be bringing our "cosmic" children, Nick and Alex, along.

As for my fear of flying, I decided not to push it, so we traveled by ship, the *Queen Mary II*, and navigated the Atlantic Ocean from New York to England.

By far the most difficult logistic to overcome was my fear of leaving home. All I could think to do for that was to perform a ritual in my backyard where I prayed for strength and courage. While I was at it, I asked the gods to please help me grow up. Told them I was done living in a fetal position. It worked. I stepped off the ship well on the way to becoming the New and Better Me.

But cures don't happen as fast in real life as they do in the movies, and what kind of bullshit is that? Sometimes when you commit to change, spirit tests to see if you're really serious. I had work left to do. The most significant was to return to my knowing, to replace self-doubt with a hefty dose of confidence — a challenge I've been working on ever since.

That said, I'm not filled with doubt when I'm making dreams come true for others. When Funk asked if I'd set up his campaign headquarters to run for mayor — something he said would take a day, a week at best, to find and furnish — I threw myself in without flinching. I had no idea that my ability to "just know things" would come in handy.

C'mon Funk, Move Your Ass

Our Little Secret

FUNK WAS GOING TO KILL ME.

Each day before leaving for work he never failed to drum it into my head that no one except our children could learn our secret for another two months. I'd honored his request. Until now, that is. Spring was the first person I had told that Funk was running for mayor. But I had to. What other possible reason could I have given her for needing the space? Believe me, I was not going to lie to my friend. Funk needed to chill. Spring was as honest and loyal as I am. The woman could be trusted.

Pulling out of her parking lot, I dialed my man.

"Hey babe, I have a surprise for you."

"You found me a place?"

"Yes, but since you ruined it, I'm not telling you anything else until dinner."

The wait would've killed me. It didn't faze him.

"Okay, Beautiful. See you at five-thirty."

What a bastard.

Later that night, flanked by my husband and son at the dinner table, I explained the weird way it had come to me to use Spring's double-wide trailer for Funk's headquarters. I don't know why I bothered with that part, as neither believed in signs, and this was surely a sign. But they perked up, or at least they stopped rolling their eyes, when I told them the rest of the story. How absolutely perfect it was. It had a reception area, and we could turn the treatment rooms into offices. It even came with his-and-her bathrooms and a kitchen! I described every little detail as it related to the interior, and also the part about telling Spring the real reason for renting it.

But I saved that part for last, after Funk was giddy with excitement. Well, giddy for him.

He hit the fucking roof. Rose out of his chair, fists balled up on the table, bottom lip exploding out of his face, spit flying everywhere.

"Gloria!"

Not letting his emotion scare me, I took a moment before responding.

"Yes, Funk."

"I asked for your help, but I have to be able to trust you."

Gathering my husband off the ceiling, I said, "Yeah, Funk. You do."

I waited for his lip to retreat to its normal position before imparting the even more fascinating points about the space — points that were unbelievably serendipitous to him and his campaign. Once I did, he saw what I saw.

"You're right, Glor. It's perfect. Are you certain Spring won't say anything?"

"Funk. She's Asian, we can trust her."

Low cost aside, the symbolism of the double-wide was incredible. All by itself, it sent a message, especially to voters who didn't know about my husband's job at city hall.

Funk had been the city auditor for going on eighteen years. And while most Americans seemed to have a big hate going for government employees, Funk was popular. He'd been all over the news for years. Still, not everyone in Kansas City could have known the man. Folks like me glaze over when they hear government talk. Funk and I knew that once the election campaign got underway, everyone would be paying more attention. And that was the amazing thing about of Spring's offer of a discount-price rental. Just by sitting ungracefully on its little plot of land, the double-wide spoke volumes about Funk and his values. All by itself, the trailer made clear how he'd administer the city as its mayor. It showed that Funk was a man who could think outside the box — he was a visionary who was frugal yet effective. And perhaps, just perhaps, having the nerve to place his headquarters inside a metal box would even make him seem like a fun guy. I can't believe I just said that. Funk, fun? But that was the point. Without having to restructure his personality, the trailer lightened up this purposeful dude.

The location was emblematic too. Without using words, it spoke to his belief that to bring a city back from the dead you had to restore its urban core, and not only by repairing and replacing infrastructure. To institute a lasting comeback in Kansas City, people, beginning with him, needed to live and work downtown again.

The double-wide was the perfect advertisement. No selling of Funk would be necessary. This was a most fortuitous point, since the campaign didn't have a dime except for what our family had fronted it. Until he quit his job at city hall on November 17, Funk's candidacy had to stay under the radar. Therefore, unlike the other candidates, no one had yet backed him — meaning, there was no money to commission a commercial or buy ad time. Even this was a symbol: Funk wasn't the type to spend ridiculous sums of money on ads whose only purpose was to shove untruths down viewers' throats.

Not that Funk would speak untruths, even if he had the money. The trailer expressed his truth. All by its bedraggled little self, it showed that Funk walked his talk. There would be no wastefulness with this guy, nothing showy. He didn't need a building or highway named after him, like every other mayor in this town. All he hoped to achieve was positive outcomes.

Over coffee the next morning, Funk gently commanded, "Glor, I understand that you had to tell Spring, but no one else, okay?"

"Jesus, Funk, enough already. I got it. Besides, who else would I tell? All I have left to do is have the lights turned on and the internet set up. Oh, and

I guess you'll need a phone. And some furniture. A desk, a chair, and a place for visitors to sit. Oh, shit. We'll have to buy a few computers and a printer. Office supplies. And your announcement party still needs to be arranged, and. . . ."

Feeling suddenly overwhelmed, I stopped ticking off items that hadn't been on my to-do list and said, "Oh, brother, I thought I was almost done with your stuff and could get back to my own life."

"Glor, there is one other thing."

Dropping my empty coffee cup into my lap, I yelped, "Funk, I'm already doing everything but wiping your frigging ass! What now?"

The man has no shame. Just gave me direction as if I were his assistant.

"Order two more copies of *The Campaign Manager*. Get one over to Jeff Simon and read the other one yourself."

"Why the hell would I read that boring shit?"

"So you'll know what I'm doing and can give me informed advice."

"Listen, Funk. I've helped you earn a couple of master's degrees and your PhD — I should have a byline on your dissertation for all the work I did for it — not to mention your thousand and one certifications *and* the grant for your book. Why would I want someone else's opinion when I've got my own? Don't worry, you'll get plenty of advice from me. This campaign is your thing, Funk. I'll finish setting up a headquarters as I promised, but then I'm outta there."

Days later, at the cozy gym in Westport, I strode atop the stair-climber, reading through the stupid *Campaign Manager*. It took quite the gymnastics too, what with me having to hide the book jacket while pedaling the machine so Funk wouldn't come unglued again.

At least the book was well done. Plenty of information there. According to the author, Catherine Shaw, all it takes to run a political campaign is planning and organizing and the ability to give commands and dole out advice. Things every competent mother is good at. And here I was, for all these years I'd been thinking the position was something big.

Funk wanted Jeff Simon, his friend and colleague, to be his campaign manager. I had met him only a few times, but to me he seemed more blow than anything else. Now that I was deep into the book, I sure hoped Jeff knew how to multitask.

21 SEPTEMBER 2006

IT WAS THE TWENTY-NINTH ANNIVERSARY of our first kiss. If someone had given me a heads-up way back when that I'd be devoting my life to Funk, I would have run the other way while I still had the chance. What happened to his unromantic declaration, "Stick with me, babe, and you'll be farting through silk"? Dozens of years after those all-too-sincere words were spoken, here I was, on the verge of an empty nest, and instead of returning to my own dreams and ambitions I was digging deeper into his, with silk nowhere in my foreseeable future.

I made it to the double-wide in time for my eight-a.m. appointment. Bored, I paced inside the grubby trailer, awaiting a Kansas City Power and Light technician, who was late. I had to change the account into my name. I asked myself again why I was taking such a risk to help Funk pursue his dream. He wanted to continue babysitting the city council for a few years longer so he could rest easier at night, knowing there was someone at city hall serving citizens. Was this something I cared enough about to risk my family's savings on?

Before I had left home that morning, Funk had implored me not to put any business accounts in his name until he quit his job. As if the electric company would give two shits that someone else was setting up a campaign. What, the technician was gonna race back to his truck and dial a tip line? "*Woo-woo*, news flash, the city auditor is running for mayor!" Nobody cared! That said, since I had agreed to the task and since I don't talk shit, I did it Mr. Does-it-by-the-book's way.

Please let the record show that when we married, Funk-the-feminist *wouldn't allow me* to take his name. I was devastated, as all I had ever wanted to be was a wife and mother. I was barely twenty-one when that edict came down, and I hadn't yet learned I had a voice. Hoo-boy, do I ever excel in that field today. If you don't believe me, ask Funk.

Everything works out in the end. Fast forward twenty-something years, and now I'd slit my wrists if I had given up my beautiful Italian name, Squitiro, for his ugly German one, Funkhouser. Can you imagine? Not only that, but sometimes, like that day, it really came in handy having two names to choose from.

As soon as the technician left, I zoomed over to Office Depot. Back at the trailer in a heartbeat, I hauled a vanload of boxes up the driftwood steps and over the buckled-up carpet, mindful not to trip. I'd sprained my ankle three times and didn't want a repeat performance, because man, that really hurt.

I turned one of the treatment rooms in the back into the supply room, and before long I had organized the shelves to perfection. Then, although it skived me, I sat down on the musty carpet and started reading the instructions for the items that needed put together. I was in the middle of assembling the first chair when Funk did something he rarely does. He stopped by to bring me a cup of coffee. I think it was really to check my progress. My husband had a nasty habit of pretending not to be breathing down my neck when that's exactly what he was doing. This got on my nerves to no end. Because if you never ask for help, you get to walk through life appearing the martyr for seemingly doing everything for yourself. Me, I'm always asking for things, which is why I live in a perpetual state of guilt. Him? Not him. Why would he feel guilty when he's always handed things he didn't ask for, yet just happened to want?

For some reason, his repugnant personality didn't bother me as much that day, probably because it was his first time seeing the trailer. And while the emotion is unusual for him, the man was excited. I didn't understand what there was to be so excited about, but seeing him like that put butterflies in my heart. So many that I made him stand behind the reception desk to snap a picture of him. Hey, you've got to record momentous occasions when they happen.

His happiness was endearing. He strolled around the double-wide openly marveling at everything — another rare emotion — and kept going on about how I'd chosen the perfect space. About how quickly everything was coming together and how it felt like home. So thrilled was my man that he placed the tablecloth I had brought from home down on the yucky floor, picnic-style, and using ourselves as the entrée, we toasted the headquarters on the spot. But only a quickie, as my man needed to get back to work.

I sent him on his way with one last kiss and went back to assembling the chair. But first, I took a look around the joint. To me, I hadn't done anything out of the ordinary. I'm a homebody, and homebodies make homes for ourselves wherever we go. Still, it was true — in one morning, I had made the place cute — at least, as cute as a brokedown trailer could be.

Each area now had a new function, with a touch of loveliness added here and there. I turned the space just inside the front door into the lobby, the focal point being an extra-long folding table I had purchased at an estate sale years earlier for $15. It had seated hordes of guests at our Thanksgiving dinners and it doubled as a buffet table at other gatherings. I chose one of my more elegant tablecloths to top it, and unfortunately, I had to bring that home for laundering. But soon it would be sitting pretty again, the showcase for Funk's campaign material, should he be able to afford to have any. For the time being, I graced it with a few of his city audit reports. Later, I'd add some buttons and sign-up forms for volunteers.

I wanted the public spaces to be sparse and inviting, so I designated the office farthest back to be used for storage of bulky, ugly items such as yard signs — again, should Funk be able to afford them. The office supply room was back there too, as well as most of the volunteer offices.

The offices had once been used for treating Spring's acupuncture patients, and their built-in cabinets were a blessing. Funk didn't have to purchase shelving, and the cabinet doors helped keep things looking tidy.

I couldn't do much to make the restrooms appealing, but I was grateful there were two. Should I decide to drop in on Funk once his campaign was underway, at least I wouldn't have to stand in a puddle of man-pee. I hated that. I chose the one closest to the entrance for the women's room. Such are the perks of being the person who is setting things up. C'mon, if you can't find happiness in the little things, you're screwed.

The room across from the reception desk was the most private, so I put Funk's office there and assigned the one next to it to Jeff Simon, who didn't know yet he was Funk's campaign manager. I didn't organize Jeff's office, but I made my husband's really nice. It was conducive to talk yet allowed him to gaze out the window the way he likes to. I almost hung a bunch of pictures, but in the end I left the walls bare. If Simon read his copy of *The Campaign Manager*, he'd know to tape the election timeline around the room.

Now that I'd seen the trailer through my husband's eyes, I was happy with my effort. Plopping my ass down on the carpet, I went back to building the chair.

Just as I was about to leave to pick up my son Andrew from school, I noticed I needed to vacuum the floor again. I had vacuumed it just the day before, but now it was riddled with tiny specks of Styrofoam packing material from the chair. That stuff is maddening. You can't flick it from your fingers to throw it away. So, despite the late hour, I got out the Hoover and flew through the place until it sparkled again. Okay, it didn't quite sparkle, but it was as clean as I could get it.

Looking around, I envisioned the place filled with volunteers cheerfully at work and believing in Funk's dream, their shared dream. Smiling, I raced to get Andrew and then home to have dinner on the table by five-thirty.

24 SEPTEMBER 2006

MY FIRST THOUGHT when I woke in the morning was that I had to stop kidding myself. When I started on Funk's project, I thought I'd be done with it in a flash. But now that I was this far into it, I understood that setting up a campaign was a major involvement. So, yeah, it looked like I'd be helping for a tiny bit longer, since Funk still needed a lot of help to get ready for opening day.

I was running myself ragged. It wasn't as if I could stop my life and focus solely on Funk's. I still had my own responsibilities to manage. It was taking everything I had to keep up with the household chores, mother my children and the stray children we'd taken in, teach in the evenings, and be on call for births. This husband of mine sure knew how to sway things around to his side.

To keep up the pace, it was imperative that I remained scheduled and organized. Once I got Andrew off to school, I went straight up to my office to pay the next month's bills. I went down to the kitchen to chop vegetables for dinner and then tidied the house. I despised coming home in the afternoon to a messy house and rushing to get meals on the table.

I was almost out the door when I had to go back inside for a phone call: A first-time mom, discomfited by pain, couldn't accept that she wasn't in labor, only pre-labor, which meant I was on the phone forever. But since it's my mission to save women from unnecessary cesarean sections, I gave her the time it took to make her feel safe and strong and heard.

I began my errands. First on my list was a stop at the Apple Store. I had just enough leeway to make Funk's purchases and still be on time to pick up Andrew from school. My son hated it when I was late. He was a senior at Lincoln High, which was located in downtown Kansas City. We wouldn't let him drive his Vespa scooter on the highway, which was why I was still on car duty. But I didn't mind picking him up. Not really. Being a mom has been the best part of my life, and I knew that role would be coming to an end all too soon.

I lingered at Apple a little too long, scrutinizing prices on behalf of Mr. Cheapola. If I didn't get the best value for the money I knew I'd be back a second time, returning and repurchasing. Might as well get it right from the beginning.

I hurried the purchases over to the headquarters. Lifting two computers and a printer from the trunk, I lugged them one by one up the brittle steps, over the buckled-up carpet, and into the supply room. After I had neatly stacked the purchases, I zoomed over to get Andrew. In the few short weeks I'd been helping Funk, I had picked up one of Kansas City's worst habits. But instead of being a drive-by shooter, I'd become a drive-by mother.

Peeling into the parking lot, I rolled down my window and yelled over to my son.

"Ange! Quick, get in."

Standing in a crowd of his friends, he tossed me a vile look.

"C'mon, Andrew. We've got to *go*!"

Not wanting further words in front of his buddies, he snapped to.

I thought he'd jump into the back to get away from me, but surprisingly, he chose the passenger seat, where I received, "I hate you, Mom. You're so embarrassing."

"No, you don't, Andrew, and that's not a nice thing to say."

"What's the fucking rush?"

"I need you to set up Dad's computers."

"Maaahm! I just got out of school! I'm tired. I'm hungry. I want to go home."

"I'm sorry, Andrew, but it would take me a million years just to read the instructions, and you can have everything set up in a snap. Besides, you don't do anything at school anyway, so what do you have to be tired about?"

Many hours later, the printer was spitting out copies next to the reception desk and the computers hummed away in selected offices. Everything looked as pretty as could be. Shiny and new, the machines glowed with anticipation. I was only coming at my husband's campaign from the standpoint of a loyal wife — helping him make his vision a reality — but boy, were things ever getting exciting. As exciting as starting a new business. All the dreams and all the possibilities were rolled into this worn-out trailer.

25 SEPTEMBER 2006

IT SEEMED LIKE AGES AGO that Funk and I had decided he'd run for mayor, yet it had happened only five months earlier while we sat on a park bench outside a carwash. I still felt unsettled by the decision, but I suppose that was a normal reaction to something so big.

One thing I made clear from the beginning was that Funk wouldn't be running a typical campaign. I didn't want a bad reflection on our family, especially not on our children. There'd be no hustling people for money and no scheming for votes. Not that my guy could do either. He's not Italian. He doesn't have the capacity. And the crazy thing is, I didn't feel bad for making the demand because I didn't view it as something that would set him up for failure.

My thinking was, if the residents who'd been intrigued by his success as the city auditor really wanted the substantial changes they'd been calling for, they'd contribute to his campaign without being asked. No one needed to shake them down for donations or deceive them into voting for him. No tricks would be necessary. No overreaching promises were needed. Besides, if Funk had to be underhanded to get elected, who needed it? Not him. Certainly not his family. Even more important, who would take a $75,000 yearly cut in pay just to be called mayor?

Well, I'm sure many in this town would.

But Funk was not a traditional candidate. He just wanted to fix the city. He already had the only title he'd ever wanted: husband and father. If people didn't like what he had to offer, he figured, they could vote for someone else. A slew of candidates were vying to be the next "pretty face" for the city. Plenty of them would be happy to carry on the traditions in this town. Plenty would allow the established few to line their pockets at the cost of the poor and middle class. Plenty would have no problem looking the other way as black people kept killing each other. Plenty didn't give two shits if residents kept jumping the border for Kansas. Plenty would keep this a tired old city. If residents preferred things to remain the same or if they'd rather not suffer the turbulence that came with big change, they could choose one of those candidates.

Funk totally agreed with me. We were opposites in almost every imaginable way but not in our values.

30 SEPTEMBER 2006

TARA HADN'T BEEN BACK AT COLLEGE for a month yet, but I'd been missing her so badly that I offered to fly her home for the weekend, and she said yes. She arrived late on a Friday evening, and the next morning I was blessed with her company on my daily walk. Everything felt right and good again.

My children were elementary students at Holliday — Kansas City's version of a public Montessori school, where 85 percent of the kids came from minority families. I was forever popping into the school for one reason or another but mostly because I missed my kids. As soon as I walked through the doorway into my child's classroom, all the heads would lift, and a moment later a passel of kids surrounded me, their arms circling my body, their faces smiling up at me from hip height. Their energy said, *Hey, look at me! Notice me. Please tell me I'm good.* Their faces shone with all the innocence in the world, but it was the tinge of fear tattered to the edges that compelled me to grab the bunch in a hug and love them up, even though I'd been called to the principal's office for doing so.

I loved Principal Becker, but he was wrong about this. I couldn't abide his request that I not cuddle the children, not even when he tried getting me to comply by dropping fear into my heart. "Gloria, you could be charged with child abuse if you keep 'touching' the students," he said.

He succeeded in making me nervous, but how could I not return their embraces? Me, forsake a child because I'm afraid? Never. It was the right thing to do, so I kept doing it. Because there are some rules in life you should never listen to — the stupid ones, for instance.

After the group hug I'd hang out for a while, offering a private word to some of the kids.

"What are you reading now, Jamal? Wow, that's pretty advanced for a little guy like you."

"When did you start tutoring the little kids, Keyarra?"

"Alex, your mom says you and Nick are staying with us this weekend." Alex was proud to be singled out in front of his classmates, but the only thing he could bring himself to do was to dip his shy, round face in the affirmative.

I didn't have the same disdain for the parents at Holliday that I did for my neighbors. Most Holliday school students lived in the East Side, with single moms. Those women utilized day care to make ends meet, not because of some misguided notion of what was important.

Our middle class and white family was an anomaly at Holliday. We had chosen the school because we felt our kids would do better learning how to relate to people from all cultures rather than just reading about the differences in a book. As they grew older, we bought into the hype that the public high schools were dangerous, so we transferred Tara to a private school. What a mistake that was. She received a better education when she was a minority, and not just in the three R's. One of the unexpected byproducts of her public schooling is that she can dance. Man, can she dance! I envy that so much. Someday I'm going to learn to dance as well as my daughter does.

17 OCTOBER 2006

THINGS WERE MOVING FAST.

Funk put in his one-month notice at work. When I called to see how it went, Dottie, his receptionist, picked up as usual, but instead of her usual bubbly greeting, she mumbled a hello through sniffles and tears.

All I'd ever heard was what a wonder Dottie was. Funk said she was a pro at editing reports, scheduled his meetings without flaw, was accurate to the penny with expense claims, and did everything with wholesome good cheer. Cherishing her as he did, I always took a little time to chat her up and express my gratitude for having Funk's back before I asked for her to transfer my call to him.

In his many different jobs, my husband's staff had always adored him. Whenever I went up for one of his outlandishly boring office parties, it was common for a staff person to inch up next to me to say that he was the best boss they'd ever had. Likely because he was one of the few department heads who hired women and minorities and didn't abuse his power. Even more unusual, he asked their opinions, and since he purposely employed staff who were, more often than not, smarter than he was, he believed their ideas were better than his own.

Dottie was gentle and loving, and hearing her tears, I forgot why I'd called and I shouted into the phone, "Dottie! What in the world is wrong?"

"Mark just told us he's quitting."

"Oh."

Sniffle, sniffle, cry, cry, blow her nose.

"I don't think I can stay once he leaves."

To console her, I said, "Sure you can, Dottie. You've been with the city longer than Funk. Besides, I'm sure he'll recommend one of the auditors up there to be his replacement, probably Gary."

"That's what I'm afraid of," she moaned.

Oh, brother. Here I was, all this time worrying about how our secret would affect our family, and I'd never once given a thought to how it would affect my husband's staff.

I soothed Dottie as best as I could before I asked to speak to Funk.

I could picture him sitting in his chair on the twenty-first floor of city hall, deep in thought, his feet propped up on his desk, alternately rubbing his beard and gnawing on his thumb.

"Your staff aren't taking your departure so well, huh?"

Funk replied, "They're fine. They'll be even better once we move up to the twenty-ninth floor."

20 OCTOBER 2006

ONLY A MONTH TO GO! On November 20, Funk would *finally* announce he was running for mayor. We were beside ourselves with excitement. It was all we could talk about, especially since my husband still wouldn't let me discuss it with anyone else.

Getting Funk ready for opening day had been more time-consuming and trickier than he first let on. It was reminiscent of the time he was writing his dissertation, the book I should have a byline on. Back then it was, "Babe, would you mind calling a couple of cities and asking these questions?" "A couple" turned out to be 219. Thankfully, by 2006 I'd smartened up. I wasn't the dumbfuck I once had been. I had a contract this time. Once Funk had his eight years in office, it'd be my turn to realize my dreams. And boy, would he be in for a shock. My list of tasks for him was long. I was gonna own that man.

In the evenings — after he'd put in a long day at city hall and spent time with any children hanging around our dining room — he'd saunter up to our office to work on the speech he'd be giving at the press event. I had no idea why it was taking him so long to write the announcement that he was running for mayor. The guy knew how to talk, particularly about dull government topics. I kept telling him it didn't matter, "just put it on paper and get it over with already," but he didn't listen.

For my part, campaign headquarters was ready to receive people. Everything was purchased and in place. The utilities were turned on and I'd stocked the pantry with healthy snacks. Funk didn't ask for that, but if he got any volunteers, it was only right that he served them something. Of course, the hick wouldn't actually offer them something, but refreshments would be available to anyone who needed a bite while they did whatever it is that volunteers do for a candidate. I had planned the menu for opening day as well. I kept it simple. We'd offer coffee and cookies.

I'd resigned myself again that I'd be working on my husband's behalf, this time, until the opening day event was over, as a million last-minute things kept cropping up. I had to make another run to Costco to purchase a coffee maker big enough to serve a crowd. It stood ready for action. I placed it off to the side of our holiday table so no one would spill their drink on the campaign materials that I had grudgingly agreed to spend more of my family's money on. I ran out of cash, so I had to use a zero-percent credit card offer to make the purchases. *I'll pay the card off once Funk's retirement check arrives. Oh, good Lord! Our retirement money! Jesus, I better not think about that, or my throat will close.*

I also agreed to loan the campaign a few dollars more — a hundred, to be exact — to have a banner made. That had been my idea. If we were doing this, we'd do it right. Pinch in the wrong places and you lose the whole thing. With Funk announcing his candidacy via a press conference, surely the news would make its way to TV. It would be wise to enhance that opportunity with a backdrop that gave viewers a taste of his platform. I tried to be smart about it, though. I designed the piece with multiple uses in mind. It was waterproof, so once the announcement was over, we could hang the banner outside the trailer like a billboard.

Because the banner had been a last-second inspiration, I had to find a designer for it quickly. I hated the rendering the artist came back with. I didn't ask for conventional, but there was no time to juice it up. The piece of crap was ready for pickup at the print shop.

Finding a printer had been no small feat. How was I supposed to keep the words spilling across the banner, "Mark Funkhouser for Mayor," a secret? I quickly learned there are printers who deal exclusively with campaigns. Did you know that? If I weren't involved, I would have never known that. But just like priests and lawyers, they're sworn to secrecy. *Yeah, right.* Still, I chose a printer across the state border in Kansas City, Kansas. Not that a few miles made that much difference, but at least I tried protecting my husband's secret as best I could. To be sure, though, I didn't bring this situation to his attention, because who needs a Nervous Nellie around when you're in rush? He had to trust that I was being as discreet as possible. Besides, I was getting pretty good at the campaign thing.

21 OCTOBER 2006

ONE MORNING, as the time to unveil Funk's candidacy was drawing near, something told me it wasn't in Funk's best interest to keep this secret so close to our chests. Yet when I dropped my opinion, he wouldn't hear of doing anything different. And then one day, while striding atop the stair-climber *still* reading my copy of *The Campaign Manager*, I came to a section that made it clear that my husband was entering the race late. Most candidates had announced their candidacy eons ago. Because he insisted on keeping his plan to run for mayor quiet, Funk was losing out on securing backers. The author's reinforcement giving me confidence, I phoned Funk on my way home from the gym and begged him to tell a few political players about his intention to run.

"Funk, listen to me. You've got to call Mr. Nutter and tell him what's up."

"I can't do that, Glor."

His refusal baffled me. I knew he'd read the book, probably twice.

"My situation is different, Glor. It's unethical to remain in my position and actively run for mayor."

"Actively run? C'mon, stop being such a Goody Two-shoes. Having a private conversation with Nutter isn't actively running."

"Gloria —"

"That's ridiculous, Funk!"

"Gloria, I can't —"

"You're always screwing us with your ultra-moralistic attitude."

"Screwing us?"

"Listen, buddy, I've just run a two-month marathon for you and I'm still running. Are you telling me I've wasted my time? Please don't tell me I wasted my time."

"Glor, if I could've told anyone I was running, I wouldn't have needed your help."

Help! What did he take me for? I hadn't helped. I'd done everything. I'm telling you, the guy hadn't lifted the first finger. Whatever. I'd done my duty. Funk had needed my "help" finding a low-cost headquarters. I did. Then he needed me to set it up. I did. Next, he had the gall to ask me to read that stupid book. Like a moron, I did. After which he wanted comment. I did that too. But now he wasn't taking my advice. If he was going to squander everything I'd done, in defense of his misplaced ethics and to the point that he crashed and burned, so be it.

Only, what about our money? By my last calculations, we were twenty-six grand in the hole. How could we get that back if he lost before he began?

23 OCTOBER 2006

THE CAMPAIGN BANNER came in and it hurt my eyes to see. It was blah, blah, blah, red, white, and blue — revoltingly predictable. I'm sorry, world, for putting something so ugly into you! I was running as fast as I could, but with everything else on my to-do list, there wasn't time to make it sing. Man, I hated doing things halfway and being a conformist. But neither of those things did I hate as much as I hated Funk at that moment. This undertaking felt as heavy as a start-up business. I was trying to help actualize Funk's dream, the way he envisioned it. I still couldn't figure out how I'd gotten sucked in. But there was no time to dwell on that. To get by, I stuck a pacifier in my mouth by looking the other way and got on with the day's business.

24 OCTOBER 2006

I'D BEEN NAGGING FUNK for weeks to write a statement that spelled out his vision for the city. He couldn't just serve coffee and cookies and have reporters walk away from opening day with nothing in hand but a ho-hum campaign button. All he had to do was bullet-point the speech he'd be giving that morning. But he hadn't finished writing it yet. How long could that take? His speech was the only thing he was responsible for in getting his own campaign off the ground.

The event was his thing to be sure, but I was excited too. This was big! It would be the press event of the century, followed a few weeks later by a kick-off party the likes of which this city had never seen. Both would be classy affairs. A million little things needed my attention if opening day was to sparkle as it should. Scatter myself too thin and there would be a dull coating on everything, and that's not the way I operate in the world.

I wanted Funk to be on his game. This being the speech of his life, it had to shine. Funk was a frequent keynote speaker at dreary auditing conventions nationwide and was often put on the spot by local media looking to scoop his latest audit report. He flew by the seat of his pants with those, and he was surprisingly good at it. But not being able to help him polish this speech of his was bringing on my case of nerves.

Whereas Funk's press event was about letting the public know he was running for mayor, the kick-off party, which I'd dubbed his Coming-Out Party, was about celebrating the news with friends and family. It was to take place at the Kansas City Art Institute on December 2 — my poor, grieving mother's birthday. I had secured the venue just before leaving for Europe the previous summer. Thank God I did, or I never would have found a classy enough place so close to the holidays.

I had settled on a caterer and was thrilled that I had found someone in tune with my vision for the night. Funk didn't care about minutiae; he just trusted me to make everything nice. That said, he kicked up a fuss when I told him the price the caterer had quoted for the menu. He said we should serve hot dogs instead. I told him since the kids and I were affiliated with him, we couldn't go along with that nonsense. And yes, we did have a say. Since our family was fronting the money until Lord knew when, we were not going to half-ass it. Either the party would be elegant or he wouldn't have one. I mean, who in their right mind would vote for a man who served hot dogs to kick off his campaign?

25 OCTOBER 2006

THE CATERER and I toured the venue together, hanging back in the lobby to nail down the menu. Then he walked me out to my van and I, ugh, shelled out more cash for the deposit. My family's future was dripping out of my hands.

When I got back to the trailer, first on my agenda was touching base with the musician because, to me, Funk's Coming Out Party was just as important as the press event. Given how unconventional our family was, the music had to wow. Funk couldn't choose predictable fare, especially not the go-to jazz that everyone in Kansas City seemed to rely on.

I picked up the phone to give Slick Ballinger a call. It gave me chills to think about the night I had met him.

~

ON MAY 2, 2006, Funk and I made the decision that he'd run for mayor. The very next day, instead of packing for our imminent trip to Europe, I placed a call to a musician I'd met the previous September, Slick Ballinger.

Funk's colleague Jeff Simon had invited us to his block party. I wouldn't know a soul at the gathering. I usually shied away from such events, and that night was no different. But because my husband's asks were infrequent, I had a hard time refusing him, especially with a request as innocuous as this one, so I agreed to attend. Yet when the night came for this homebody to walk out her door, I tried wheedling out of it.

I was standing in front of my bedroom mirror applying the finishing touches to my outfit when I asked, in the lightest way possible, "Funk, wouldn't you rather just sit on the porch tonight? It's so beautiful out."

He was standing directly behind me combing his just-washed hair, staring at my reflection. Knowing how I get, he had a glint in his eye when he said, "Glor, it'll be all right. You're just getting cold feet. Once we're there, you won't want to come home, just like always."

Now that I'd had the courage to broach the topic, I felt slightly more comfortable about digging my heels in. "You're out of your mind, Funk. I already want to go home. It's going to be so boring."

"Glor, you always say that, and then you end up having fun."

"Fun? C'mon, Funk. What fun could I possibly have?"

The glint left him.

"Gloria, you're already dressed. Let's go. Get in the van."

Funk always speaks my full name whenever he's irritated with me. But I didn't let it scare me. Just groped for something else that might appeal to him.

"I wouldn't mind if you went by yourself. Think about it. If I stayed back, you could talk to your heart's content about government matters without feeling bad for leaving me out."

"Gloria—"

This test of wills went back and forth for a while in all the silly ways of long-married couples. In the end, Funk had to drag me out of the house. In the van, we headed south toward Romanelli—a gaggingly upper-middle-class neighborhood in the heart of Kansas City. Funk and I found Simon's toney address just off Ward Parkway. There were a million cars parked on his street and, seizing the opportunity, I made one last attempt to toss the evening.

"Well, Funk, there's nowhere to park. I guess we'll have to go home."

He replied with a very sour "Gloria."

I shot back, "Whatever, Funk. Don't be so weird."

As usual, my husband didn't bother trying to find a spot close in. He just chose the first available, which was three blocks from where the Simons lived. I lugged myself out of the van and kissed the door goodbye. We reached the party just as the four-piece band was warming up. Surprised to see such extravagance, I looked up at my husband and said, "You didn't tell me there'd be live music. Are the Simons rich or something?"

With his hand loosely on my hip, he briefly replied that no, he didn't think the Simons were rich, and then he left me standing at the edge of the makeshift stage while he went in search of a beer. I watched him leave, staring at his back until the crowd swallowed all of him up except for his head. Hundreds of people milled about, and just as I had expected, I didn't recognize a soul.

I stood alone with nothing to do but watch the band tune their instruments, after which they took the beers the host pushed on them. Tapping my foot on the asphalt, I impatiently waited for them to guzzle down their drinks and get on with it already. The sooner they started, the sooner I could leave.

While waiting, I made small chitchat with the couple standing next to me, the conversation mindless enough that I had time to listen and respond and also wonder what the hell was taking Funk so long to find a beer and get back. He'd been gone for twenty minutes. The only thing that could've kept him away was that he was engrossed in an all-too-titillating conversation about work. If that was the case, and it likely was, then I was just as happy to be over here by myself.

The band finally placed their cups in the trash can and walked to their places on the stage. They were a strange-looking lot. Obviously not from around Kansas City. They had too much expression on their faces for that. The person who appeared to be the leader seemed like just a kid. He was ridiculously dressed in suit at least five sizes too big for him. Perhaps he was from around here after all. Maybe he was Jeff's nephew or something. That would make more sense than Jeff shelling out big cash to hire a band for a block party.

One of the sidekicks was also on the young side and pasty white, though he was balding and tall in comparison. The other two musicians were black and probably the only people there with any shading to them except for me with my Italian skin. One seemed a few years older than the white kids and was a little Tubby Two-shoes, and the other was miles older than the rest. I thought he might be blind, though I couldn't tell for sure. He wore sunglasses even though it was dark out, and he hadn't moved from his seat since I'd arrived.

I was curious to learn where the band hailed from and what type of music they'd play. I hoped it wasn't country. Funk loved it, but I couldn't stand it. The musicians were taking forever to tune their instruments. I was waiting to get my wonderings answered when the leader nodded to the kid behind him, whispered, "Les' go" to the old guy, and off they went. The music erupted with such intensity that it felt like a meteor had just shot through the sky and landed at my feet.

I had been expecting all the normal formalities to take place — a punked-up kid in love with the mic, trying to act the part by holding it too close and breathing a too-sexy greeting: "Evenin', everyone! We're the Blah-Blah Band, in Kansas City tonight to *rock* your world! *Whahhhhh!*" — but this kid had no time for such things. With all the confidence in the world, he bypassed the preliminaries and went straight for an intimacy that usually takes most bands an entire evening to coax from an audience.

All of five-foot-four at age twenty-three, Slick presented like a five-year-old playing dress-up in his father's zoot suit, yet the façade completely belied the power radiating from him. He was a ball of untamed energy, every cell in his body cranked to the max. He was everywhere at once. All over the street, moving and gyrating among the crowd, his feet a whirl of action keeping up with the fast beat, his microphone cord a tail jumping behind him like spit on a cast iron frying pan. And that voice. My God. What a voice. From out of that diminutive frame came a voice that was pulled from the depths of the Earth, and if there was someplace deeper to go than that, Slick would have pulled it from there. Throaty, southern, scratchy, his voice was all that and more. The kid couldn't begin to open his mouth wide enough to let out all of the sound. Yet as commanding as he was, his passion couldn't have been more incongruous to the mood on the street. A mostly Catholic crowd, not enough drink had been poured yet to allow their bodies' release. Since I had all of my drinking out of the way by the time I was fifteen, Slick had me mesmerized with the first Elvis-like move of his feet.

Two seconds earlier I'd been standing in boredom, and there I was, riveted, watching as Slick called it down from above. Wrapped up in his emotion, I couldn't move. My eyes pierced his being, and I couldn't look away, not even when he noticed me staring and I embarrassed myself. Between the impact of his voice and the frenzy of his suit flying about, by the time he'd finished belting out the first tune, Slick's vitality had captured the attention of the crowd.

I didn't think it could be possible, but he only ramped it higher from there. His two-toned patent leather shoes took on a life of their own, dancing atop the volcano he'd just summoned from the earth. From the audience who now engulfed him, he allowed only the most primitive behavior, as we all moved like entranced revelers at a Beltane fire.

Spellbound by his essence, Slick's bluesy moaning transported me to a place I wasn't prepared to go. He evoked a mood that brought to the surface just how utterly strange my life had just become. Drenched in the force, life questions whirled inside me, with accompanying answers that I felt, rather than heard.

It had been a terrible autumn. By any measure, I should have been deliriously happy to be making the arrangements for my upcoming trip to Europe. But instead of spinning through my days in joy, I had undergone a meltdown, brought on the minute Tara left for her year-long study-abroad program in France.

Please don't get me wrong. My daughter going out to see the world was the most wonderful thing I could've hoped for. In fact, all summer long our family had helped her prepare for her adventure. By the time that August departure morning rolled around, parents and daughter drove to the airport abuzz with excitement. Yet as soon as we approached her gate, my nerves started cracking. When we reached the head of the security line, I couldn't let go of Tara's hands. I had to keep calling her back for just one last kiss, relinquishing her only when the guard gave me a stern, "That's enough, ma'am." And planting the true one last kiss on her lips, I uttered a final goodbye and watched her disappear into the Jetway from behind the plate glass window. The last glimpse of my child was the tiniest sliver of her purse as she rounded the turn.

And that's when my world went upside down and I became a desolate mess on the floor.

Unbelievable! Hadn't I just given birth to her? The last thing I should've been seeing was her little pink backpack disappear as she walked through the door of her kindergarten classroom. That had been traumatic enough, but this was preposterous. I'd wanted to scream for her to turn around and get back inside my womb. Instead, I stood in agony outside Gate 57 of Terminal B, my life tumbling down, comprehension hitting like a perfectly placed fist to my kidney. Normally not one to shed tears, I turned to my husband and fell apart in his arms. Even though he was unfamiliar with this sort of display, he cooed to me like a mother. I was ashamed to be sobbing, in public no less, but I couldn't make myself stop.

I'd always wanted to be a wife and a mother. Having achieved those things, I'd never given it more than a passing thought that I'd one day be the owner of an empty nest. Somehow — and I know this sounds crazy — for the previous twenty years I had just assumed my family would carry on as we always had. Even when I found myself lost in a daydream about what life would be like when Funk and I were old and decrepit, the picture that always came to mind was the two of us skinny and gray-headed, rocking on our same chairs, on our same porch, our children still young and tucked safely away inside their bedrooms.

Devastated by a reality that I could no longer deny, not even planning for my lifelong dream of going to Europe had helped ease my sorrow. Ever since Tara had left, I'd been walking through my days unfocused and anxious. At times the anxiety became so severe that for the first time since I was a child, I had the vaguest lack of a will to live. It's not that I wanted to kill myself — never that — I just couldn't fathom how I'd ever be thrilled by life once my children were no longer in the picture on a daily basis.

So it was that I had arrived at the Simons' party all crumpled and small. And Slick's explosion knocked me down further. But just for a moment.

Suddenly I understood that the universe wasn't pounding on me again, only surprising me with an offering. With each note Slick strummed I felt my soul filling with hope. Raising my children had been my greatest joy on Earth, but maybe there was something more for me. It would not be as thrilling as having my children around all the time, but could it be almost as good?

I had no idea my miseries would turn themselves around that night, but that's exactly what happened as I watched Slick express himself to the universe. As my husband had predicted, he had to drag me away from the Simons' party. I had been a bedraggled mess walking out the door of my home, yet by the time I returned to the van I was excited to be living again. I'm not talking an instant cure here. Apparently, that only happens in the movies, and what kind of bullshit is that? However, I left the Simons' party with a renewed connection to spirit, and because of that, I knew I would be okay.

The party and the chain of events that followed eventually lifted me to a higher state of wellness. But when you're living something so dark, "eventually" feels like a really long time. That said, I was confident that if I could just bide my time, my darkness would retreat.

I'd remained anxious for the rest of that autumn, but blessedly, the beast didn't have the same impact on me as it had earlier. I still walked my days deeply afraid — because anxiety is a ferocious emotion. The visions I'd tried to shut down as a child had returned, but now they didn't scare me as much.

To show the universe my gratitude, I gathered my tits about me and hunkered down low. Forced myself to be brave and searched for that elusive silver lining. For what the anxiety was supposed to teach me. Tough love — what an overrated bunch of crap that is. Why couldn't God just give me a good talking to, like I do with my kids? Then again, where's the gratitude in that?

I pushed my remaining anxiety into submission by going to therapy three times a week, talking being the only thing that helped me figure things out. I told Shelley about my experience of listening to Slick and his band and about the visions that'd been waking me in the night ever since. Everything came out on Shelley's couch.

Finding the door to her office ajar, I strode right in, waving my arms in the air emphasizing my news, "Shells, you are never going to believe this."

She waited as I went through my typical maneuvers of making myself comfortable. I flung to the carpet any pillow that had bad energy on it, the leftover from the tortured soul who'd been in before me, and rearranged the uncontaminated few into a comfy nest on top of her couch. Before settling in, I remembered my manners and asked, "Shells, do you mind if I open the door and pull up the blinds?"

"No, I love that you feel at home."

I propped the screen door open with a rock and, going to her desk, gave her papers a nosy once-over before lifting the blinds. But not too high, because who wanted the people in the house next door watching me shed my burdens? Once I had arranged the environment to my liking, I kicked off my shoes and sank to the couch.

For my existential musings, I couldn't have found a better recipient than Shelley. Sitting opposite me — her hair a golden bush framing her face — looking at Shelley's beautiful face was like looking at an angel. Her gaze spoke volumes. She was taking inventory, the same way a mother does with a child. Knowing her assessment would show my energy had changed, I let it rip.

She listened intently about my experience of hearing Slick, but she was more interested in the visions that had come to me afterward. Shelley never wavered in her belief that my visions were real. Her steadfast confidence encouraged me to explore the subject.

Yet, each time I made room for the possibility that I might have an inclination toward the spirit world — that my "visions" really were messages rather than just some sort of peculiar daydream coming in the middle of the night — my mind turned to self-doubt. I fought hard to accept Shelley's opinion over that of my family, who believed that I was completely full of shit. My cosmic whip brought to the surface all the other opinions I harbored about myself. If you must know the complete truth, my worst fear is that I am a fraud. A fraud as a mother. A fraud as a childbirth instructor. A fraud as a Sensitive.

How could I not feel a sham?

I gave birth to a daughter and then to a son, and because I did, that allegedly made me a mother. But mothers are supposed to know everything about everything, and I barely knew a thing. I had no apprenticeship for the most important job in the world — yet, *poof*, I pop out a kid and I'm suddenly called a mother? I had no idea how to be a mom except to act like one. So I did. And I'd been pretending ever since, even though it felt incredibly dishonest to do so. Like when I repeated all the things good mothers were supposed to say, such as "Eat this, it's good for your health." Man, did I ever feel like a sham with that one. I mean, how in the world would I know if eating something was good for them? What? First I'm a mother, and now I'm a scientist?

The same sense of shame came over me whenever I said I was a birth instructor. I'd read countless books, medical textbooks, and research articles, had attended dozens of births, and even caught many of those babies in my own arms, yet my understanding of the subject barely fit on the tip of a needle. I felt horrifically dishonest when I sat on my dining room floor lecturing a roomful of expectant couples and said, "Hey guys, listen to me good. If you use labor for the opportunity that it is, you'll shave five years off your therapy bill." Because how did I know if there's an opportunity lurking out there for them? Other than I just knew it. My gut told me it was so. But I couldn't rightly say that, could I? Hell, no! If my students knew that the material they were the most captivated by came more from my observations at births — from looking and listening and soaking it in — than from a textbook, they'd have rebelled. My word-of-mouth business would have dried up faster than a vagina in menopause.

This is where things got confusing. Because to the extent that I trusted anything, I trusted my gut more than what I read in a book. Because, think about it: books are written by a person, and how did that person come to be an expert? In this century, knowledge begins with observation, and it snowballs into fact the minute it rings true to the masses.

I'm sure you can see why I'm in therapy.

I'm a walking contradiction. I vacillate between doubting myself and trusting my instincts, and that's the same way I judge how other people think and feel and act — or, God help them, how I judge them if they *don't* think and feel and act. I'm critical of anyone who believes what they're told without doing a little research on their own. When one of my parents-to-be asks, "How do you know that?" my first inclination is to say, "Trust me, I just know," because most times, I do. Yet if my student swallowed that, I'd be secretly berating him: *Okay, you've only known me for six weeks, but please, be a pansy-ass, trust me the way you shouldn't trust your doctor.*

Although I'm critical of others, it doesn't compare with how critical I am of myself. Even with Shelley's bolstering, I had a tough time believing the visions weren't just a pile of crap that my fraudulent self had made up. Shelley reassured me that what I divulged wasn't the makings of a crackpot. I believe this was partly due to her skill level and partly because I was a living, breathing science project sitting right in front of her. And who could resist something like that?

That was only me judging myself. Shelley's bottom line was that I should stop trying to understand things with my head and, instead, accept them in my bones.

Therapy wasn't easy. As good as it was to finally be discussing such existential perplexities, our talks produced an inner tug-of-war that made my anxiety shoot right back up. I wanted to ditch the whole topic. Yet, between Shelley's guidance and my renewed connection to spirit, not to mention plain old curiosity, I gulped down the fright and stayed on course.

Why is it that whenever you say you're going to do something, the universe seems to test you to see if you mean it? And why is it that change, even when you're the one initiating it, makes things worse before they get better? Are the gods having fun at our expense? It felt as though the heavens were having a rollicking good time watching me struggle. You know how these things go. It's the first day of a new diet, and all of a sudden everyone's showing up on your front porch with a cake and then laughs about how you have no willpower.

Well, whatever the answer, I was done with being afraid of myself. Yet each time I got the tiniest toehold of confidence, a serving of doubt plopped into my lap.

After a particularly profound set of visions one night, I finally turned a corner. Shelley's faith in me gave me the permission to consider that someone from above was trying to tell me something. But who? What? And why?

I feel stupid describing them, because if I were reading this, I wouldn't believe what I'm about to write. But I also know you'll scream if I skip over it, because that's what I'd do if I'd come this far and found it was missing. So here you go. And laugh away. I can feel you, so don't even try denying it.

My first vision was of our ancestors, back when we still lived inside the Earth. I dropped into their lifetime just as they were witnessing light for the very first time. I watched them being drawn to a glow they'd never seen before, curious but afraid to go near. One courageous soul finally crept close, despite throat-clenching fear. When he did, I saw what he saw: the world as you and I know it. A world filled with vegetation and other living things. A world that is green, lovely, and bright. Awed by the discovery, he shouted for the others to come see. They tiptoed slowly and when they finally arrived, my heart did flip-flops watching them experience the wondrous sight. Watching their fear melt into peace.

The only sense I could make of this scene was that I had a few things in common with the first guy that I needed to learn about myself. I was a sniveling coward, yet something in me couldn't back away from things that intrigued me, be it a curious light or some other fascinating new thing, even when it made my throat slam shut in fear. And when people looked to me as an authority and I pretended I was capable, even though that made me feel like a phony, I still did what needed to be done. So perhaps the message meant that being afraid had nothing to do with leadership or courage.

Shelley believed the vision spoke to leadership, and she also believed the message indicated that my role would escalate. Hearing her say that blew me away, as I hadn't told her yet about Funk's decision to run for mayor. Her interpretation made me wonder whether the visions were preparing me for Funk winning the election.

Are you laughing yet? I'm sure you are, so let's get this over with already.

The next vision brought me to the place I'm most terrified of finding myself: in the middle of a sea of black muck. This scene wasn't new to me. Anytime I'm truly afraid, I disassociate and off I go into the darkness. The difference this time was that I heard a message being whispered that the muck was just a ruse and that all I had to do to rid myself of blinding fear was to lift myself out of it. Wanting very much to heal, I tried. And, wonder of all wonders, my mind decided to help me for a change. Provided a soft chant to work by. After hearing it intoned fifty million times, I began to rise from the blackness. I rose so high that I scared myself further by meeting up with my higher self, the part of me that is timeless and holy, peaceful, and good.

Turns out, the New and Better Me was nothing more than the Earthly counterpart of my powerful, spiritual self.

And before you go saying anything — yes, I know, this sounds like a load of horseshit. I agree. Whatever. I'd been shown a path out of misery, and I was frigging taking it.

My next attempts at lifting myself from the muck weren't as successful, but I'm no quitter. To access my chiropractor's office for my monthly appointment, I had to ride in a coffin-like elevator. The elevator's interior walls were designed to resemble fine wood, yet all I saw in the fake burled knots were thousands of tiny, screaming faces. Instead of allowing that image to anchor me in terror, I practiced rising from the muck. It worked, but only gradually. Any small victory soon gave way again to doubt, and anxiety would bulldoze right back in. The next time I rode in the elevator, the screaming faces seemed familiar. Were the faces there to warn me about something, or was this just one more test to see if I had the courage to change? I had no idea. All I can tell you is what happened the last time I had stepped into that elevator. The faces grew claws that grabbed at my legs to keep me stuck in the muck. The audacity of that brought out the New Yorker in me. How dare someone, something, it, or whatever this was, try to keep me down?

That hard-won mettle helped me build on my successes. Each day I stacked up small bits of confidence and rose higher than the day before. But not without a fight. The higher I rose, the deeper the claws dug in. And then, one day, they slid down my legs and finally lost their hold. Unleashed, I floated in the air. I was a bloody mess, but at least I was free.

To this day, whenever I'm too afraid or need to stand my ground, I chant my way into strength. I "throw my glamour high," and up I rise.

THIS IS HOW IT CAME TO BE that three weeks before leaving for Europe I hired Slick to play music at Funk's Coming-Out Party. It wasn't a difficult decision. If Slick had the power to restore my hope in a matter of minutes, I knew Funk could use his help in bringing that same hope to his soon-to-be new bosses — the 450,000 residents of Kansas City. Like me, our city had lost its way, and if anyone could bring it back, Funk and Slick were the ones to do it.

27 OCTOBER 2006

I WAS GOING TO KILL FUNK.

Just as I had feared, his high-and-mighty attitude had just cost him the support of Kansas City's most influential political kingpin, mortgage broker Jim Nutter Sr. After wrestling with Mr. Ethical for hours on the porch the previous night, I had finally convinced him to let his elderly friend in on our little secret.

Funk drove to Nutter's before work. After handshakes, their conversation went like this:

"You're looking well, Mr. Nutter."

Nutter's husky body grandly perched behind the desk in his office, which hadn't seen a renovation since he'd bought the place God knows how long ago. Leaning forward in his chair, he bellowed, "Good to see you, Mark! What brings you in today?"

"I've been thinking about what all we've accomplished for the city, especially for people most in need."

"Yes, Mark, we certainly have gotten a lot done together."

"You helped me win the fight to audit the police department for the first time, eliminate the city stickers, and open more community centers in the economically challenged parts of town. I couldn't have done any of that without your support."

Nutter pointed to the miniature streetlight sitting on the corner of his desk, which Funk had given him. "Don't forget the streetlights."

"Indeed. Getting those was almost as difficult as getting to audit the police, yet both had a major impact on the city's crime rate."

"Word is you're retiring. Congratulations, you've earned it!"

"I'm not exactly retiring."

"What's next for you?"

"That's why I'm here. I haven't told anyone my plans, but Gloria's been urging me to tell you, and I think she's right."

Funk's stomach was tied in knots from going against his better judgment. Still, he ran with my instinct and divulged the secret that was not to be told to anyone else for another twenty-four days. His stomach twisted even further when Nutter told him, expressing deep regret, that *just the previous night* he had agreed to support Councilman Jim Glover's run for mayor.

"Mark, why didn't you come to me sooner? I would have backed you in a heartbeat. But it's too late now. I never go back on my word."

Funk sank miserably in his chair.

"We can talk again if Glover loses, but don't bank on that because I never back a loser."

Minutes later, still in Nutter's parking lot, Funk phoned me from his Toyota Corolla. Never in my life had I heard him sound defeated.

"Glor, you were right. I should have gone to Nutter sooner. He just signed Glover."

He sounded like he was ready to puke, though he'd never say anything unmanly like that. I could picture him, though, slumped in the driver's seat, a sack of bones, his face drawn from holding back bile. Knowing this, I skipped past what I wanted to say: "You frigging idiot! See? What did I tell you?" Instead, I shouted into the receiver with great cheer, "Glover? Are you fucking kidding me? That's so great, Funk! Holy shit. There's no way that guy will win the primary. Don't worry, Nutter will back you in the general election."

30 OCTOBER 2006

THE LOSS OF NUTTER'S ENDORSEMENT sat like lead in Funk's belly. We were sitting on our porch when I grew tired of looking at his bottom lip protruding into Kansas.

"Funk, you've got to stop with this holier-than-thou shit. There's no law that says you can't run for mayor while you're employed at city hall. If you're as concerned as you say you are about losing other support, you can't take this to such extremes. Besides, if these people are your friends, they'll keep it to themselves."

He shot back grouchily, "Gloria, I can't lead if I don't hold myself to a higher standard."

"Oh, get over yourself, Funk. Remember when your staff wouldn't take vacation time because you never would? You finally had to take time off so they could."

"I forgot about that."

"Well, this is the same thing. You're too rigid sometimes. It makes people uncomfortable. They don't understand the leadership thing you've got going on, probably because it went out the door with Abraham Lincoln. Give it up already."

"Gloria, I'm not running until I retire my position at city hall."

"Jesus, Funk, catch up with me already. Keep this up and you'll lose before you even get started."

He was dug in. I hated when he got like this. But Christ, why did I even care? Maybe because I'd been working my ass off for a million months on his behalf.

3 NOVEMBER 2006

FUNK FINALLY RELENTED.

He realized that if he was going to do this, he'd need financial backing *plus* a few other "little things," such as organizing volunteers to help run his campaign. The price of my getting through to him was that he asked something else of me. I had to find those volunteers. When he made that latest request, an ugly thought popped into mind: *What if Funk is just pretending to be ethical to get me to do the grunt work for his dream?* But the suspicion dissolved in my next breath. I forgot. Funk doesn't have it in him to come up with a scheme like that.

Relieved, I phoned a few potential volunteers who I felt were trustworthy. The first call went to Funk's longtime secretary, Dottie. She and I chatted a few times a week on the phone, but we'd never spent any time together except at Funk's office parties.

She picked up in her usual chipper way. Thank God we were conversing over the wires. She had the sexiest voice alive, and it was jolting when it collided with her Midwestern attire. Since I couldn't physically see her, it didn't throw me off my game.

"Good morning, city auditor's office, this is Dottie, how may I help you?"

"Hey, Dottie! It's Gloria. How goes it today?"

"I'm fine, how are you?" she said with a gravelly laugh.

"I'm good. Thank you for asking."

"What can I do for you, Gloria?"

"I have the oddest request, Dottie, but I don't want to ask over the phone.

Would you mind meeting me in person? I can swing by city hall later this afternoon and we can talk in my van."

The unusual question scared the Midwesterner. She stammered, "I — I . . . guess so."

Four hours later I picked her up on the north side of city hall. Downtown being a wasteland, I had to drive a only few blocks before finding a deserted enough street to begin our Deep Throat–style meeting.

I had hardly been able to contain myself while driving over to city hall, that's how excited I was to *finally* be telling someone our secret. But Dottie was so nervous when she climbed into the van that she made me nervous. What a let-down! I'd been waiting an eternity to spill the news, and this is what I got? Her hands held onto each other for dear life, her body tiny and white-faced, her eyes staring straight out the windshield.

Concerned she'd start gagging, I let it rip, "Thank you *so* much for meeting me, Dottie!"

My exuberance didn't help. Her eyes remained unfocused, not giving the least indication she'd heard me say something. To help her feel more secure, I dropped into my fraudulent, authoritative self. "Dottie, everything's fine! I just want to tell you something that Funk and I have been keeping to ourselves for the longest time."

Still nothing.

In fact, my tactic seemed to heighten her discomfort. It was as if I'd just said, "Dottie, I'm here to kill you. Do you have any last words I can bring to your family?" Her demeaner worsening by the second, I pushed on.

"Dottie, you've been upset ever since Funk said he was retiring, so I just wanted to tell you that, actually, he's not."

Zilch.

"Before we left for Europe last summer, Funk said the city was floundering and he felt obliged to fix it."

Still nada. Like, not one muscle twitched. The only movements from her were waves of anxiety ringing the air, like heat rising off a highway. I felt ridiculous continuing a one-sided conversation, but I had a mission that needed to be taken care of.

"But since he's gone as far as he can as the city auditor, he thought maybe he should run for mayor."

Finally! She swiveled around in her seat and smiled at me. "I thought that's what you were going to say, Gloria."

Surprised by the turnaround, I squealed, "Really, Dottie? What made you think that?"

Catching up to my excitement, she chilled even further, "I've always thought Mark would make a good mayor. He's just what the city needs."

My heart melted at her words and I kind of choked up. "What a nice thing to say, Dottie."

"Oh, Gloria," she giggled.

Now that we were back to the Dottie I was more familiar with, I let out the breath I didn't know I'd been holding.

"Well, here's what I wanted to ask. But before I get to that, please promise you won't answer on the spot. You're too nice, and I'm about to make a big ask. I don't want you feeling pressured in any way. Funk will treasure you always, whatever your answer."

"What did you want to ask, Gloria?"

"I've been setting up Funk's campaign headquarters. Initially, Funk just asked if I'd find a rental, but then it snowballed into a million other things. I can't tell you how much work it's been. Most of it's behind me now, but once he announces he's running, he'll need someone in charge down there."

"What do you have in mind?"

"You know, someone to handle all the stuff that comes with running an office. Who can take care of all the little nuisances that crop up in a day and, God willing, can deal with the voters who come in or call."

"I see."

"And you know Funk. He won't be the usual candidate. Before I sign off from helping him, I want to make sure that anyone who contacts his headquarters is greeted properly. That's what made me think of you. Your caring voice is exactly the welcome mat Funk needs for the campaign."

"Thank you Gloria," she said, smiling sweetly.

"I know it's a lot to ask, but would you consider moving from your current position to his headquarters? I don't know where he'd get the money to pay — "

"Yes."

"Wait a minute, Dottie, I haven't told you everything. It would mean — "

"I said yes, Gloria," she replied with the hugest grin and the color back in her face.

Dottie had gone from passive to assertive in five seconds flat. I was having a difficult time assimilating the change. "No, Dottie, please don't answer now. I don't know if Funk could pay your salary. Ever. What if he doesn't get any donations? Or, worse, what if he doesn't get elected and you have given up your job at city hall for him? Then what? Really, Dottie. Please go home and think it over. Call me on Monday with your answer, okay?"

Laughing her joyous laugh, she gave me a determined reply. "Okay, Gloria. I'll do as you say, but the answer will still be yes."

Shock and goodness soared through my being. Funk was even more adored by his staff than I knew. I don't know how he garnered such loyalty. And with Dottie's so resolute, I sat heavy in the driver's seat, looking just the way she had a few minutes earlier.

The experience with Dottie seemed like a portent of what was to come. I had the flash of a vision: as soon as Funk made his announcement, just as with Dottie, hope would bound throughout the city. The vision was only a flare, but I saw it. I could feel it in my soul. Yet I knew that hope leads to change, and change takes courage. I wasn't sure Kansas City had enough courage to see Funk's campaign all the way through to success.

Back at city hall I gave Dottie a hug. She came around to my side of the car and stuck her head inside my window to say another goodbye, her face all aglow, just as mine had been ever since that day at the carwash.

Dottie gave her notice at city hall and was soon working full-time on

Funk's campaign. She was betting that Funk would raise enough money to match her salary and would have a job waiting for her at the end of the ride.

4 NOVEMBER 2006

MY COSMIC CHILDREN, Nick and Alex, slept over again last night. They were brothers whose single mom had a job that required her to travel part-time. They lived with us for at least two weeks out of every month. I loved the boys, so I didn't mind the "situation" or that their mom paid me *oogotz*, which is Italian for "absolutely fucking nothing." I referred to them my cosmic children because I felt as though the universe had made them mine, in a certain way.

It was incredibly warm outside for November, so we took our morning coffee to the porch and the family hung out for the longest time. The kids were pretty blasé about Funk's run. Even though the loose ends for his opening day were crowding my mind, I steered the conversation to things they were interested in. But mostly, we just kidded around like we always do. I have many favorite parts of the day, but this one was right up there.

After we dispersed I went inside and began chopping vegetables for dinner while Funk hopped into his Corolla and ran a few errands. An hour later he sauntered into the kitchen, his hands full of his dry cleaning, sacks of groceries, and Saturday flowers for his girl, me. My husband isn't the romantic type. Once he alights upon something that delights me, he just repeats the action for all eternity, expecting my same initial response. Still, he did well that week. He gave me a single stem, just as I like. Today's edition was a pink rose with the sunset still glowing inside.

"Wow, Funk, this is gorgeous. Thank you. It smells wonderful." Up on tiptoes, I kissed his mustached lips, the bristles scratching my face.

"I made sure I got it right this time, considering the additional work I've put on you."

"Well, if that was your intent, buddy, this isn't enough."

Turning back to cutting up vegetables, I said, "Give me fifty-two little reasons why you adore me or sixteen big reasons, and you might hit the mark."

"Sixteen, huh? Okay, let's see." With his frame towering above me, he held up a hand to begin the count. He jabbed the air with an index finger and started ticking off, "Belly, boobs, and butt." After which he unraveled two more fingers and said, "That's one, two, and three."

"Oh no you don't. You're not stealing your son's lines. Start over."

"Okay. One, being a source of constant wonder and surprise. Two, teaching our children to have conversations that matter. Three, helping me achieve everything I've ever wanted. Four, fighting with abandon without abandoning any of us. Five, pushing your dress up off your thigh when I put my hand on your leg. Six, choosing the porch over TV. Seven, staring uncompromisingly at the world and not flinching at your own truth. Eight, refusing to fly — and so allowing us to experience the fun of ships and trains. Nine. . . ." The list went on until he reached seventeen, because he always gives me one more than I ask for.

Satisfied by his effort, I let him off the hook and turned the Grateful Dead back up high for company. We always had an early dinner on weekends, so the family was back on the porch at two on the dot. The kids gobbled down their food and off they went, which was when Funk and I started on my to-do list.

15 NOVEMBER 2006

OH, SWEET BABY JESUS, there was no more putting the brakes on. No more chance to turn this ship around. We were in this for keeps. I felt trapped inside a live freeze-frame shot of our life. The scene looked something like this: A cat was practicing a kill with a ball of yarn. The yarn was beginning to unravel all over the floor. That poor ball of yarn had become our life.

Tomorrow was the day we've been waiting forever for. The curtain would finally part on our little secret. It was the beginning of the end of Funk's days as the city auditor. I still didn't get what was driving him. Who would want to be mayor at a time like this, with Kansas City approaching bankruptcy and our nation at the edge of a recession? It had to be a hand from above because no other reason made sense. Oh well. I could obsess about it until my throat closed, but it wouldn't change anything.

His first goodbyes begin in a private lunch with his staff. The fare-thee-wells continued later that afternoon in the chambers deep inside the belly of city hall, where the city council was going to present Funk with a proclamation for his outstanding years of service. That sounded nice, but if any of those thirteen elected officials were truthful about it, their fare-thee-wells would sound like, "Don't let the door hit you in the ass on the way out, Mr. City Auditor."

In his eighteen years at city hall, this last one has been Funk's most trying year. Working for an ever-changing set of bosses had been difficult. Most councilmembers had egos that reached higher than a nuclear plume. This current council had forgotten they were there to serve. They had been spending taxpayers' dollars like fiends and hiding dirty backroom deals behind false smiles. The result had brought the city to her knees. The situation kept my husband awake at night worrying. The only resolution he could imagine had brought us to the ledge my family was currently standing on.

I have to tell you a little something about those backroom deals. TIF is an acronym for "tax increment financing," a measure designed to lift up economically disadvantaged (i.e., poor) areas of the city. Yet the funding had gone mostly to projects in the wealthier parts of town, to the council's rich supporters. The practice, which had depleted the city's general fund, explained Kansas City's inferior basic services and was one reason residents had been moving across the state line to Kansas. The council had been tossing out TIFs like dime store necklaces.

His tough year had affected him, and it put pressure on me and the kids too. Each night at dinnertime, the holy hour in our home, we had to feign interest in Funk's professional life so he could blow off steam. The conversations were more boring than you can imagine. No one at our table other than Funk had much interest in politics or in running a city, and yet we were lectured into oblivion on all things essential to government. This is how it came to be that we became experts on subjects we didn't want to know about. Trust me when I say that I shouldn't have known what a debt ratio is, much less how to balance one, but God knows I had become a specialist in the field. I could repeat verbatim my husband's thinking on any governmental subject, be it moral or financial, though not with his zealousness.

Very soon now, Funk's dream would take us deeper into a story we wanted no part of — the continuing saga of his white hat versus the councilmembers' black hats.

Still, family is family and dreams are dreams, and even when they're stupid dreams, you support family. The kids and I had lived for years dodging the fallout from Funk's ethical code, so I figured we'd learn to live with whatever came of this. That said, knowing something in your head was easier than living it, which was why I lay wide awake at night in the sacred bed when I wished to sleep. My mind churned over all the things the council might do to Funk once they learned the reason behind his decision to retire early. I was sure they'd never considered the possibility he might run for mayor. How I wished I could see their faces when they first heard the news! But boy oh boy, did I ever fear what would come next. It was never a good idea to pull one over on the council. The man they mockingly called the "Almighty City Auditor" had hindered them for years. I was sure his retirement, the hour in which they'd finally run him off, couldn't come fast enough for them.

It was three thirty in the morning, and I'd been twisting all over the bed. My mind kept vacillating between thoughts of all the horrible things the council might do and excitement over the bigness of this day. Funk was on his back, lightly snoring. It was his big moment, so why was he sleeping and not me?

Worried about the hour and how I'd need my game face on for most of the day, I nudged my man gently. "Funk? Wanna put me to sleep?" Instantly conscious, he pulled me to him and said, "I'd love to."

16 NOVEMBER 2006

I FELL ASLEEP shortly after what Funk calls "the festivities" and woke after nine a.m. I had to rush to get ready or I'd be late for the real festivities.

I couldn't believe this day was finally here, yet what a bittersweet day it was! After six months of preparations, I was raring for Funk to pull the trigger on this. The problem was, I was sentimental. I hated goodbyes, even though I knew this goodbye was really a hello.

With no time for my morning sauna or to get a headstart on dinner, I grabbed a quick shower and hurried to dress. At the last second, I put on Funk's favorite earrings — the sterling silver wires with the beaded dangles — before racing off to city hall.

As I was locking the door of the house, I saw my next-door neighbor in her front yard raking leaves for the bazillionth time that fall. Opening the door to my van, I shouted, "Hello, Mrs. Musser! I'm sorry you're out here working again. You should make Jack hire a lawn person."

"Hello, dear, *ha-ha-ha*," she twittered in her creaky voice. "No, honey, I'm fine. I'll leave Jack's money alone."

"Whatever you say, Betty. I'm late for Funk's event. I'll tell you all about it if you're still out here when I get back."

"Okay. Have a good time."

Have a good time? I repeated to myself as I strapped my seatbelt on. I didn't know which would be worse, raking leaves or attending a boring-ass city function.

I sped up Southwest Trafficway and careened onto the exit lane for city hall. As usual, Funk had made arrangements for me to park behind his car, knowing how much I hate the lot across the street with its creepy staff. I pulled in behind Funk's Corolla, nosing his bumper. I walked up the dank staircase and through the carousel doors, coming to a dead stop in front of the elevators.

Ever since I'd noticed the screaming faces staring at me from the fake paneling in my chiropractor's elevator, I'd been leery of getting inside elevators. I passed on the first three that came down, opting to wait for the express so I could ride straight up to Funk's floor. The security guard noticed my hesitation and likely guessed the problem, since he brought it down without me asking. Sucking it up, I stepped inside and held my breath, praying the whole time the elevator car wouldn't get stuck. As soon as the doors opened I bolted out, and before entering the auditor's suite I took a moment to re-apply my game face.

I always felt like I was living inside a dream when I went up there. Funk called me from work each day at ten and two, but I only visited city hall for the auditor's annual Christmas party or for something the council wanted to get credit for acknowledging the city auditor for. Most times, I just viewed the place from Southwest Trafficway, where I made the kids wave to their dad as we zoomed past his building.

Dottie greeted me with her typical sunny hello but gave nothing away. Man, was my husband's staff ever going to be shocked come Monday. Perhaps some had an inkling as to why he was retiring, but so far, no one had let on.

I went from booth to booth, giving each person a kind word, before going inside my husband's office. It was the only way I knew to show my respect for them working so hard on Funk's behalf — really, on the city's behalf — because getting a thanks is terribly lacking for government employees.

My husband's office was the only one that was walled in, but this was the first time I had ever closed the door behind me. Funk sat behind his desk, his feet propped up on the table as always.

"Hey, babe," I said as I went around to give him a kiss hello.

"Hello, darling. Did you make your rounds?"

"Of course," I said as I plopped myself down in the chair across from him. Excitedly I whispered, "Funk, isn't this is so *fucking* unbelievable? I can't believe this day is finally here! My God, it's been *forever*! I'm surprised that I'm nervous. Are you nervous?"

"Nervous? Fuck, no! Bring it the hell on!" he roared.

"Funk!" I said in a reproachful whisper, "Keep your voice down. Do you want your staff to wonder what you're talking about?"

"They'll find out soon enough."

"Jesus, Funk. You've had me in a chastity belt all this time, and you're gonna blow the secret in the final forty-eight hours?"

He didn't respond. Just gnawed on his thumb and raised his shoulders in acknowledgment, and then he stood up and began pacing.

I stared at him. Something was different. His aura had changed. I wish you could see him. He was as pumped up as a warrior going into battle. Confidence oozed from every pore. His stance was daring, like a man secure of the outcome of that battle. I'd never seen him look so . . . geez, how does he look? Euphoric? Funk never looked euphoric.

The luncheon was sedate, the usual up here, them being auditors and all. Still, it was even more low-key than normal. I could hardly believe it, but his staff seemed sad. Before long, the group of us walked down to the council's chambers to watch Funk receive his proclamation. And oh, the BS that followed! On sacred ground, no less. The grand hall that had been built for truth, service, and justice was decimated with fiction.

The mayor stood queenly at the podium, her phony smile frozen to her face, her trademark boutonniere hanging limply atop one deflated breast. She gaveled the meeting to order and asked the city clerk to call the roll. Eight of thirteen councilmembers were present. Of these, four were running for mayor.

The clerk announced, "Zero-six-one-two-seven-three special action, a resolution honoring Mark Funkhouser for his eighteen years of service as city auditor of Kansas City, Missouri. Dr. Funkhouser is here to receive the resolution." Funk was escorted into the bullpen to stand beside Madam Mayor, at which time said mayor's painted smile cracked a bit, as if she were forcing out a long-constipated shit. Putting it quickly back to rights, she declared, "We have a resolution before us." *Pause, smile, smile, star-gleaming-off-an-eyetooth smile.* "Councilman Eddy."

And around the room they went, each councilmember posturing for the media. Most had the biggest hate going for Funk, yet publicly they spoke with gusto about the wonders of my children's father, the People's City Auditor. They lamented his much-too-early retirement and what a loss for the city it was. They had to. They were on TV. With not a care in the world for the audience, they drew the ceremony out long, exploiting the coveted airtime. Some mixed their mock-praise with arrows aimed at my husband's heart.

By the time they wrung the ceremony dry I was beyond upset. For the sake of your nerves, I'll provide highlights:

The facts: Councilman Eddy. Short. Round. Running for mayor. Didn't have a chance in hell of winning the mayoral election.

A mix of comments and myth: "Dr. Mark Funkhouser! You've always been very straightforward, and I've always enjoyed working with you. Your charisma, your ability to cut to the chase, has always been appreciated. You've been controversial, however, and we've enjoyed that at times. Your caring devotion to the city is unswerving and it shows in all that you do."

My thoughts: *You've enjoyed working with my husband? Yeah, right. You squealed like a stuck pig every time one of his audits came out.*

The facts: Councilwoman Nace. Running for mayor. Might win if that damn city auditor didn't throw his hat into the ring.

A mix of comments and myth: "I have always appreciated your audits and have agreed with them 99.8 percent of the time. . . . What you have done most of all for the people and taxpayers of Kansas City is that you have identified ways to better serve them, to save them money. Your audits have saved millions of dollars for the people of Kansas City, and that says a lot about your commitment to the people of Kansas City and to this council."

My thoughts: *Oh boy, councilwoman, come Monday are you ever gonna want to eat those words.*

The facts: Councilman Glover. Running for mayor. Is there a word to describe someone who has less than a chance in hell of winning?

A mix of comments and myth: "The purpose of the auditor is to monitor what goes on. We need that professional, unbiased analysis on how city government is performing its services. I enjoyed working with you and look forward to working with you in the community in the future."

My thoughts: *Believe me, Mr. Glover, you'll soon be wanting to kill him.*

The facts: Councilwoman McFadden-Weaver.

Her comments: "I've learned much from my conversations with you and in seeking information from your office. Kansas City is different just because you're a part of it. Thank you so much."

My thoughts: *What a cordial thing to say. You exemplify the way leaders should behave.*

The facts: Councilman Fairfield. Running for mayor. Still. Even though the rumor was that he'd just been caught with his pants down. At city hall. Precariously perched, half-on and half-off his citizen-loaned desk. Inside his citizen-loaned office. Astride his citizen-funded employee. Yes, that councilman. The elected official who for no good reason gleefully voted against salary increases for my husband. And Christ, the crap that came dribbling out of him. And yes. I know. Those aren't the best-chosen words considering what I just told you.

The myth: "I've enjoyed your candid discussions with us. We don't always agree, but we could always have a good conversation about it. Now there might be time to play that game of chess."

My thoughts: *Uh-huh. Sure thing, councilman. I'll pencil that game into his calendar.*

The facts: Councilman Riley. Running for council reelection.

His comments: "Thank you for all the oddball requests that you went out and got for me. I know that you will be busy doing many other things, probably joining a whole crew of other people doing something around Kansas City."

My thoughts: *Oh my God, he knows! How the fuck does he know?*

The facts: Councilman Nash. Extraordinarily eloquent and by far the most suave, gracious politician in the room. I adored Nash's jab at his council-neighbor.

His comments: "Dr. Funkhouser's commitment to Kansas City goes without saying. Others have spoken that he has been a strong, independent voice as part of this government. But I do want to point out a few other accomplishments. Mark also holds a master's degree in social work." Here, with (black) Councilman Nash's eyes still trained on my husband's, Nash began directing his oratory to (white) Councilman Skaggs, because Skaggs's voice sounded clearly over Nash's. "That might be where he gets that social agenda from, that is reflected, Mr. Skaggs, in many of his audits." Nash turned to speak directly to Skaggs — the gentlest way of scolding the man — and glided into the rest of his commentary. "Dr. Funkhouser is probably one of the country's leading performance-auditing experts, and he's here in our midst."

My thoughts: *Is this guy smooth, or what? And did I mention that he's astonishingly handsome, too? Like, in take-your-breath-away handsome?*

The facts: Councilman Skaggs is a favorite of mine at city hall.

His comments: "Mark, there's not much left to be said. I think my colleagues have covered it all and I agree with them. Good luck in your next endeavor. We'll miss you around here."

My thoughts: *I love you to pieces, Councilman Skaggs!*

And finally, it was Mayor Kay Barnes's turn.

The facts: In her defense, I believe the elementary-school-teacher-turned-group-sex-educator began her first term sincerely. Yet, as they did to most mayors in Kansas City, the media ate her alive. The harassment was so unrelenting that she tossed her campaign promises, succumbing to the self-serving agendas of the ill-begotten establishment. It takes courage to stay pure with that type of bullying going on. The abuse she endured in the media was probably where her disdain for my husband originated. He continued pointing out all the areas where the citizens were being screwed. If I were Barnes, I'd probably have an intense hate for Funk too.

More facts: To approach the microphone, Mayor Barnes had to come near my husband. That proximity being less desirable than a colonoscopy, she moved her face a few inches forward but, like an acrobat, arched the rest of her body backward, keeping herself as far away from him as possible while still being able to press her lips to the mic. I don't know about television viewers, but I could easily hear the sharp spring of that recoil reverberating off the consecrated walls of the Council Chambers. Through teeth clamped so tightly that it showed in her temples, the mayor proclaimed, "We have a resolution before us." *Pause, bright smile.* "All those in favor say aye. . . . The resolution is adopted."

Lost-in-my-head thoughts: *Lord, I don't want to go here, but I suddenly feel sorry for the woman. With the proclamation now behind her, she has no other formality to delay her repugnant task. The only item remaining is to heap her unheartfelt praise onto the city auditor.*

As quickly as my empathy presented, it left in a flash. For when the mayor got on with it, she did not swallow her bitterness and assume the dressings of a leader. She did not tell how Mark Funkhouser had embodied the essence of a public servant. She did not say that he'd held the government accountable in using resources in a way that maximized effectiveness and productivity. Or that his work improved the quality of life for residents of Kansas City and restored their trust in city government. She said . . .

The myth: "Mark, it's my honor to present this resolution to you for many, many years of service. We all know that you care deeply about the city. You believe strongly in the approaches that you promote, and we do respect that."

More lost-in-my-head thoughts: Mayor Barnes was still talking, but I couldn't listen anymore. I was too appalled by it all.

What the mayor said about Funk was true. The problem was, she didn't believe a word of it. She said it for the camera and only because she knew the positive regard citizens had for my husband. The dishonesty gave me a sick, depressed feeling in my gut.

I was angry at all the terrible things Barnes had done to my husband over the years, yet I also feel compassion for the brokenness inside her that would make her do such things. I also felt sorry for all the other lost souls who were sitting in a horseshoe shape around the mayor. Hardly any of them seemed to be getting pleasure from serving. They were clinging fiercely to a title, but only to make themselves feel important, and how sad was that? I have heart for those who've been hurt in unimaginable ways, but seeing people choosing not to rise above their hurts made me feel disillusioned. Weren't honor and valor supposed to be the hallmarks of our elected officials? Shouldn't telling a lie never cross your mind once you've been chosen to lead? More, shouldn't a councilmember be more than an ordinary peon like me?

Drowning in bitter reflections, I consoled myself with unbecoming thoughts: *Wait till Monday, guys. Payback is a bitch. Karma is coming to get you.*

Oh my God! I had a sudden insight. The council had just fucked themselves. Their glowing testimonials about the outgoing city auditor had been captured on film, which meant they'd all just endorsed him for mayor, and they couldn't take it back.

Final words from Mayor Barnes: "I think you have made an enormous contribution to the city, so please know that we deeply appreciate it."

My thoughts: *You look tired, Mayor. I'm sorry to have to tell you this, but before you can lay your head down tonight, even though you'll feel exhausted, you're gonna have to recite the Act of Contrition for that load of crap you just disgorged.*

Finally, Madam Mayor stepped away from the podium, with what I'm sure she thought with relief was my husband's last fifteen minutes of fame. She stood stiff-backed to have her picture snapped with the almost-gone auditor, shaking Funk's right hand and placing the proclamation in his left. I could see right through her gesture. Because more than anything in the world, the mayor would've preferred to stuff that proclamation right up his ass.

With that last formality behind her, she waved Funk toward the podium. My husband looked surprised but at once stepped up to the mic, with the aura of a mayor. A true mayor.

The facts: City Auditor Mark Funkhouser. Husband. Father. Social worker. PhD. Honorable. Unconventional. Dependable. Courageous. Shocking as it is, extremely gullible and doesn't know how to scheme.

His comments: "Thank you for all the kind words. I have been stunned ever since I announced my retirement. I mean, I see my work as kind of like a plumber or carpenter. I go to work every day and try to do the best job that I can. I guess I didn't realize some of the views that people had of me, and I'm very grateful — *Oh my God, he actually believes what the council just said. See what I mean about him being gullible?* — and I guess the overwhelming sensation that I have is that I am grateful to you, the city council. I serve at your pleasure, and it's been my good fortune to have the opportunity to work for the citizens of Kansas City for eighteen years. I'm very grateful for that. I'm grateful to my staff because — *Here, my man tries to make a joke, but it falls on the council like a limp dick* — I'm just the pretty face. They do the excellent work that we have been recognized for. These are smart, capable, competent, caring people, and I am grateful to them. As I leave, I want to say two or three more things. Councilman Fairfield, Tuesday nights at the Flea Market you can get a cheeseburger and a good beer and a good game of chess, and I'll be there just about every Tuesday night.

The final thing I want to say is, thank you so much, I'm grateful to the council for having the good judgment to decide on Gary White as your next interim city auditor. I think he's going to be great."

With those words, my husband stepped down from the podium. But just for a little while — of that I was certain.

17 NOVEMBER 2006

FUNK WAS HOME at five-thirty sharp. What with more goodbye parties, he didn't get a lick of work done on his last day as the city auditor.

In bed that night, just after he turned off the light, as usual, I scooted myself into a spooning position with him. And, not quite as usual, I backed straight into the Big Whoop. It stabbed me in the thigh, and I thought to myself, *Oh brother, is he ever going to be a handful with this happiness thing.* But nice wife that I am, I said, "Hey, big guy, I have a ton of work tomorrow to get your invitations out the door. You remember the kick-off party, right? For your dream?"

He moved closer and started rubbing my leg.

I elbowed him away and said, "Good Lord, Funk, do yourself. I'm busy over here."

18 NOVEMBER 2006

THE WEEKEND was going to be busy as all get out. Funk wouldn't let me send the invitations to his campaign kick-off until his last day of work. It was customary to provide two weeks' notice for a shindig of this size, so I should have dropped off the envelopes at the post office the previous night. But I'd barely had time to design the card and place the print order.

I hopped out of bed at the first ray of light and was at the print shop as soon as the door opened. The owner of Marthabelle's was a real creepolla. I asked to see a sample before giving him my credit card. He made it seem like that was the most unusual request in the world. Given his reaction, I was pleasantly surprised with the results. If the first faux pas of the campaign had to be that the invitations were late, at least they were classy. I couldn't stop thinking about how astonished people were going to be when they found one in their mailbox.

No time for the usual Saturday fun of taking in an estate sale or window-shopping at Anthropologie. Instead, I raced home, took the stairs two at a time up to my office, and grabbed the whittled-down guest list from my desk.

We were going to hand-address the envelopes, much to Funk's dismay. At the dining room table, with all the pens and envelopes in place, Funk griped, "Gloria, you said we're running late with this mailing. I don't think we are, but you seem to know the rules."

"And?"

"Looking at your to-do list, I see three weeks' work piled into this one weekend."

"What are you saying, Funk?"

"Why don't we print address labels, slap them on the envelopes, and start tackling the rest of the items on your list?"

"*My* other items? Christ, Funk, I can't believe you're complaining. I'm helping you, remember? I should be out enjoying myself right now. No, we're not half-assing this."

For some reason, my husband had been bolder lately.

"What's wrong with — "

"Get back inside your box, Funk. We've gone over this a million times. Labels look tacky, and you agreed to run your campaign elegantly. The kids and I are associated with you, and we don't want your hick persona bleeding onto us. You're engaging regular folks, and you need to show them the respect they've never gotten from any other candidate. That's why we're not slapping on a label," I said, swooshing the air with my hand.

"I've been working for folks in this city for years, Gloria. They already know I respect them."

"Yes, Funk. But if you want to win, and I think you do, you have to continue demonstrating your regard with the only thing you have: class. Well, you don't have any, but thank God, I've got enough for you. Pick up a pen already. All you've done this morning is sit on the couch with your feet propped up on the coffee table reading that stupid newspaper."

Abashed, he grabbed the pen closest to him.

The guest list included three hundred and fifty people from all walks of life — Funk's fraternity brothers and colleagues, our friends, family members, exchange students, neighbors, and even some of my birth students. Everyone invited was meaningful to our family in some way. This was going to be a campaign opening like none other. We were kicking it off with a celebration. There would be nothing political about it. No shaking our guests down for money. No television crews tipped to the event. Funk wouldn't work the room to schmooze with politicos, because we hadn't invited any. I did have donation envelopes printed, but they'll be placed off to the side, along with the ugly campaign buttons and my pretty volunteer sign-up sheets. But that was the beginning and end of it.

Many hours later, we still hadn't finished addressing the envelopes. Damn. I wanted everyone to receive them on Monday, as the garnish for Funk's press event. But the task would remain undone because it was time to get ready for our dinner date with the Wolfs. I was excited about the evening. Funk was *finally* going to tell someone else his big news! He and Ed Wolf had worked together at city hall. Wolf had headed the Department of Public Works for years but retired a few years back.

According to Funk, Ed was a dedicated public servant. I liked the guy, but I liked his wife more. I sometimes called her Gwennie, and she seemed to like my affectionate name for her. Her husband was Midwestern down to his tasseled loafers, but Gwen had *pizzazz*! I bet her closet didn't have a single beige piece of clothing hanging forlornly within it. I had a strong feeling she was a witch. I didn't know why, other than she had sparkling green eyes. I didn't give two shits whether she was or not, I'm just curious, is all.

Gwen was more than an acquaintance. I hung out with her and Ruth Bates at city-related functions. Ruth, who I called "Ruthie," was as un-Midwest as Gwen, except that she didn't possess Gwen's sizzling personality. Ruth had a lot of other good qualities, though. She dressed as well as any New Yorker. And although she was shy like me, once you got to know her, Ruth's quiet nature disappeared. She loved having fun.

I was almost dressed when Funk came into our bedroom, naked from the shower.

"You look beautiful, babe."

"Thanks, Funk. Er, you don't," I said as I flicked his balls.

He was toweling his hair dry when I did that and drew a knee up like a little girl, yelping in surprise.

"What did you do to him, Mom?" yelled Andrew's voice from his bedroom down the hall. Andrew loved playfulness just as I did.

"He's naked. What do you think I did?"

"Gross, Mom! Leave him alone!"

Soon Funk and I were out the door. Blessed with an unexpectedly fabulous weather day, we walked to our date. Along the way, a strange thing happened. Drivers honked their horns as they passed us, some even slowing to give Funk a thumbs up. It was normal for city residents to recognize my husband on the street, but this was entirely different. The sentiment exhibited for a newly retired public servant was crazy to behold. Like, who gives a shit about a city auditor? If I weren't married to one, I certainly wouldn't.

The weirdest thing of all happened as we rounded the corner to the restaurant. A guy in an expensive car came to a dead stop and started leaning on his horn like a maniac. Having gotten our attention, he lifted himself out of his window and shouted, "Mr. City Auditor, you should run for mayor." Then he burned rubber and peeled away.

I had a lot of feelings about his actions. The first was annoyance; I hate being startled. Next was a bad taste in my mouth on account of yet another interruption to our private time. Then came wonder. Because other people were on our wavelength. On the heels of that came a quiet acknowledgment. It was just so obvious that Funk was going to win the election.

My husband waved at the guy, escorted me into Avenues Bistro, and the two of us settled into the booth where the Wolfs were already seated. The Wolfs were as giddy at our news as third graders who had been sneaked candy beneath their desks.

We lingered after dinner talking and laughing until I said we had to leave. It wasn't late; I just felt guilty for being gone so long, with the kids at home. We spoke on the sidewalk before saying a final goodbye. After a round of hugs, Funk and I waited at the curb as Ed and Gwen pulled away in their gigantic SUV, waving at us like two youngsters setting off on a field trip. I looked up at my husband and said, "Well, there go a couple more in Kansas City who can't wipe the smile from their face." But as soon those words hit the atmosphere, my smile turned into a frown. I'd had a week of wildly swinging emotions — first up, then down, but never neutral — yet in my next heartbeat, my hyped-up feelings went from happy to panic. I could feel myself standing on top of something big. I could sense the curve of the Earth, feel her power emanating beneath my feet. Funk was on the verge of being the mayor of a large metropolitan city. Yet now that we were immersed in a reality that couldn't be changed, the horizon felt really scary. I hated feeling trapped, and Lord, did

I ever feel trapped. Funk had quit his job and couldn't get it back, and while I was no clairvoyant, it wasn't hard to predict what was going to happen on Monday, after the press event.

This city loved my man to pieces. Well, the establishment didn't, but its residents surely did, and the media were gaga for him, especially *The Kansas City Star*.

I'm not talking about mild gaga. The newspaper had such a lovefest going that they'd all but turned him into a celebrity. Sometimes Funk's head was so big he could barely fit through our front door, and we had double front doors! Whenever Funk released an audit report, the media immediately requested an interview with him. Why those reports made headline news is still a mystery to me. From the saturated news coverage, Kansas City's auditor developed a reputation as a tough son of a bitch. Funk was one of those rare government officials who held a highly political position yet was open and honest in interviews. When you coupled that with Funk's preacher-way of speaking, you could see why the media ate him up with a spoon.

Funk was so chummy with some reporters that he'd asked me to add a handful of their names to our annual Christmas Newsletter roster. You had to be more than an acquaintance to get on that list. Many journalists said they looked forward to receiving those newsletters, and a few even left me messages to tell me how funny they thought a particular installment was. Some even called me a writer. *A writer!* Imagine a big-time reporter thinking that of a little nothing like me! Attached to the newsletter was an invitation to our annual New Year's Day party, which meant that the families of those reporters became regular guests in our home. My daughter even babysat the children of the business section editor of *The Kansas City Star*.

The media exposure was so prolific that Funk became an easily identifiable public figure. With that, a lot changed for our family, the most significant being the loss of our privacy. Normal, everyday things just weren't normal anymore. I loved hanging out with my kids, but I looked forward to the moments when Funk and I had time as a couple, even if we were only running errands together. After the media exposure, it didn't matter where we went — we could be grocery shopping or perusing the goods at Home Depot — and strangers would approach, act like old friends, yuk it up with Funk, and ask him to introduce them to "the wife." Before you knew it, we'd be trapped in the nuts and bolts aisle with citizens complaining about "that damn mayor and council," the tête-à-tête ending twenty minutes later. The interruptions made it such that I had to go off by myself to look for the items that we'd come out for. This was a loss for both of us, but Funk's dance was more intricate than mine. He not only had to deal with my disappointment over the forsaken outing, but he also had to deal with the public, not an easy thing. Funk respected authority. He couldn't rightly join in with them dissing the council, yet he didn't want to come off as snooty either.

I can understand how Funk's manner supported his mayoral endeavor. He was not just gracious; he was on the road toward being graceful. I could hardly believe it, but my husband was a natural. His evolution had surprised me. Being from the sticks, Funk wasn't the greatest at social niceties. He loved people, he'd just been brought up inelegantly.

Even folks on the other side of the state line had been cheering him on. It blew my mind. Why all the fuss? Because Funk had the balls to stand up to the establishment? Because he tried stopping the council from screwing the city sideways? Because he didn't let raises withheld from him keep him from whipping city hall into shape? Had there really been no others who did such things?

My biggest worry concerned the media. They'd created an image of Funk not totally steeped in reality. It's true that my husband *is* a fearsome straight shooter, a champion for the underdog who is chinked in iron. It bothered me, though, that the image-making seemed to be intentional, as if they'd been using Funk to talk shit on the city council — the shit being the controversy that sells newspapers. Even seedier, they had an agenda. By glorifying Funk, the newspaper essentially directed the way the city was run. And in the same way they had created a positive image of Funk-the-auditor, they could take him down once he was Funk-the-mayor.

Such were the reasons that I landed in that dreaded sea of muck. Funk was high on yin now — the savior of the working class — but yang was always lurking around the corner. And that was not my Italian talking. I knew from running my own business what it felt like to be placed on a pedestal. The problem is, up was a long way back down.

20 NOVEMBER 2006

WE WERE READY to jump off the cliff. The press event would begin at eleven a.m., and I'd been at the trailer since early that morning getting everything ready. Actually, I'd had everything ready the night before, but I couldn't sit still. I was too excited or agitated — I couldn't tell which. I needed to keep moving or I'd go mad.

I hit Send on the press release seconds before leaving home and did the same with the email inviting our friends. Those messages were the first public acknowledgments that Funk had thrown his hat into the already-crowded ring. I wished I could see people's face when they opened that email. I was sure no one had suspected, especially not the press.

I'd been putting finishing touches on the finishing touches for hours. The fifty-cup coffeemaker stood ready for action. All I had to do was flip the switch to start it brewing. I wanted to put the cookies out, but I was afraid they'd go stale, so I was making myself wait. It was Funk's first day of being an ordinary citizen in over thirty years. I was staying as far away from him as possible. I couldn't stand being around him when he was nervous. Of course, he said he wasn't nervous, and hearing him say that only made me feel more disagreeable toward him. But I kept that to myself. I didn't want to hate him on this momentous day. Why have that be the takeaway? I'd deal with my jumping nerves on my own.

I was doubly excited. With Funk *finally* working on his own damn campaign, I would be, as of later that day, a free woman! I still had his announcement party to organize, but I'd do that from home, far from the dumpy old trailer.

Pacing, pacing. Bending over to pick up lint. Wiping tables of just-fallen dust. Gathering stacks of handouts, shuffling each to the sharpest edge, and setting them down just so on our family's holiday-turned-campaign table. Flipping each campaign button right side up — the blue Funk stars looked cheap — but hey, Funk had no financial backers, so we were grateful for whatever we had. I hadn't eaten. I couldn't eat. My empty stomach was contributing to my jitters. Funk passed by on the way to the bathroom. Again. He'd been in and out of there a million times already. But, no, he wasn't nervous. And he wasn't grouchy either. I was trying not to take even the smallest peek at him, because no matter what he told me, I knew he felt ten times worse than I did.

The toilet flushed and he went back to his office, the one that I'd made homey for him. I loitered in the reception area wiping dust off the coffee table so I could spy on him. He was reading his speech with his dirty shoes propped up on the clean desk. Geez, what was it with him? Was he not even thinking? I'd have to race in there to clean it again after the press arrived.

We'd stayed up until the wee hours editing his speech, making fifty billion one-last-changes, every time promising the last would be the last. Hopefully, he wouldn't change it again. I had it double-spaced on card stock for easy reading and turning of pages. There was no time to redo it as pretty as I had it now.

Almost showtime. I stepped inside the office where I'd worked since this project first began and closed the door. I needed to compose myself. And pray. The little bells on the front door, left over from Spring's acupuncture clinic days, were tinkling away. Dottie was the first one in. She stood at the entrance greeting visitors, but I wouldn't go back out until the media arrived. When they did, I'd leave my hidey-hole and perform my wifely duties. Welcome everyone kindly, offer refreshments. Until then, I had no capacity for small talk.

I had begun my second round of prayers when I saw the first of the media cruise into the parking lot. I was sure Funk was going to win, so all I was doing was asking the deities to help him do a good job presenting himself. I closed my appeal with a kiss skyward and popped a few balls of *Argentum nitricum* for my nerves. The little blue tube said the homeopathic remedy was for treating stage fright, and that seemed appropriate for what I was feeling. I glanced in the mirror one last time to ensure my hair was becoming, my nostrils free of ghastly debris, and my dress smoothed to rights before I turned the handle of the door and leaped. Toward what, I did not know.

Game face on, I walked to the lobby and greeted the reporters. Their expressions were grim, as if they were stopping by a funeral. This wasn't their big day; why so serious? No matter. I gave each a smile, directions on where to set up cameras and equipment, pointed out the his-and-her bathrooms, and offered a coffee and a handout. Most looked right through me, so intent were they on getting their own bead on the place. The only media who were personable were the "waitstaff," the cameramen and such — especially a big, burly dude named Jeff. He seemed Italian, like me. Kissed me full on the lips, though we'd never met before. People don't act like that around here. But it's the way New Yorkers respond, so the gesture brought me comfort. Even he refused my refreshments, opting instead to grab a front-row position for his camera in the staging area. At least he acknowledged me. After this kiss he dropped a few funny words that broke the tension before scurrying off to set up his tripod. I didn't know how he knew, but he chose the best spot in the room. Because, at the appropriate time, that was where Funk would stand. *If* he remembered. We'd gone over it a million times. He needed to stand exactly in that spot if the cameras were to catch the backdrop that I had commissioned for the occasion. It was embarrassingly conventional, but it was the only thing we had to make the campaign appear legitimate and to get Funk's message out there. With no donations as of yet, he had to milk this media exposure for all it was worth, so I hoped he'd remember.

Friends keep coming up to me, saying things like "I can't believe you didn't tell me." "Why didn't you tell me?" "When did you decide?" The reporters were asking the same questions, but of each other. "Did you know?" "No, I didn't know until this morning." "Did he just now decide?" Unlike our friends, who were excited to be part of something this colossal, the reporters seemed miffed that we hadn't notified them sooner.

One minute to go. Funk sauntered into the room, speech cards in hand.

Reporters surrounded him like little ants, tacking microphones to his lapel. The mics weighed his suit down, making it look funny. I wanted to rearrange them into an orderly configuration, but I didn't dare go near him. He'd have a cow, and he was already having a cow. Thank God it didn't show.

Friends insisted that I stand beside them, kept grabbing at me, pulling me to and fro. But I couldn't be near anyone. I perched against the entrance to Funk's office, hoping the door jamb would hold me up. It was as far away from everyone as I could get, yet still close enough to my husband to send him good energy. It was also out of his line of vision. Like a workhorse, he needed blinders on so he wouldn't spook.

Cameras jammed in his face. Funk called the time. Took possession. Didn't look at the cue cards in hand. Just came roaring out of the box. Full-blown preacher mode. He knocked it out of the fucking park.

I didn't expect that. I'd seen him speak hundreds of times, but this was different. It was as if his whole life had directed him to this moment. He was beaucoup confident, dignified, uncommonly sexy — *Where the hell did that come from?* — just doing what he does, laying out the facts and slaughtering camouflage with the truth. Passionately. Using words that common people can understand. Finished, he opened the floor to questions.

Curve balls came one on top of another. Funk stayed rooted. Met each with a quick, honest, cogent comeback. No normal politician, this one. Surprisingly, the questions were pretty much the same ones he got when he was the auditor. But now, the reporters were asking whether Funk-the-mayor would make good on the recommendations in his audit reports. Would those be his agenda if he got elected? *Would? If?* Couldn't they see? I'd never been to a press conference before, but why else would Funk be running mayor if not for that?

C'mon, ask him something meaty already. Besides, were they even paying attention? That's only what he'd been saying he'd do for the past hour now.

Oh shit. The room had just stilled. The reporters were standing at ramrod attention. Funk must have said something! What did he say? Ruminating on all the peculiarities, I had stopped paying attention. *Oh, I get it.* It made sense that his response had piqued their interest. The media loved Funk's distinctive turns of phrase. The kids and I had heard them a thousand times over, which is likely why my mind had drifted, but these guys heard that line for the very first time. Man, are they ever zoned in on it, like tigers tracking prey.

"I've always thought the talk I heard from community leaders about making Kansas City a world-class city was just silly. Heck, I just want us to be metropolitan class. Forget Paris; let's try to compete more effectively with Prairie Village!"

The press were creaming themselves over the Paris to Prairie Village comparison. We'd been in discussion about it for twenty minutes. It had gotten boring. *C'mon, Funk, move it along already.*

None of the questions tossed out that morning was unique. It was just the same old drivel, except for a question posed by Joe Arce. He was from the *Hispanic News* and was the only media rep in the room using antiquated equipment. But Lord Almighty, was this little man ever bold! All by himself, he changed the subject, and as he did, he shoved his tape recorder right up Funk's nose. I was shocked Funk didn't bristle.

I don't remember Arce's exact question, but I remember his sentiment, which was something like this:

"Mark, what made you choose the West Side for your campaign headquarters?"

"My wife chose the place for me." *Jesus, Funk! Really? Do you always have to be so honest?*

"There's never been a campaign on the West Side before. Why did you locate it here, Mark?" *Wait a second. Didn't Arce already ask that?*

I held my breath, waiting to see how Funk would respond the second time, figuring he'd just go to the next-most-truthful answer. The one that told how the double-wide was the only place he could afford. Instead, he responded with a truth I'd forgotten.

"Because if the city is to survive, Joe, we need people living downtown again."

But little man Joe wasn't having it. As the other reporters had done with Prairie Village, Arce was beating this question into oblivion. He asked it over and over in different ways, hoping, I think, the response he was looking for would come spilling from Funk's tongue. Funk was so literal, he was oblivious to the between-the-lines happenings. I wished I could whisper to him what was going on. There was nothing I could do about it. Funk kept responding with the same answer. Because that's how it is with someone who speaks the truth.

But Arce was hanging in there, fishing for something, even as the other reporters were beginning to shuffle. Fifteen minutes had ticked by, and Arce didn't seem to give two shits that he was hogging the time. I was surprised the others were putting up with it. It took a lot for Funk to lose his patience, but once he did, it was over. Aware now that he'd answered Arce in full, he was ready to move on, but Arce wasn't having it. *Uh-oh, that's a mistake, Mr. Arce. Now you've done it. C'mon, Funk, don't lose your cool. You've been doing good so far. Don't let this little man make you lose your stride.*

My husband gazed at the sea of heads squished into the tiny reception area and was about to call on a different reporter when Arce fired off another question. Actually, the same question. Just asked in another different way.

"But Mr. Funkhouser, there's lots of places one could call downtown. Why the West Side? Are you trying to say that you support the Hispanic population? Are you asking for our support?"

Funk was agitated, but he remained levelheaded. I scanned the reporters' faces. Thank God, I don't think anyone had noticed his simmering mood.

From a primal stance, Funk responded like an old chieftain, grandfatherly but no-nonsense: "I'm asking for everyone's support, Joe. Here. Over on the East Side. Up north. Down south. From anyone who wants the same thing that I want: a city that works for regular folks."

"Are we regular folks, Mr. Funkhouser?"

Oh, fuck. Don't step in his trap, Funk. Watch yourself, boy.

But Funk wasn't watching anything. He just wanted to give the other reporters a turn to ask questions, and Arce was blocking that. Funk boomed, in a vexed tone, "No, Joe. What I'm saying is what I've been saying. There's nothing hidden here. I want to level the playing field for the people of our city. Spread the wealth. Does *that* answer your question?"

"Mr. Funkhouser, are you a Republican?"

Fucking hell!

Clearly pissed, Funk said in a very unfriendly way, "Joe. I know you're aware this is a nonpartisan race, but if you're looking for my values, I'm fiscally conservative and socially liberal. Next person."

Oh, Lord. There it went. My husband just lost the election. He had it in his pocket, but now it was gone. All that work, down the drain. What was he thinking! There are some facts a person can skirt, you know.

Oh my God, what was I saying? Funk did exactly what our family had agreed to do. He spoke the truth, with the corresponding emotion. He was not in this for anything other than fixing the city. If that was what citizens wanted, they'd vote for him. If it wasn't, he'd find a different job. Yay, Funk! You did good. Bring it home, boy!

I don't know what poor Mr. Arce was after, and I don't think he got it. And it's too bad, because even though he stressed Funk out, at least his questions had weight. They were way more significant than the gibberish other reporters asked of this unexpected and late-getting-into-the-game candidate. You'd think that fact alone would have sparked more meaningful exchange. But what did I know? Maybe this was what politics looked like. Talk about uninteresting.

The event broke up shortly after Funk put a stop to Arce's endless probing, lasting twenty times longer than we had anticipated. Just as quickly as everyone had slammed into the trailer, is just how quickly they slammed back out.

It was well past lunchtime, and I was beyond spent. My blood sugar was low because I had not eaten that day. Funk always noticed me going down before I did, and for his own self-preservation he hopped into the car to get takeout for the three of us who remained: him, me, and Dottie. As soon as he left, I began cleaning up the mess, beginning with the fifty-cup coffee maker. I went to lift it, but it was as heavy as when I had first set it down. The press had taken barely a cup of the coffee, and the cookies were mostly uneaten too. What a waste of money! Oh, well, what can you do? The expense was already on our credit card, whether the food was in anyone's belly or not. Once I had set the lobby back to rights, I vacuumed the joint. After that, I gave the bathrooms a once-over As expected, there was pee on the floor in the men's room. Don't guys know there's this handy little thing called toilet paper they can use to dab themselves dry? Or better yet, how about they sit down and take a load off? It's the same principle as when they're dropping a load in. I clean our bathrooms at home because I like every inch to sparkle, but that's my family's pee. It skived me to be wiping up after strangers.

When the trailer was as perfect as it had been before the event, I began gathering my belongings into a neat pile. Having spent more time in the trailer that fall than I had spent at home, the few items I'd brought in each day had amounted up to a sizable pile. But no matter. In just a few hours I'd be off wife-duty and my things would be back where they belonged.

I set the bundle by the front door, but since Funk wasn't back with the food yet, I grabbed my computer and went to my office to rest for a while. I was in the middle of responding to emails when Funk arrived, shaking the trailer with his heavy footstep. As he stopped into my doorway, his arms loaded with greasy bags of food, I said, "Funk, what the hell took you so long?"

"People kept coming up to shake my hand or to tell me to go get those sonofabitches."

"Wow. The news is already out? That's amazing!"

"They say it's all over radio and TV."

"Geez, that was fast!" I said brightly before disappointment set in. "But Funk, you were gone for so long that I barely have time to sit with you now."

"Why?"

"Christ, Funk! Do you remember? We have a son. I have to get Andrew from school. I have an hour, at best."

If I had used that tone three months earlier, his bottom lip would've protruded so far that I'd have been drowning in a sea of drool. But on this day? Nothing. He just gave me a breezy "Okay!" as if it were a small thing that I'd be missing out on the most fun part of the day, the rehashing of everything.

Trying to shake off my mood, I went to his office and unpacked our lunch. Setting a bag of french fries on his once-again-clean desk, I said, with more uplift than I felt, "Oh well, we can talk about everything while we're eating. But hurry, Funk, I can't wait to hear what you thought about everything. You looked nervous but stoked. Were you nervous? I would've been so scared. I don't know how you stood there like that. Hey, what did you think about those reporters lighting on your Prairie Village piece like that? Don't they know the city is going down? They acted like they heard the news for the first time today. And what was it with that Arce guy? Can you believe he was using a cassette recorder? My God, Funk, he almost had that thing shoved up your nose. I'm surprised it didn't piss you off. And what about the question he asked fifty thousand ways? That was so weird, wasn't it? And who was that pasty-white dude? Dave Helling? I never heard you mention him. Which station does he work for? That's strange, if he works for the newspaper, why did he have a video camera? Man, he's one angry sad sack, huh? What's his story? Oh never mind, tell me later. I want to hear what you think about Cauthen. Funk, you better not fire the city manager straightaway. That would be way wrong. Who knows, Barnes probably forced him to be as incompetent as you say he is, what with her forcing TIF projects on him, and all. . . ."

My husband barely answered my questions because that's how he rolls. He had to think first. And the man can't think when he's hungry. Me? I can respond on a dime to any question.

When I had set the food out I invited Dottie to join us, and we three dined together at Funk's desk. Well, Funk and I ate. Dottie just sat there folded in on herself, looking as pale as someone who has just come down with the flu. She merely nibbled at her burger. Every once in a while, she'd set it down and pick up a fry, only to have it hang from her fingertips like an after-market hard-on. For some reason she'd reverted to being a deer in the headlights, same as at our Deep Throat meeting of a few months earlier. Or had that been a few weeks ago? Things had been moving so fast I couldn't keep track. All I know is the whole time we dined, the phones were ringing off the hook and Dottie, although she wasn't eating, never stopped picking at her food to answer them. When I couldn't listen to them go unanswered a second longer, I grabbed my sandwich, ran back to my office, and began answering them myself. It was a relief. Dottie seemed so nervous that she was making me nervous.

I threw my sandwich onto the desk and didn't even bother sitting down, just grabbed the receiver as if I knew what I was doing and started putting callers on hold. After taking a second to situate myself in my chair, I picked up the first caller and gave him my full attention. Minutes later, you could have blown me away when I answered a line and heard my son's voice. He'd been calling me on my cell phone, which I hadn't heard over the ringing of the office lines. As usual, he was brief. He asked that I not come to the school to pick him up for another hour. Dottie must've overheard me talking because she came charging out of Funk's office and began picking up calls. After I finished my conversation with Andrew every phone line was still blinking, so I felt compelled to continue helping, even though I badly wanted to use the extra hour to talk over the event with Funk.

When the ringing slowed, my mind drifted to the situation with Dottie. I didn't get it. She had been her normal perky self during the event, but now that it was just the three of us, she seemed nervous again. When I had suggested that Funk make her the office manager it was because he'd told me a million times how she managed the auditor's office like a champ. I was banking on that, but in Funk's campaign headquarters she wouldn't make a move without checking with me first, even when I told her there was no need. She acted as though I was the boss, but I wasn't, nor did I want to be.

Around and around I went with circling thoughts. Should I help Funk for a few more weeks? Just until he and Dottie established a routine? Even if I made myself available until after the Coming-Out Party for our friends next month, how could I be Dottie's boss, given that I sucked at being a boss? I could direct children with ease, but I expected too much from adults, or so I'd been told.

When BirthWays grew so large that I couldn't attend all the births asked of me, I had added a doula-training program to my business. I'd worked plenty of service industry jobs — from selling cosmetics door-to-door at age ten, to cleaning houses at fifteen, to waitressing just before I went to college. I expected my doula staff to take the job as seriously as I did. You couldn't just up and leave a woman in labor, no matter how tired you were.

You should have heard some of the things those doula trainees said to me. I still didn't get it. When I picked up their three a.m. calls, with the doula boo-hooing about the labor taking too long and threatening to go home, I just lay in bed and rolled my eyes. Funk's staff worked for him for years on end, but mine never stuck around. That was why I knew that having me supervising Dottie would never work. Besides, she was the one who'd be running the headquarters. It still awed me what she'd done, following Funk to a new job. Few people would've taken such a chance. I believed in my husband with my entire being, but Dottie believed in his dream. For that alone she deserved my respect. But that might be the problem. She was looking to me for direction, and I kept pitching the decisions back to her. She seemed to feel as if she was in over her head. I was worried for her but more so for Funk. How would they manage if things continued this way?

I could hear Dottie's flustered voice from the other side of the room. Though every phone line was blaring, I got up and walked over to her desk, only to find her half crazed because of the Apple computer. Meekly she asked me if Funk would be willing to replace the computer with "something normal." But I couldn't return the computer. Funk couldn't afford to piss money down the drain by paying Apple's restocking fee. I said this gently, and Dottie responded by gazing at the computer as if it were of a creature of higher intelligence. Realizing she was stuck with the thing, she reached for the little white manual and blankly began flipping through the pages.

The whole time I'd been standing there, straining my back talking over her desk, the phones had been ringing like mad and no one had answered them. I glanced at the phone by her elbow and saw one of the lights lit solid, which meant Funk was on the line with someone. But Jesus, shouldn't he be placing them on hold and catching the other lines?

As much as I didn't want to leave Dottie in her despondent state, the unanswered calls were making me crazy, and I couldn't have both of us go down. Gently I said, "Dottie, how about I go back inside that office and we both keep answering the phones? It's getting late. Surely the calls will stop soon, and you can figure out how the computer works then."

In a kind but defeated voice, she said, "No, that's okay, Gloria. I can manage the phones myself. You'll be late picking up Andrew if you stay."

But when she didn't pick up the phone and went back to staring at the manual, that's exactly what I did.

Slamming my ass back into the chair that I'd built a few weeks ago, I punched a button on the phone and said, "Mark Funkhouser for mayor. How may I help you?"

"Hi, I'd like to know...."

More ringing, and still no one was picking up lines but me. I interrupted the first caller, saying, "I'm so sorry, but can I put you on hold for just a minute please?"

I waited until the man agreed before answering the next line, because I hate when people ask me that and don't wait for my answer.

But the same thing happened when I answer that line, so I put that person on hold and picked up the rollover. When every line was blinking on hold, I got my purse from its hiding spot, pulled out my cell phone, and dialed my son.

"Why are you calling? You should be here."

"Dad's headquarters is going nuts."

"Mom. Can you be more specific?"

"The phones are going crazy."

"Just say what you have to say, Mom!"

"Andrew, there's not enough people here to answer all the calls and I feel weird leaving with this going on. Is it possible for you to get a ride home, just for today?"

"Fine."

"C'mon, Andrew! You know I'll come if you really need me to."

"I said fine."

"Yeah, but you said it in a way that lets me know you're not."

More kindly then, he said, "I'll get a ride."

"Thanks, babe. Okay, listen fast. When you get home call for takeout, because obviously I won't be making dinner tonight."

"Obviously."

"Please be nice. Oh, one more thing. Please put the vegetables I prepared this morning back in the fridge. I hope they're not rotten."

"Whatever, Mom, I'm going now."

"No! Wait a minute. Use the credit card that's in the wood box on top of my desk to pay for the food and please don't forget to tip the guy."

"I know where we keep the credit card, Mom."

"Okay. I'll be home soon. I love you. I'm sorry."

As soon our conversation ended, I glanced at the bank of callers I had put on hold. Unbelievably, no one had hung up. Beginning with the first caller, I picked up the line.

"I am really sorry to have kept you waiting. This is Gloria. How may I help you?"

"Is Mark Funkhouser there?"

"Yes, but he's on another call. Is there something I can do for you?"

"Yeah, bring me a yard sign. My address is. . . ." *Click.*

I said, "Of course!" but the guy was already gone.

That was how it went all afternoon: "I want this" and "I want that," most of which we didn't have. And I doubted Funk ever would have any because not one person said, "Where can I send a check?"

At one point, I ran to take the pee that I'd been holding in ever since I had plopped my ass down in the chair. On the way back, I saw Dottie on her hands and knees fooling with the printer.

"Jesus, Dottie, what are you doing on the floor?"

"I'm trying to figure out how to set up the printer."

"It's already set up."

"Well, it's not working."

"Oh, shit! You've got to be kidding me. Let me see."

I walked over to her desk. It was not a normal desk. It was one of those half-open, half-closed-in contraptions like you see in a doctor's office, probably because in its former life the trailer had been a clinic. The desk part was built into a chest-high wall, likely meant to add privacy. But it's not private. It has always annoyed me to see people having to sit so low behind one of those things, yet this is what Funk had in his headquarters. To get to Dottie's computer, I had to open the gate — *That thing has to be removed. It's absurd. It has no purpose but to get in the way* — make a sharp right turn, and walk to the end of the enclosure. When I stood directly in front of her computer, I warily tapped the Print icon and the printer whirled into action.

"How'd you do that?" Dottie said through that sexy laugh of hers.

Well, what do you know? A smile and *a laugh!*

I let out a deep sigh before responding, "Don't worry, Dottie, you'll get used to everything."

"No, Gloria, you're better at this," she responded, a little embarrassed, though still smiling and somewhat laughing.

"Dottie, I'm telling you, you should have seen me two months ago. I was a complete basket case. I had no idea what I was doing or where to start. But this is just like managing a household. You just throw yourself into the mayhem and somehow everything gets done. You'll find your stride, just as I did."

The phones ringing maniacally, I raced back to my office, shouting behind me, "Keep answering the phones. Once everything dies down for good, I'll help you figure out the machines."

I waited for Dottie to pick up the first call, put that caller on hold, and pick up the next. But instead of placing the second caller on hold, Dottie just hung onto it, the other callers be damned! Which is when I started picking up and putting everyone on hold again, all the while wondering what the hell had happened to the manager who Funk said beat all others. Oh, well, what did it matter? She talked so sweetly and respectfully, and that was what Funk needed. Dottie was a gem. I just had to figure out how to boost her confidence so things moved a little more quickly.

A million hours later, Funk ambled past my office and did a double-take. Stopping, he stared into the room as if he was a widower and his beloved wife had returned from the dead.

"Gloria! What are you doing?"

"What do you mean, what am I doing? I'm answering your frigging phones. My God, Funk, don't you hear them ringing?"

"I thought you went home."

"Funk, when have I ever gone home without kissing you goodbye first?"

"I don't know."

"Well I do. Never! Jesus, Funk, everything has always been all about you, but this is getting ridiculous."

"I'm sorry, Glor. This morning you said you were leaving as soon as the press event was over, and I assumed you had gone home."

"Funk, we ate lunch together. Or we started to, and then the phones started going nuts. How was I to leave with that going on?"

His bottom lip began testing the pressure in the room.

"I don't know, babe, but last week I said I wouldn't burden you further — that today would be your last day."

"Oh really, Funk? Today would be my last day? What you said last week was bullshit. I just didn't have the time to tell you so. What about everything I still have to do for your Coming-Out Party? Don't make me mad by talking stupid."

"Gloria, you're already mad. You can finish putting the party together from home. You can go now. I've got this."

Feeling bad for making him feel bad, my mad left me.

I rolled my eyes toward where Dottie was sitting. Lowering my voice, I said, "Funk, I can't go home. You don't have enough people here. Someone's got to answer the phones. They're out of control."

"Dottie will answer them."

And getting mad again, well, not really mad, more like exasperated, I said, "Funk, do you see Dottie answering them? Are you answering them? The phones are ringing off the hook. I'm barely greeting one caller before putting them on hold and picking up the next. This is crazy. I shouldn't have ordered six lines. Don't people know we're not totally set up yet?"

By this time, Funk was fully inside my office. Turning in a slow circle, he replied in typical husband-fashion — like a man who knows nothing about the mundane workings of a stay-at-home mom. "We're set up. Look at everything you've done."

"Good Lord, Funk, yes, the trailer is set up, but what about all the activities that are supposed to be taking place? Dottie just got here. You can't expect her to keep this pace yet, and there's no one else here to help you. This is the most frustrating thing I've ever lived through. People are calling wanting long, drawn-out conversations. Surely they can hear the phones ringing in the background, but they're lingering on the line, asking for yard signs, buttons. I don't know why they can't just come and pick the stuff up, but when I hint at that, they act like this trailer is in the ghetto and I'm crazy for suggesting it.

"And, white boy, I hate to break it to you, but you don't have yard signs because you don't have any money. You do have buttons, but who's here to stuff one into an envelope and mail it off? Besides, where would the money come from for stamps? Don't even go there, you're not getting any more from me."

Not pausing for a response, I continued freebasing into the atmosphere, with as much ferociousness as a dog gnawing on a bone, thoughts that I'd been unconsciously worrying over.

"Funk, I've done more than you asked to get you squared away, but it never occurred to me to find more volunteers than just Dottie. You certainly need some, but even if you had people calling with that intention, how would I know what task to give them? Is there a "Give the Poorest Mayoral Candidate Some Money" category? And even if people were signing up to volunteer, how could I possibly make an organizational flow chart, with the phones going berserk like this? And, buddy, what's with this "we're set up" business? I keep telling you, there's no 'we' in this. This is your thing, not mine. And I'd say I've done enough."

Having worked myself into quite the tizzy, I withdrew into my head. *Man, I can't stomach this guy.* He knew I could never leave him in a lurch, yet he also knew I had missed picking Andrew up from school. And deadbeat father that he is, he didn't see a problem with it. The poor kid had to beg a ride home. I can't tell you how guilty I felt to have slacked off in my duty to my son. Up to this point, the kids' needs had come before their father's, because Funk was an adult.

The bastard I was married to watched me roam around in my head, but when he saw me growing more frantic, he got a bit frantic himself. "Gloria, go home! It's fine. Dottie will catch on. She's good. I know. I've worked with her for years."

I said, with an edge in my voice, "I'd love to go home, Funk. And if I hadn't seen this mayhem I could have, but now I can't. And you know that, so don't pretend like you haven't put this on me. I can't go anywhere until Dottie gets the hang of things. You need more bodies here or you'll come off as unprofessional, and you know how much I hate that. And Funk, what the hell have you been doing in there? You haven't picked up any of the lines!"

"I've been talking to the people that Dottie's been transferring to my line. I also arranged a meeting with Jeff Simon."

"Finally! At least something's gotten done. Did you tell him what it's about?"

"No, I thought it would be better in person."

"Well, you're right for a change. You can't ask something like that over the phone. I hope it's soon. The book says the campaign manager is the most vital position in the campaign. When is the meeting?"

"Later this week. He said he'd call me back with a time."

"Was he shocked to hear you're running for mayor?"

"More like perturbed that he had to hear about it on the news."

"Oh boy, there's going to be a lot of that. Prepare yourself. The last thing you need is a million hurt feelings. When you tell people, be gracious about it. Mention why you had to keep it a secret, so no one thinks something worse. Remember, more words are better than less."

Funk went back to his office and, as I'd promised, I showed Dottie the differences between an Apple operating system and the one she was familiar with.

She caught on quickly, and since it was way past dinnertime, I shooed her home. After that, I grabbed my copy of *The Campaign Manager* and returned to my office. My ass felt as sore as if I'd been riding a horse for twelve hours. I opened the book and reread the chapter about volunteers, taking notes so I could develop a chart. The whole time I was embroiled in this activity I felt like a mad scientist, as if I was pulling something over on someone by being prepared for the next day.

At about ten p.m. Funk walked me out to the van, stepped into his little red Corolla, and the two of us headed down the Southwest Trafficway for home. Soon I was pulling into the driveway I'd vacated early that morning. Turning the ignition off, I leaned on the steering wheel, taking a moment to collect myself before going inside to face my son. I drove faster than Funk, so I had a good five minutes to myself before we walked together into the house.

"I'll be home soon!" came my son's sing-song, sarcastic greeting.

Spent beyond belief, I couldn't rise to the gibe. Instead, I flicked off the television and apologized again.

"What the hell have you guys been doing? I thought you were coming home after Dad's press conference."

I threw myself down on the couch next to my son — but not too close, lest he hightail it up to his bedroom to get away from me. Funk returned with a beer and, jazzed from the day, sat perkily in the chair across from us. And there in our living room, parents and son discussed everything that had gone down and how different the reality was from what we'd envisioned. Funk and I had worked long and hard to get him ready for this momentous day, always holding the date in sight because that's when we thought things would calm down and return to normal: I'd go back to doing what I was doing before his dream edged mine out. I'd teach and attend births. I'd put fingers to a new business I'd been itching to start, building little houses in the woods for just-dumped women to live in. And Funk, no longer working at city hall, would be able to gather himself for the task ahead.

We had never anticipated the blitz of opening day. We never imagined that the preannouncement days would be the languid phase of the campaign.

"We thought we'd be coming back directly afterward," I told Andrew. "Well, Dad never said he'd be coming right home, though he never expected to stay as late as we did. Ange, you wouldn't believe how crazy it was down there."

"I don't care."

"Yes, you do, Andrew. I'm sorry for not coming to get you."

Having conversed as much as he could tolerate, my child turned the TV back on, and he and Funk watched nonsense while I tidied up the house and got ready for bed.

An hour later, Funk was sliding into bed next to me, asking what I was reading. But I knew what he was really asking.

"Are you fucking kidding me? My God, you're insatiable. Not on your life."

"Okay. Goodnight, dear. Thanks for helping all day and for offering to stay until Dottie learns the ropes."

"*Offering*? Good Lord, Funk. I've had enough of you today. Go away already."

21 NOVEMBER 2006

A LOT WAS WRITTEN ABOUT FUNK'S PRESS EVENT, but I didn't have the time or inclination to read more than a few pieces that someone brought into the double-wide.

The first was penned by someone who called himself Capt. Spaulding — *what a weird name* — and he did a rather decent job of summing up Funk and what he stands for:

> Joining a field of what seems like more than a thousand candidates — *A thousand? Jesus, what hyperbole!* — former Kansas City auditor Mark Funkhouser has thrown his accountant's hat — *Hey, buddy, he's not an accountant. Get your facts straight.* — into the ring to be KC's next mayor. I have long liked this gentleman and his no-nonsense "Harry Truman–like" approach to the city's fiscal matters. I liked him even more after getting into a tiff with Mayor Barnes earlier this year over

the city financial issues. — *Okay, you've redeemed yourself, I forgive you for everything.* — I heartily endorse this man to be our next mayor. — *Wow, would you look at that! Funk's already been endorsed. By a blogger. Whatever a blogger is.*

The second piece was a bunch of comments made on *The Kansas City Star*'s Buzz Blog.

Heidi says: Whoo hoo!! First time to actually be excited about a mayor's race here." *Thank you for being excited Heidi — I am too!*

Ryan says: Oh crap! I will have to reconsider my vote for the other Mark F. *You'll be glad you did Ryan. I promise.*

CWG says: I'm very impressed with Mark Funkhouser's web site, credentials, humor — *Humor? What humor?* — analysis of the city and its challenges and his ideas for governing. Yes, there are other good candidates as well. But Mark's approach is so different than what I'm used to seeing in a mayoral race. *Yay, you got the rest of it right, CWG!*

FBCn says: THE SEWER SEPARATION, LIGHT RAIL, NEGLECTED NEIGHBORHOOD, INFRASTRUCTURE NEGLECT, ETC. SOMETIMES SOMEONE COMES ALONG TO FIX PROBLEMS THAT HAVE HAPPENED FOR YEARS. AS AUDITOR, MARK FUNKHOUSER HAS THE EXPERI-ENCE OF LOOKING AT THE CITY WITH A MAGNIFYING GLASS AND SEE WHAT HAS WORKED AND WHAT HASN'T. HIS KNOWLEDGE AND INTEGRITY ARE JUST WHAT KANSAS CITY NEEDS AT THIS TIME. *Nicely put, FBCn, BUT WHY ARE YOU SCREAMING?*

The commentaries calmed my nerves, reinforcing to me that Funk was going to win the mayoral race.

25 NOVEMBER 2006

I WORKED AT THE DOUBLE-WIDE until the eve of the Thanksgiving holiday, arriving a little after nine each morning. While I wasn't necessarily early picking up my son from school, you better believe that my ass was waiting in the parking lot as he walked out the door of the building.

Even in a normal time, Thanksgiving is a miracle to pull off, and this year wasn't normal. Like every mother across America, I had a hundred things to do. Thanksgiving was the holiday our family loved the most. We always invited stray guests who had nowhere else to go, and it was one of the few times that we served a traditional American menu. In addition to the meal, we shared a family tradition: after we cleared away the dinner dishes, I set out pens and fall-themed notepaper that I purchase just for the occasion. All of us wrote down five things for which we were thankful. One by one, I read the lists aloud, embellishing each with words the person should've said — such as how much they adored their family, especially their mothers — and the crowd guessed whose list was whose.

As usual, the day was a load of fun. Only two things were different about our Thanksgiving holiday that year: first, the balmy weather — and I had nothing to do with that, but man, can a girl ever get used to temperatures in the high sixties, in November, in Kansas City. Second, the kids and I had to go out to collect petition signatures the next day, and I had nothing to do with that either.

I'd learned about the signatures requirement only a few days earlier. I still couldn't believe that a candidate needed permission from fifteen hundred voters to run for office. So, on Black Friday, instead of shopping the sales rack at Anthropologie, the kids and I stood outside the grocery store begging, pleading, and cajoling signatures from customers. By the time the kids cried uncle I thought we'd surely collected five hundred names — but all we had was a measly one hundred.

Before I blinked, the weekend was over and Tara was leaving home to return to Pittsburgh for her final exams. I drove her to the airport. Funk usually did that because I hated goodbyes, but as I said, nothing was normal that year. We wrestled her luggage out of the van and, sentimental fool that I am, I tugged her back a hundred times for one last kiss. Unsentimental fool that she was, she pushed me off with a scowl, and I drove teary-eyed to the double-wide. I'd decided to help Funk until after his Coming-Out Party.

When I entered, all I saw of Dottie was the tip of her head over her desk. She appeared to be deeply engrossed in an electronics manual. When she looked up, I noticed right away that she was back to her chipper self.

"Hi, Dottie! What are you doing here on a Saturday?"

"Trying to understand this thing," she said, grinning and pointing to the computer. Turning bashful, she asked, "Do you mind showing me how something works again?"

I replied with a playful "Yez, ma'am." When the tutorial was over, I encouraged her to go home, "Dottie, all this will be here come Monday. Go on home. Jack's waiting for you."

"Are you sure you'll be okay?"

"I'll be fine! I've had my fingers crossed all morning that the phones would be quieter today, and look, they are!"

"I mean, do you feel safe being here alone?"

"Of course! Besides, you were here all by your lonesome before I came in."

"I know, but I feel bad leaving — "

"It's all good, Dottie. Please go home to your hubby."

After she left, I walked through the available offices, trying to decide which one to work in, the whole time thinking about Dottie's safety comment.

Many people thought of the West Side as the slums. That was because the West Side was home to non-white people and various ethnicities. Having grown up in a neighborhood where people from various countries lived on my block, I felt more at home in West Side than I did living among the repressed lily-whites in my family's Kansas City neighborhood. Still, I was not stupid. New Yorkers develop street smarts at an early age. I routinely hid my purse in the cabinet just in case some loser walked through the door.

I chose to work in the office I'd used during the preparations for Funk's announcement and began unpacking the items I'd brought to decorate the space. Once I had positioned everything just so, I sat back in the chair I had assembled a hundred years ago and admired my work. The office had better energy now, with my talisman hanging in the window and my rocks peeking out from nooks and crannies. Not only did everything look pretty, but the items drew attention away from the brown, water-stained ceiling and wrinkled carpet.

My eyes lighted on the photographs I had placed on the corner of my table — my favorite one of the kids, one of Funk, and one more: a photo of my dad. Ever since I had stepped off the gangplank of the *Queen Mary* last summer, I'd been running flat out. I'd had no time to reflect on our big trip to Europe, much less to process my father's death. But now, his round face smiling back at me kept me from starting in on my to-do list.

My dad would've gotten such a kick out Funk running for mayor, just as Funk's father Chet would have. I missed both something awful and thinking of them turned my spirit melancholy. My mind swirled with thoughts about the illness that had taken my father. Even if he had still been alive, he couldn't have enjoyed this moment, what with his Alzheimer's and all.

At first, his only symptoms were his magnified personality traits. The negative ones, especially his propensity toward quick anger. As the illness progressed, it became clear that his horrific moods correlated with his memory loss. It seems thickheaded that no one caught on sooner, but then again, my father hid things he perceived as character flaws. He finally couldn't hide that he forgot *how* to take out the trash. Then, his flares of temper made perfect sense. Who wouldn't be angry for forgetting how to do something so simple?

My mother never acknowledged his illness. How could she when she was losing her love of fifty years? For me, once I'd learned about the trash incident, I had no further illusions. I just started thinking of how to be of service from fifteen hundred miles away. I was deep in the throes of raising my own family and couldn't trot off to Florida at every twist and turn. My parents would have to come to Kansas City. And they did, every few months.

During one of their lengthier stays, I noticed that my dad's ability to hold conversations exponentially increased the longer the visit lasted. Like me, my father loved children, and I made my family's home the kind of go-to place for teens that my childhood home had been. Between the constant activity and the endless bantering, my dad's voice magically began to return.

I took him to Spring, my acupuncturist — the one whose double-wide we later rented for Funk's campaign headquarters.

Each visit went the same way. Spring would ask, "Mr. Sqweetearwoh, can you pwease show me your tongue?"

My father complied by opening his mouth, just as a baby bird does when accepting a worm from its mom. Spring would note the flaccidity and color of his tongue and whatever else she checked for in there.

Next: "Can I check your pulses, pwease?"

Taking my father's proffered wrists, Spring grabbed both and began her journey around them. My dad pretended not to notice that she was checking his pulse "incorrectly," the whole time making crazy eyes at me to let me know that he wasn't so sick that he didn't understand that Spring was a quack. His goo-goo eyes said what his voice couldn't — that he still had game, that no one would be pulling one over on him anytime soon. He never understood that Dr. Fung was checking his pulse the Eastern way, retrieving more detailed information than his Western doctor ever could.

Watching my dad alternate between reverting to a little boy — obediently going along with the doctor's request — and the man who still resided in him, was too much for me to take. Try as I might to keep the visit on the straight and narrow, I couldn't help laughing over the bizarre situation. The treatments helped balance his moods, but not much else. Yet the laughter we enjoyed during the process was restorative.

My next approach at keeping my dad alive was to shovel food down his throat. It had only been a few months since their last visit, yet when my father stepped off the jetway, his complexion ashen-green, he was so weak he couldn't talk. Shocked by his condition, I asked what had caused such a drastic decline. My mom said he'd lost his appetite.

Had it been his time to die, I might have accepted this as my father's fate, but his lack of appetite had everything to do with his doctor forbidding my mom from feeding him his favorite foods, supposedly because of a heart ailment. The doctor insinuated that my mom would kill him with a heart attack by feeding him the wrong foods. I had no such fears. Well, actually I did. It's just that I didn't let them stop me. Something was going to kill my dad, and I didn't give a shit what his death certificate read, only that he was happy and comfortable while still among us.

My mom wouldn't budge from following the doctor's orders. Not even when I reasoned that my dad would eat if only she'd feed him something fun. She responded to my logic the way she always had: "Gloria, would you leave well enough alone? You're driving me crazy!"

Leave well enough alone? My father was about to keel over. As if that wasn't bad enough, have I told you how much I hated being yelled at by my mother. In my forties.

"But Mom, don't you see? Dad will die a different death if he doesn't eat."

"Gloria! Stop talking such morbid shit! Your father's not going anywhere unless you keep saying that!"

Well, fuck me. We had just entered a field I knew all too well. The world of superstition. The realm where I could never win. It transported me instantly to that black sea of muck. That is why I disregarded my mother's wishes on how best to keep my dad alive. I know. Maybe I'm a terrible daughter. Maybe payback will be exact when the time comes for my daughter to be wiping my ass. Then again, she'll likely stick me in a nursing home.

Anyway, with my mom's back trustingly turned away, I played the Grateful Dead on high volume, knowing full well that she'd never come into the kitchen with "Box of Rain" blasting from the speakers on top of my fridge. Once the room was rocking, I'd seat my dad at the table, dose him with a hit of Rescue Remedy to steady his nerves from the pounding blare, while he watched the squirrels run across the electric lines and I prepared the first of the three lovely little snacks of his day. I cringed to think that I'd kill my kids if they ever went against my wishes. But I couldn't stop myself, not when I saw my father's wilted body spring back to life from the infusion of calories from the food he loved.

Later, I'd hide the evidence of his binge in the dishwasher and turn the music down to a more soothing Pavarotti. Day by day, plate by plate, my father's ashen cheeks tinged back to pink and my disappointment with Western medicine grew ever wider. If only there was a confidence-boosting remedy to dose my mother with.

With this enterprise going swimmingly well, I moved to my next cure: helping my father not to forget. Borrowing from Pavlov's experiments, I exercised his brain by doing the same thing, the same way, in the same place, and even with the same squirrels, each day. Once I'd gotten the kids home from school, I'd have them join their grandpa at the table and served them all a nutritious, delicious snack. For my dad's serving, I always used the same plate, the one serendipitously manufactured in his mother country, Italy. It was edged with painted, life-size strawberries.

From my place at the counter, the kids knowing full well what I was up to, I'd smile mischievously at my dad and yell as loudly as I could, "Hey, mister! Have you tasted one of those strawberries yet?"

Without saying a word, he'd look at me and then down at his plate, and then warily back up at me — vaguely remembering this was a hoax. Not quite able to recall if it truly was, he would shake his head no.

"Well go ahead, try one already! They're delicious!"

Suspicious, yet trapped inside an illness-induced state of childhood, he'd obediently stab a berry. And as his metal fork rang against the plate, the kids and I would burst out laughing. Thank God, the trick didn't trigger his Italian macho. Instead, four merry voices filled my kitchen with joy. Well, it was really only three voices. My father's laugh had always been silent, just like Curly's on *The Three Stooges*, his favorite television show.

I hate confessing this, but I liked my dad a lot better after he came down with Alzheimer's. With his defenses gone, his real, sweet nature poked through.

I don't know how long I sat in the chair, lost in memories, but when the campaign phones began again, I returned to the here and now. For once, their incessant ringing was a relief. Shaking off my sadness, I picked up the phone and said, "Mark Funkhouser for mayor. This is Gloria. How may I help you?"

Later that evening, while cleaning dinner dishes, I turned my music on for company. And wouldn't you know it, iTunes shuffled straight to Brent Mydland's heart-wrenched soul singing "I Will Take You Home." Why *that* Dead song when I was already wrung out?

> Little girl lost
> In a forest of dreams.
> It's a dark old wood
> And it's damp with dew.
> Ain't no way the Bogeyman can get you,
> You can close your eyes, the world is gonna let you,
> Your daddy's here and never will forget you,
> I will take you home.

My "daddy" hadn't been that kind of father to me. He had hardly ever made it such that I could close my eyes in peace. Still, he'd been something. And I missed that something. Terribly.

Funk's Coming-Out Party

THE MOMENT FUNK AND I MADE THE DECISION that he'd run for mayor, we were both absolutely certain he would win. Yet even with that knowledge, we knew it would be hard work to cross the finish line. Funk and I had never worked so hard on so little sleep in all our lives, not even when our children were infants. Everything about the campaign was fast and furious, and we were always two steps behind where we wanted to be. While we didn't exactly half-ass anything, some tasks sure went by the wayside.

The first faux pas came when we mailed the invitations to the Coming-Out Party with less than the customary two weeks' notice. It activated the insecurities that always loiter inside me. I'm a dichotomy. How does my heart know that whatever I'm worrying over will turn out fine, when my mind is casting doubt? I've had a lifetime of therapy and I still don't know how this contradiction exists within me.

All that remained of the planning was to apply finishing touches — the most crucial details. To give them the attention they deserved, I had to stop answering the blasted phones. I felt guilty about shrugging that duty onto Dottie, but if the Coming-Out Party was to be classy, I had to.

"Dottie, I'm really sorry to be handing the phones off to you, but I don't know what else to do. I've taken work home every night, but there isn't any night left by the time I get there."

"I know. This is crazy," she said with her gravelly laugh.

"Well, I just wanted you to know why I have to close my door to work, and not pick up the phone."

"It's okay, Gloria," she giggled.

Relieved but with no time to chat, I began checking items off my to-do list. I was approaching the bottom when I saw the line that read "Practice speech." The one I wrote. Or really, the one that wrote itself when we were living in the slums of Barcelona the previous summer. The speech that I'd give at Funk's party. The one that introduced him as the next mayor of Kansas City. Oh, Lord, could I really go through with it?

28 NOVEMBER 2006

FUNK HAD HIS MEETING with Jeff Simon. *The Campaign Manager*, my campaign bible, said the most important position in any campaign is the campaign manager. Yet here it was — eight days *after* the press event — and Funk was just now getting around to assigning the job. You can't imagine how much I hated such dilly-dallying.

Jeff was Funk's closest friend in Kansas City, which was probably why he wanted him in the role. For as long as I can remember, they'd had a standing lunch date at Cascone's, a greasy spoon convenient to both their offices. Month after month, over cheeseburgers and fries, Funk had learned a lot about the guy. Which meant I'd learned a lot about the guy too. He was fun and charismatic, emotional and caring. As much as Funk could love anyone outside our family, he loved Jeff Simon. This is likely why he asked him to be his right-hand man.

Jeff turned Funk down flat.

Said he was too busy at work to do justice to the campaign.

While it was strange enough that Funk had a close friend that I barely knew, it was plain as day that there was something to read between the lines with his answer. Well, it was plain as day to me and to anyone else capable of reading between the lines. My husband, quite obviously, is not numbered among those people.

I couldn't take too much credit for deciphering Jeff's unsaid diction, as his rationale was at the kindergarten level. It was pretty simple to break the code. I wish people would just say what they mean. It would make things much easier, particularly for people like my husband, absent-minded professor types, who are clueless as to what's going on two feet in front of them. What Jeff meant to say was that he couldn't be Funk's manager because he didn't think Funk would win.

How did I know this? My first impression of Jeff had been that he was charming but excruciatingly conventional. Not the sort to take risks. Not for someone else. So there was no way he'd risk the embarrassment of backing a loser.

I was at the double-wide drafting templates when Funk and Jeff met. I could hear Jeff's boisterous laugh through the shared wall that separated my office from Funk's. I also knew when Funk popped the question, because the room went quiet. The next thing I knew, Simon's car was pulling away, which just happened to be the exact moment that Funk walked into my office and closed the door behind him. He didn't even ask Dottie if it was okay to do that. He was so impolite sometimes, and it discomfited me to no end. And get this. He didn't apologize for interrupting my work either. I'm telling you, the mistake I'm married to doesn't realize how lucky he is to have me. Normally, I would have given him what for, but at that moment he looked upset — and Funk never looks upset. So I held back, and I'm glad I did. Because, surprisingly, the correct read of his emotion was disappointment. He had never expected Jeff Simon, a service-oriented Catholic, to turn him down. I don't know why, when there was a lot of talk and no action going on in this town. But Funk, who took the spoken word at face value, was unprepared for the brush-off.

This character flaw has always boggled my mind, particularly when you consider Funk's line of work. Because a good auditor looks more at what *isn't* being said, rather than what is. Or, at least that's what my husband has always told me, as if I cared to know.

I'd never asked Funk why he'd wanted Simon in the role. All I'd ever heard was that Jeff would be Funk's manager and a reporter named Joe Miller would be his writer. Probably because I hadn't grilled him on the decision, it was now biting him in the ass. This was more my fault than his. Sometimes my eyes glaze over at the things Funk thinks are fun to tell me, because it's usually some head thing he's talking about, whereas I like talking about heart things.

But since the guy had forced me to read *The Campaign Manager*, I felt obliged to give him feedback on what went down with Jeff, because looking ahead, Simon's rejection of the job had the potential to create many problems for Funk's just-begun campaign. This wasn't the best time to be ruminating on an alternative for the position. The three of us were so busy that it had been difficult to break away even to eat or use the restroom. Instead of the phones quieting, they'd picked up in velocity. The calls were about everything under the sun, including just lonely people looking to chat. The front door was swinging with folks wanting to volunteer. That sounds great, but Dottie and I could barely stop long enough to give them a task, much less train them. Funk should have had a manager in place eons ago, just to deal with the volunteers.

Also, the campaign needed to maintain a veneer of tradition. Kansas City citizens loved the novelty of an un-politician candidate for mayor. But beige was still their color. Funk couldn't be all-innovative, all the time, not if this campaign was to fly. People said they want change, but change can be scary and it's surely ugly. Most folks don't factor that in when they're dreaming of things being different.

The only thing ordinary people know about election campaigns is what they've seen on TV: loads of smiling volunteers working diligently for their candidate. Funk's campaign had the loads part down, and they were smiling. Well, mostly they were sneering, in a way said, *Look out, world, the people's mayor is here and he's gonna destroy you.* What he didn't have was volunteers doing real work. Organizing and training them would involve more hands than Dottie and I possessed. If Simon wouldn't lead the volunteers, then who would?

From the pages of *The Campaign Manager*, I'd surmised that the manager's job wasn't the big-deal position I had once believed it to be. It was simply the role of an organizer. Any mother could handle the job.

Funk had to unwind this pile-of-shit situation graciously. To avoid hard feelings, I advised my husband to offer Simon a different position in the campaign, something that wouldn't give the man heartburn yet would stroke his you-know-what.

Chairman.

Asking Simon to chair the large committee headed off several problems. "Chairman" suited the guy better than "manager" ever did. From the little I saw of him, Jeff loved being the big cheese. And since the guy was also risk-adverse, being chair wouldn't cause him a problem in the world. The title was often just an honorary designation. It didn't necessarily imply that the friend believed in what his friend was doing.

So, perfect, right?

Nope, not if you live with Mr. Clean.

"What happened, Funk? You look upset."

"I'm not upset."

"Geez, I guess that look on your face is one of sheer joy. Sorry. My mistake."

"Gloria."

"Oh, for God's sake, what happened?"

"Jeff said no."

"I figured that. What else has you upset?"

"I'm not upset."

"Oh, okaaaay."

"I'm disappointed."

"Disappointed? What the hell?"

"Jeff's always said I'm the only one who's doing anything for the city. I thought he'd be on board."

"Lots of people think you're God's gift; it doesn't mean they're gonna get off their fat ass and help."

"I'm disappointed, Glor, what can I say?"

"Well, you've got bigger problems than that, Funk."

"What do you mean?"

"I mean you've got to corral this. It won't be long before Jeff starts feeling guilty for turning you down and does something stupid to absolve himself. When people go there, watch out because they usually make the injured party look wrong."

"Jeff's not like that."

"Yeah, right. And he wasn't going to turn you down either."

"Gloria."

"All I'm saying is you better plan as if he *is* like *that*."

"Gloria."

"I'm telling you, Funk, you don't really know about these things. You're focused on doing the work, but this new world you've just entered has moving parts you have to contend with. This is politics, Funk."

"I know politics, Gloria. My job as the city auditor was political. It took politics to push my recommendations through the council. It took politics to change audit standards nationwide. I know politics."

"Not this kind you don't. This is seedy. You have to think seedy. We're not talking audit standards anymore. You're no longer dealing with 'head' people. This is about human nature. People and relationships — their emotional baggage, inadequacies, personal flaws. You're not a schemer. With this campaign, you gotta be a schemer."

"Gloria, I'm running a clean campaign. I'm not going to do things the same old dirty way. It's not what people want. They're tired of the games you're talking about."

"Jesus, Funk, you're a chess player. I don't know how you can't see what's needed here. You've got to be two moves ahead. You're dealing with the heart now, with people like me. With how people view themselves. If Jeff starts thinking he's anything other than what he wants to think he is, it'll fuck you up the ass."

I could tell my husband was starting to take me seriously because his hand went up to his beard and he was kneading it, the way a cat paws at things. I hate cats. Maybe that's why I hate my husband sometimes.

"Glor, is what you're saying in the book? Is that how you know this?"

"Funk, I'm Italian. That's how I know. But how do you *not* know this? I don't play chess, and I know these things."

"What things?"

"You've got to head this off. Offer Jeff another position. Something that speaks to how he sees himself."

"Like what?"

"Well, I was thinking he could chair your committee."

"I don't need a chair. I need a campaign manager."

"I know that Funk, but you've gotta give Jeff a dignified way out. You also have to give the world the impression that even though you have unconventional ideas, you're running a normal campaign."

"But I'm not."

"Jesus, Funk! Are you trying to lose?"

"Gloria."

"C'mon, Funk. It's no skin off your nose to add a chair to your committee. Even if I'm wrong, what could it hurt?"

"It can't. Okay, I'll call him."

"Well, hurry up already. Make that call and then appoint a campaign manager. Dottie and I are dying over here."

29 NOVEMBER 2006

YAY! IT WORKED! Jeff was officially Funk's campaign chairman. I don't think Funk recognized the brilliance of my plan; he just went along with it. But I felt as though I should be blowing on my fingers and rubbing them on my shirt for thinking it up.

After updating me on that news, Funk asked if we could have lunch to-gether in his office to discuss a few things. He was having pizza delivered, which was a bad thing. It was a fast and easy meal, and that's why he'd been relying on it, but if I continued eating junk food, I was going to gain back the pounds I'd shed in Europe.

As usual, Funk was using me as a sounding board. He was mulling over the other candidates for appointments to his two committees. It seemed like just a second ago I had to convince him he needed to appoint a chair. Now he wanted to add a slew more positions, as well as make the appointments required by the Missouri Ethics Commission. I hated it when he did a one-eighty like this. When I complained, he said only close-minded people stick to their guns once they're aware the gun is shooting blanks, and then he asked why I bothered arguing a position if I was going to be upset when I persuaded him to change his mind. Whatever.

It was weird, working together. We'd always collaborated on projects, but I'd always been the lead. It was strange having Funk in my role. Worse, he was a man of few words. Except for when he wasn't. And Lord help me either way. But at least I didn't have to listen to boring auditor and city council stuff anymore. The campaign was forcing Funk to talk about the "heart" matters I love.

Funk had recruited an accountant to keep track of the finances, though the ethics commission didn't require it. My Excel spreadsheet tracked every nickel and dime coming and going — mostly going — but that wasn't good enough for Mr. White Hat. It had been good enough for our family's finances, which to my way of thinking were way more important than this, but he didn't see it that way. He wanted to set an example for how to run an upstanding cam-paign. Okay. But he wasn't the one doing the work. Was piling more shit onto other people's plates an example of how one saves the world? Funk stood up to my sarcasm by declaring he had done me a favor, but I didn't see it that way. I still had to keep track of the books, or I wouldn't know where the campaign finances stood on a moment-to-moment basis. Now I'd have to keep track of the CPA too.

The commission required a campaign treasurer and deciding whom to appoint was weighing heavily on Funk. Up for grabs was Evert Asjes. His claim on Funk's heart was that Evert was one of a few who served on the city council who actually tried to do right by the city. By council standards, Evert was as honest as those types get, and that was likely why his colleagues frowned on him. Funk believed Evert wouldn't fight him on following the election commission's rules.

I liked Evert. He was an older gentleman, and I have a thing for old people, especially old men. Unlike most councilmembers, Evert wasn't pompous. His family owned Rosehill Gardens, my favorite nursery. Because I liked the man and since my husband had good reasons for appointing him treasurer, I seconded the choice.

Next up were Ed Wolf and Mike Bates, two of Funk's former colleagues. Their résumés included a passion for governing that was similar to Funk's. I didn't have much input except to inquire about their wives.

"Ed and Mike seem fine, but what about Gwen and Ruth?"

"I'm asking you which positions Ed and Mike should fill."

"How would I know? What skills do they have?"

"They—"

"Funk, we don't have time for a long diatribe. You know you want them on the team. Figure out the best places for them later."

"Good point."

"So, what about their wives?"

"What about them?"

"How are they supposed to feel when you ask their husbands to be on the committee and not them?"

"I've worked with their husbands."

"So?"

"I didn't work with them."

"So?"

"What are you saying?"

"We've socialized as couples at your horrifically boring work functions. Don't you think excluding them will hurt their feelings?"

"This isn't about feelings, Gloria."

"No, this isn't *only* about feelings, Funk. I'm quite sure both women are extremely influential in their husband's work lives.

"And?"

"Funk, are you slow, or what? We don't have time for this. Let me put it to you in a way that appeals to 'Mr. Feminist'. It seems that, so far, only men are associated with your campaign, yet in your career you've hired mostly women. Don't you think you need some women on the campaign?"

"Yes."

"Well, at least I know these two. And since I'm stuck working here for God knows how long, it would be nice to have them on board."

"I was thinking of asking Dana Laiben to be my campaign manager."

"Jesus, Funk, not another man!"

"She's a woman."

"Dana is a woman?"

"Yes."

"Why does she have a man's name?"

"The name is unisex."

"That's stupid."

"Perhaps. But Dana is a woman. And you and Dottie are women. So, there are women on my campaign."

"Funk, Dottie is your office manager — which is a pretty name for receptionist — and I'm your wife. What's it to you to include Gwen and Ruth?"

"Adding frivolous positions to avoid hurt feelings will make the committees too large."

"Is there a law about how many people can be on a committee? I don't remember reading about a limit in *The Campaign Manager*. Which chapter did you find that in?"

"Okay, put Gwen and Ruth's names down."

"Oh, I didn't know I was your secretary now. When was I promoted? How much do I get paid?"

The bastard didn't acknowledge my scorn. He just started rubbing his beard in thought, and when he tired of that he went to gnawing on his thumb.

Finally, the king spoke.

"What do you think of Maria Kuntstadter?"

"Our dentist? Why are you considering her?"

"She's connected to the Democrats."

"I don't know about that, but she's just an average dentist. I only go to her because I'm terrified of Novocain, and she'll numb only one tooth for me. You have no such impediments. I said you needed more women on your team, but not any old woman. Besides, what does Maria have that Gwen and Ruth don't?"

"Influence with the Democratic machine."

"Whatever."

My husband continued running through a list that clearly needed to escape from his head. I'd never heard of the other people he was considering: some union guy named Javier Perez and a few Catholic buddies of Simon's, Dan Ryan and Leland Shurin. The way Funk had been droning on, believe me, I wasn't about to ask for details. Funk had it down anyway. He just needed to voice his thoughts to be certain of himself. The minutes had been ticking by for over an hour by now, so I rose to leave, said it seemed like he'd put together a couple of fine committees, and left him with his fingers and thumb for company.

Back in my office I could hear him singing "Life Is Like a Mountain Railroad." Funk sings when he's happy.

> Life is like a mountain railroad
> With an engineer that's brave
> We must make this run successful
> From the cradle to the grave
> Heed the curves and watch the trestles

Never falter, never fail
Keep your hand upon the throttle
And your eye upon the rail

How the two of us had hooked up I'd never understand. I mean, is that a song to be singing in happiness? I wondered what Dottie thought. I was sure she could hear him. I'd bet you anything he never sang in the auditor's office. This must have been a totally different side of him than she'd ever seen. I just hoped full-frontal Funk didn't embarrass her.

2 DECEMBER 2006
MY MOTHER'S BIRTHDAY

WHAT THE FUCK!

All autumn, Kansas City had been as balmy as Florida, and on the day of the party of the century, this is what happens? When I awoke in the morning I needed to put sunglasses on, my bedroom was that bright. And not from the sun alone — mainly from the weather having just given over to an ice storm. The quaking aspen tree outside my window was quaking away, albeit slowly, what with the weight of the icicles hanging from its limbs. Everything outside my window glistened with an icy coating. The trees. The electric lines. The sidewalk. The street. Even my neighbor's gutters and downspouts. The world looked fresh, new, and clean. It wasn't beautiful. It didn't make me feel one with God. In fact, the brightness felt as dark as a bad omen.

Everything about Funk's Coming-Out Party had gone wrong, beginning with sending out the invitations late. We were deep into the holiday season, and by the time people received them I was sure most had accepted a different offer. I was already planning on being mortified by the low turnout, and the ice was sure to further dwindle those numbers.

The caterer phoned five times to discuss separate disasters, though they didn't sound like disasters to me. I suspected he'd gotten attached to me and just wanted to hear my voice. This happens to me a lot. People tell me their innermost thoughts, exposing their dark side upon first meeting. I'm used to it, but I couldn't deal with it on that day. I already had too many balls in the air.

I'd driven to the airport and back three times before noon. The first trip was an aborted attempt at picking up Anna, our former exchange student, because of course the storm had delayed her flight. I kicked myself the whole way home for not checking the flight status before leaving home. But done was done.

I thought of Anna, who lived in Italy, as my daughter. Over the years, Funk and I had invited ten exchange students into our home. I like most people, and I especially resonate with those from other cultures. I had given Anna my credit card points to fly in for the big doings, and she was going to stay with us for the weekend. Could you imagine flying across the ocean twice in three days? I couldn't.

Shortly after arriving home without Anna, I drove the forty-five minutes back for Tara and, after that, to pick up Slick and his band. To save money, the band was going to stay in our home instead of at a hotel. They arrived without speakers — I hadn't known I was supposed to supply them — so I carved a spot into my packed calendar to drive the band to a shop to rent some.

The only good thing about all the running around was that I didn't have much time to obsess about my speech. Why did I ever think I could give a speech? And to a cavernous room filled with either three people or three hundred and fifty? It was a stupidest idea I've ever had. I had to be on my game in the biggest way at the event, and I couldn't be the Welcome Wagon Lady when my mind was fretting over a speech. And then I had a great idea: I'd ask Simon-the-chairman to introduce Funk, instead of me. It would be right up his alley.

The day flew by. Finally, I showered and dressed for the party. All I had to do then was stay clear of Funk. If you think my nerves were bad, hoo-boy, you should've seen his! I honestly didn't know what his problem was. He was barely responsible for anything that night. I was the one who had to make sure the event went off without a hitch. And give that stupid speech . . . or not.

An hour before showtime my husband and I pulled up to the Kansas City Art Institute, the venue I had secured before we left for Europe the previous summer. Not a single parking space was open in the parking lot that I had paid extra to reserve for our guests. After scrambling around for a bit on the ice and nearly falling on my ass, I went back to the van and got on my phone to find out what the problem was. Many calls later I learned that people attending neighborhood parties had stolen our parking spaces. Nothing could be done about it. Just then, I noticed a security vehicle idling nearby. When I suggested that the guards knock on party hosts' doors and order folks to move their cars out of the lot, they looked at me as though I were menopausal.

The situation added to the bad omen from the morning, and I was beginning to obsess. I kept picturing our guests pulling up to the venue, finding no parking spaces, and deliberating their options: *Should I circle the block and ice skate to Funkhouser's party, or should I turn this car around and return to my comfy, warm home and have a drink in front of the fireplace?* I knew what I'd do, given the choice, and I feared our guests would do the same.

There wasn't time to dwell on it. Having no other option, we parked in the "No Parking" zone in front of the venue. Screw the Art Institute and its rules, or their lack of enforcement thereof.

Blading up to the front door, we entered the building, only to be smacked in the face by a ninety-degree wall of heat. None of the staff knew how to turn the thermostat down. With things continuing in the wrong direction, I steeled myself for further problems, especially an embarrassingly paltry turnout.

Sweat running a river of mascara down my cheeks, I snapped my fingers and shouted orders to my children: "Nick, Alex! Move the table over by the entrance. No, not there! Are you crazy? Put it over here! Tara, go out to the van and bring the tablecloth in and drape it *nicely* on the table. Wait! Be careful of the icy pavement! Ange, bring me that box of campaign buttons. Don't look at me like that — do it with a happy heart."

The kids fell in line, and when everything was where it needed to be I began setting up the information table. I arranged the uninspiring blue "Funk for Mayor" buttons into a pleasing pattern — because you've got to make the best of what you've got, even if it is ugly. I stacked, in the straightest line possible, the volunteer sign-up sheets. I placed the donation envelopes in the least-prominent position on the table because there'd be no shaking our guests down for money on that night — or on any night, for that matter. How insulting would it be to invite people to a party, only to turn around and ask them to pay for it? It would be the same as asking someone to BYOB. Classy? Nope.

I had scarcely finished arranging things to perfection when the first guests drifted through the door. Funk's frat brothers from both coasts had flown in for the occasion. I loved them to pieces, especially Crutch, but I didn't have time to linger because the next guests were on their heels.

They were Sonia and Melvin Brown, two of my favorite doula clients. Now *theirs* had been a fun birth. Thirty-six hours into the labor, Melvin banished his Cuban mother-in-law from his home. The woman was making her daughter crazy, enough to stall the birth. But instead of driving off in a huff, the woman hid in the bushes beneath her daughter's bedroom window. Only she didn't hide herself so well. Melvin and I had followed her moaning straight to her hidey-hole. And here we were together again, laughing and hugging as we recalled the memory. The fun lasted for just a moment, as more guests arrived. A half second later, more came in. And more after them. Soon there were too many to count. Not only did our guests attend despite my late invitations, but they'd come out in an ice storm and in such numbers that I couldn't think of anyone we'd invited who wasn't with us. I'd feared a scanty showing, but we'd packed the house.

I spent the next hour giving each person a hearty greeting, and after making sure everyone was fed and watered, I grabbed Tara and we snuck off to the restroom so I could practice my speech. I'd decided earlier that the smartest thing would be to hand the job to Jeff Simon, but it was a mere thirty minutes from showtime, and Mr. Chairman still hadn't made an appearance. I have no choice but to give it. *Oh the nerves!*

My daughter stood across from me, in front of the bay of sinks, from which eagle-eyed view she could report if I was doing anything wrong. I had the speech written on index cards but tried not to look at them. Fifty million recitations later, I had it down to two minutes. The only interruption was that I had to keep going into a stall to pee. My daughter, having never seen me this nervous, was amused. Her laughter helped calm my nerves. Breathing a titch easier, I recalled something intrinsic in my personality that put the whole thing in perspective: it has always been easy for me to talk to people, even strangers. The only real difference tonight would be that I'd be talking to skatey-eight thousand of them. All at once. Away from my environment. So, no biggie.

Ten minutes to eight. Before I could chicken out, I marched back to the party and directed my family up onto the stage. Simon was still nowhere to be found. It was just me and Funk; our children Tara and Andrew; our cosmic children Anna, Alex, and Nick; and Slick, the musician I had met at Simon's block party.

Once everyone was in place, I gathered my tits about me and walked across the stage, assuming an authoritative stance at the podium. It was the same posture I took with my birthing students. Like those folks, no one here knew I was a fraud — except for me.

Bing! Eight on the nut! I was bending the microphone down to mouth level when, out of the corner of my eye, I saw Jeff Simon walk in, half a moment too late to take over for me, though it appeared that he planned to join us onstage.

Laying my speech cards out on the lectern — not because I planned to read them, just to waste time so I could catch my breath — I gripped the mic tight. Taking a deep breath, I looked straight into the gorgeous eyes of Sonia Brown, just as I'd done on many occasions when she was attending birthing class on my dining room floor. Just as she had done then, she beamed rays of love at me, so I let her love be my beacon and began to speak, ad-libbing the first few lines.

Well, this is scarier than I thought it would be. (*Oh, great! I just began with a lie!*) If I can't finish, I'll let Funk's campaign chairman, Jeff Simon, take over. You won't mind, will you, Jeff? (*Just as I thought, Jeff came on stage, and also as I figured, he loved the limelight. Jeff threw a hand high in the air and waved, giving a big, cheesy smile of acquiescence.)*

I'd like to introduce our family to you. I am Mark Funkhouser's wife Gloria, and these are our beautiful children, Tara and Andrew. Along with them are the children of our hearts, Alex, Nick, and Anna.

Over here is your musician for the evening, the best blues and gospel artist this side of the Mississippi and fast becoming another child of our hearts, Daniel Ballinger.

When my husband told us one awful evening not so long ago that he had gone as far as he could as city auditor and that he could now best serve the citizens of Kansas City in the capacity of mayor, I knew that, just like anything else that has been big in our life, getting him elected would be a family event.

So, on behalf of my family, I would like to thank you for being here with us tonight, and . . . since I don't want to bore you to death, I'd like to introduce you to my husband, who is known at home as "Funk" or "Little Daddy-poo," who is known by his friends and co-workers as "the doctor of Funk," who is known at city hall as "that son of a bitch," and who will soon be known as "the next mayor of Kansas City" — your obedient servant, Mark Funkhouser.

Oh my God, I did it! I couldn't believe it was over. I only got tunnel vision once. And the audience laughed in all the right places. Taking in air, I gathered my notes and stepped to the side to let my husband at the mic. I stood beside him, shaking off my nerves.

Soon he was three minutes into his speech, and to tell you the truth, he wasn't doing well, which was strange. He'd made hundreds of speeches to much larger audiences, and although he was coming off as he usually did — full of integrity and smart as hell — his demeanor was as grave as when he was giving a keynote to a roomful of auditors, and that didn't seem appropriate for this new field. But maybe it was just me. This audience seemed enthralled. They were pumped that Funk was doing this most unexpected thing — running for mayor — and didn't seem the least bit bothered by his style. Still, his rational, dependable, dignified delivery had me worried. He didn't embellish himself. This audience was part of our inner world. Given that most politicians were prancing around town like celebrities, wouldn't residents expect the same from our understated Funk?

Kansas City was teetering on the brink of bankruptcy. Even though voters said they wanted someone who would whip city hall into shape, they were accustomed to a cheerleader in office telling them everything was okay. Our friends were aware of Funk's many sides, but all the citizens knew was what they'd read in the newspaper or seen on TV. And we already know that profile lacked dimension.

To offset that image, we needed to inject some life into his campaign. Let voters catch a glimpse of the auditor who wept at old movies. Allow them to hear the little ditties he sang to our children, the jingles our family groaned over. It was not what they'd be expecting from their staid auditor, and I was betting they'd find the juxtaposition amusing. To round Funk's personality out, we needed to paint a picture of a straight-talking, dollar-watching mayor — a secure, grandfather-type for the city — who had a fun side! *Hey! I just had a comforting thought.* Maybe letting the world know in my speech that I called my husband "Funk" had been a good start.

Wait a minute. What was I thinking? Getting Funk's softer side into the hands of the public wasn't my job. With this party almost a wrap, I'd be going back to my own life. Surely our guests would throw a few dollars at Funk, even if I had placed the donation envelopes off to the side. Surely there would be enough money to pay our family back for this little shindig and for everything else we'd loaned to the campaign. And surely there'd be a little bit left to hire a person to do the menial tasks I'd been helping Funk with so I could slip out of the double-wide without feeling guilty. Fingers crossed and legs uncrossed on that one.

Oh, Lord. Funk was droning on and on about how the city issued a billion dollars of debt without doing a rigorous analysis of costs and revenues. *Blah, blah, blah, put me to sleep, why don't you?* Luckily, he was nearing the end, at the quote from Teddy Roosevelt: "Far and away the best prize that life has to offer is the chance to work hard at work worth doing."

Yay! We were almost done. Now he was ad-libbing, saying how much fun it was going to be to go after the skeletons he hadn't been able to uncover when he was the city auditor. I inwardly rolled my eyes, but Christ, if the audience wasn't giving him a standing ovation! Okay, so maybe they liked his speech. Still, I promise you, my delivery was way better.

Funk left the stage before the applause quieted and was immediately swallowed up by the crowd. And me? Well, me and my party notes folder, which I had glued to my right arm for the entire evening, walked toward the entrance to see if anything on the table needed replenishing. The caterer was on my heels imploring me to eat, but I couldn't. I couldn't make small talk either. Trying not to be rude, I began fussing over the table — for longer than necessary, as I needed a few minutes to collect myself. Everything was going swimmingly. Really, much better than swimmingly. I was just a tad overwhelmed, was all.

Sooner than I wanted to, I headed back into the hall. Slick was scheduled to get the music going in fifteen minutes, and I wanted to go over his schedule one last time before he hopped onto the stage. It was the first attention I'd paid to the kid all evening, so after we had concluded our business, I asked him about his recent wedding. Slick was sharing stories about that life-altering event when Jeff Simon's wife came stomping up to the table looking loaded for bear.

A few months earlier, as I was taking my morning sauna, she had phoned me out of the blue to discuss this event. I barely knew her, yet she had pressured me to break my contract with Slick because of a mix-up between the two of them the previous year. To most folks, Amy appeared tiny and cute, but I saw hardened. I don't know if that came from her being Catholic or if it was the consequences of a horrific childhood embedded on her face. Whatever the cause, it took away from her looks. Still, judging by her frame, she'd probably had easy births. Why do thin girls get to be skinny and also have fast labors? It's an unjust world us fatties live in, I tell you.

Amy seemed stuck in middle school. If she was mad at someone, she wanted you to be mad at that person too. I heard her out, after which I immediately dialed Slick, and then his agent, to check out the story. By the time I hung up, my intuition assured me Slick had been on the up-and-up.

On a business level, I never questioned my decision. Besides, who in their right mind would disregard a message from above that Funk needed Slick's help to win the election? Since I wasn't seeking a relationship with Amy, I wasn't concerned on a personal level either. All the same, when I called her back, I tried to be gracious, saying the mix-up seemed to have originated with Slick's agent rather than with Slick.

She didn't buy it then and wasn't buying it now. Amy pulled a chair next to Slick's, and the ensuing conversation went something like this.

Big, brawny Amy — *How did she transform like that?* — said, "You were a no-show at my party."

Slick's southern drawl had her twang beat by a mile: "Yes, ma'am. I was sure sorry to hear about that. I — "

"Sorry won't cut it, *boy*. You cost my family a lot of money. We had t-shirts made. My kids drew pictures for you and hung them on trees."

Looking ashamed, Slick replied, "My, my, I am so sorry. My agent made many a mistake like this, and that is why I am no longer with her."

Amy's face was so close to Slick's, he would've needed a fly's eyes to take all of her in.

"This is your band. You're responsible, not your agent," she screeched, her face transforming into Cruella de Vil's.

The twenty-three-year-old didn't flinch from her spit.

"I'd sure like to make it up to you, ma'am. I'll come play for you anytime. At no charge."

"Of course it would be no charge. But I'd never have you back. My husband is a lawyer. You'll reimburse me, or I'll sue you for every penny we lost that night. For the food, the drink, the t-shirts, everything!"

During the interchange I sat frozen, staring at Amy, my jaw gaping by a mile wide. What in the world? Amy had all the time in the world to chew this kid out. But this brazen-hearted hussy had chosen Funk's party to make the entertainer squirm, minutes before the kid was due onstage! Seven months in the planning, and this woman was about to screw up everything? No frigging way. Not on my watch. Not on my dime. Not on my husband's big night. Funk might be a hick, but no one messed with my family.

I stood up, sallied around the table, and positioned myself between Amy's and Slick's chairs. With as much aplomb as I could muster, I said, "Amy, Daniel seems sorry for what happened. And as I said before, I believe the problem was his agent's, not his. But either way, can you please settle this another time? Tonight's pretty important."

I didn't allow a response, just acted as if she'd follow my instruction. Dismissing her, I put an arm around Daniel — aka Slick — and leaned down to whisper in his ear.

"Please put this out of mind. I don't know Amy well, but I've heard she's like this with everyone."

He didn't stir, just sat staring at the floor.

"C'mon, Daniel, put it behind you. Get up on stage and sing your heart out for Funk. For the people of Kansas City."

At that, he turned halfway around in his chair to look me in the eye. I don't know who he thought was crazier, me or Amy Simon. But gentleman that he was, all he said was, "Yes, ma'am. I surely will."

And he did.

When the band began to play, the same sultry voice that had mesmerized me a year ago belted forth. Funk's guests, who had been sitting just moments before, moved and grooved to his music. Relieved, I peeled my eyes away from

Slick and walked over to where my husband stood. And, just like a Midwesterner — yes, after fifteen years, I'd learned how it works — I planted a smile on my face as I ranted to him about Jeff's wife. Once that poison was out of my system, Funk and I went from table to table thanking everyone for coming to celebrate with us.

Our friends were so sweet I could have died right on the spot from too much love. They flattered Funk to no end — as if his head needed to be any bigger. Said how lucky the city would be with him running it and said how impressed they were that I'd arranged the event all by myself. Some mentioned that I was a natural at giving speeches. If they had only known what my insides had felt like. . . .

Finished with my duties for the moment, I let Slick's voice carry me away. It did, but not for long. A meaty-looking dude, with hair the color of a metal lamppost and curls permed as tight as an old grandma's just back from the beauty parlor, came up behind me and screamed in my ear, "You're Mark Funkhouser's wife."

It was a statement. What was I supposed to do with that? No matter, the dude went on without me.

"I'm Britt Nichols, a former student of Mark's."

The name rang a bell, and I racked my brain. Oh, I remembered. It had been Funk's night job. He taught graduate-level public finance classes at universities in the metro area. I had helped grade his students' papers. Well, I didn't grade them. I just did the time-consuming work of pulling them from the computer and printing them out for him to grade.

"Yes, I remember seeing your name on my computer. Nice to meet you!" The music was too loud for conversation, so I smiled and turned my attention back to Slick.

Instantly, Curly's mouth was at my ear again. His body was so near that he was almost spooning me — *ewww* — his mouth so close that my ear felt all humid-like, and it hurt from his shouting into it. I stepped forward to relieve myself of the pain, but his bulging eyes came at me. The dude was going to say what he'd come over to say. Boiled down, the message was that he wanted to be Funk's campaign manager.

I had hoped to be off duty for a second to enjoy the music. But I dropped into diplomat mode to tell Mr. Nichols that although I had nothing to do with such decisions, I'd be happy to pass his message along to my husband. A moment later, I thought better of it. Because Funk was in desperate need of a manager, I suggested that Curly speak with him immediately. To facilitate that, I pointed to my guy, as if Nichols couldn't locate Funk for himself, Funk being a head taller than everyone in the room. Thinking our business complete, I shifted my eyes back to the stage.

The dude wouldn't go away.

"You're Mark's wife."

I thought to myself *yeah, we've already covered that* but, nice person that I am, I just smiled and nodded my head.

The beefy guy turned aggressive. He began lecturing me, like a parent to a child who has done something wrong. "Every candidate's wife is involved, Gloria, whether they want to be or not. Get used to it. Soon, lots of people will be trying to get something from you, especially if Mark makes it into office."

Now he'd gone and activated my inner New Yorker. If there was anything I hated, it was being told what to do — by a stranger, no less. I hated that almost as much as I hated negative talk. Any glimmer of hope I'd had for this guy being associated with Funk's campaign flew out the window when he said, "*If* Mark makes it into office. . . ." What kind of manager says that? I'll tell you what kind: the losing kind!

Not entirely relinquishing my obligation as hostess, I told the guy as nicely as I could to please go fuck off. "Oh, my husband will make it into office all right, but I know nothing about the other thing you speak of."

"Well, I do. I've had years of experience. I've gotten many candidates elected and have worked in their office afterward. I know how this works. I'll explain your role later — what you should do publicly, what you should do but fib to the press about."

This distasteful stranger said that last part with an evil grin.

Nichols rambled on to such an extent that I had more than enough time to size him up. If the man had so much experience, why was he trying to sell a lowly wife on his qualifications? Wouldn't candidates be seeking him out, not the other way around? Plus, he didn't know a thing about my husband if he thought Funk would have me lie to anyone. And hiding my true self isn't the way I operate in the world.

Without the least bit of encouragement, the man blathered on about how wonderful he was. This guy was more boring than Funk in work mode. But at least my husband was honest. And smart. And charismatic. Well, sort of charismatic. On rare occasion. He *is* charming though, no doubt about that.

I backed up again, but Nichols moved nearer. His eyes were a mere inch from my nose. He was speaking so animatedly that his curls were having a riot on top of his enormous head. Some were springing forward, brushing my face, as he demanded five grand a month to be my husband's manager.

"Five thousand!" I yelped, unable to stop myself. Man, was this guy fucked up or what? By this time, I wanted to tell him as much. There was no use trying to enjoy the music. Nichols demanded my full attention.

"I'm sorry, Mr. Nichols, but you're probably unaware that my husband is running a grassroots campaign. Most of the work will be done on a volunteer basis, by people who believe in what Funk is trying to accomplish. He isn't part of the establishment. There's no one funding him. But thank you so much for the offer. I'm sure you're worth every penny, and I'll be sure to let Funk know, in case I have it wrong."

The dude responded with a Midwestern smile.

Jesus! Why did I attract the weirdest people? The man was creeping me out with his screeching and those bouncing curls. I'd already extended more time to him than to anyone else, so I stopped with the hints and excused myself, saying I needed to tend to things.

He followed me.

I walked over to my personal-trainer-turned-girlfriend, who I knew understood signs.

"Hey, Teense!"

I had hired Tina to make sure I didn't set foot in Europe looking like another fat American.

"Thank you so much for coming, Tina. Can you believe the friggin' ice?"

She grabbed me in a hug and said, "You look great!"

"Tina, let me introduce you to Britt Nichols. He's a former student of Funk's."

She ran with my unsaid words.

"Nice to meet you, Britt." Winking a thank-you to Tina, I took the opening to escape this nuisance.

Finally, the night came to at a close. Fried beyond belief, I herded our guests to the front door to avoid the Art Institute's overtime charge. Funk and most of the kids hopped into his Corolla, and the musicians squeezed themselves and their equipment in the van with me.

Alex rounded the corner just as I was about to pull away. Seeing my front seat empty, he jumped inside, buckled up, and proceeded to dry heave. I looked at him in astonishment and saw that he was dead drunk. A sixteen-year-old boy, the boy we claimed as son — always the practical one, ever the responsible one, the boy now associated with a candidate running for mayor — *that* boy was in my van, drunk out of his mind.

"What the hell, Alex? Don't tell me you snuck a drink inside Funk's party!"

In his typical lazy but surprisingly sober-sounding voice, he replied, "I didn't drink inside. I made sure to drink outside," after which he proceeded to gag again.

"Who gave it to you? Never mind. Get out."

He looked at me, hurt.

But I didn't care, just screeched louder, "I said get out!"

I'd never spoken to Alex like this before. Andrew, yes. Alex, no. Alex's face registered horror at provoking my anger. I felt bad for how crushed he seemed, but I reached an arm across his chest, unlocked the door, and threw it open.

He stumbled out of the van and flagged someone else to give him a ride.

I was fuming mad, especially since the blues-turned-gospel-singer had witnessed the whole thing, including my cursing. He didn't know this was an unusual occurrence. Well, Alex's drunkenness had been unusual, even if my cursing wasn't. Cursing was an extension of my people's vocabulary, and I had no shame about it. Still, I tried never to let loose in front of people I didn't know.

Glancing in my rearview mirror, all I could think to say to Slick was that I was sorry. That Alex had never done anything like this before, and to please not judge him for it. I didn't mention the cursing part. I just put the van in gear, drove home, got the band and the family settled into their rooms, fell into bed, and was instantly asleep.

4 DECEMBER 2006

I'D BEEN SO IMMERSED in the party and my kids that I hadn't been to the double-wide for two whole days. I had skipped going to the gym, too. That was going to haunt me, but I couldn't go or I'd never catch up with work.

Four hundred emails were waiting in my inbox. The number had been increasing ever since Funk had announced. I began each day by sorting through them and forwarding each to its rightful owner. Without pre-thought, I'd assigned the three of us specific jobs. I handled the emails that concerned Funk's calendar and volunteers; those pertaining to running his office went to Dottie; and the largest number, the personal missives, went directly to Funk. I didn't know where he found the time to answer them all.

Also waiting were thirty-five voicemails, but it had become my habit to have Dottie pull those off the machine and return the calls. She was better on the phone than I was. Besides, I was dying to open the donation envelopes from the party.

We had crested the thirty-grand mark. No, not in campaign donations — in the amount my family was in the hole to achieve Funk's "dream." We had spent about twenty thousand on the Coming-Out Party alone. I was hoping against hope that the donations inside the stack of envelopes would be enough to pay us back for everything we'd fronted the campaign.

I didn't want a million paper cuts, so I exited my temporary office and walked over to Dottie's desk.

"Hey, Dots. May I use your envelope opener?"

Not as shy around me anymore, she laughed and playfully squealed, "Gloria! Would you stop calling me that?"

"I can't, Dottie. I have a special term of endearment for everyone I love."

Blushing but seeming delighted at my profession of feeling for her, she said with resignation, "Okay." And then, pointing a scolding finger at me, she added, "But you're the only one allowed to call me that, okay?"

"Sure, Dots."

I had no time for chitchat. I went back to my desk and began ripping into envelopes. My plan was to remove the contents without looking at the amount, but like a child, I couldn't help peeking as I pulled each donation from its envelope.

The first was a check for $500. *Yay! Not a shabby start!* The second was a five-dollar bill. Next, a $10 bill. Then a dollar after that. Seeing a one-dollar bill in my hand, I laughed out loud. Who would give Funk a buck? Maybe because Slick had sung gospel songs that night, the donor thought they were sitting in church and didn't want to get caught not tithing something. I wanted to know so bad who had given a dollar, but the donor hadn't filled out the form on the envelope. I'd never contributed to an election campaign, and I couldn't imagine giving, even though I was now in the campaign business. I was just hoping for more donations so my family could get out of the red.

Bills and checks sorted into neat little piles, I glanced at my father's photograph, blew him a kiss, and began tapping my calculator.

Oh, brother.

The bottom line totaled less than 10 percent of the amount our family had placed on our credit card. Shit. There'd be no paying us back for anything. And forget about Funk hiring someone to replace me. We got barely enough to cover a month's rent on the trailer. Funk had estimated there would be at least fifty grand waiting inside those envelopes. I put my disappointment out of mind because if I danced with it, my throat would strangle shut and I wouldn't get anything done.

I drove Andrew home from school and shoved a meal down his throat — the whole time pretending to be listening to the happenings of his day, when really, I was obsessing about the lack of donations. After cleaning the dishes, I drove back to the trailer to wrap up work for the day.

Later I broke the news to Funk. I wished I could have softened the blow, but I didn't pussyfoot around. My husband's face went from happy anticipation to crestfallen, but we couldn't discuss what our next step would be, because Jeff Simon arrived in the middle of that conversation.

That guy entered every room belly first, and man, was he a talker. I made a few pleasantries so as not to appear rude and then excused myself before the tiresome banter got underway. Back inside the water-stained walls of my office, I hurried to finish my tasks. I didn't know which mound to tackle first. How could it be that everything was important and of the highest priority? I decided the thank-you notes had to come first, as every penny given to my husband was a blessing and was to be treated as such. The only way I could think to show our gratitude was to hand-write each card. Even the $1 donor would've gotten a thank-you, had the person given his name.

I was the middle of composing those letters when I discovered that half the donors hadn't provided the information required by the state ethics commission. And damn if I didn't let a curse word slip for all the trailer to hear. I had included a simple information form on the back of the donation envelope. Why didn't people fill it in?

The contributions via check didn't pose as big a problem as those made by cash. I could pull most of the information I needed from the front of the check. For the rest, I could either do a quick internet search or telephone the donor and ask for the info. Better yet, I could ask a volunteer to make the call. I was always looking for tasks I could delegate because there weren't too many of them. Most of what I did could only be done by me or Funk, and my husband was usually out talking to people.

He and Jeff Simon were still yakking it up in his office. Jeff Simon worried me. It seemed as though Funk's campaign was just fun and games to him. As far as I could tell, he didn't do anything. He just dropped in for entertainment. Well, that's not entirely true. He'd done one thing: he had taped a handwritten sign on Funk's wall that read "Sennyhow." Apparently, Funk said that a lot and Simon thought it was funny. *Tee-hee.* I couldn't think of a single time I'd heard Funk say that, but that was beside the point. I'd spent my entire marriage trying to un-hickify my man, and Simon was luring him back to his podunk ways.

My husband was enjoying himself with Jeff. That's why I hadn't fussed about it. Not yet. Give me a day or two. Because Dottie and I couldn't keep going full steam as we were, only to have those guys just horsing around. Jesus, what nerve, the two of them!

5 DECEMBER 2006

JOHN MEARA, the CPA my husband brought on board, had been Funk's fan for a long time now. At the scheduled meeting—guess who arranged that—the minute my husband asked him, John said he'd love to lend his services to the cause. Personally, I would never help a candidate who wasn't part of my family. I wish I was as good and generous as other people.

Each day brought more volunteers and donations to Funk's fledgling campaign. Smack me in the mouth for saying this, but how I wished the donations were as prolific as the volunteers. Still, money came in at a trickle, and it was enough to get us to the next day. Each time we needed another ream of paper, *poof,* another buck or two rolled in and we could purchase it. The volunteers were signing up by the bucketload. Most we didn't know from anywhere. They came unbidden. It blew my mind. It was as if my husband was the leader of some sort of a revolution. I barely knew what to do with them all, as there was barely time to think. But most were finding ways of being useful on their own. I think they preferred it that way. They were nice, if a smidge quirky. Some had outlandish ideas on the path the campaign should take, and they loved telling me about them. Someone drew an abstract of Funk's face and wanted that on the yard sign — no words, no nothing. Just the abstract. Others wanted to "call out" the establishment out by name, accusing them of stealing from the city. Talk about a nontraditional campaign!

Not all the volunteers were eccentric, though. One day I was going to the stockroom for supplies and noticed a woman sitting in a back office. It stunned me to see her, for two reasons. First, she was black. *How was Alvin Brooks going to feel?* Brooks was an older man who'd served the city for a long time. He also happened to be one of only two black candidates running for mayor, not to mention the expected winner. If he finds out she's here, God help her. But I was more shocked for the second reason: that someone from the campaign had stuck her in the back of the trailer. I mean, the symbolism of that was so bad.

The door to her office was open, but to show my respect, I knocked on the doorframe. Looking up from a phone book resting in her lap, she gave me an engaging smile.

I smiled back and said, "Hi, my name is Gloria. I'm Funk's wife."

"I know who you are."

"Oh, I'm sorry, have we met before?" I usually never ask this question. I just try to draw the conversation out until I can figure out how I know the person. It's my greatest fear that it's a former birth student that I've forgotten. With my classes as intimate as they are, I don't want to hurt anyone's feelings by not recalling a face.

"No, we haven't met, but I've seen you on TV."

"Really? I didn't know I was on TV. That's a first!"

"Yes, just the other night. They filmed you standing beside the next mayor's car. My name is Imani."

I had an instant liking for this woman.

"What a beautiful name. Are you here to volunteer?"

"Yes, I came in on the spur of the moment."

"Geez, that's really nice. Thank you so much."

She gave me another dazzling smile.

"Well, I don't know who put you back here, Imani, but there are plenty of offices up front. How about we find one closer, so you feel like part of the group?"

"That's okay. I chose this space. I don't have much time, and I'm hoping to lend a hand for a couple of hours before I have to go to my job."

I was liking this woman more and more. Not only was she committed but my God, was she beautiful. Like, model gorgeous, and dressed the part. Her outfit reminds me of the Chanel suits Jackie Kennedy used to wear, and this woman looked every bit as dramatic as Jackie had. But it wasn't just her appearance that was striking. Imani emanated a beauty from deep within her soul.

"What do they have you doing?"

"I'm looking up names in the phone book."

I was surprised again, this time by the tedious task assigned to the woman.

"That sounds really boring. Can I find something else for you to do?"

"I don't mind this. The way I see it, everything I put my finger to does some good."

"I never thought of it that way, but you're right, the smallest tasks lead to the highest good."

I walked back to my office in dazed amazement, an emotion I'd experienced fifty million times that week. The double-wide was beginning to feel like a holy place, and the ragtag people associated with the campaign seemed like angels. Imani knew Funk only from what she'd heard in the media, yet her devotion was what you'd expect from kin. I can't tell you how many times in the past few weeks my heart had let me know that it's there, beating inside my chest, because it brims over each time I encounter another unexpected outpouring of help like this. Of love, really.

As Funk and I dedicated longer and longer hours to the campaign, the time we spent with our son Andrew grew shorter and shorter. I felt miserable about neglecting Andrew and also for rushing Tara off the phone when she phoned me. She probably thought she'd need to be bleeding to get the attention of her mother anymore. Our talks had been the highlight of my day, but now they just made me feel like a loser. I practically cut her off mid-sentence. I'd talked to the kids about the situation and although both said I shouldn't feel guilty, I hoped that soon I could go back to just being their mom and running my business. I didn't know what was driving this. I don't even like my husband near as much as I like my children. I mean, it's not even close.

It was after ten p.m. when Funk and I gave it up and drove our separate cars home. After we spent as much time with Andrew as he could tolerate, Funk and I collapsed into bed. Lying there in the dark, Funk began telling me about a conversation he'd had with Jeff Simon, an everyday occurrence now. Kind of like a daily special in a restaurant. We were both way too wired to sleep yet way too tired for many words, so our pillow talk went something like this:

"Simon was in tonight."

"Yes, I heard him through the wall again. Does that guy ever shut up?"

"He says I need a campaign manager."

"Wow, really! I didn't know that. What else?"

"I need to pay the campaign manager."

"Pay?"

"Yes."

"Why?"

"To appear legitimate."

"How do you figure that?"

"Jeff has it figured out."

"Oh, okaaaay."

"He wants Britt Nichols."

"The curly-headed dude from the party?"

"Yes."

"Are you fucking kidding me? That guy seems dense."

"He's actually pretty smart."

"You like the weirdest people."

"Smart people are typically weird."

"Does Simon know you're running a grassroots campaign and that Nichols wants five grand a *month*?"

"Yes."

"Well?"

"He says I need to show the movers and shakers that I have an experienced manager handling me."

"Movers and shakers?"

"Yes."

"Handling you?"

"Yes."

"What the fuck?"

"He says my clothes are shabby."

"Oh, my God!"

"That I need to buy a few thousand-dollar suits and wear them at all times."

"Okay, so now you're kidding, right?"

"No."

"Does Simon know you're not rich?"

"He knows we don't come from money, but he probably assumes we're well off."

"To use your stupid word, have you *disabused* him of that notion?"

"No."

"Well, did you ask your chairman if he'd be purchasing those suits?"

"No."

"What did you say?"

"Not much. It's hard to get a word in."

I shot up in bed, sleep no longer in my desired future. Inside our darkened room, I turned and leaned down toward Funk's prone face, my annoyance boiling over.

"Yes, Funk, and that's a big problem. You, me, Dottie — none of us have time for the amount of gabbing that's going on between you and Jeff Simon. Jesus, Funk, you're not even giving that kind of attention to your son anymore, and that's really bad. It's a slap in the face."

Defensively, my husband said, "Andrew barely came out of his room tonight. He's a teenage male. He prefers keeping a distance."

"That's bullshit, Funk, and you know it. No, our son doesn't want to talk for long, and he doesn't want to be around us much — except for when he does! But believe me, he likes us being in the house, and don't think he isn't keeping score. I don't know how he got those macho Italian genes, what with me raising him the same as I did his sister and with you being a hick from West Vagina, but trust me, the Italian goes deep."

"Gloria — "

"I could understand your having fun with Simon if he were lending a hand, but he's not doing anything, and that means you're not doing anything when he's at the trailer, and he's there every night now. He just saunters in after work like he owns the joint, probably as an excuse not to go home."

"Gloria — "

"Funk, he's taking time, not giving any. He isn't helping with any of the work that desperately needs to get done, work that Dottie and I are buried under. He hasn't organized the first volunteer. Hasn't arranged the first meet-and-greet, even though you say he knows *everyone* in town. Jesus, he hasn't even made the simple timeline of events *The Campaign Manager* says you're supposed to have."

"Gloria — "

"For fuck's sake, Funk, I bet you anything he hasn't even read his damn copy of *The Campaign Manager*! The book your *family* purchased for him! What a waste of money!"

"Gloria, he's read — "

"Oh, give it a rest, Funk. I know the man doesn't want to be seen publicly hooking up with you, but I thought you'd be working privately, from inside."

"We're working."

"You're working? All I hear is cutting up."

"We're strategizing."

"Strategizing?"

"Yes."

"I thought we agreed at the carwash that you'd just be who you are? Is this why you wanted him for your campaign manager, to strategize you into something you're not?"

"No. Jeff says I have to strategize. I wanted him because I thought he knew more about setting up a campaign than I did."

"Setting up a campaign? What the hell are you talking about! That's spelled out in the book: step one, step two, step three. Have *you* read the friggin' book, or am I the only asshole who has?"

"Gloria — "

"Does Simon know you're not running a traditional campaign? Does he know you're trying to turn the city around, not win a popularity contest?"

"He says I'm exactly what the city needs. That I'm ballsy and in all the right places. Gloria, he knows me, and he likes what I stand for."

"Well, Funk, it doesn't seem that way to me."

"Glor, he's a good man. The type you typically go for. A do-gooder and funny as hell. He'll come around. When we really need him, he'll be right there with us."

"Funny thing is, Funk, I thought you really need him *now*. And would you stop with the *we* shit? I've told you a million times, there's no *we* in this campaign of yours. And stop yakking it up with Simon every night. One night, two nights, fine. Not every night. Put him to work, and then use your freed-up time to bring some money into the campaign so I can frigging go home already. I can't take the guilt anymore."

"Is that what this is about?"

"Don't make me mad. This is about everything I just said!"

Finally, my man agreed to all my demands. Then, as nonchalantly as only a puffed-up rooster in search of a tasty hen can be, he rolled halfway onto me and started rubbing his hand up and down the length of my body.

Knowing where he was going and that it wasn't meant to be the comforting gesture the situation warranted, I spat, "Get off me, crazy man. You've got me working like a slave. I'm too tired for that." I threw his hand off my person and conked out.

6 DECEMBER 2006

WELL, BLOW ME AWAY, it was early morning and Simon had just walked past my door with Curly. They barely paused to say hello before going inside Funk's office and slamming the door shut. They'd been in there for an hour, Simon cackling away as usual. Each time he did, my skin crawled in tidal waves.

I was trying to like Jeff Simon, really. Mostly for my husband's sake, since he enjoyed the man so much. You probably don't know this, but I loved watching Funk have a good time. I also loved watching him eat. And I loved looking at his beautiful hands. Sometimes when we're driving to the cabin, I held one of them and turned it this way and that, just looking it over. They're a work of art, those hands.

Anyway, Funk was right. Jeff Simon was a lot of fun, even if it had been hard getting to know him. He was a man's man except for when he was a lady's man. He was a big flirt, like I am — but still, the man didn't even come close to the kind of person I'd take a detour for. Actually, I'd never met anyone who I felt was worth it. That's kind of sad, when you think about it. Like, Funk is the high bar?

I had heard many stories involving Jeff before I ever laid eyes on him. One that stood out was how he sat at Senator Harry Wiggins's bedside for weeks before Harry passed away. I'd never had much interest in politics, but I respected Senator Wiggins. When I was stomping to get a midwifery bill passed, he was one of the few legislators who supported it. He had taken a stand, a rarity among politicians, in favor of midwives, another rarity, so I had a lot of heart for the man. Years ago, when Funk told me Wiggins was dying, I was relieved to know someone as charming as Jeff was comforting him in his final hours. It moved me enough that I sent Jeff a note to say I admired him for his actions.

But now that same Jeff Simon was pressuring my husband to hire Britt Nichols to be his campaign manager, and I had no idea where Funk would land on the issue. Funk and I were with each other more than we'd ever been, but we were seldom together. We just breezed past one another, stopping only to remind the other about things we needed to do or to check that they had been done. There was no question that Funk needed a manager, but ever since Jeff had turned him down, Funk had been of the mind that Dana Laiben was the right person.

Moments after Jeff and Curly left Funk's office that day, Dana knocked at the entrance to the double-wide. I introduced myself and then escorted her back to the king's domain, because why would Funk get off his ass to let her in? Can you believe this is what I've been reduced to? An usher.

Dana appeared to be a few years older than I was, which was bad. She was from that generation of women who believed they had to act like men to get ahead, the ones who channeled the worst attributes of the male breed. I found it distasteful. I didn't like macho men, and I didn't find their traits becoming in my species. Besides, I don't get it. We women have plenty of our own strengths; we don't need to borrow any ugly traits from our male counterparts.

Later that morning, between his other meetings, Funk stuck his head in my door to say Dana was interested in the position and even willing to work on contingency, as Dottie was. By Funk standards, he was delirious with joy. I think he wanted to stay and discuss the conundrum of Jeff wanting Nichols and him wanting Dana Laiben, but I shooed him out of my office. I couldn't stay inert while he pondered that again. He just needed to *choose* someone and get on with it already! But not someone who was demanding five grand a month, because where would he get the money?

It had been stupid crazy around headquarters. Volunteers were coming out of the woodwork, yet between instructing them and answering the phones, Dottie and I were so tied up that we couldn't fully utilize their help. By the time we finished showing a volunteer the ropes, we could have done the job ourselves, twenty times faster. It was like when your kid wants to help you cook — only worse. With the constant interruptions, we started the same pile of work fifty thousand times a day. It was maddening.

I didn't want to wait another second for Funk to get a manager. We needed to whip the headquarters into shape, right away, or Dottie and I would never get off our treadmill leading to nowhere. I was not going to leave the brokedown shack until I had systematized the place. Whoever Funk's campaign manager turned out to be better come to my office on their knees to thank me. Then again, they'd never know what Dottie and I had been through, so we'd probably get oogotz.

I started with *the* most important element in campaigns: getting a handle on the volunteers. I planned to list all the tasks the book said we needed help with and then pen a step-by-step description of how each task was to be carried out. Then I'd draft a spreadsheet that matched volunteer skills to tasks. Most supporters had been gracious, saying they'd do anything to get Funk elected, but I knew things would go more smoothly if I assigned them to a job that suited their personality. It meant I'd have to spend more time getting my husband organized, but it would pay off down the road.

By the time I had worked through the list I was congratulating myself because here it was, done, and it wasn't even time for me to pick up Andrew from school! Two heartbeats later, I realized congratulations weren't in order. Not at all. Like everything else around this joint, one job just led to another. You can't put a period at the end of anything. There was no clearing off your desk so that the fake wood surface would show again. No coming in the next morning to a clean slate. No talking to your daughter without hurrying her off the phone. There was none of that. Campaigns are full on, all the time. And you'd better get with it or get out.

There was a gaping hole in my plan.

Even after a campaign manager was in place, Funk would still need a volunteer to manage the volunteers. This person would schedule workers, ensure that tasks were being done, and see that they were done correctly. The job would require forty hours a week, and no one had offered to donate that kind of time. The database also needed a person to work on it full time. It had grown large and unwieldy. And even if we found noble types willing to donate long hours, we'd still have to train them.

If Funk got enough donations, yard signs would take planning too. We'd need someone with a background in graphic design to put Funk's vision to paper. Another person to research print shops for the best quality at the cheapest price. Dozens of people to install and maintain the signs. I wondered who at city hall had decided it was a smart idea to hold elections in wintertime.

Several professionals had joined Funk's campaign. Some, who worked in advertising, said they could find the best radio and TV slots for commercials. Others wanted to develop print ads. But there wasn't even a blip of money on the horizon for them. *Wait a minute*, I thought. I should accept their offers and have them waiting in the wings, ready to go if and when Funk could pull the trigger. Of course, that day would *never* come unless my husband started moving his ass with getting a campaign manager. I didn't know what was wrong with him. This was his dream, yet he was moving as slow as shit. Not my shit. His shit. My shit moves fine.

Another thing: the campaign needed a tracking system for every type of contributor. A few supporters made cash donations, but most just wanted to show their allegiance with a button or a yard sign, *but only if* the campaign planted the signs, which we didn't have, or mailed the buttons. Which reminded me, I still needed to change the design on the button.

Others wanted to host a meet-and-greet. I had never heard of those before, but basically, they were a pretty way of saying that Funk would go to someone's house and try not to appear as if he was begging for money, and the host got to feel important without forking any over. Believe it or not, people had been calling in like mad for them. Funk would never be able to meet the demand. A lot of work went into setting up meet-and-greets. A packet had to be prepared for each event. It included getting a bead on neighborhood-specific issues; printing driving directions because Funk couldn't afford the luxury of getting lost; documenting donations, which had to be deposited and recorded in the database; and the coup de grâce, writing and mailing thank-you notes.

See what I mean? We were drowning in work, yet the more tasks I organized, the more things needed doing. If I had been putting this kind of effort into my little house business idea, I'd be freaking rich. A million things demanded my time and attention. We needed to build a professional website to replace the rudimentary thing Andrew had slapped together. And the copy for it needed to be written in Funk's voice. We were not going to message what we *thought* people wanted to hear, no matter what anyone, including our campaign chairman, said. We needed to hunt down legal papers. I was supposed be able to pull information from the city's website, but it was a piece of shit. When Funk got into the mayor's office, he'd have to fix that too. We needed to schedule debates, but first someone had to figure out how to set up a Google calendar. I didn't have time to learn, and I thought it would drive Dottie insane to try. And Funk had to nail down his choices for committees so I could ask each person about meeting times.

Man, just laying out the list of tasks gave me agita. How would I remember everything that needed to be done, *and* done well, when there weren't enough hours in the day to do most of it? I had to quit thinking. If I kept this up, I'd start fretting. And if I started fretting, it'd be only a blink before I spiraled down into the black sea of muck. If that happened, I'd never get the campaign sorted out.

C'mon Glor. Focus on your work. You'll get everything done and you'll do it well. Don't look up, or you'll notice you have tunnel vision and that will scare you, and then what? We can't keep scheduling people when we don't know what to do with them. Not that I'd ever volunteer, but if I did and I saw this dysfunction, I'd turn around and be out the door quick. Fuck. Quit thinking. Just keep working on the outline. The Campaign Manager *explains everything. Follow the instructions and all will be well. You're a New and Better You. Don't regress to your sniveling old ways. You're more capable than before you left for Europe. You can do this. You* are *doing this. The New and Better You can stop obsessing and organize this mess into a workable condition. You have the mind for it and the energy of a teenager, wherever that came from. Gloria! Stop obsessing!*

Okay, I'm back. But Jesus, shouldn't the campaign have been structured eons ago? If I had known from the beginning that I'd be doing this, I would've put a system in place from the get-go. But no, here I was, months since I'd started, the place was a wreck, and I was spending precious time unraveling things. *I've been nervous all day about getting out of here tonight, but that's a joke. I couldn't do this in a day. I'd be at it for weeks, and that was only if I did nothing else.* But honestly, why had this worry fallen on to my shoulders?

Christ! I just realized something. Funk had me doing all the tedious shit his campaign manager should have been doing! Maybe that's why it was taking him so long to choose. I mean, why make a difficult decision when you had someone slaving away in the interim? Jesus, how could I have fallen for such —

Gloria! That's enough. Put your damn head down and get to work, or you'll never get out of here today.

Much, much later — I don't think you could even call it later that evening, it was more like early the next day — I was finally home and in my sacred bed, trying to fall asleep, when Funk brought up his latest conversation with Jeff Simon. I wanted to wait on that until daybreak, but I'd been dying to know why Jeff had brought Britt in, so I couldn't resist listening. Turns out, the two had come to tag-team Funk into hiring Curly. It made me think Jeff didn't know my husband very well if he thought it was okay to spend $5K per month on the guy.

But that was nothing compared with the other thing Funk told me: at the time of Senator Wiggins's death he had no heirs, so Jeff inherited the senator's lake house. I wish Funk hadn't told me. I'd never get to sleep. Not for wondering if Jeff hung out with the senator in his final days for that. Man, I really hoped not, or poor Harry.

7 DECEMBER 2006

IT WAS PEARL HARBOR DAY. For as long as I could remember, Funk had made note of the day. Even though the war with Japan had ended a long time ago, my eyes popped open in fear as I awoke in the morning. Funk was staring at the ceiling, blinking a slow blink. He does that when he's deep in thought, as does my daughter. She's been taking the world in like that ever since she was born. Since I like her, it melts my heart. On the monstrosity lying beside me, well, it's not as cute. His innocent gaze allowed the fear I woke up with to explode from my mouth.

"Funk!"

"Yes, Glor," he said, barely acknowledging me.

"Have you heard from the University of Missouri?"

"About?"

The mayor's salary was going to be an enormous cut in pay, not nearly enough to support our family. Funk would need a second job to get by — just as every other mayor of Kansas City had, including the rich ones.

"Establishing the Center at the university, UMKC. What else?"

"I thought you meant the campaign."

"Jesus, Funk, not everything is about your damn campaign. You have a family. Remember us? Helloooo. Your children are asleep in their beds."

He went from being pensive to looking excruciatingly uncomfortable.

"Well, have you touched base with them or not?"

"With whom?"

"Oh, my God! I feel like I'm living inside a fun house, only I'm not having fun. Have you followed up with the university?"

"No."

"Don't you think you should?"

"No."

Anger ignited and lifted me from the bed.

"What the fuck!"

Funk deplored being summoned into action first thing in the morning, and since he wasn't on his game yet, he stood up to my emotion.

"Gloria, we've been through this a hundred times. They've repeatedly said the Center would be funded within a year. It hasn't been a year."

"Hey, buddy, don't talk to me like that." Then, like an imbecile, I parroted the imbecile's words back to him, "We've been through this a hundred times."

He said nothing.

"Why aren't you following through?"

"I have followed through. The ball is in their court."

"What the hell are you talking about? You quit your job so you could run for mayor, but you need another job."

"I'll have one shortly."

We had a plan. We had firmed it up the previous May at the carwash. One reason I had agreed to Funk's dream was because he had promised to secure a second job.

"Are you talking about the Center?"

"Yes. That's my second job."

"You have a signed agreement?"

"I have their word."

"You need more than a handshake, Funk. You've got to stay on top of this, or the university can just as easily fall in love with someone else's project, and that'll be it for yours!"

"And a meteor might fall from the sky too, Gloria."

His words did me in and I started screaming, "You're pissing me off. This doesn't even sound like you. Have you gotten yourself possessed overnight, or what?"

Finally, my husband joined the conversation.

"Gloria, the Kansas City campus has pledged themselves to me and to the Center. I can't call the university and ask for that same information again. I'd look like a fool."

"That's ridiculous. Checking to see that things are progressing is smart, not foolish. You've got to nudge this forward. If you keep waiting on UMKC to make a move, you know where you'll end up? Standing in front of our family boo-hooing, telling us how sorry you are. Screw that. I don't need a bunch of I'm sorrys. I need you to make enough money so we can pay our bills. Get something in writing from them or start looking for an alternative."

"Gloria—"

"I'm serious, Funk. Work the fucking plan."

"Glor—"

My words weren't getting through to him, so I tried a different approach.

"You probably don't know where we are with our finances. BirthWays isn't pulling in the same income it used to. I can barely make it home to teach my birth classes, and I've been turning down doula clients because I'm dedicating myself to helping with your work."

Softening, he said, "Babe, I know this scares you, but everything is fine. UMKC wants this as much as I do, maybe more. They're not funding the Center to be nice. They're funding it *because* of me. They need my reputation and connections to get it off the ground, and they want to get it off the ground. It's a niche field that no other university has. It will attract top scholars from around the globe. . . ." *Blah, blah, blah,* on and on he went in professor mode. But I didn't resist; I just let the fucker ramble on. ". . . Adds prestige . . . sets the Kansas City branch apart from Columbia . . . I see UMKC *becoming* the main campus . . . think how that will play out for the city . . . solve our financial mess . . . put us on the map. The establishment likes to say we're world class, but the university will *make* us a world-class city."

"Funk, I could give two shits about UMKC's status or the city's economy. All I care about is your family staying financially afloat. What's wrong with having a backup?"

"It's a waste of time to chase another job, with everything else going on."

"A waste of time!" I roared. "What the hell is going on? I've never heard you say such stupid shit before."

"Jeff about lost it. He says I can't run a campaign and also look for a job. He says I had to choose the campaign, or I won't win. That I can look for a job once I'm in office."

"Are you fucking kidding me? How is our livelihood any of Jeff Simon's business! Are we even talking about the *same* Jeff! The Jeff who's not doing anything except getting a hard-on from an empty title! You're listening to *that* fat fuck about what's best for us? And without discussing it with me? When was the last time we didn't discuss something? Oh, that's right, Funk. *Never!*"

Our bedroom fell silent. My words all used up, I could only stare at him in horror.

As always, he composed himself and took back adulthood before I did.

"You're right, Glor. I've been stupid. I'm sorry. I'll call UMKC as soon as I get to the double-wide."

He reached for me, but I jerked away. It takes me a while to calm down after being upset. Leaving him in bed, I went downstairs to make coffee and get a head start on dinner, but mainly to fume as far away from him as I could get.

The kids were already awake, probably because of our exchange. As soon as my feet reached the landing, all eyes went from the TV to me. They hated when Funk and I argued yet were fascinated by it all the same. I ignored the questioning stares, just raised my hand in hello and slipped into the kitchen to be by myself. I wasn't alone for long. For reassurance or perhaps just out of train-wreck curiosity, likely both, in and out they came with one made-up excuse or the other, but mostly for the skinny on what had just happened.

I was usually dying to spill my guts as much as they were dying to know. But this day was different. Today was the rare occasion I didn't have any words for them. If they had asked, I would've answered, but they didn't, so I didn't.

My children were so different from each other, especially in the way they handled conflict. Of the two lounging in my living room that morning, my cosmic child Nick was the first to need propping up, even though he was usually too embarrassed to ask for it. Whenever he got anxious he came looking for me, just the way Ginny-dog did at mealtimes. She gave me a long-suffering look, hoping I would notice her woe and do something about it. I understood Nick because he and I were the same in that regard. My obsessive mind wouldn't reroute to peaceful thoughts until I'd expressed myself verbally. This time, I had nothing to give him. Each time he came into the kitchen I'd look up from the cutting board, but when he received my blank stare, he averted his eyes. If I'd had the energy to speak up, he would've been on my side. Nick was good that way.

Not Andrew. Andrew always took whatever side I wasn't on. He despised conflict and has to blame it on someone. He behaved just like my family of origin did. I'd told that kid a million times that just because someone brought an issue to the surface, it didn't mean they were starting things. But he didn't listen. Not even when I told him his logic was ass backward. That pointing to the elephant in the room took guts. And that anyone who risked it, anyone who was brave enough to allow a situation to fall terribly apart in order to get it resolved, was *heroic*, not to be blamed!

I'd made a decision to raise my children opposite to the way my parents had raised me, because I hated pretense and cowardice. I hated people who pretended everything was oh-so-peachy when, really, they were dying a thousand deaths inside. That was such a waste of God-given time. If you are broken, you should suck it up and fix yourself! I'd been in therapy ever since leaving my childhood home, the home where I was *forced* to pretend. The home where my physical needs were met but not the emotional ones. Where I never felt like I mattered. Where no one took delight in me. Where I wasn't protected from the violence inside my home, much less the violence outside. Where I was blamed for things I didn't do and where pointing out the accusers' faulty logic only made things worse. Having my voice shut down had contributed to my anxiety issues.

But even if there hadn't been anything from my past to untangle, I still needed to be genuine, even if it sometimes made the kids and Funk uncomfortable. Because what possible joy could be had from living on the surface, where nothing was real?

10 DECEMBER 2006

FUNK HAD MEETINGS SCHEDULED even on weekends now, so he was apart from the family more than ever. I always cooked an elaborate meal on Sundays, and we often had visitors at our table. To keep the peace at home, Funk asked if he could invite a guest to dinner to avoid going to the double-wide for the meeting.

The guest of the day was Joe Miller, a reporter from *The Pitch* newspaper. I could have bet he had no idea why Funk had summoned him, to our home of all places, and I'm even more certain Funk didn't clue him in that it was about volunteering. My husband was socially cumbersome that way. He provided very little information for people to go on.

Funk knew Miller from his auditing days and said he was a pretty good reporter, which was why he was going to ask him to be the volunteer writer for the campaign. Funk liked the oddest people, so I was curious to see what surprise this guy had in store for our family.

The day's entrée was beef bourguignon, served with homemade peasant bread and a green salad. Our family didn't normally consume much meat, but since I didn't know our guest's eating habits, I figured I'd better cater to the Midwestern diet.

I put effort into preparing the meal, even though I hadn't an iota to spare. I felt scheduled down to the minute. I was missing important obligations. My household accounting books had gone to shit. All I did was pay the bills instead of scrutinizing the statements the way I usually did. Whereas my children had always been my highest priority, they'd become just another line item on my daily to-do list. I strapped on my phone headset and rang up my daughter at college so we could chat as I cooked.

Tara was in the middle of sharing a juicy tidbit and I was in the middle of living vicariously through her when the doorbell rang. Given that the men in my family knew my hands were deep in dough, do you think one of them thought to answer the door? Nope. I had to click off with Tara, rinse my hands, and run from the kitchen to the front of the house to welcome our guest. Along the way, I shelved my annoyance and steeled myself to greet the weirdo. But one look at Miller told me that my hostess duties were about to be challenged.

The guy just wasn't what I was expecting.

I'd anticipated a clean-cut, all-American preppy type with a narrow notebook clutched to hand. Miller was the opposite.

He was dark-skinned and unbelievably hairy. His unshaven face made him look short. His khakis—*My God, what was with all the beige in this town?*—were loosely belted at his hip, the foundation for his button-down shirt. If his outfit hadn't been soiled, you could've said he looked preppy. However, that notion would've been erased ten seconds later. Because after I opened the door and smiled at him, his smile back seemed to apologize for his existence, and what preppy did that?

To put him at ease, I said something I hoped was encouraging: "Hey there! You must be Joe Miller. I've heard so much about you." He looked surprised at that. Thinking him to be insecure, my mothering instincts kicked in. That happens whenever I meet a gentle sort. I don't like seeing anything suffer. This guy being an aching wound of a human, I shifted from hostess to Earth Mother to feed his soul.

"Funk tells me you're a great writer, that you have a lot of guts!" The compliment made his smile brighter, if a little shyer, so I stopped at that and waved him inside.

Andrew and Nick were sprawled in the living room, and after introducing them to the reporter I shouted upstairs for Funk to come down. Once the males were gathered, I left them to it and went back to the kitchen to finish dinner preparations, racking my brain trying to recall what else Funk had said about this scruffy guy.

Oh, yeah. Joe Miller was one of a group of reporters who regularly came sniffing around Funk's office looking for an off-the-record comment or to learn how government worked — or was supposed to work. Joe was uncommon in that he read whatever Funk suggested, including books, journal articles, and audit reports in full. Joe didn't need to be spoon-fed information, and, like Funk, he strove to do good in the world. The problem was, my husband's summation of the man didn't equate to the guy I had just invited into my home.

When everyone was seated in the dining room, I took a moment to consider Joe's physique, or what I could tell of it from beneath his shapeless attire, before dishing up the meal. Sensing him trim, I didn't heap his plate to overflowing. My children did me proud by remembering their manners. They didn't take up their forks until after Funk gave the blessing. Our family never forgoes the blessing, even for company, though it does make things a bit awkward sometimes. To dispel the quiet, I shifted back to hostess mode and began a conversation so Joe wouldn't feel uncomfortable.

I don't remember the nature of our talk, only that the kids picked up my thread, and Joe soon relaxed enough to chime in. The first time he did, I noticed his plate was already empty. So empty that it looked as if he'd washed it in the sink.

Rising from my chair, I asked, "Would you like seconds, Joe?"

"Yeah. That was really good!"

Back from the kitchen, I set a fuller plate in front of him. He inhaled that one too, so I offered a third and then a fourth. It was as if the guy hadn't eaten for days. Andrew and Nick gave me maniac eyes, letting me know they'd observed the reporter's behavior. I winked in understanding but then made them clear the table so they wouldn't get out of hand with it. When Joe refused a fifth helping, I excused myself to clean up the kitchen.

Funk and Joe followed me.

My husband grabbed a few beers from the fridge, and the two of them sat at my kitchen table and discussed Joe joining the campaign. Unlike Jeff Simon, Joe seemed honored by the request and instantly agreed to serve — albeit with a few strings attached. If Funk won the election, Miller wanted to be his communications director.

If my husband had a gavel in hand, he would've struck it on the table to signal a done deal. Instead, he slapped his hand on the table with such exuberance that it made Miller jump. Seeing him startle like that, I had to try my hardest not to crack up.

I don't know about Funk, but I liked Joe Miller way better than I did Jeff Simon, even if Joe was messy around the edges. He couldn't seem to hide the pain accumulated from living, and that trait made me believe he was more honest than the lawyer. But, man oh man, why did our family always attract these types? Couldn't some normal, everyday folks be drawn to us?

Funk's campaign now tallied four primary volunteers. Dottie was his office manager. John Meara was his CPA. Jeff Simon was chair, whatever that meant — interferer in family affairs was more like it. And Joe Miller was his writer. All in all, Funk wasn't doing too badly.

I tidied up the house for the following day. And, wonder of wonders, I got to bed earlier than I had in ages. It felt great not to be so tired that I couldn't read my book. That blessing lasted all of twenty minutes before I had to turn out the light.

Unless he was after something, Funk usually came upstairs to bed later than I did, but not this time. The two of us settled down together in our darkened room. I pulled him toward me, the way I always do when he gets into bed. But instead of grabbing his hand, which he always rests next to his face, I unknowingly grabbed his nose and began pulling it and him across his pillow. It was only after I heard him cry out "Hey!" in what sounded like a cold-infected voice that I realized what I was holding. I laughed myself wide awake over it — to the extent that the kids were grossed out, thinking something amorous was going on in our bedroom.

As if.

Still, I kept it up, just to get on their nerves.

From Demure Little Wife to
Campaign Manager, by Default

11 DECEMBER 2006

JEFF SIMON HAD BEEN VISITING the double-wide every night after work, heading straight for Funk's office. After they shut the door, although I couldn't see what was going on, I didn't sense that any work was getting done. I double-checked my hunch with Funk one morning and he said I was right, that Jeff's visits were mainly about upping the pressure on him to hire Britt Nichols to be his campaign manager.

Jeff was certainly running with his title of chairman. To him, that meant he got to direct the show. But as far as I could tell, he didn't even know what the show was. I considered it rude that he'd not once acknowledged that Dottie and I had been shouldering the load for umpteen weeks, nor had he asked us to catch him up to speed. He hadn't asked to see the plan of action I had produced to coordinate the campaign efforts. And since the campaign was still without a manager, I was sure we were duplicating tasks. That made no sense, given how little time we had.

I hadn't asked about Jeff's plan because for some reason, I felt intimidated by him — as if he knew more than I did, him being a bigshot lawyer and me just a stay-at-home mom with a small business on the side and a bachelor's degree in psychology. Everything I knew about running a headquarters came from the pages of *The Campaign Manager*. Mostly, though, I was just winging it. I didn't know how much campaign experience Jeff had, but surely it had to be more than mine. Why else would Funk want him on his team?

So far, Jeff hadn't told me what to do; he only made "suggestions." That stuck in my craw like you wouldn't believe, but what bothered me more was the way he treated Dottie. He ordered her around as if she were his paid helper. Christ, Dottie was the one who needed help. Could you imagine the fallout if she quit? We'd be friggin' sunk. Since my husband didn't notice interpersonal issues that were two feet in front of him, the moment that I could get a word in, I planned to bring this to his attention. He'd be as horrified as I was and would hopefully put a stop to it.

12 DECEMBER 2006

FUNK FINALLY MOVED HIS ASS. He gave in to Jeff's demand and hired Britt Nichols. But he appeased himself too, by hiring Dana Laiben as well. We'd gone from zero campaign managers to two!

I wondered how long it would take for Britt and Dana to get their feet beneath them so I could beat it the hell out of there. It would be so great if my last day would come before the Christmas holiday, even by a day or two, as I hadn't done a thing to prepare. But whatever. Until Spring's doorbells tinkled on the day of my departure, it'd be fun watching the dynamics between Britt and Dana unfold.

Funk had asked for my opinion about his decision. I told him it was fine by me to hire both, provided he made it clear that no one was getting paid unless enough financial donations rolled in. "Enough" meant we would pay the monthly bills first, including Dottie's salary, and also what the campaign owed to our family. Funk agreed. Strangely enough, the managers agreed too. That seemed odd because both of them said Funk didn't have much of a chance of winning. I couldn't understand why Funk wanted people on his team who didn't believe in him. But I'm no fool. Bring that shit up and he'd keep me here until the bitter bloody end.

The "Brain Trust" — the chairman and the two campaign managers — were sitting inside Funk's office. On his way back from the bathroom, Funk walked briskly past my door and beckoned me to join them. With my desk piled high with work, the last thing I wanted to do was to be part of a circle jerk. I had never been among those three as group, but I had a strong feeling that's what it would feel like.

Rolling my eyes, I grabbed a notebook and started for Funk's office. As soon as I walked in, the Brain Trust froze in place. As in, pencils held in mid-air. I felt so uncomfortable by the halted conversation that I tossed the note-book onto Funk's desk and left. Before I was fully out the door they had resumed their conversation, talking about how to brand my husband.

Brand Funk? I thought my man was a trademark in and of himself. Sad to say, those three didn't seem any brainier than the other volunteers hang-ing around the joint, and especially not brainier than Funk. This was strange, as it had always been Funk's habit to surround himself with people who were smarter than he. Why he was changing things up now was beyond me. But I didn't have time to ponder it.

Funk returned to my office a few minutes later looking Ginny-dog ner-vous, asking why I had left, whether something was wrong. I reassured him that everything was fine. I said I just had too much to do to sit there bullshit-ting all day. I figured he and I could discuss the real reason later, after I'd sorted through it myself. If I'd broached the subject at that moment we'd have gotten in a fight, and I didn't want that to happen in front of the volun-teers. Funk bought my excuse and leaned across my desk for a kiss, at which time I couldn't help but clutch his shirt to whisper in his ear, "What the fuck are they talking about, branding you?" He didn't reply, just scrunched up his shoulders as if he didn't have anything to do with it before closing my door and returning to his team.

His closing my door annoyed me. How many times had I told that man it was ill-mannered to shut the door on volunteers? But it seemed as though my words didn't sink in anymore. Ever since Jeff had come on the scene, they just fed off one another's bad habits. In a huff, I swung my ass out of the swivel chair and opened the door. And, surprise of all surprises, who should be standing on the other side but Joe Miller? I yelped, and that made him yelp, and we both started laughing. I liked this guy. I hadn't seen him since he'd sat down to dinner with my family, so we stood on my threshold and talked for a while.

Unlike Jeff, Joe was eager to hear about the efforts the campaign had made and where it was headed. I gave him a brief rundown of everything Dottie and I had accomplished thus far but said I didn't know where it was headed because, with Funk having just absorbed not one, but two, campaign managers, my obligation was almost over. As soon as I was able to turn the job over to the managers, I planned to hightail it out of there. Joe looked disappointed to hear that I was leaving — a sentiment he shared with Dottie. She was barely able to entertain the notion that I'd be leaving. Each time I brought it up, she said, "Oh, Gloria, you're not going anywhere. What would I do without you?"

I was having a ball talking with Joe, but I had work to do. I walked him over to Funk's office, knocked on the *closed* door, and ushered him inside. Because, with Joe being the writer, it sure seemed like he needed to be in on whatever was being said.

Twenty minutes later Joe was back in my office. He just walked in, plopped himself down in the seat beside my desk, and started talking as if we'd been friends forever. After a while I asked, "Joe, why aren't you in there with the rest of them?"

"I don't know. I didn't feel comfortable, I guess."

"Oh God, Joe, what did Funk do? He's not the greatest at social niceties. Honestly, if he made you uncomfortable in any way, that's the explanation. I know he's thrilled to have you on board."

"It wasn't him. It was the others."

"What did they do?"

"They didn't do anything. They just seem *bougie*."

"*Bougie?*"

"You know, bourgeois."

"Oh, that!" I said with a laugh as I leaned back in my chair. "I know what you mean."

Joe smiled but didn't say more.

"I just met Dana Laiben," I continued, "so I can't say much about her, but the other two seem as old-school as you can get. Funk always sees the good in others before I do, though, so they must have something going for them."

"If you say so."

I laughed again, this time at Joe's look of outright confusion. He must have read my lightheartedness as permission to settle in because he began talking nonstop about the path the campaign should take, acting as if the two of us would be working at headquarters until Funk won.

"So, Gloria, I have a few thoughts."

"Truly, Joe, I won't be here much longer. You need to go back in there and tell it to Funk. Better that he hears it from you, instead me trying to repeat your thoughts back to him."

As if I hadn't said a word to this wary but forthright little soul. Joe kept on without pause. I felt edgy with the need to get back to work, but on the other hand I was having a load of fun listening to him. Joe was like reading a really good book: he captured my attention with the very first line. The more he spoke, the more I liked him. He had the best ideas! He was impressively smart and was in step with the values Funk and I held important.

Joe spouted a surprisingly accurate picture of who Funk was, going on to say *we* could get his candidacy discovered. Talking with Joe came so easy that I felt comfortable sharing the branding discussion I'd just overheard and asked what he thought of it. Thank God, he felt the way I did: that it was crucial for Funk to remain true to himself, since Funk already represented what voters were looking for. I was relieved to know I wasn't alone in opposing the direction the Brain Trust was taking — as always, I'd been doubting myself.

I really needed to stop doing that. I needed to trust my instincts, in all areas of life, including this thing. When it came right down to it, organizing a successful campaign took common sense, and you didn't need a political degree to grasp what was going on. You could see for yourself that Kansas City voters were gaga for Funk. What else could explain the public excitement over him running for mayor?

Joe and I danced from that subject to the next topic whirling in his mind: Funk had no significant financial backers. More to the point, since the campaign had no money to pay for advertising, how would we get Funk discovered by citizens who weren't his fans? Joe had a solution. He called it "earned media." He described it as a free path to getting Funk's message out. Even better, my husband would control the agenda. If Funk held press events targeted to address specific issues, we would essentially force the other candidates to speak to Funk's platform.

The longer Joe sat there, the more excited I became. Was this guy brilliant, or what?

Knowing he had my attention, he outlined how we'd engage in earned media. There were ten weeks between the start of the debate season and the primary election. First, we'd make a list of the ten most critical problems facing the city, linking each to one of Funk's past audit reports. The reports would show that Funk had not only identified the problems a long time ago, but he already had the solutions. Using the reports, Joe would design a series of press events, one on the eve of each debate. Funk would highlight a problem that was clearly identifiable to the neighborhood in which he was standing. And just like that, *poof*, later that day Funk would be all over the airwaves, and the next day he'd be in the newspaper. And, because he had brought the issue to the voters' minds, Funk's platform would be discussed at the debate.

No campaign money? No problem. Earned media to the rescue! Funk would get "discovered" without paying a penny.

Next was the kicker — the really fun part of Joe's plan. Many of Funk's opponents were current or former councilmembers — and had therefore been Funk's bosses. Joe would obtain their voting records on Funk's audit recommendations and would use those records as a trump card. It wouldn't be pretty. The best part is, Funk wouldn't have to say a single negative word about his running mates. History would speak for itself. Their records would show that even when Funk had alerted them to the issues and they had the power to effect change, they had often ignored his warnings. I loved this plan so much. Payback is a bitch when the karma isn't coming for you.

My God, what was coming out of Joe's mouth was so exciting, I adored this guy. His mind worked like Funk's, not like mine. Still, I knew a good idea when I heard one. I felt it in my bones when something was right, and what Joe was saying rang true. I'm telling you, the call to start the Beltane fires was clanging to no end. I'm no brain, but there are a few things that I do do well. *Do-do?* Well, I do do doo-doo well, and thank God for it, but that's not what I meant. What I meant was, I'm Italian — and therefore I'm great at plotting and planning. Tell me a great idea, and my mind immediately starts working like you wouldn't believe, trying to figure out how to turn it into a reality.

I didn't know what the Brain Trust were cooking up on the other side of the wall, but the plan on this side was to synchronize the press events with the debates that were just around the corner. Joe wanted my help with that. Although my time at the trailer was running out, I figured Funk might as well gain from the Italian side of my personality while I was still there. So far, the only thing he'd gotten from me was my work ethic. Funk could reap the rewards of Joe's inspiration and my ability to set it in motion.

My first task was to get the debates onto the calendar; Joe would decide about which issues the campaign would focus on. He wanted my help with that too. I knew little about government, but I could tell Joe what Funk thought the worst problems were. Once we did that, Joe would grill me so we could link those issues to the most relevant audit report. He said that since I was schooled in that area, he'd prefer to get the information from me instead of wasting Funk's time.

If I was schooled or I had any information, it was only because my kids and I had listened to my husband's boring government talk for the past hundred years over dinner. We had learned all about tax incentives and the reasons the council gave away so many of them. I'm fairly sure we could have balanced the city's budget — and in less time than it would take the city council to agree on how to finagle the hell out of it to their advantage.

What Joe was asking for would be easy to provide. But honestly! Here I was, being used again. This time it wasn't by my daughter as she walked to and from her college campus, calling me for companionship. And, amazingly enough, it wasn't by my husband as he flitted to yet another dream, suckering me in to help. This time it was by someone I barely know.

I must have had a blinking light on me or something. Must have been some human form of a lighthouse. Really, didn't I have enough to do? I liked Joe, but there was no reason he couldn't look that shit up for himself. Why is it that men always need a woman to look over their shoulder as they work? Did a reporter really need me to tell him which report to pair city problems with? All he had to do was phone the new city auditor and ask for copies of Funk's past audits. The titles would tell him everything he needed to know. Whatthefuckever. Joe was working for free. I'd feed him the information he needed, and I'd do it good-naturedly.

Joe stopped talking and asked if I had any ideas to add to his plan. I was surprised he wanted my opinion, but I did share a few thoughts. The first was that Funk should maintain the identity he had developed as the city auditor — but a softer version of that persona. I explained how I'd been nurturing that by referring to my husband in public as "Funk." Joe loved the Funk-the-city-auditor part but didn't understand what I meant by softening up his image. Worried about the time, I skipped over that part and shared another idea. It was nothing really, just that Joe should hand the media a parting gift at the conclusion of the press event: a printout of the corresponding audit report, which just so happened to be dog-eared to the recommendations page. Joe liked that suggestion too, so blow on my fingers for thinking it up.

This was the plan for the media rollout: Ten weeks. Ten problems. Ten audits. Ten debates. Twelve candidates. All of them forced to speak to Funk's platform and wishing they were dead. Wasn't that the most kickass thing you ever heard of? I loved outsmarting cheaters and fakes more than anything else in the world. And the establishment was full of those types.

And, see? My husband didn't need branding. So, c'mon, you Brains in Funk's office, get with it. Everything he was, everything he believed in, was documented and verifiable. No one had to make anything up to get him elected. The other candidates had nothing to set them apart, nothing to define them. They were the ones who needed branding. Funk's campaign had to resort to advertising only in order to reach constituents who weren't yet familiar with his efforts at city hall. Joe's earned media would create a natural buzz that reached their ears.

Now that I understood what Joe had come in to say, I wanted him out of my office so bad. Because, Lord, what he was asking for was going to take a lot of time, which meant, enough of this talk already! Back to work!

But Joe didn't leave. We sat together in my office working his plan because he wanted to present the entire golden nugget at the first campaign committee meeting. After a few hours had slipped by, I remembered something urgent that needed to be done.

"Joe, would you mind if we stopped for the day?"

"Why? We're going so good."

"I have to get something out the door."

"Do you have anything to eat?"

"Eat?" I said, taken aback by the complete off-trackness of his response. "Like what?"

"Oh, I don't know. A snack or something."

"We have a few things in the cupboard, but I don't know if you'll like anything. It's mostly health food."

"I like health food."

We walked to the snack room and I pulled items off the shelves, looking for something to satisfy his hunger. He took everything. I left Joe sitting on the futon sofa across from Dottie's desk, snacks snuggled beside him, his laptop balanced on his knees.

Alone again inside my temporary office, I stared up at the water-stained ceiling to gather my thoughts. I needed to call the committee members and ask them to specify a couple of days and times that would work best for the weekly meetings. That sounded simple, but it wasn't. I had to come up with a quick spiel that didn't sound overly businesslike yet wouldn't keep me dawdling on the line too long. Some days, God is on my side. When I began making the calls, most people didn't pick up, so I left a message on their answering machines asking them to call Dottie with their response.

Even with the help from above, I was fifteen minutes late leaving to pick up Andrew from school. I raced to pack up and grabbed my cell phone to call to let him know I hadn't even left the double-wide yet, but then I thought better of it. Who needed to listen to moaning on the other end of the line? I knew I was late. Again. I was already beating myself up for it, and I didn't need him piling on.

Ten minutes later I rolled into a deserted parking lot at Lincoln. The only students remaining were Andrew and Nicholas Bates, a friend of the family whose mother — I'd only recently noticed — was also always late.

I ignored Andrew's evil stare, rolled down the window, and called out in a singsong voice, "Hey, it's Everyone-Waits-for-Nicholas-Bates!" Nicholas smiled. Funk had thought up the nickname many years earlier, when the Bates kids had played on a soccer team with ours. Invariably, we had to wait for Nicholas to get to the van so we could blow out of there. After soccer matches, Nicholas and his sister Jessica often hung out at our house.

I was fond of Nicholas. He had the sweetest personality, and like his sister, he was gorgeous enough to be a model. The only thing keeping him from a high-action career was that his head was too big for his body. But I was sure he'd grow into it.

As Andrew hopped into the van, I received Nicholas's shy, dazzling smile, pulled him to my window, and planted a kiss on his cheek. I bumped his enormous head on the door frame on the way in. Nicholas took both good-naturedly — the bump and the kiss — but having no time to waste, I threw him out my window and drove home like a mad woman. After dumping Andrew on the curb and instructing him to use the credit card to order takeout again, I zoomed back to the headquarters to finish the pile of work that Joe had interrupted. On the drive I was racked with guilt, obsessing about how I was becoming the mother I'd worked my entire life not to be. What Italian mom didn't put her children first? I was going to be punished for this, I just knew it. And for what? That bastard I called husband?

At the end of the day, when Funk and I were the only two remaining at the now-darkened double-wide, we sat on the futon together, my feet in his lap, catching our breath. I told him about Joe's marvelous idea to use his audit reports to earn free advertising. As expected, the plan delighted my husband. He said it was a far better idea than the directives the Brain Trust had given him earlier. Britt and Dana had agreed with Jeff's nonsense that Funk should wear thousand-dollar suits and stay plastered to his chair for two hours daily, making calls to a list of rich people he didn't know, begging for money. It sucked to be Funk.

Our conversation turned to the reason for my hasty departure from Funk's office meeting that morning. As I unraveled it with my husband, I figured out what had been eating at me. I had felt dismissed. Like a little girl. Funk saw it plainly and felt bad about it. I also told him the ways in which Jeff had been treating Dottie as if she were his personal maidservant. We had no idea how to approach that problem, but at least Funk was aware that he had one.

My husband usually handled the problems that occurred outside our home. Not that he was better at it than I was — quite the opposite. He yielded too much, too quickly. I tended to yell whenever I was upset, and I couldn't rightly yell at people who weren't family, Funk had to deal with those situations. But I didn't know if his usual approach would work. He normally had to sit with a problem before he acted. By the time he did, the campaign would likely be over.

I needed to get one last thing out of my system before we returned home to our son. I saw the genius in Joe's plan, but something about it didn't sit right. After talking it through, my nagging feeling grew to an even bigger worry, because Funk and Joe were both missing something key.

My husband was a gifted orator, especially when he dropped into what I called "preacher mode." But if this campaign was to work, Funk couldn't just be the city auditor anymore. His passionate side had to poke through. I tried to explain why, but I could tell he wasn't getting it. I paused to think about how to express it better when he suddenly raised my legs off his lap and started unfolding his six-foot-eight frame from the futon.

"You ready?"

He was so rude sometimes.

"No, Funk, I'm not ready. If I were, I would've said something to notify you."

He gazed at me intently, still holding my legs in the air. This guy was so annoying. He had two modes: either he never stopped talking or he didn't talk at all. I popped my eyes wide, giving him a look that said, "*Seriously?*" and he responded by lowering my legs back down.

I pushed past my aggravation and took up where my mind had left off.

"I'm worried that you and Joe don't see the need to soften your image, but I'm even more worried that I give two shits."

"Gloria. We've already established that I won't be something I'm not, just to get elected. But Glor, we already know voters want me. You're just getting cold feet, like always. And you care because that's who you are."

"Funk, of course your fans want you to be the next mayor, but what if there aren't enough of them to get you elected?

"What are you proposing?"

"I have no idea. Right now, I'm just trying to figure out how to get you and Joe to take this seriously."

"Tell me more."

"The whole point of earned media is to get you in front of the people who haven't been following your work as city auditor. But you can't just project the hard-driving image the media have pushed for all these years, because people here are used to a mayor who feeds them horseshit."

"People know they're being lied to, Glor. They just don't know what to do about it. They've never had a choice before. This time they do. *I'm* what to do about it."

"I know citizens want something different, Funk. But they're used to a mayor who behaves like a cheerleader — smiling, rah-rah, everything is fine — while the city is falling apart. Buddy, I hate to tell you, but you're the opposite of that."

"Gloria, I'm running as the former city auditor."

"Yeah, uh-huh Funk, and who said you should? Appearing one-sided was fine when you were the auditor, but if you want to be mayor you have to tone that serious shit down. Add a little glow."

"Okay."

"Okay? You agree?"

"I don't know if I agree, but your intuition is usually right."

"Usually, Funk? It's always right."

"So, what's the plan?"

"It's been five minutes, Funk. I still have no idea. But I'm thinking it has to do with the new wave of politics. You know, how Americans are starved for politicians who will get something done and how they are hankering for a real connection to elected officials. Joe's plan shows you'll get the job done. What it doesn't cover is how to make your hard-driving persona seem more approachable."

"That sounds a lot like Jeff Simon's branding plan. I thought you didn't like that."

"Jeff wants you calling up millionaires and acting all chummy with them, wearing thousand-dollar suits you can't afford. That's phony. I'm just asking the campaign to show your other side. The Funk side. Show the part of your personality the media has never reported because it didn't fit the story line they've been making a killing on."

"A personality trait would be hard to convey in a twenty-second clip."

"What's so hard about it, Funk? It's Christmastime. Next time you're in front of a camera, just make an offhand comment about how you've watched *It's a Wonderful Life* a dozen times. If a reporter bites, say how you still boo-hoo over it."

"I'm not doing that."

"Okay. How about showing the after-effects of standing up to the city council? How your family bit their nails each time you were about to blow another raise?"

"How would I do that?"

"Jesus, Funk, I don't know! I'm just throwing shit out there."

"I don't see how I'd — "

"Funk, you're getting caught up in the logistics. First decide if this is the direction you want to go. Then figure out how to do it. We both love Joe's plan, but even if earned media works, it doesn't guarantee people will blacken your name in the voting booth."

"Glor, we don't want people blackening my name, we want them to put a mark next to my name."

He's so literal sometimes. But since he was getting it, I told him I was ready to go, so he walked me out to the van and waited as I buckled myself in. On the drive home, my thoughts kept going back to the weird world of politics.

It seemed crazy that many Kansas Citians could be skeptical of government leaders yet simultaneously treat the mayor as a celebrity. How was it possible to be skeptical *and* starstruck at the same time? They didn't trust the leadership, but they had grown accustomed to the mayor sugarcoating the dire circumstances in which the city found itself, particularly in matters related to safety. Whenever I caught a snippet of whatever news program Funk was watching, it blew my mind to think that people were buying the leadership's story. Because I don't know how you could whitewash the fact that Kansas City had been ranked the third-most-violent city in America, far more dangerous than New York City.

The puzzle got even weirder.

When Funk was the city auditor, residents rooted him on because he stood up to the city council. But maybe that adulation had more to do with residents loving to hate the council than it did with Funk pressuring the council into fixing the city. Now that my husband was a mayoral candidate, I feared that in voter's minds he would be seen as *part of* the city council, that he'd go from being a beloved public servant to a despised politician, and only because they'd lost all hope that a politician would bring change. Would voters be able to wrap their head around a hard-driving auditor as their next mayor? I thought so, but only if Funk gave them a big dose of rah-rah to help make the medicine palatable.

Shortly after Funk announced he was running for mayor, a reporter for *The Pitch* had come to our house to interview my husband. After their business concluded, she said she was disappointed that Funk had gone over to the "evil" side. My husband and I were astonished. What a crazy-ass thing to say. Did she think all politicians were evil and always would be? That no one could fix the system? That no one should even try?

Funk had always spoken highly of this reporter, but if *she* could hold this opinion, what about the city's residents? Would they forget Funk's eighteen years of dedicated service? Would they stop trusting Funk-the-auditor because they now viewed him as Funk-the-politician? How would he win a grassroots campaign, when most campaigns in Kansas City were purchased? My only calming thought came from a phrase Funk often repeated: "Voters aren't stupid." I hoped he was right.

My family lived in a community called Brookside, one of the nicest neighborhoods in the city. Three-story, turn-of-the-century homes, most of them rehabbed to keep the charm while adding in the upscale, graced the streets. Yards were meticulously groomed, and neighbors were, for the most part, neighborly. They didn't do intimate, but some would lend a hand if they saw a need.

Our family settled there because the Brookside neighborhood was an anomaly in Kansas City. In addition to providing us with a big front porch, it was one of the few neighborhoods within walking distance of shops and parks. But our reasons for being there weren't the same as our neighbors'. They lived in Brookside because the violent crime rate was relatively low. Yet here was the rub: if you head east just eight-tenths of a mile, you come to Troost, the dividing line between the white (west) and black (east) parts of town. The East Side was where most of the gunfire was taking place. A mile away was pretty close. Yet my neighbors felt safe because the mayor told them they were, even when the truth was just up the street.

I wished I could stick my head in the sand and believe that all was well, but experience had forced me to deal with harsh realities head on. At forty-eight years old, I understood that if I was seeking change, then I better damn well batten down the hatches, because change would make things uglier before they started getting better. The only way around a problem was to go straight through it. But that was *my* way of thinking — it wasn't necessarily Kansas City's. Funk's campaign needed to speak the language of the Midwest. And honestly, it shouldn't be that hard. A candidate called Funk couldn't be all that heavy, could he?

How would we get the word out, given that Joe didn't see what I was seeing and Funk was just going along with me?

13 DECEMBER 2006

WITH SO MUCH WORK HANGING OVER MY HEAD I couldn't enjoy any part of my morning at home, I figured I might as well give it up already. I drove to the double-wide.

As I wheeled the van into the parking lot, I saw that Dottie had beat me there. That woman was as dedicated as they came. We were getting along swimmingly. The tension that had been present in the beginning was totally gone. I think my playfulness with her had helped turn the situation around. Humor makes everything better, doesn't it? We were having a wonderful time, even with Funk running us ragged.

Though I was eager to start in on my work, I headed first to her desk. Dropping my bags on the guest side of her weird-ass desk, I smiled and said brightly, "Hey, Dotsie."

"Gloria!" she hollered with her sexy laugh. "You have a new name for me every day."

"That's 'cause you're so sweet, Dots. One name just won't do!"

She blushed at my affection but didn't turn shy.

"How's your hubby?" I asked.

"His ankle is still bothering him, but he's fine."

"I'm glad. I know you've been worried about him. Hey, when are Labia and Britt due in?"

"*Gloria!*" she gasped, scandalized at my nickname for Dana Laiben, yet laughing all the same. But then the phones started ringing and we had to stop horsing around.

I walked to my office, put my belongings away, and then started in on email. The campaign's inbox was growing. Almost one hundred and fifty messages had come in overnight. I groaned. It would take me hours to direct them to the right party and even more time to respond to those I was responsible for. Before opening the first one, I took a quick look at the Sent folder. I saw that Funk had emailed someone late last night, probably after we'd gotten home.

I was so horrified that I cried out," Oh my God!"

"Are you okay in there, Gloria?"

Barely able to respond, I gave a weak, "I'm sorry, Dottie. Yes, I'm okay," as I reread the email chain.

Some stranger had poured his heart out to my husband — like, the guy had rained cats and dogs with his feelings, so much that his tears were dripping down from my computer and rolling all over my desk. The man had closed his missive by saying he was voting for Funk, get this, because Funk was his "savior"!

Funk's reply?

Four words: "Thanks for your input."

If the asshole I called husband had been in his office, I would've gotten out of the swivel chair I built a hundred years ago and slapped him upside the head. What the hell! Funk *loved* regular folks and had spent his entire career working for them, yet he had no idea how to be one himself.

I stewed all morning, waiting for him to come back from the meet-and-greet that I'd scheduled for him. When I heard his car's muffler, I hurried outside so we could talk in private.

Not noticing my mood, the ignorant bastard said, "Hey, babe." And with as much delight as any happily married man has for his wife, he added, "This is nice, you coming out to greet me. I like this new arrangement of us working together."

As he leaned in for a kiss, I reared back and bellowed, "Funk, are you crazy!"

"What?" he said, his voice unperturbed.

"I can't believe you spoke to that man that way."

"What are you talking about?"

"I'm talking about the email you sent last night."

"Which email?"

"The one where the man called you his savior and you responded with a dum-dee-dum 'Thanks for your input.'"

"What's wrong with that?"

"Honestly, Funk, you might as well have told the guy to go fuck himself!"

"Gloria."

"C'mon, Funk, you're running a grassroots campaign here. Put some effort into it."

He didn't respond, just started looking concerned. I eyed him for the Ginny-dog look, and thank God for the two of us, it was nowhere in sight.

"I shouldn't be working harder than you. This is your dream, for Christ's sake."

"Gloria, I'm working every hour that I'm not asleep. I can't give this any more effort. I responded to the guy. That's good enough."

"Good enough? No, Funk, what you did is damaging. Can you imagine how that poor man must have felt when he opened your email? He handed you his soul, and all you could come up with was 'thanks for your input'? If you can't respond like a normal person, then don't respond at all."

"I responded."

"I said, 'like a normal person,'" and I added a threat. "If you can't get it up more than that, I'll have to start responding to your emails for you."

"You're working around the clock already."

"Well, Funk, someone has to respond properly, so I guess I'll to have to work more. At least until you get Dana and Britt settled."

"Okay."

"What do you mean, 'okay'?"

"You said you wanted to answer my emails. I said okay."

"Would somebody please slit my wrists already? Funk! That was a threat, not an invitation!"

My husband had gone off the deep end.

He had no qualms anymore about the amount of work he was asking me to do — in his usual non-asking way. I couldn't think of anything more to say, so I walked away and left him standing in the parking lot, looking befuddled.

Later, I was heading for Funk's office to place some papers on his desk when I overheard the Brain Trust, minus Dana, discussing strategy. Except for Funk's, "Hey, beautiful," the room went quiet upon my entrance, but it didn't grow totally cold this time.

It was just one scheme after the other with those two. They were as macho as all get-out, and their behavior had grown worrisome in other ways as well. They'd bonded. It seemed as if they were operating separately from Funk. When I walked into the room, they had been in the middle of working Funk over good, practically scolding him for not tying himself to the phone to grub money from the establishment. What a ridiculous waste of time! Funk was running *against* the establishment; why would they give him money? As I was leaving, the Brains were talking some old-school bullshit about how Funk's way of doing business had to change. Every scheduled meeting going forward had to be over a meal in public so that he could work the room.

Funk, work the room? How phony was that?

Citizens craved authenticity. Jeff and Britt were demanding exactly what voters were running from. Their strategy sessions were beginning to get on my nerves, and I didn't like it one bit that they thought they knew more than Funk. But I remained quiet because if Britt had truly worked on many campaigns, then I guess he did know better. I didn't know how much campaign experience Jeff had. But even if they both had experience out the wazoo, it seemed to me like stupid experience.

The second I was out the door, Jeff and Britt resumed their fast talk. But there was more than one way to gather information that others don't want you to have, and that's where my Italian roots came in nicely. Leaving the door to Funk's office ever so slightly ajar, I stood innocently working at the copy machine, eavesdropping on the conversation.

Their topic went from working the room to chiding Funk for meeting with people without deep pockets — in other words, the regular folks who this campaign was about. You couldn't imagine how much I wanted to run back in there and tell those guys to take a seat. Ask them why they needed to resort to such madness when a diamond was sitting in front of them. It was frustrating to hear them doling out bad advice, knowing my husband was sucking it up. The Brain Trust should've been out there trying to raise money from Funk's supporters instead of pressuring him to milk cash from establishment people who were working around the clock to make sure he *didn't* get elected.

Actually, I was probably wrong about that last part. Quite a few of volunteers were working for Funk because they hated the city council and the insiders who were joined at the hip to the councilmembers. From what the volunteers told me, the establishment wasn't trying to make sure Funk lost, because they didn't for one second see him as a threat. The establishment were laughing behind his back for thinking he had a chance of winning.

Having heard enough, I took my copies, returned to my grimy little office, and tried to focus on my work. But those Brains were really hyped-up today. Their voices carried through the wall loud and clear. Not Funk's. He hadn't made one little peep. I could picture him, though. He'd have his feet on the desk and be rubbing his chin and gnawing on his thumb, listening to the schemers. He was probably having a high time of it, too. Funk loved being part of a group and he accepted everyone, flaws and all. Not me. I knew that stupid people were just stupid people. Hearing Jeff and Britt one-upping each other in their disgustingly macho way, thinking they were oh-so-funny, oh-so-witty, had me rolling my eyes to such an extent that I felt like I had a sinus headache.

I wish you could've heard what I was hearing. I'm telling you, there was a dick-bumping festival happening on the other side of my wall. How was a girl supposed to get any work done?

Our crew of volunteers spanned generations, ranging from college students to grandparents. Some were scraggly around the edges; others were Midwestern prim and proper. About twenty of these helpers could fit into the trailer at a time.

A slew of volunteers showed up at headquarters one afternoon. Most of them shyly peeked inside my office, first to see if I was there and then pausing in the hope of getting some guidance. The campaign managers still hadn't assigned them tasks, so that duty still fell to me.

Thank God, the system I had set up worked. All I had to do was hand volunteers an instruction sheet, and they'd know what to do. But now a different problem arose. After I gave them the sheet they just stood there holding it, shifting from foot to foot. I'd come to know what that stance meant: they were hoping for a private conversation. Of course, I had to yield to it, since they were giving their time to Funk. Still, how was it possible to have a twenty-minute tête-à-tête with every person who tinkled Spring's bells and still get my own tasks done? I couldn't take work home anymore, because I was working in the double-wide from early morning until late evening. My home had become a place to briefly say hi to the son I'd forsaken before collapsing into bed. I wasn't even cooking anymore, and man, was that ever gonna bite me in the ass. I hadn't dared step on the scale lest I curl into a fetal position upon reading the number. I had no idea what to do about any of this, as I had no time to even think. The needs of the campaign reminded me of the time I was raising my infants, a phase when I could never finish a thought for tending to their constant needs.

Just as I was getting up to mingle with the volunteers, Joe dropped by my office. It was important that I give him my attention, so I plopped back into my chair even though my ass hurt from sitting all day. Joe was needy, but as far as I could tell, besides Funk he was the most essential person in the campaign. It didn't hurt that Joe and I had a lot in common, and he was a ball of fun!

Because Joe was Italian, like me, I gave him a hearty, ethnic greeting: "Hey, Giuseppe!"

He smiled at my delight for him.

"Why aren't you in there?" I asked, pointing to the wall that separated my office from Funk's.

"What do you mean?"

"What do you mean what do I mean? The meeting."

"No one said anything about a meeting."

"Britt didn't email you?"

"I don't think so but let me check." Joe fired up his Mac, and I sat there wishing I'd never opened my mouth. I placed my hand under my desk so he wouldn't see me tapping my knee with impatience as he sorted through dozens of unopened emails.

"Nope. Nothing's here. Are you sure I'm supposed to be in there?"

"Geez, Joe, you're the most necessary one of the bunch. Yes, you're supposed to be in there."

"I don't know about that," he said bashfully, his face alight at my compliment. "Besides, I don't really see where I fit in."

"You're the writer, Joe. How are you supposed to know what to write if you don't know what's going on?"

"I know what to write. You're a surprisingly good parrot of your husband."

"It seems that I am. Though the thought is kind of gross."

Joe laughed at the imagery.

"I won't be in this chair much longer, Joe. But even if I were, the campaign is moving too fast, and it can't remain disjointed like this. We need coordination from within, and those guys," I said, pointing to the wall, "need to take you seriously."

"They're on a different path from ours."

"Yes, it's like we're on parallel tracks—but you're on Funk's wavelength. Trust me, your input is more valuable than theirs."

"What can I do if I'm not invited to the meetings?"

I thought for a moment before saying, "This situation is so weird. They make me feel uncomfortable for giving my opinion too, but I thought it had to do with me being a girl."

"They probably think of me as a girl too," he said, his face contorting into a thousand unusual positions, while trying to hide them all.

I smiled at his struggle, knowing he was probably right, and promised to take care of the dilemma when Funk and I were alone. God only knew when that would be, since Evert Asjes had offered to host the first committee meeting that evening, in the community room of his newly renovated condo in Brookside. Evert, who had sat on the city council, supported Funk's run for mayor. At the meeting, Jeff would make opening remarks and Dana would unveil the plan of action. I had let out a cheer when Funk told me that. It was about time. Past time, in fact, for the curtain to be drawn open on the campaign. I hoped the plan would focus on the nuts and bolts of running the campaign, not just fanciful "strategy" talk.

Funk had asked me to attend the committee meeting. We both believed that two sets of ears were better than one on any matter of importance. But there was no way I'd agree to this request. Even though I was dying to hear the ideas the managers were going to present, I found those sorts of meetings incredibly boring. Plus, why waste my time, when I could get the skinny on the meeting later from my husband?

14 DECEMBER 2006

YOU WON'T FUCKING BELIEVE THIS.

Yes, of course I went to the committee meeting. I'm an absolute chump, what can I say? And yes, it was excruciatingly boring, just as I had known it would be.

But guess what I didn't know? Guess what plan the Brain Trust unveiled? More specifically, what tasks would bring the campaign to a successful finish line?

Recently, the situation in the double-wide had deteriorated because Funk *still* hadn't chosen a campaign manager. One day I grew so frustrated with him that I put my overflowing pile of work aside so I could systematize things myself. I ignored my son so I could draft a temporary plan of action for the campaign to follow until Funk chose a stupid campaign manager. I'd been holding my breath ever since, waiting for the Brain Trust to draft the *real* plan so I could beat it the hell out of there.

Well, that bitch — I mean, Dana Laiben — didn't unveil a new plan. She unveiled *mine*. She had the gall to sit at the head of the table reading directly from *my* eight typewritten pages of notes, assigning committee members tasks that *I'd* bullet-pointed, ticked items off *my* outline, yet never once mentioned that I had produced the desperately written piece of shit!

My God, I thought campaign managers were supposed to be *so* smart. *So* organized. *So* sexy. I'd been waiting an eternity for Funk's team to lend a professional hand to the campaign. I anxiously anticipated the day when I could return home to where I belonged, mothering my children. And for what? This? I was dumbstruck. The managers had done nothing more on my husband's behalf other than reveal the plan that I had culled from *The Campaign Manager* — a plan they were calling their "winning strategy." I could've done that. Wait a minute! I did do that!

From the moment Dana began going through *my* outline, all I could do was stare at her, my mouth hanging open like a fool.

Dana glanced at the audience as she orated, yet she never once looked my way. She didn't dare. She could feel me.

It got worse. She never revealed the author — not even when the committee went on and on about how well-thought-out *her* plan was, how far-reaching *her* ideas were. For that, Funk was going to compensate the woman five grand a month?

That wasn't the only shock of the night.

The other came when Funk and I entered Evert's community room and saw City Councilwoman Aggie Stackhaus, one of Funk's former bosses, sitting there as if she belonged. I gave my husband a quick scan to get a bead, but no, he indicated he hadn't asked her to be on his committee. Neither of us knew why she was there. I didn't know what Funk was gonna do about that sordid little situation. I was glad I didn't have to concern myself over it.

Even better — or worse — the minute Joe walked in and saw Aggie I thought the room would explode in a fireball. Joe had a history of reporting the truth, and Aggie, as a former councilmember, had hated the heat that brought to her position. I hoped Joe would be at the double-wide the next day because I couldn't wait to hear what happened between those two. Next to enter were Gwen and Ed Wolf, followed by our dentist, Maria Kuntstadter. Then Jeff and Britt strolled in — and even though they weren't exactly holding hands, they might as well have been. Those two were as thick as thieves, kind of literally. They continued dreaming up schemes, and scheming was the exact opposite of what my husband was about. Me, I was Italian, and scheming is what we do. Before you go thinking poorly of me, remember that there are law-abiding schemers in this world. I'm one of them. I believe in taking things right up to the edge. I didn't know Jeff and Britt well, but I guessed they fell on a shadier, but still legal side, of the equation. But my kind, their kind, what did it matter? This was Funk's campaign, and everyone associated with it should have been doing things his way: on the straight and narrow, completely by the book.

Next to arrive were Dan Ryan, Javier Perez, and Mike Bates, with Ruth Bates bringing up the rear. Funk and I didn't know anything about Dan Ryan; it was Jeff's call to place him on the committee. I'd heard Javier Perez's name mentioned around our dinner table, but all I could remember was that he was Union.

Mike had worked with Funk at city hall, and our kids had played soccer together. Ruthie had become a pal. And since she was the only black person in the room, not to mention incredibly fun, I patted the chair beside me. Whenever we were at one of our husband's boring-ass work functions, we'd pass the time by whispering lewd comments behind covered hands, unobtrusively cracking each other up. I loved making Ruthie laugh. Her whole face lit up, and she already had the most gorgeous face. She was one of the few people in the Midwest who made me laugh. I about died when she pretended to be oh-so-scandalized whenever I one-upped her gossipy comments with juicy comments of my own, and her answering laugh told me she was enjoying the hell out of our time together too.

Other than having fun with Ruth and catching eyes with Gwen Wolf whenever someone said something so banal that my entire being quivered in reaction, the meeting ground monotonously on. I did my part as the dutiful wife, greeting each person as they entered, offering refreshments, and separating those who clearly shouldn't sit together. I tried hard not to look at the clock, as I didn't want to see the second hand moving at an agonizingly slow pace. I didn't want people see me fidgeting as I listened to the predictable banter, all the while fretting because my son was home alone. Again. Waiting for me yet pretending not to be.

Instead of assigning tasks, Dana asked the committee members to choose their own. After an embarrassingly long pause, a few hands hesitantly went up. Councilwoman Stackhaus-Who-Wasn't-Supposed-To-Be-Sitting-in-the-Room said she'd draft a list of names for Funk to call for donations. Most of the group heartily endorsed Jeff's mandate that Funk spend most of his day tied to the telephone, begging for money. The word begging is mine, but it's essentially what they were saying. I didn't know why Funk hadn't spoken up against it, as we both disagreed with that typical, squirrelly campaign tactic.

Dana then gave Britt an assignment.

I wondered how her ordering him around would go down. Thinking about the possible ramifications had been one of the highlights of my night. Dana tasked Britt with emailing every supporter who'd contacted the campaign, petitioning a donation. I was even less happy about that because, just as I'd threatened, I'd taken over responding to emails from Funk's supporters. Now that I had been doing so, I'd begun to feel protective of those supporters.

And just so you know, I didn't pretend I was Funk in those emails, although I could easily have gotten away with it. I begin each email by introducing myself as "Funk's wife" and by apologizing that he was too busy to respond personally. Then I answered their questions, assuring them that my response was indeed what my husband would say, and I closed by saying I'd copied him just in case I was wrong, in which case he'd follow up with them directly.

Responding to Funk's emails was work I didn't need, but it had been uplifting. Often, the supporter immediately responded, graciously saying they understood how busy Mr. Funkhouser must be. Many had thanked me for my devotion to my husband. Given that loveliness, there was no way I'd allow anyone to abuse those supporters, not even the Brain Trust.

Another positive note came when Councilwoman Stackhaus offered to schedule the meet-and-greets *and* make the arrangements for them. That lightened my load like you wouldn't believe. I almost let out a shout, but I tamped myself down in the nick of time and just profusely thanked her for taking work off my hands.

The committee got lost in the woods after that.

The majority wanted the meet-and-greet practice stopped. They said Funk had limited time and he needed to meet with the movers and shakers — enough with the ordinary folks already.

Here, my husband finally said something.

Funk *loved* meet-and-greets! Loved being in the thick of regular folks. And, gaggingly, he loved their adulation. I'd accompanied him to most of those events because someone had to set up the table with the campaign buttons and whatnot. The attendees hung on his every word, fawning over him. It was nauseating — not their reaction, my husband's. When we left the meeting, Funk's head was so big sometimes that there was hardly room for me in his Corolla.

The sad news is that the good news stopped there.

Dana had added a few other conventional old-school jobs to my outline, most of which also fell on Britt's shoulders. I was appalled by what she'd done, but I had loved watching her make Britt twitch! He took it well, though. Didn't act the least bit bothered that a woman had ordered him around. Just complimented himself on how good he was at persuading voters. Hearing that made puke rise in my throat, even though I hoped he was right. Persuading voters was a great idea.

Funk needed his campaign platform printed out in bullet points on a handout. What bothered me was the way the committee wanted to go about it. The longer I sat there, the more I wondered why Funk had chosen this team. Except for Joe and a few others, the group seemed cliché to the highest order. And man, were they ever into spending. I managed the financial books and made them available to anyone who wanted a peek, including Funk's supporters. The Brain Trust clearly hadn't given them a glance; Dana told the committee that Funk's team would produce a professional brochure, even though I knew his budget didn't have that kind of money.

This was when I had to add my two cents.

Meekly, I told the group the bottom line, financially speaking. Said I didn't have a problem with informing voters about Funk's platform, but I wondered where the money for a professional print job would come from. Before I could whip out my spreadsheet to show them the numbers in black and white — or, in this case, red — Dana contradicted me. She interrupted me to tell the committee the brochures were going to save the campaign money, thanks to their multiple purposes. No doubt because she was the campaign manager, the committee saw her idea as brilliantly thrifty. Thrifty? Funk's campaign had $10K in the bank and still owed my family close to $30K.

No matter. The committee bulldozed on into the night.

Dana asked for a volunteer to draft the document. No one stepped up, but that didn't faze her. She told Britt to target it to voters.

She directed Funk to canvass the neighborhoods with it. He was to wander through every inch of Kansas City, knock on doors, chat with whoever answered, and shove the piece into their hands when he took his leave. If no one was home, he'd wedge it in their doorjamb. Lord Almighty, if the committee didn't go crazy for the idea.

I saw problems with the plan.

Common sense told me a few things. First, how the hell was Funk supposed to canvass neighborhoods when he was also supposed to be tied to the phone all day? And, assuming he could be in two places at once, Dana had overlooked a few other key facts. Kansas City numbered 450,000 people and encompassed 318 square miles. That would require a lot of walking. If Funk set out that night, he wouldn't be back until the election was over. The second problem had to do with safety. Kansas City had the third-highest crime rate in the country, even though it was the thirtieth-largest city. With the crime rate as high as it was, who opened the door to strangers anymore?

Still, it was a relief to hear that Funk's campaign was finally putting his platform on paper. A simple flyer would provide something constituents could take home with them from the trailer or a meet-and-greet. But where would the money come from to pay a professional printer for a brochure? And because Dana eventually wanted to send that glossy piece by mail, how would we pay for postage? Worse, she was calling the mailer a "push piece," a name that pretty much said it all, didn't it?

My last problem with Dana's plan was that it was a misuse of Britt's time to ask him to target voters. If the committee had asked, I could've easily pinpointed the neighborhoods where Funk was most likely to pick up supporters. It was simple: Red Bridge, just south of Brookside. And anywhere out east. That was where the working class resided, and those were the citizens who would resonate most with Funk's message.

Toward the end of the meeting, Dana directly assigned the two most important tasks from my outline, and both were good decisions on her part. Endorsement questionnaires fell to Ed Wolf and debate prep to Joe. Ed had worked at city hall even longer than Funk, so he understood how governments work. And Joe had recently authored a book about his experiences coaching an inner-city debate team. Their competency was an important rationale for conscripting those two, but I was happy about Dana's decision for another reason.

Loyalty.

I barely knew Ed or Joe, but so far, they'd passed the loyalty test. They were okay with handling the campaign Funk's way. Ed had a military background, so it was ingrained in him to offer help where it was needed. And although Funk valued free-thinkers, he had rejected many of Joe's ideas for being too far out — yet Joe had been able to roll with Funk's vetoes.

Many tasks in terrific need of attention went unassigned, the exception being the multitude of tedious jobs. Can you guess whose laps those tasks landed on? Yep, mine and Dottie's. Dottie wasn't even at the meeting to say yay or nay to taking them on, and I'd be leaving the campaign soon.

15 DECEMBER 2006

I SEEMED TO HAVE CAUGHT a touch of Dottie's shyness. Sucking it up, I sheepishly told her about the tasks Dana had assigned to us the previous night. I couldn't think of another way to be sure Dottie was asked, not ordered, to do yet more. Doll that she was — even when Funk hadn't paid her a cent yet — she kindly said she'd be happy to add the tasks to her repertoire. Hearing that, I busted through the gate of her weird-ass desk to give her a big hug before heading into my office to start in on the emails that had come in overnight.

Once again, I started my workday with a scream.

In my inbox sat a message from Britt that included a mock-up of the campaign's first email newsletter, soon to go out. He must've gone home directly after receiving his marching orders from Dana and begun working on the draft that I was viewing. I didn't know why he was calling this thing a newsletter when all it did was encourage donations from Funk's supporters. And trust me, I use "encourage" in the lightest sense of the word.

"Holy shit!" I said to myself, but apparently loud and pathetic-sounding enough that Dottie bolted out of her chair and was at my side in a flash.

"What happened, Gloria?" she cried.

"Oh my God, Dottie! Have you seen Britt's newsletter?"

"No," she said with a slight whine, "I didn't receive anything from Britt."

"Dottie! Stop letting him get away with keeping you in the dark," I said crossly, then instantly took it back, for my frustration was with Britt, not her. Besides, I couldn't blame the woman for being herself.

"I'm sorry, Dottie," I said with a sigh. "It's just that you're gentle, and this campaign is dog-eat-dog. Britt won't stop disregarding you unless you force him to, the way you did the other day." Recalling their outright argument right in the middle of the trailer, I smiled and added, "Geez, Dots, I never heard you yell like that before. I didn't know you had it in you!"

"I'm sorry, Gloria. I shouldn't have yelled."

"I would've done that and more if he had been bossing me around. Listen, forget this. Everything's fine. I was just surprised by his email. I'll forward it to you, for a laugh. Actually, it's not funny. Christ, wait till you see it. The newsletter is so *not* Funk. And don't worry, I promise to let Funk know that those guys are still excluding you from important emails."

"Don't do that, Gloria. He's busy. I don't want to be a bother."

We couldn't finish the exchange because the phones lines began ringing like mad and Dottie ran back to her desk to catch them. This was the way it went around here. No one got to finish a conversation.

I went back to reading Britt's newsletter. Thank God he had sought my input before sending it. Funk must've said something for him to suddenly be including me on the Brain Trust's email chain. It's crazy to me that I had to guess whether Funk did something or not, instead of just asking him. But we'd been reduced to this kind of communication. The pace in the campaign headquarters was so great that everything having to do with our family dynamics had changed. But I wasn't moaning. Because aside from feeling guilty about neglecting my kids, I was having fun working on the campaign, especially with Joe. And, surprisingly, I found I was sort of good at it too, maybe because the field was mostly instinctual and my instincts were pretty honed.

I put aside the task I'd planned to do that morning and contemplated

Britt's newsletter instead. With his Word document open on my laptop, I clicked Track Changes and began the arduous process of editing. Britt popped his head in my door just as I was about to make the first change, so I gently closed the screen of my laptop.

"Any luck finding volunteers to write letters to the editor?" he asked.

I shrank in my seat. Withering was my initial reaction when I was in the presence of the Brain Trust because they had undermined me at every turn. They scoffed at any opinion I articulated — and there hadn't been many — making me feel silly for speaking up. Funk's managers thought the same way some doctors do — that you shouldn't have a viewpoint unless you have "proper" training. It's such bullshit. When I was in doula role at the hospital and told the doctor — who typically arrived on the scene twenty hours *after* contractions had started and *after* I'd been up all night with the mom — where we were at with the labor, I typically got back "Do you have a medical degree?" I wanted to reply, "No, but with the baby's head bulging out of our mutual client's ass, I really don't think I need one." Yet, for my clients' sake I didn't utter a word because the poor women had enough to deal with.

I winced each time the Brainiacs made similar off-putting comments. But now I was done with that. The previous night, when I was trying to fall asleep, I had one of those visions I sometimes get. A presence from above seemed to think I needed a shove, something to remind me that I had become a New and Better Me. Recalling the message, I "threw my glamour high" and said what needed to be said.

"We're not asking volunteers to write letters to the editor, Britt."

"Who said?"

"No one said. Well, I guess I just said."

He gave me a long look, as if I were a moron, which to him means the same as being a woman. When I couldn't take him staring me down anymore, I explained my rationale.

"That's a hundred-eighty degrees opposite of who Funk is. Besides, Funk doesn't need to enlist people to write phony letters. Supporters are already professing their love for him, all on their own."

"Gloria, I realize you and Mark are into transparency, but this is what the other campaigns are doing, and we need to keep ahead of the game."

"But Britt, we're not *like* other campaigns. Funk's different. He's not in this for personal gain or ego."

"Gloria," he said and then paused dramatically, "he's got quite the ego."

I laughed. "Yes, Britt, you're right about that, and it's growing by the minute! But Funk's competency and honesty are his niche. They set him apart from the other candidates. Besides, if he's not confident in himself, why would anyone else be?"

"You won't feel the same way when you see support for the other candidates lining the editorial page, ten to one."

Okay, so this guy didn't even do humor.

Losing mine, I countered, "Funk's not posing, Britt. He's here to do a job. Once he wins, that job will mean a lot of work. He's not doing the ribbon-cutting thing that mayors here love to do. He's not building more monstrosities downtown that the city can't afford, and only to pay supporters back or as a tribute to himself. Voters are calling for a revolution, so we don't really know what the ratio of letters to the editor will be by the end of this."

Britt didn't roll his eyes but believe me, cosmically speaking he rolled his eyes.

I felt uncomfortable with his energy but carried on anyway. "Britt, if it turns out you're right — if Funk isn't what citizens want — the bottom line is, he'll be happy to go back to the life we had before. My knowledge is limited in this area, but it seems to me that people are craving a mayor who will look after *their* interests for a change."

"That's a novel thought, Gloria, but voters aren't as intelligent as that."

"They're not stupid, Britt. They have eyes. They see the city going downhill. They might not realize it's almost bankrupt, but they know we're in bad shape."

I cringed after I said all that because, fucking *ewww*, I sounded just like my husband.

Britt cringed too, but he cringed as if I were a child who was trying his patience.

His macho came after me harder. His steel-gray curls bobbed maniacally with each word he spat. "This is how it's done. Honesty is for *after* the win, Gloria. *If* Mark wins. Which is unlikely. I'll ask your husband what he thinks when he comes in."

With that, Curly turned on his heel and was out the door before I could shout, "Be my guest!" But I'm glad I didn't get a chance to say it. That guy made me doubt myself. And when I doubted myself, I got upset. And when I got upset, I usually had to say something. And there was no telling what would've come out of my mouth, as tired as I was.

I shook off the exchange and went back to editing Britt's newsletter. I was no writer, but there was no way I'd let this thing out the door reading the way it did. I couldn't find Funk anywhere in it. It was "in your face" and it came off as a reprimand. It went something like this:

Dear Supporters,

If you're serious about supporting me, PROVE it.

SEND MONEY! **NOW!!**

Any amount. Even five bucks will do.

The campaign is in its infancy, so I can't divulge our secrets. But all you need to know anyway is that if you're serious about change, then you need to back up your words with a donation.

DO IT! **NOW!!**

Respectfully yours,

Mark Funkhouser

The Former City Auditor

Sending them that thing would have been like punishing Funk's supporters for being supporters. Didn't Britt see that? The newsletter read, "I can't divulge our secrets." My husband's campaign was about transparency. What the fuck?

Editing Britt's piece was mighty tricky. I didn't care much for the guy, but I didn't want to insult him either. I needed to make an honest attempt to communicate his message, in Funk's voice. I printed out his draft. Many attempts later, after grinding my teeth to aching proportions, I balled up the copy and threw it into the trash. There was just nothing there that sounded like Funk. All I could do was keep Britt's message in mind and begin anew.

I hadn't known the campaign was going to send a newsletter until Dana had blurted it at the committee meeting. Therefore, I hadn't had time to ruminate on it. I was leaning back in my chair pondering how the newsletter should begin when something told me to just write it the way I did our family's holiday newsletters. Those were not fluff. They were intimate and newsy. I held nothing back. Funk loved them. Shockingly, recipients loved them too.

I titled the newsletter *Notes from the DoubleWide*, similar in style to the way I spelled the name of my business, BirthWays. And since I was conscious of the way Kansas Citians were riding the new wave of politics — seeking a greater connection to elected officials — I opened the first paragraph with something personal, a small snapshot that showed readers how the dynamics in our little family had changed with Funk's run for office. After that, I got down to business and the piece practically wrote itself. I gave a rundown of where the campaign stood and where it was headed and provided information about "volunteer opportunities," even though I hated that term. It was really just another way of saying "working for free."

Just as I was about to wrap up the writing, I thought to list the times and locations of the upcoming debates, hoping that if I made it easy for them, people would come out to show support for my husband. And while I didn't ask for donations outright, in order to wave a white flag at Britt, I included the address to which people could send a check. It took me a while to find a way to include that tidbit without slamming it down the reader's throat, but class takes time. I concluded with a hearty thank-you for everyone's support of Funk in thought, word, prayer, and deed.

Scusi. Notice anything?

I found another way to get my husband's "softer" name out to the public. Referring to him as Funk came naturally, because that's how I always signed our family's holiday newsletters: "Love from the Funks."

I willed myself to let the fear wash through me instead of stopping me from sending the newsletter back to the Brainiacs. Holding my breath, I hit Reply All.

My nerves were shot.

I had taken this step without discussing it with my husband. I also knew the Brain Trust would think my version was hokey and their chiding would be merciless. Whatever. I couldn't worry about this anymore. Funk could decide which newsletter he preferred to send to supporters, Britt's or mine.

Oh Lord, I thought, *please let me out of this trailer already. I can't take the pressure.*

16 DECEMBER 2006

NEW VOLUNTEERS were streaming into the double-wide in ever-growing numbers, yet Funk's campaign managers still weren't welcoming them in. Perhaps Britt and Dana believed their status was too important for that. And if my hunch was correct, they hadn't read their copy of *The Campaign Manager.* If they had, they'd have known that volunteers are the heart of any successful campaign and that fussing over them is a big part of the manager's job. I suspected they were shying away from the duty because of the types of people Funk was attracting to the campaign. Most were working class or outcasts of society. If I had to describe their most predominant personality trait, I'd say they were the walking wounded. But who isn't?

The campaign managers weren't tending to the volunteers, so Dottie and I were forced to. Dottie did it because she was just plain nice. I did it because, the same way I couldn't ignore a crying baby, I couldn't let broken souls go unnoticed. Someone had to make them feel as though their breath mattered. If they couldn't help themselves, someone with more strength had to lift them up. Otherwise their pain would continue. And that doesn't only affect them personally; it negatively affects civilization.

Whenever I heard Spring's doorbells tinkle and the hesitant footsteps of a volunteer walking across the buckled-up carpet, I hauled my ever-growing ass up to greet them. Most had never been part of a campaign before, so they were wary. Others were as cocky as all get out, in a way that made it abundantly clear they were the worst off. But I treated each the same, although I must admit I had my favorites.

A woman with the most intense blue eyes came in one day. Boy, did she strut her insecure self boldly through the world. She opened the lobby door with such force that Spring's bells clanged instead of tinkled, and her footsteps shook the trailer almost as much as Funk's. She was at the reception area asking Dottie which office was mine before I even had a chance to drag myself out of my chair. She was standing at my desk a moment later.

"Are you Gloria?"

"Hey there! Yes, I'm Gloria. How may I help you?"

"I'm Betty Lou, and you can help me by getting your husband elected and making him fire Wayne Cauthen."

"The city manager?"

"Yes."

"Okay, what's up with that?"

"I worked for the brute, and now I'm going to set him on the street where he belongs. You have me forty hours a week. What do you want me to do?"

"I'd love to have you here full-time, Betty Lou, but perhaps you should talk to Funk before making such a big commitment."

"Why would I do that?"

"Well, I haven't heard him say much about the city manager, so I don't know if he plans to fire Cauthen. I don't want you to be disappointed if he doesn't."

"I'm starting today. Once Mark gets into the mayor's office, he'll see what I'm talking about and get rid of him."

The woman seemed intelligent and the campaign needed more full-time hands, so I handed her a list of jobs. I nearly flew out of my chair with joy when she said she'd manage the database. Every time I opened the spreadsheet a wave of nerves came over me. I was tending it in only the barest way, yet it was the most integral component of the campaign.

We documented the activity of every volunteer and supporter. The database listed the tasks volunteers preferred and the shifts they were willing to work. It recorded the names of supporters who had requested a button or yard sign and verified that we had delivered the items to them.

Mr. Goody Two-shoes wanted a paper trail of every penny donated and how that penny had been spent. I put controls in place to ensure we recorded contributions according to Missouri Ethics Commission rules, because the commission was as big a pain in the ass as Funk about tracking donations. I added a million other controls because there were just too many things to remember on my own. I even inserted a column to make sure I'd written a thank-you note to donors — because you know that hick from West Vagina wasn't thanking them properly.

The database really *was* the most vital element of the campaign. And I didn't think this because I was a compulsive organizer. *The Campaign Manager*, my bible, said the key to a successful campaign was to keep it structured.

"Do you have experience managing a database, Betty Lou?"

"I can do it in my sleep, Gloria."

"Geez, that's great! Let me introduce you to Dottie."

I was beside myself with happiness to have another full-time volunteer, but I became hesitant as I walked Betty Lou back to Dottie's desk. How did I know this woman was trustworthy? The database wasn't just any old spreadsheet. It could be disastrous to Funk's campaign if it fell into the wrong hands. How can you delegate with assurance to people you don't know?

"Dottie, I want to make an introduction."

"Hi, I'm Dottie," she said in her usual bashful but vivacious way.

"Hi, Dottie," Betty Lou monotoned.

"Betty Lou is heaven-sent. She just volunteered to help out here full-time."

"That's wonderful," Dottie said, beaming.

"Can you show her the ropes?"

"Which ropes, exactly?" she asked nervously, having been called to action without knowing which action I sought.

"The ropes we're going to hang ourselves with."

Dottie was stunned to silence, her penciled-in eyebrows frozen in place, two sharp angles pointing toward the top of her head.

"I'm just kidding, Dottie! Betty Lou is going to manage the database."

"Oh, that's great. Thank you, Betty Lou!" And welcoming person that she is, Dottie was up in a flash, unlatching the stupid gate that corrals her inside her fake office. "I'll get another chair, Betty Lou. There's room for both of us back here."

When she said that, I thought to myself, *Good move not to stick her in an office, Dots. We need more people answering the phone and greeting volunteers.*

Before leaving them to it, I made sure Betty Lou understood that Dottie was in charge. Then I thought to lighten Dottie's load further and asked Betty Lou if she'd be the first responder to the phone. She agreed, and I left the two of them to work out the pecking order.

Funk came in directly afterward with lunch for everyone who was working at the now bulgingly staffed trailer. Most volunteers donated an hour here and there, and sometimes they really loaded down the double-wide. No one stopped to chat; they just diligently shoveled down food as they worked. Takeout was from Pizza 51. Again. We had a barter system going with some of Funk's supporters. The pizza restaurant's owner, Jason Pryor, was one of them. I was grateful for any campaign contribution, but what with all the carbs, no doubt about it, I was gaining weight. Since there was no time to go to the gym or ingest nutritious-but-delicious food anymore, I was screwed. I kept thinking I'd cook a vegetable and bring it to headquarters or I'd take a quick walk before hopping into the van before work, but I didn't. Each morning I made my son his breakfast, dropped him off at school, and headed straight to the trailer, arriving at the double-wide by seven-thirty. Driving was one of the few times that I got to converse with Andrew anymore. I dumped him back on our home curb at four o'clock, headed back to work, and returned home after ten. By that time, I was too beat for anything other than reading a few pages before falling asleep. What was a wife and a mother, one who was worried about gaining weight, to do? Being one, I can answer that: I didn't cook at home. I didn't go to the gym. Nope. I just took on more of Funk's responsibilities, including driving Andrew to school, and just so I could talk to the kid who didn't want to talk. Funk owed me bigtime. The man didn't have enough life left to repay me for everything I was doing.

I had barely finished my lunch when Funk bellowed for me to come into his office.

Was the guy losing his mind, or what? If there was any ordering around in this family, I did it. My husband had grown quite the set of balls, and they were getting bigger every day. Maybe his run for office wasn't such a good idea, and not just because of all the work that was ahead of him. It was his head I was worried about. It'd take me years to chisel that thing back down to size.

I reluctantly rose from my chair and went to the reception area. A new set of volunteers had come in, and I wanted to say hello to everyone before seeing what my husband needed. After a thousand repetitions of "Hey, how are you, thank you so much for coming in," I stepped inside Funk's office.

My man was leaning back in his chair with his feet propped on his desk, staring at his laptop with the biggest shit-eating grin on his face.

"What do you want now?"

"Babe, this is great!"

"What's great, Funk?" I said wearily, tired of this guy's happiness and insatiable needs. Why is it that both his cheerful and dour states elicited the same response in me?

Since the man can't read a room, he responded gleefully, "Your newsletter!" And in his deep baritone voice, he pontificated in a professorial tone, "Notes from the DoubleWide! I love it! It has a personal touch, just like our Christmas newsletters."

And seeing as he was tossing me a crumb, my weariness left me. What can I say? I'm a whore for a compliment.

"What made you think of doing this?"

Oh shit, I'd forgotten to talk to him about it. "I didn't, Britt did."

"Britt asked you to write a newsletter?"

"No, he wrote one. But he included me on the email chain that asked for comments. Didn't you get it?"

"The only emails I've looked at are from you."

I shook my head and said, "Jesus, Funk. You should at least be glancing at your emails." Turning away, I walked back to my office and grabbed Britt's newsletter from my trash can. I threw the wadded-up paper across his desk. He smoothed it out and started reading.

"Oh Christ."

"Mm-hmm, that's what I thought too."

He didn't say anything more, just held the creased sheet in his hand, giving it another read. Frowning, he asked, "Has this gone out?"

"No, I stopped it. Told Britt that you had to sign off on anything that has your name on it. He wasn't happy."

Again, he just stared at the page, gnawing on his thumb.

"You're welcome, Funk."

"Thanks, babe."

To repay me for saving his ass, he asked that I not only send my version of the newsletter — today, as if I didn't have anything else to do that afternoon — but that I send one out weekly.

He asked as if it was no biggie.

"Funk, I don't mind writing a newsletter, but what will you tell Britt?

"Nothing."

"Are you crazy?"

"Gloria, he works for us."

"Yeah, but he doesn't have a problem with *you*! You're making things really hard on me. You know I'm no good at telling people what to do. And Britt certainly doesn't think he's working for *us*."

"You're pretty good at telling me and the kids what to do."

"Don't be stupid, Funk."

"Do you want me to talk to Britt?"

"No, that always makes things worse. I'll friggin' deal with it. Now goodbye. Don't bother me again today."

At home, I had no problem telling my family what to do, but with outsiders other than my birth students, I found it tough. And Funk, off in his little red Corolla most of the time, was relying on me to carry out his wishes at the double-wide, much to the irritation of his Brain Trust. He'd put me in a terrible predicament, though he couldn't see it. He thought I was stronger than I was. In truth, I was a chickenshit at heart. I had to force myself out of my comfort zone. He knew I couldn't watch shit going down and not do something about it, and I was pretty sure that's what he was banking on. This wasn't sinister behavior on his part. He was simply too busy to deal with all the minutia that went on around headquarters, and he knew I'd have his back.

Still, it seemed a little much to ask that I write a weekly newsletter, whether or not it got me crosswise with Britt. Then again, I could see his point. Because who could you really trust besides family? And even that was sketchy in some families.

I'd resigned myself to the obvious: no way was I was getting out of that joint until after the election was over, even though Funk had hired not one, but two, campaign managers. Returning to my normal life was just a daydream. Now that I understood the inherent chaos of the campaign, it made sense that Funk hadn't made it easy for me to go home. And I was too loyal to just up and leave when he needed me. Needed *me?* What was I saying? The guy needed twelve more of me.

At the end of the day, as I was packing up to leave, I received an email draft of a press release. Those were Joe's responsibility, so I couldn't understand why the sender had included my name in the long-ass address chain that invited comments. At the last minute, Joe had probably thought to add me. I'm telling you, that guy loved me to pieces. And thank God for it, as you should have seen the thing. The press release was majestic in how shitty it was. I was surprised Joe could write such garbage. Maybe he had been rushed. Whatever. It couldn't go out.

Nervous beyond belief, I stopped packing up and dialed Joe.

"Hey there. I'm sorry to bother you at home, but I just received the press release."

"What press release?"

"Uh, the one you just sent."

"I didn't send anything."

"Well, Giuseppe, I have the draft open on my computer."

"Hold on. Let me look at my inbox."

I waited an eternity before he spoke again, "Okay, found it. I didn't write this."

"Oh, man. You have no idea how glad I am to hear that."

We both laughed with relief. Me, that Funk's writer hadn't gone mad. And Joe, because he could tell I had been disappointed in the press release. It was amazing how comfortable we felt with each other. I felt as though I knew him on a deep level, and I'm pretty sure he felt the same.

"Joe, I thought you were in charge of press releases, you being the newsman and all."

"So did I."

"Well, we can't send this. How about we both edit it in Track Changes and send it back and forth until it's right?"

"Sounds like a plan."

"Can you do it now?"

"It's kind of late, Gloria."

"I know, and I'm sorry. But if we don't do it tonight the Brainiacs will think it's good to go."

"You're probably right. I'll look it over."

I was so ready to leave headquarters, but I tossed my car keys on the desk and sat back down. It pained me to see substandard work bearing my husband's signature, particularly *after* it had been sent out, so not going home was actually less punishment than letting that pile of shit fly.

Turns out, Joe and I made a marvelous team.

After a few rounds of emails the piece looked great. My contribution was to add phrases that were particular to Funk, but Joe did the bulk of the work. He polished the whole thing up with his journalistic flair. When we were both content with the finished product, I hit Reply All. But just before I did, I noticed that the Brainiacs hadn't included Funk on the email chain, so I copied him as well.

I wondered what the Brains would think. First I rewrote Britt's newsletter, and now Joe and I rewrote the press release. I didn't hear them grumble about my rewrite of the newsletter, but I wasn't slow. I saw them whispering to each other and could sense they were conversing about me. If they viewed this latest development as a personal rejection of them and their place in the campaign, they might act even crabbier with me as a result. But Lord, really? Why did I have to worry about such things? Couldn't we work together for the good of the cause? Did we really need this competition between us? I thought the real race was happening outside, not inside, that brokedown trailer.

17 DECEMBER 2006

AS USUAL, I WOKE UP AFTER FUNK. I went downstairs to find him sitting on the couch, his gargantuan feet on the coffee table, the newspaper in his hand, and his laptop opened at his side.

What a sight to see first thing in the morning.

"Good morning, babe," he said merrily.

"Hey, Funk," I said indifferently. I'm kind of a grump when I first get up.

"Did you sleep well?"

"I guess."

"Great press release."

"That's because Joe worked it over," I said as I plopped myself down on the couch, moving his computer to the coffee table so I could sit beside him.

"Doesn't he always?"

"No. And I just found that out last night, too."

"What do you mean?"

"Joe is supposed to be in charge of press releases, but the draft didn't start with him."

"Gloria, we need a chain of command at the trailer."

"Wow, that's insightful, Funk." The guy had gotten on my nerves lately, so I moved to the other side of the couch.

"Funk, this is ridiculous," I continued. "Communications are being sent in your name, yet you're not even being consulted. I don't know why your people suddenly included me in the message thread but thank God they do. You should have seen the original. Nothing in it was what you think or the way you say it. After Joe and I got done with it, I even had to add your name to the email chain. That's the only reason you're seeing it now."

"Thanks for catching that, babe."

"That's not the point, Funk. *You*, not me, should be monitoring your team. I'm not good at supervising people."

"Glor, you're fine at it, and I can't do everything."

Did this guy really say that?

"Let me tell you something, buddy-boy. You are barely doing anything. You've got the easy part. Just going around town getting stroked all day, leaving me to deal with your chairman and managers. Christ, their egos are as big as yours, maybe bigger. I can't deal with it. I was so nervous editing the draft last night, wondering what they are were going to say."

"You helped edit it?"

"Joe did the bulk of the work. I mostly added your stupid phrases. But Funk, you're still missing the point."

"Glor, I'll tell them again this is what I want."

"Funk, they're blowing me off and they're not exactly listening to you either. Do you realize they're still not including Dottie on emails? She and I double-check each other's work, but how can we do that when she's not copied? It's senseless. I shouldn't have to wonder whether Dottie's received something or not. There's too much to keep track of, and there's no good reason I should have to bird-dog everything."

"Do you want me to make you some eggs?"

"My God, Funk," I growled, "my blood sugar isn't low. You're just aggravating me."

"Are you guys fighting again?" said our son as he came down the stairs.

"We're just talking, Andrew."

"It sounds like you're fighting."

"We're not. It's just that things are really busy at the trailer. There's no time for nice talk, only to-the-point talk," I said.

"When is this going to be over?"

"After Dad wins."

"I hope he doesn't."

"Andrew!"

"What? It's just going to get worse if he wins."

"Jesus, Andrew, no it won't."

"He'll be even busier, Mom, and it will be really stressful."

"Andrew, it's not possible for Dad to be busier than he is right now, and once he's in office he'll be in charge. His new job will be a breeze compared with when he was the city auditor."

"If you say so."

"I say so."

The phone rang, and since it was my daughter Tara calling, I took the phone to the dining room and sat in my rocker looking out the window at my neighbor's mustard-colored house. I'd told Funk many times that hell for me would be having to look at that color for all eternity. He said hell for him would be having to listen to me looking at it. But that was neither here nor there.

Our daughter was flying home from college, and I was all a-twitter about it. She was a-twitter too, but not for the same reason. She was calling from her airport layover in Cincinnati because she was nervous about getting onto the twenty-seat airplane. I'd been using credit card points for her travel, and it wasn't a great flight. But because Funk still hadn't secured the contract from UMKC, nor was he looking for a backup job as he had promised, our daughter had to suck it up because we couldn't spring for a real ticket right now. Thinking about Tara's uneasiness fueled my loathing for her father even more. Right in the middle of me talking her down, said father placed a plate of scrambled eggs on my lap.

Don't tell him, but it turns out that my blood sugar was low after all. I felt happier within minutes of consuming them. Why could he tell I was going down when I couldn't?

After reassuring Tara a bazillion times that she'd be okay, I said I had to go or I'd be late picking her up. The flight from Cincinnati took forty minutes, the same amount of time it took me to drive to the airport.

I loved being with my daughter. There was no one in the world I had more fun with. She thought I was funny, and I melted at her laugh — a heavenly, two-tone flutter that started high and ended low. Andrew could be a load of fun too, but only when he was in the mood to be around people. Funk? Meh.

I shouted a goodbye to Andrew, gave Funk a hug, and told him I was relieved he was glancing at his inbox again. In a flash I was in the van racing up Southwest Trafficway, barely able to contain my joy over seeing my daughter. When I arrived at the terminal, I had to drive around five times before I saw Tara in my rearview mirror. As I pulled up to the curb she hopped into the van and planted a kiss on my cheek. We drove straight home, yakking the whole way. She dropped her suitcase on the bench in the hall, kissed her papa on the lips, said hey to her brother, and off we went.

I'd been waiting eagerly for Tara to come home, for our family to be normal again, for us to do all the things we loved doing together. I was thrilled to be walking to the Plaza again, shopping the sales racks at Anthropologie, and calling Funk to join us for coffee under an umbrella outside Latte Land. We asked Andrew to join us, but of course he said no. Despite that disappointment, adding to the joyous day was the weather had turned warm again, a delightful bonus in mid-December.

Funk's Corolla pulled up just as the barista set our drinks on the counter.

We had only thirty minutes to relish the moment, as Funk and I needed time to return home to dress for Councilwoman Aggie's holiday party. But we enjoyed ourselves, Funk drove home with a cookie for Andrew, and Tara and I walked back, talking and laughing.

Funk had to drive around Aggie's neighborhood a few times before we found a parking place. Her home was jammed with guests. I wondered what was up with that. I was relieved to see my pal Ruth in the living room, so when Funk went to get a drink, I made a beeline for her, squishing my ever-growing ass down on the settee beside her and Mike. I rarely saw this husband and wife together, but tonight they were sitting so close their hips were touching. Even more shocking was that Mike was kidding around with her, flirting almost, and Ruth was blushing at his words.

Mike was like Funk, noticeably crazy about his wife, but Ruth had always been cool whenever she spoke of her husband. Before long, Gwen came up behind me and began playing with my hair. I loved Gwen. She was interesting and fun, not the ordinary beige that was way too prevalent in the Midwest. Mike stood up to let her sit down, and instead of our normal girl-talk, my friends focused on city gossip. Ruth and Gwen were hooked into the players in town and were more interested in those happenings than I was, so I mostly just listened to them dishing dirt. Because they'd arrived at the party long before me, etiquette said they were allowed to leave first, which left me all by myself in Aggie's crowded and overly decorated living room.

When I could no longer tolerate the claustrophobic feeling or the revelers' personalities, I headed outside to breathe in the night air. The only space available was on the porch ledge, where Councilman Ford was sitting. My husband always referred to him as Thoughtful Ed — unlike the many councilmembers who wouldn't think for themselves, who just went along with whatever their sponsors told them to do because that ensured reelection. I'd been around Ed plenty of times but had never conversed with him. I was sitting within inches of the man and I had to say something, so I began with dreadful small talk.

"Hello, Councilman. I hear you're running again."

"Yes, I am," he said without enthusiasm.

"You don't seem very happy about it!"

"I am. I just wish I had a competitor," he said flatly.

"You do? Why in the world would you wish that?" Although I didn't say it aloud, I thought to myself that I'd have given anything if Funk didn't have eleven people running against him.

Ed answered my question surprisingly honestly, "So I'd know that it's me who people are electing."

"Ah, I see."

"No, you don't," he said bluntly. "My father has very little regard for me, and I'd like to prove that I can be elected on my own merits, not because there's no competition."

Oh, brother. Why did people always divulge their innermost thoughts to me?

For instance, I once had a student who revealed to me her penchant for sexual threesomes a mere thirty seconds before I was to begin teaching my birth class. Like, what was I supposed to do with that little tidbit? I wanted to tell her that given her situation, she'd better damn well let the hospital put silver nitrate in her baby's eyes — something I vehemently opposed for most newborns — as her child really could go blind from an STD the mother might have picked up. I had to ring her up later in the week to delicately have that conversation.

I didn't sit in judgment of anyone. As long as no one was causing harm, differences didn't bother me. Growing up in New York, I learned to get along with people from all walks of life, even if my friends and I did notice differences and snicker over them. The politically correct set at Aggie's tonight would have said that if you were a good person, you'd never notice those differences.

Yeah, right. Those differences were the reason for the mass exodus from Missouri into Kansas whenever children in my neighborhood came of school age. You could get yourself killed on Shawnee Mission Parkway from the stampede of Kansas City plates fleeing the border to the lily-white schools each September.

Midwesterners were more judgmental than any people I'd ever met — and I'd lived in lots of places. These folks hid behind nice. They would say all the right things with a big smile on their face while viciously knifing your back so you couldn't see who was doing it. There was a lot of repressed rage. If they had spoken their truth, they wouldn't have had such horrible darkness loitering beneath the surface. It *is* possible to speak your mind in a kind way.

Ford had to be nearing fifty. Wasn't it time he shelved the daddy issues? I contemplated giving him the phone number of my therapist because I knew he'd feel much better if he sought her aid. But we were only acquaintances, so I kept it to myself and tried reassuring his soul instead.

"I'm sure your father thinks you're terrific, Ed! You're a lawyer, after all."

"That means nothing to him," he said in a shockingly dejected tone, his eyes staring unfocused at the floor.

"Well," I said, "maybe someone will enter the race at the last minute."

"Like your husband did?" he said with derision, which took me aback.

I mean, honestly, I *was* trying to be nice to the man. Not knowing how to respond, I replied lamely, "Perhaps."

He looked up and said in the most condescending way possible, as if he were closing an argument at a trial, "Mark is embarrassing himself. He doesn't have a chance in hell of winning."

Lord Almighty! What a thing to say! And to Funk's wife! Thoughtful Ed Ford, my ass!

Thank God, I'd placed myself in diplomat mode on my way to the party, because that was the only way I was able to respond as neutrally as I did. "I'm pretty sure my husband is going to win, Ed."

We sat in uncomfortable silence for a while, but then Ed retracted his claws. Turning docile and appearing almost like a little boy, he swung his legs on the ledge and said with yearning in his voice, "It's nice that you're supportive of your husband. My wife would never help me."

"So I'm told. About my help, that is. Not your wife."

I didn't know how people knew I was helping Funk with the campaign, given that I was behind the scenes, glued to the trailer fourteen hours a day. I rarely ventured out, except for the meet-and-greets. Other than signing my name to his newsletter — which was only proper etiquette — no one should have known my name.

Redirecting the conversation to safer ground, I asked how many children he had and how long he'd been married. But Mr. Ford was done with me. "Important" people had just stepped onto the porch, and the councilman couldn't have made it plainer that he wanted their attention. If he were a dog, his tail would've been thumping on the wooden floorboards, begging to be noticed.

Mr. and Mrs. Important said hello. To appear well mannered, I joined the conversation. At least, I tried to. To Ford, it was if I had just disappeared. I got the impression he was afraid to be seen associating with me, so I did disappear.

I walked through the house, room by crowded room, looking for my husband. Many "please-excuse-me's" later I found him standing in a circle of partiers, a drink in his hand, a rare smile on his face. I squeezed my way over and pulled him down to whisper in his ear, "C'mon Funk, let's get out of here. We've got children waiting at home for us."

18 DECEMBER 2006
MY ITALIAN EXCHANGE DAUGHTER'S BIRTHDAY

IT WAS DOTTIE'S HABIT to arrive at the trailer a few minutes before I did, and thankfully, we had the place all to ourselves for a few hours. The first volunteer to tinkle Spring's doorbells was Betty Lou. She ambled in at around ten a.m., coming straight to my office. She didn't speak, just stood in front of my desk as if reporting for duty.

Looking up from my calculator, I said, "Betty Lou, you have the most brilliant blue eyes I've ever seen."

"Why, thank you, ma'am."

"So," I said, leaning back in my chair, "you're back!"

"What did you think?"

"I didn't think anything, just hoped."

She smiled at that.

Not wanting to usurp Dottie's authority, I got up and walked Betty Lou over to the reception desk.

"Dots, we have help today!"

"I see that," she said, smiling. "Welcome back!"

Betty Lou looked slightly perturbed at being handed off. But in addition to my need to reiterate that Dottie was in charge, it wasn't possible to have drawn-out conversations with every volunteer. I was mindful to share a few private words with each, especially those who had the greatest need — which was, like, all of them — but because of the workload, I wasn't able to give everyone as much time as they wanted.

The notion that I should parent the way I did had come to me in a message from above when my children were young. BirthWays had taken off like wildfire, and I was working sixty hours a week to keep up. But on a drive to Colorado one year with my family, spirit asked me which I wanted: a booming business or children raised in such a way that they'd feel seen, loved, heard, and wanted. After that, whenever my children came up to me, which was around a thousand times a day, I forced myself to stop whatever I was doing and focus my eyes on their sweet little faces.

Thank God I listened to spirit's message and made that choice, because think of all the joy I would've missed out on. At this point in the campaign, though, my time was so fractured that I wasn't giving anyone the attention they deserved. Many of our volunteers came from the fringes of society, and it was nearly impossible to fill the deficits in their soul. Between neglecting my children and shortchanging the volunteers, all day long I felt guilt, guilt, and more guilt.

The morning Tara and I had walked at the Plaza, she told me she felt sad that she couldn't talk to me whenever she wanted to anymore. I was horrified and instantly shot off to that black sea of muck — but thank the Lord, just momentarily. Once I landed back on Earth, I told the universe that I was done with the situation; I was going to quit the campaign. I stopped in the middle of the sidewalk and turned to face my daughter, saying that my children's needs came before my own and certainly before her father's. I said I was no longer going to help her dad with his stupid-ass dream. I was going back to being just her mother. I kind of freaked. And that made my daughter kind of freak.

"Jesus, Mama! You don't need to quit. Daddy needs you! You're always wondering if I love and miss you. Well, I was only trying to tell you that I love and miss you."

"No, Tara. I knew this was wrong from the beginning, and I can't take it anymore. The guilt is killing me. You guys come first. End of story. Dad's a big boy. He'll manage."

"Mama, it's okay. It's good what you're doing. You and Dad will help so many people. Andrew and I will be fine. We *are* fine!"

"Christ, Tara, I'm not working my ass off like this for *other* people, I'm only doing it for Dad. I don't even like other people. Well, I do, but not the way he does. You know what I mean: I care about my little circle and the band around us, and that's it. I don't give two shits about anyone else."

Finding humor in my angst, Tara smiled. "Right, Mama. You're always indignant about some injustice that befalls people."

"That's not true. That's Dad's M.O., not mine. And don't tell me what I think."

"You get incensed by the things that happen to your birthing students in the hospital."

"That's different, Tara. They're my responsibility. Plus, I don't want them going through what I went through, getting sliced open for no reason other than to put more money in their doctor's pocket. Besides, someone has to make sure that families bond, or there's going to be complete mayhem in the world. I'm just protecting me and mine by looking after my students."

"What about the man you saved at Sam's Club?"

"What about him?"

"Everyone just stood there looking, afraid to go near, but you got on the ground and helped him."

"That's a stupid example, Tara. That guy was going to die right there on the concrete floor if someone didn't help, and at Sam's Club, of all places! Jesus, that's no place to die!"

"C'mon, Mama. You're helping Dad save the world because that's your M.O. too. There's no reason to feel guilty over it."

"I'm not trying to save anyone. I just feel immense pressure to help Dad. You know I hate his guts for this, don't you?"

She ignored that last part; she'd heard it too many times to get upset over it. She just continued lecturing me.

"All those kids you loved up at Holliday — I guess you weren't trying to save them either."

"That's different too. You know how I feel about children."

"Holy God, okay, let's forget the examples. Last week you said that you were surprised you were having fun with the campaign."

"I am having fun, but I'm not going to forsake my children just to have fun."

I didn't quite land back in tunnel vision, but my throat closed up from hearing myself say I was forsaking my kids, because to me, that was the worst sin in the world.

Seeing me distraught, my daughter chose her words carefully. I abhorred that my children could see a fuller view of me now, especially when all I am is flaws, flaws, flaws.

"You're not forsaking me. I love college, and it's okay for you to have fun too."

"But sis, Andrew is alone most of the time," I said, the guilt crushing me.

"I hate to tell you, Mom, but he likes having the house to himself."

"Yes but . . . my God, I'm so confused. Fuck it all!"

Losing patience, my daughter barked, "Mama, please! I shouldn't have said anything."

And since I always get mad at my loved ones whenever I'm torturing myself, as much as I didn't want to, that's where I went.

"Don't talk to me like that, Tara. Not saying how you feel is the same as lying. Don't make it that I can't trust you."

"Oh Lord, Mama."

I can't even describe how much I loved hearing my daughter refer to me as Mama, yet I didn't feel less confused. We walked past the row houses on Wyandotte that I loved so much, each of us lost in our own thoughts. Sensing I'd gone too far, I forced myself out of the tunnel and made myself act like a grown-up again.

"Just the other day Betty said this was the best thing that could've ever happened to me."

"What's the best thing?"

"When I apologized for not spending as much time with her and Jack, she said I shouldn't worry, that she understood. Said I'd been overwrought over you being away at college and I needed something to take my mind off my empty nest."

"She's right. Please keep doing what you're doing. I want you to be happy. I'm okay. I just miss you sometimes."

As if I were cutting a deal with God to save her life, I responded, "How about if I always answer the phone whenever you call, and if I never hang up first?"

"It would be nice if you can do it. But I'll understand if you can't. This won't be forever."

"What about Andrew?"

"Make him some food or let him get takeout and he'll be fine too."

"That's what Dad says, but it's not true. Andrew's going to crucify me over this. That kid keeps score. How the hell did he get so Italian, when I raised the two of you the exact same way?"

She laughed and said, "I don't know," which made me laugh too.

I'd left the reception desk eons ago, but all I'd done since then was stare up at the stained ceiling in my now permanent office, reliving that conversation with Tara. I tried shaking off the guilt. About Andrew especially, but also for shooing my daughter off the phone on too many occasions, for not giving enough attention to the neediest volunteers, for not being as helpful to my aging next-door neighbors, and, good God Almighty, for not focusing enough on my newly widowed mother.

Surprisingly, it wasn't as hard as it normally is to closet my cosmic whip. Not with the phones going the way were, my inbox dinging every few seconds, volunteers walking in and out with questions, and trying to tackle my own to-do list. Who could dwell on anything with all that going on? To be sure, though, guilt sat like a rock in my gut, reminding me of the horrible person I was becoming.

Soon, the bastard I called husband was back from his latest meet-and-greet, bringing lunch for everyone. My skin crawled the moment I heard the rumble of his car's muffler. I suspect my annoyance with him stemmed from my feeling of shame. Thank God, Funk knew me sometimes better than I knew myself, and his self-worth was rock solid. He was aware that my attitude had to do with my inner struggles, that it wasn't about him. That said, just as with PMS, it didn't mean my feelings had no basis in reality. I had been quick to get agitated with him, partly because we weren't spending enough time together. Realizing that, I walked to his office to have lunch with him. I didn't pull the door closed, but I hoped the volunteers could tell we needed time to ourselves.

As soon as I walked in, my husband looked up from his newspaper and said, "Hey, beautiful!"

And that was as good as it got, because as usual, Funk proceeded to bore me to tears. He talked about the latest endorsement screening. Nothing had changed. Regular folks loved him and the establishment hated him. *Tell me something I don't know.* I was grateful we weren't talking auditor shit anymore, but it would've been nice to talk about something other than him.

Detecting my mood, he tried saving himself. "You look nice today, darling."

"If you're trying to get on my good side, it's not working. You'll need to do better than your typical refrain."

"Nice press release. Those are getting stronger every day."

"It's still not working. Besides, it's mostly Joe's hand with those."

"Babe, you're good at this. Why don't you see it?"

"Funk, I've been doing *this* for years. I've run my own business while raising your kids, editing your work, and organizing your life and those of our children — you just haven't been around to see me in action. Everything just magically happens for you. How do you think things have gotten done when all you do is go for one academic degree after the other — and now this enormous thing? Jesus, think of what I could've become if I had a wife like me."

"You're amazing, babe. Someday you'll see that."

"All I see is that I'm helping you when I should be at home with the kids and dealing with my students."

"Glor, the children are fine. They said so at dinner last night."

"I know what they said. I was there. And unlike you, I pay attention to them. But they only said that because they're good kids. They don't like this. I'm telling you, Funk, I can't take the guilt anymore."

"It won't be much longer."

"There's three more months!"

"Only if I win."

"Stop being an idiot. You know you're going to win."

Just then, Dana and Britt walked in, pizza box in hand. Never mind that Funk and I were having a moment. Still, I understood. Everyone needed Funk's time. His team probably thought we talked at home every night. But of course we were hardly there, and when we were, we were either paying attention to Andrew or dropping into bed.

After Britt had shoveled four slices of pizza into his meaty head, he got down to business.

"Mark, in the past few days we've received a slew more questionnaires. Ed's filling them out as fast as he can, but some require contact information for your campaign manager. Whose name do you want to put down, mine or Dana's?"

I could see Britt teetering on the edge of his seat, hoping Funk would choose him, and I waited for it too, wondering the same thing.

"Put Gloria's name down."

I thought Britt and Dana would projectile-vomit their pizza across the room. In fact, I could see the ghost of it flying right past Funk's head and whap against the back wall, and the contents of my stomach weren't far behind. All jaws except Funk's stood agape. I took the freeze-framed moment to skedaddle out of my husband's office, because just like his managers, never in a million years did I expect Funk to say that. Britt and Dana would never believe that I hadn't put him up to it. They thought Funk doted on me. He did, but not the way they assumed. Funk gave me the strength I needed to evolve, but he didn't allow me to become stagnant. But how would Britt and Dana have known this? They didn't have a clue about what our relationship was like.

Still, what a dumb thing for Funk to say. What was he thinking?

I found out a short while later. Funk stepped to the threshold of my office and crooked a finger at me.

Again.

Like, how many times did that make?

I walked over to Dottie's desk and told her I'd be back in a minute. I followed Funk out of the trailer — the whole time asking him what the hell was going on. He had the audacity not to respond. He headed to the van and opened the door, signaling me to hop inside.

We settled into the front seats. I turned to him and said, "What are we doing? I can't go anywhere. There are tons of people here today."

"We're not going anywhere."

"What the hell!"

"We need to talk."

"We couldn't do that inside?"

"Not about this."

"What now?"

"I—"

"Wait a minute! First, tell me why you said that ridiculous thing to Britt and Dana!"

"Because I need someone to manage the campaign."

"Well, Funk, you've hired two campaign managers."

"Hiring Dana and Britt was a hasty decision that turned out to be wrong."

"Hasty? Seriously?"

He ignored the sarcasm, "Glor, we're learning how to do this. I need someone who knows what I want, someone who's working the plan."

"That's only what I've been saying for a million years, Funk."

"Okay, I've caught up to you. You're my campaign manager."

"That's not what I meant. I don't know the first thing about the job."

"Glor, you've been running the campaign from day one."

"Jesus, that's not true! I read *The Campaign Manager* and did what the woman said to do because no one else was doing anything. Has anyone even read the damn thing besides me?"

"Glor—"

"Honestly, Funk! Don't you think we should've discussed this before you blurted it out to the entire world?"

"Glor—"

"You put me in such an awkward position in there."

"Babe—"

"What are they supposed to think?"

"I don't care what they think. I—"

"I know you don't care, but I do!"

"There's no time for etiquette, Gloria. Putting them in charge was a mistake, one that I didn't understand until I read Dana's email. I have to correct my error."

"Which email? She sends a thousand of them."

"The one about the budget. Have you seen it?"

"No. I probably wasn't copied."

"Which is partly why I'm getting rid of her."

"What? You can't do that!" I shouted, my head spinning, because when my husband makes a decision, he makes a decision.

Of course, he didn't notice anything, just carried on as if I weren't having a heart attack.

"I'm letting her go, Glor."

"Oh my God! Whatever. But that still leaves Britt."

"Britt can't be my manager either. In a traditional campaign, maybe. I'd still like Jeff in the role, but he continues to say he doesn't have time for it."

"Funk, Jeff's more conventional than Britt. If you told Britt what you wanted, he'd do it."

"There's no time to teach — "

"Hold on. What the hell was in Dana's email?"

"I told you, the budget. She said I had to raise a hundred grand in the short run and three hundred by the end, or I couldn't win."

"That's bullshit."

"Exactly."

"But Funk, I can't be your campaign manager. I have no idea what it involves, and I'd be too scared."

"You don't have to know. Just keep doing what you're doing. All we need is a plan to follow, and you've already created that. We've got this."

I slumped in my seat, staring straight ahead, digesting everything he'd said. Meanwhile, volunteers were streaming by, pretending not to look but failing.

After a minute my husband broke the silence.

"It seems you've decided to stay on."

"Funk, how could I go home with this craziness going on?" I said, gesturing at the brokedown trailer.

"Are you okay with me?"

"I'm resigned. And don't get that look. I'm mostly fine with everything and with you."

He brightened at that, visibly relieved.

"Glor, you're good at this. Your instincts are right there. You work well with Joe. I only saw him as the writer, but he's become much more. If you don't mind staying on, I'd prefer you in this role."

"Jesus, Funk. I don't know."

"I know."

"You're actually going to fire Labia?"

"Yes."

"When?"

"Soon."

"It's almost Christmas."

"And?"

"That's really mean, Funk."

"Gloria."

"What about Britt? He's not going like this. And Jeff, holy shit!"

"Britt will keep doing what he's doing — crunching numbers, analyzing voter data — and Jeff just wants me to win."

"No, that's not all Jeff wants, but whatever."

So it was that we suffered two campaign managers for a full two weeks. Although none of us could see it at that time, each day the campaign had fallen apart a little more, and each time it was I who had picked up the pieces, I went from being just a demure little wife to a campaign manager.

19 DECEMBER 2006

WHAT WITH ALL MY COMPLAINING, you probably wouldn't think it, but Funk and I made a pretty good team. We came at things from totally different angles, each adding fullness to the other's ideas.

A few weeks earlier, I had been sitting on the porch with him, listening to him drone on about how he wanted the campaign to reach out to people of all persuasions. As usual, he was so verbose that I could listen to what he was saying and at the same time trip through my mind, turning over ideas. An idea sprang to mind.

To pursue his candidacy, Funk was required to file petitions. That usually meant standing in front of grocery stores asking shoppers to sign on a dotted line. It amazed me that anyone was willing to do that, given that shoppers were rushing in and out to grab one last item for their holiday menu, yet they cheerfully stopped to help us out. Well, most of them.

At the neighborhood grocery where my kids and I stood collecting signatures, one lady was really nasty. She shouted behind her as she scurried by, "Not on your life! I'm voting for Alvin Brooks." I wanted to shout back, "Hey, nobody's fucking stopping you. You don't have to be so mean!" But I was trained in diplomat mode so, like a good Kansas Citian, I just smiled and chewed on my tongue to stop foul words from spilling out. I hated doing that. I felt weak when I didn't stand up for myself. I particularly hated throwing good teaching opportunities away, because it was my job to show my kids how to be brave, and I could do that best by walking my talk. Encounters like that always brought me down.

Before the family moved to Kansas City, all I'd heard was about how friendly Midwesterners were. I'd since learned that was a big fat lie. People in Missouri could be vicious, yet it was their culture to hide behind nice. Sometimes I parted from a simple interaction feeling as if I'd been punched in the face, yet I had no idea why I felt that way. New Yorkers could be mighty offensive — my God, they could be downright cruel — but at least they said things to your face. The behavior of the woman at the grocery store took my breath away, even though I'd lived in Kansas City long enough that it shouldn't have. Not when Meiners grocery was located in the heart of Brookside and most of its patrons were uppity white, bleeding-heart liberals. Those types got their rocks off hearing themselves shout to the world they were voting for a black man, when in reality they were saying it to convince themselves. The truth is, many of them would have nothing to do with the black race. They didn't want *that* kind in their backyard.

That Meiners shopper who shouted that she was voting for Alvin? Well, on the face of it, that seemed okay. Alvin was nice — that's what Funk said. However, if that woman *actually* voted for Alvin, it wouldn't be because she thought Alvin would be good for the city. It'd be because Alvin was one of those "safe" black people who white Kansas Citians loved to love. But Alvin had ties to the establishment. The mothers living on the black side of town didn't need another mayor who catered to those sorts. Christ, I didn't know how those moms had the courage to live in that district, much less let their children play outside. Not when their loved ones were being shot up left and right over there.

If you're afraid of people who are different from you, throwing money at a cause won't pardon your truth. And if you can't sleep at night, it's because *you* see that too.

Brookside was full of phonies — I hated phonies — who said they supported black people. Many of my neighbors would never think of sending their kids to a school filled with black children. As soon as their little bundles of joy came of school age, they charged across the state line to lily-white Prairie Village, Kansas.

I was a liberal too, but not that kind of liberal. Support by word, not by deed? Man, I couldn't stand that.

Anyway, my idea for how the campaign could extend Funk's reach was to harvest the names we had collected on the petitions and mail each person a thank-you note for stopping to help. The notes would mostly touch the rich voters, and my hope was that sending them a gracious card would put Funk on their radar.

The Orange Revolution

I ARRIVED at the trailer long before anyone else. What with the holidays being just around the corner, I was apparently the only crazy person who felt a need to be there. I didn't know what was happening to me. I usually had every Christmas present bought by October and wrapped by November. By the time December rolled around, all I had to do was focus on cooking.

Our holiday meals had become a tradition. I used the same menus year after year. We had Betty's Bread and a thick salad on Christmas Eve. The recipe for the bread came from my second-oldest brother's first wife's mother — a woman I never really cared for. On Christmas morning I made crêpes. But this year, we had done nothing besides hang up holiday lights. I had not bought or wrapped a single gift. I had not stocked the pantry with a single ingredient.

As we were having coffee together one morning, my daughter took pity on me and offered to help. She probably wouldn't agree that she offered. She'd say I guilted her into it, but I'm nothing like my mother. Not one time have I ever stooped so low as to use Italian guilt tactics to parent my children. It's just that when she asked about our plans for the day, in anticipation of the question, I pulled a massive to-do list from my folder and handed it to her.

Good daughter that she is, Tara dropped me off at the double-wide and headed for the mall to start on Christmas shopping for me. With the place to myself and the phones blessedly quiet, I started on the items that required my full attention. By the time Dottie arrived, I had written thirty-nine thank-you notes — one for every person who had donated that week, including re-peat donors — and one to each new volunteer.

I heard the front bells tinkle followed by Dottie's voice. "I'm sorry I'm late, Gloria. I stayed home to do some baking."

"Please don't be sorry! I'm glad someone is behaving normally. Besides, Funk hasn't paid you a cent yet."

"I'm not expecting to be paid."

"Are you that sure he's going to lose, Dots?"

"That's not what I meant, and you know it," she said, dipping her smile into her shoulder.

"I know. I'm just messing with you."

I dropped my voice to a whisper, even though no one else was in the trailer. "I need to tell you something, Dottie. You are *never* going to believe this!"

"What?" she asked conspiratorially.

"Funk is getting rid of Labia," I said, still marveling.

"My goodness, what happened?"

"Funk is upset about the budget she emailed him and miffed that she's not following his directions."

"Like what?"

"Like, she's still not copying you on emails — "

"Gloria, he shouldn't fire her over that!" she shouted, aghast.

"He's not firing her over that, Dottie. It's that piled on top of everything else. It's mostly because she doesn't understand that we're running a grassroots campaign, or she doesn't know how to. The final straw came when she emailed fundraising numbers that aren't possible to achieve, yet she said Funk would lose if he didn't. Funk is tired of his team telling him he's going to lose."

"How much money?"

"A hundred thousand now, and three or four hundred total."

"That doesn't seem like much for a mayoral campaign."

"Really?" I said, worrying that she might know something about it, her having worked in government and all.

"It seems right to me."

"Right or not, Funk doesn't think he can raise that much money. Donations aren't exactly rolling in. Anyway, I wanted to tell you before you heard it through the grapevine. I can't believe how quickly shit spreads around here, and it's always distorted. I didn't want you fearing for your job, er, I mean, your *volunteer opportunity*!"

"Oh, Gloria, you're too funny."

"Well, that's it. I'm going back to my office so I can catch up on a few more things because I really want to get out of here early today."

"You leave early, Gloria, even if you don't catch up," she said, as reassuringly as any good mother.

Before long, despite the approaching holiday, the trailer was bustling. Making my first round, I greeted all the volunteers. Their care and feeding completed, I answered their questions while I made copies at the printer.

Everyone at the headquarters assumed that when Funk wasn't present, I was in charge. I'd evolved into that role, even though I was terrible at being a boss. But, terrible or not, in the campaign world you either surpassed your limitations or you failed. In the brief time I'd been keeping an eye on things for Funk, I had learned a few things. For example, I knew that any appeal would be better met if I said it came from Funk. I asked my husband why he thought people responded better to my requests if I invoked his name. Was it because I was female or his wife? Or was it because he was the former city auditor?

He gave me a stupid answer. He said my problem was that I wanted people to like me, but no one liked being told what to do. Therefore, just as with my staff at BirthWays, I shouldn't expect to be liked at headquarters either. I considered Funk's advice useless. I was determined that his campaign would be remembered for its manners and class.

On that day I had to act on some concerns about our volunteer Betty Lou. As agreed, she'd become the first responder to the telephones. I was thrilled we had relief, but I was stressed about it too. I never had to say boo to Dottie about the proper way to greet callers, but I had to coach Betty Lou. She handled the phones professionally; it's just that I had certain ideas about the way I wanted things done.

Boy, did I hate confrontations! I had agita all morning thinking about having a talk with Betty Lou.

Creeping slowly to her side of the reception desk, I said, "Um, excuse me? Betty Lou?"

"Yes, Gloria?"

"I'm sorry to bother you, but would you mind talking for a sec?"

"Of course not," she said with a big smile, feeling special that I had singled her out.

"In my office?"

"What's up?" she asked, a little nervously.

"Nothing, really, I just need to ask you something."

She stood, opened the stupid gate that led to nowhere, and followed me to my office.

I sat down, welcomed Betty Lou into the chair opposite mine, and got up my courage to begin. But when I turned my attention fully on her, I discovered that she looked even more anxious than I felt.

"Betty Lou, please don't look so distraught! Nothing's wrong. I just wanted to ask if you wouldn't mind answering the phones a little differently. Funk wants—"

"How so?" she blurted defensively.

I added an upbeat lilt to my voice in response. "Funk wants us to refer to callers as 'Mr.' or 'Ms.' or 'Mrs.' and to respond to their questions with a 'yes, sir' or a 'no, ma'am'. That's all."

She pulled a face, so I said, "I know, he's a complete pain. He still has the city auditor in him."

"That's a little much, Gloria."

"Perhaps, but that's what he wants. He says his supporters are mostly elderly and working class, two groups that have never gotten much attention from the powers that be. Now that I've explained his thinking, can you do it his way?"

Her back was still up, but she begrudgingly said, "I guess so. I just think it's kind of . . . different."

To defuse the situation, I gave her a quick "Thank you so much, Betty Lou" and then asked about her husband. On safer ground then, we chatted a while, but when the phones began going nuts, she scooted back to the lobby to catch them. And then, instead of slaughtering the work on my piled-high desk so I could beat it the hell out of the trailer, my mind drifted to the meaning of respect.

I had a hard time with the concept of respect because it came with a yin and a yang, and God didn't grant me the comfort of seeing things in black and white. All I get is murky lines. What a relief it would have been to decide on a path, take it, and be sure of it. Typically, as soon as I reached a conclusion, I bombarded myself with questions: *Uh, Gloria, have you thought about* this? *What about* that? *Fool, what were you thinking?*

Blessedly, some matters weren't as confusing. For example, my baby daughter walked through toddlerhood with two balls of snot hanging from her nostrils because I couldn't bear her crying when I tried taking them out. The result was that she remained comfortable in her three-year-old body, even if my peers viewed me as a neglectful mother. But who cared?

Most times, though, I didn't get off that easy.

I could hardly believe I had imposed my will on Betty Lou, but I had done so because I considered it disrespectful to greet supporters informally. That was why I was still at the trailer when I should have been at home with my children.

As I got ready to leave for the day, Funk came sauntering into the trailer, the Brain Trust trailing in his wake. Once again, he crooked his finger at me. I finished gathering my belongings before going in to see what he wanted. Britt and Jeff greeted me as if they were happy to see me, though I could see right through those two. They'd just as soon I fell off the Earth. Funk, though, expressed true pleasure upon my entrance.

"There she is! The best campaign manager this side of the Continental Divide." His sentiment was met by horrified looks from his macho bookends and a full-body cringe from me. Thank God, Joe came in a moment later, followed by Evert, because they liked me. A lot.

"Why are we gathered?" I addressed the roomful of men.

"We're having a one-on-one before the large committee meets tonight," came Jeff's chipper response.

I couldn't understand why we should waste time hashing through an agenda that we'd be talking about in a few hours. But that's what we did. I stayed for a little while but then said I had to get home to my children. Keeping my eyes on the buckled-up carpet, I walked from Funk's office into my own, wordlessly letting the volunteers know I was off duty.

My son barely said hello when I walked in the door, but I knew he was happy to see me. He was on the couch watching TV, and I sat as close as he would allow, tearing through a stack of backed-up mail, leaving him only to run upstairs to grab the office supplies I needed to pay bills.

In normal times I never let a month go by without matching purchase receipts to credit card statements, searching for discrepancies. Now, I just wrote the damn check. Funk was right: there weren't enough hours in the day. Something had to give, and that translated to ignoring matters at home. To keep myself on this side of sane, I promised myself that I'd go back and justify our accounts once Funk won the election.

I had paid almost every bill when Tara pulled into the driveway and began honking the car horn like a maniac, her signal to us to help carry in the groceries. It was weird to have my child doing the same thing I'd done for many years. Weird and annoying. Of course, I didn't go out. I just made Ange do it, ignoring his protests.

"Home early, eh?" said Tara as she walked inside clutching several shopping bags.

"Sorry, sis. You know how it is at the trailer," I said, with my cosmic whip in full view.

"It's okay, Mama," Tara replied. "I'm just fucking with you. I've been busy with your list all day."

"Is everything done?"

"Mama! It's not humanly possible to get everything on the list done today."

"What's left?"

"I have to put away the groceries and then wrap your presents."

I let out my breath. "That's a relief. Those are the biggest jobs. We'll get to the rest of the list later."

"There's not much 'later' left before Christmas Eve."

"It'll get done. I'll put the groceries away; you go upstairs and start wrapping."

She was so good natured that she started for the stairs.

"Tara, wait a sec. What time are you going out with your girlfriends?"

"They're coming to get me at nine."

"I forgot that Dad has a committee meeting tonight. Do you mind if I head out to the meeting at seven?"

"No, I'll be getting ready anyway."

"That's what I thought. You're a love."

"Ange, do you mind if I go to the meeting?"

"Don't care."

"Nothing like turning the knife," I said to my son as I exposed my wrists to his sister to slit for me.

Unable to rip myself away from my kids by seven p.m., I ducked into the committee meeting late. Jeff had almost finished going over the stuff I'd heard a few hours earlier. I didn't miss anything, but most of the group didn't know that, so I received some harsh stares. Normally, I can't stand it when people think poorly of me. But in this case, I could give two shits what those people thought.

Jeff went from talking about "who-maybe-perhaps-might-eventually support Funk" to the next item on his agenda. The man was in his element, holding court, asking everyone for thoughts on the prototype for Funk's yard sign. I had drafted a design, but it was too ho-hum. The only thing good about it was that I had the foresight to put a line drawing of Funk's face beside his name. My husband's campaign had no money for advertising, yet I knew that many people would recognize him from his many years in the city spotlight. It made sense to me that putting his name and face together on the yard sign would trigger recognition. I admit, it looked hokey. But hey, you had to be crafty when you were running a grassroots campaign. Surprisingly, there wasn't much commentary about the sign, so Jeff moved to the next item, Funk's slogan: "A City That Works for Regular Folks."

Funk had thought it up. He first mentioned it when our family was shooting the breeze after dinner one night, months before he went public with his candidacy. After he recited it, the kids and I just sat there staring at him, waiting for the punch line.

There wasn't one.

Andrew was the first to say, "Is that it?"

"Yes," my husband said, his enthusiasm diminished by only a hair, as it was clear he thought it was Andrew who was off-kilter, not him.

My son went on, "It sounds like it's supposed to rhyme, but it doesn't. Does something come next?"

"No, that's the whole thing, Andrew." Turning to Tara and me, he asked confidently, "What do you think?"

Tara and I echoed Andrew's sentiment, but Funk wasn't fazed. He thought his prose ingenious, that it stated his platform in the fewest words possible. The committee's expressions at the meeting mimicked our family's clueless gaze. But they didn't leave the matter alone after their stun wore off. They spoke volumes about how much they disliked it, although their concern wasn't the same as mine and the kids'. They said Funk was playing with fire by stating he was for common folk, because what would the movers and shakers think? Now it was my turn to sit in stunned silence. Here we were with the movers and shakers again.

A tumultuous discussion ensued, in the midst of which I turned to Ruth, covertly rolled my eyes, and said under my breath, "We're never gonna get out of here tonight."

Ruth responded by pulling me across the arm of her chair to whisper in my ear, "You can't put Mark's face on the yard sign."

I had been half kidding with what I'd just told her, but she responded without her usual smile, so I asked, "Why not?"

"It's racist."

Never in a million years did I expect her to say that, and it would have taken a million more for me to understand how having Funk's face on his yard sign could signify that. Ruth and I were not close friends, but we'd known one another for over a decade. And since she was a person of color, I tried hard to grasp what she meant.

"What do you mean, Ruth?"

"I already said. It's racist."

"I don't understand. How can a yard sign be racist?"

"Not the sign. Putting his white mug on it is racist."

We had never openly acknowledged that our skin tones were different and so, ever so slightly uncomfortable with the topic, I walked into the forest with her.

"What about the drawing could be taken as racist?"

"The only reason Mark wants his face on there is to let everyone know that he's the white candidate and Alvin Brooks is the black one," she responded as if Funk had been caught out.

"Jesus, Ruth, that's not true! And the drawing was my idea, not Funk's. He hates it, by the way, though he understands my reasoning."

"It doesn't matter whose idea it was. It's still racist," she said, crossing her arms over her chest.

Seeing that she was serious, I said, "C'mon, Ruthie, it's me! I thought the combination might spark in people's minds that Funk is the former city auditor — more than just his name would."

"Mm-hmm," she said, in a disbelieving tone, scrunching down in her seat.

I preferred talking things through, even when it was difficult. I found it upsetting that she didn't believe me. But I didn't say that. What I said was, "Besides, everyone running is white except for Brooks, and there are twelve candidates.

"So?"

"So . . . the race isn't just between Brooks and Funk."

I got another "mm-hmm," so I leaned back to see if she was kidding. Surely, she was kidding. But no, her face was closed, an expression I'd never seen on her before.

That made me nervous on many levels.

The committee was still in heavy discussion about Funk's slogan, and I needed to pay attention. But I couldn't. This topic trumped that need.

Gently, I tried explaining myself again, "Ruth, voters might not remember that 'Funkhouser' is the name of the former city auditor, but if they see his face next to his name, I'm hoping they'll put two and two together. Funk doesn't have money like the other candidates do, so we have to use whatever assets are at our disposal."

"Uh-uh," she said, still with that clouded face.

Thinking I finally understood what was happening, I grabbed her arm and shook it playfully, sticking my face close to hers, "Oh my God, Ruthie, are you messing with me like you do with that neighbor of yours?"

"What neighbor?" she said, coming back to life a little.

"You know, the lady you go running with. The one you told me you love keeping in tears. The one you tell that everything she says is latent racism, just to get her reaction?"

"No. I'm serious with this," she said.

"Christ, Ruth. I wouldn't lie to you, especially not about something this important."

"You would if you were covering for your husband."

"Covering for my husband!" I gasped.

"I know why his face is there, and so will everyone else," Ruth continued. "You better take it off. Your husband can't win without the black vote."

I'd been hearing a variation on that theme a lot. My husband couldn't win without this group or that one. Couldn't win without the folks who lived up north — the farthest you could get from the black part of town. Couldn't win without the Ward Parkway Corridor — the richest section of the urban core. Couldn't win without the Hispanics — and how very smart of your husband to put his headquarters where he did. It was crazy, but it didn't seem like anyone on Funk's team, except for Joe, understood that Funk was going to win. And when my husband did, it'd be for one reason only: his eighteen years of standing up for the common person. End of story. I'd placed his headquarters in the West Side because the trailer was the cheapest rental I could find. That it was in the Hispanic part of town was a stroke of luck, not genius. But now that I thought about it, why would anyone consider that move ingenious? Like, percentage-wise, how many voters did Hispanics amount to? There weren't enough to make or break Funk, and the same went for the black populace. I was no brain, but this election wasn't going to be called on color; it'd be called on class — the working class. To me, the problems in Kansas City had more to do with economic injustices than with racial injustices.

The conversation with Ruth was beyond troublesome, but it was time to set it aside.

"Ruth, I really want to understand, but we've gone round and round with this and I need to pay attention to the discussion again."

I'd had my ear half-turned to the group while I was talking with her. With a playful smile I added, "Honestly, Ruth, have you heard some of the slogans this group has been tossing around? 'Short-term deals instead of long-term solutions'? 'We can't afford *not* to elect him'? 'He just adds up'?" With an exaggerated sigh, I whispered, "Gag me, why don't you? Funk's slogan sucks, but those are worse!"

Ruth nodded in agreement and chilled out. Just like that. Even gave me that beautiful smile of hers, which made me feel relieved.

"How about we talk more tomorrow?" I asked.

"No, I'm good," she answered.

Such was a day in the life of a campaign. Issues arose out of nowhere, and we had to stamp out those fires at once. Being part of this experience was enough to give you a headache. The campaign wasn't like running a business, because it involved working with friends like Ruth and Gwen or with supporters who were fast becoming friends. And that made the situation harder to manage.

Over the course of the next few days, Ruth and I spoke more about her concern with Funk's yard sign. Ruth said the problem harkened to what white real estate agents did. Having a white person's photograph on a For Sale sign was code that a neighborhood was white — in other words, safe from black people. I'm white, and I hadn't known that.

Ruth could've explained the concept a hundred more times and I still wouldn't have gotten it. My definition of a racist was a person who not only hated someone but also wanted them dead, and only because of the country they originated from. Besides, it seemed as if racists *wanted* people to know where they stood, because they were damn proud of it.

Because Ruth was on Funk's committee, I had to look at the situation from her point of view. I didn't do this because I feared Funk would lose. It was just that I didn't want to hurt anyone's feelings. My husband's campaign was a trumpet blare to lead the oppressed away from oppressors. To my way of thinking, the oppressed weren't limited to people of color. Plenty of whites had been held down, their tax dollars going to make a few wealthy people wealthier instead of toward educating our children. But I didn't think it would go over well if I told Ruth I thought the city's problems had more to do with economics than with social issues, because I was fairly sure she'd feel it was only her kind who were being tromped on. If I were a black person, I'd probably have felt the same way.

Since I came from an Italian family, I heard stories about the discrimination my parents endured in New York City in the 1920s. It made me mad to think about. But white oppression or black oppression aside, keeping Funk's face on the yard sign didn't seem worth the risk of offending the people he was trying to serve. And so, much to the tsk-tsking of Funk's committee, we kept Funk's weird-ass slogan and we dropped the picture of his face from the sign.

Two things about this issue were noteworthy. First, when Funk had a strong feeling about something, he was usually right. His slogan caught on like wildfire. Second, when Ruth said something was racist, you'd better watch out.

21 DECEMBER 2006

I COULD HEAR MY LITTLE CABIN in the Ozark Mountains crying for me. Our family had been going there for a long weekend every month ever since we'd bought the place in 2000. I wished we could take just one weekend off from the campaign and catch our breath there. But you know what they say, wish in one hand and shit in the other and guess what you'll be holding?

The committee had decided to meet one last time before the holidays. Before I could leave for the meeting, I had to race from the trailer to Meiners to collect more petition signatures. They were due by the end of the year or Funk couldn't stay in the mayoral race. None of the volunteers wanted any part of this during the holidays, so it was one more job that had fallen to me and the kids. Today, it would be just me standing outside Meiners like a beggar. Oh well, I was pretty good at it. I collected twice as many signatures as my kids did, but that was only because they were shy about approaching strangers. Actually, I was too. But I was more horrified at the thought of standing out there a million more times. It was better to be bold and get it over with already.

I was on a roll, collecting names, when I had to take back my clipboards to dash to the meeting on time. I could've put the matter to rest if I'd had another hour or two, and I was tempted to take them, but I wasn't in the mood to get more disapproving looks from Funk's committee for my tardiness.

Pulling up to Evert's place was always disconcerting. His building had been a college dormitory before real estate developers converted it to condos. They took a gorgeous old brick building and added a few more stories to the top. They went mod with the new floors, which featured yellow siding incongruous with the period of the structure. The building had the vibe of two-tone patent leather shoes — just not right. It was Brookside's version of hip and cool, which, let me tell you, was not San Francisco.

The community room's décor targeted the tastes of the nouveau riche. The developers had ripped out the charm and replaced it with fake features. The place was supersized, just like the McMansions over in Johnson County, Kansas, yet for some reason I felt squished inside. At the end of each meeting I said something complimentary to Evert about his digs, just to see his face glow with pride. It was a lie, but in my world, that was okay. Joy begets joy, you know.

Jeff Simon opened the gathering with another discussion about Funk's slogan, "A City That Works for Regular Folks." Most of the committee hated it. What floored me was how intensely they seemed to hate that it took a stand for "regular folks." Everyone on Funk's team was a "good Democrat," all for serving the underserved. They just didn't want Funk saying it out loud. Why risk offending the folks who *really* counted?

Next on Jeff's agenda was listing Funk's strengths and weaknesses. The group spoke mostly of his weaknesses and the ways in which those weaknesses would impede his electability. And with his wife sitting in the room!

I agreed that Funk could come off as dour and we needed to soften his image. That said, I also knew that trait drew his base to him. They liked that he was a hard-ass, that he went to the mat with the enemy.

As for Funk's other perceived weaknesses, boy, did they ever get my back up with what they said next: "He's deaf in one ear." I wanted to ask if they could name a time he hadn't heard them but I didn't get a chance because, just like that, they moved on to his next flaw. I had to listen to *them* drone on and on about how verbose Funk was. Yes, Funk could be kill-me-now wordy sometimes, but I think what really bothered them was that he spoke in simple words. Maybe they viewed that as a low-class trait, a perspective I found annoying because Funk was probably the only person in the room with a PhD. Well, the dentist had an advanced degree, but you know what I mean.

I viewed Funk's skill at plain talk as a gift. He could break down complex ideas and put them into terms that were easy to understand. Dozens of times I'd sat in some hotel ballroom where Funk was giving a keynote speech and noticed that the audience was captivated by him. Like, not another sound came from the room except for the tinkling of a spoon against the edge of a coffee cup. The first time I saw him in action, the audience's response shocked me. There I was, bored out of my mind, yet the crowd couldn't get enough of him.

Just as I was mustering the courage to speak up, the committee skipped to yet another perceived weakness: "Funk is anti-growth." What a load of crap! Funk knew he had to heave Kansas City into this century to bring it back from the dead. He had a plan for doing it, too. The city had to increase its tax base to provide the basic services its services citizens expected, such as cops, quality education, and roads that weren't paved with metal plates. The way to grow a tax base was to encourage people to live and work downtown again, because where people go, grocery stores, dry cleaners, schools, and transit follow. It would create a snowball effect. Businesses would produce tax revenue, and tax revenue would fund the services citizens longed for. Once the city was repopulated, the arts would follow. Kansas City would become a place people wanted to call home again.

Funk said this sort of natural progression was sustainable. The *only* growth Funk opposed was the way the movers and shakers had gone about their so-called renaissance. He said it was absurd to rid the city of its local flavor — the niche for which it was known around the world. He believed that tearing down established, homegrown businesses such as Lil' Jake's Eat It & Beat It BBQ, and Harold Penner, Man of Fashion, only to replace them with chain stores, bordered on corruption.

A gigantic, city council–approved tax giveaway, TIF, had funded the renewal of the city's Power and Light district, creating an area downtown that resembled a Disneyland theme park. The developer put in a couple of bars, a bowling alley, and a few restaurants. Funk's audit had revealed that the developers had falsely portrayed the benefits of the project in order to get citizens to sign on to the idea. If you did the math, the money P&L was supposedly going to bring in just didn't add up. The project had been designed to line the developer's pockets at the expense of citizens, and so Funk had tried to block it. It was one of the few fights he had lost as the city auditor and was one reason he was running for mayor. Funk simply wanted to grow the city with an approach that would stand the test of time. Power and Light sounded sexy, he said, but if there had been a true need for it, developers would have invested without relying on the city's money.

I had to admit, Funk's vision for revitalization sounded mighty beige. I much preferred Mayor Barnes's build-build-build mentality to Funk's blah-blah-blah approach. I mean, which sounded like more fun, Barnes's glitzy new downtown or Funk's working sewers and more cops walking the beat? Funk's approach was like a homeowner taking out a second mortgage to bring the plumbing and electric up to code, versus getting a new kitchen. Give me the kitchen!

When I allowed for a wider view, though, I thought it was smart that Funk wanted to use the city's inherent strengths to make the comeback. I just wish he had unveiled some of the fun things he was planning for, as those things would give people hope. But my husband wasn't into starry-eyed promises.

This was one item on Funk's plan to grow the city, in a nutshell: Kansas City was located in the center of the country. Because it was the second-largest rail hub in the United States, he was going to market it to shippers around the world as a better export option than the jammed-up port of Los Angeles, California. By utilizing the railroad tracks that ran from Kansas City to an underused port in Mexico, shippers could bypass California and cut days off their shipping times. That equated to more profit for them and a bucket-load of untapped money for Kansas City. Just as the cattle boom had brought prosperity to the city in the twentieth century, Funk was planning to capitalize on the city's strengths.

Were his ideas sensual and fun, like new bars and a bowling alley? Nope. But they were a viable means of steering the city away from financial disaster and of slowly rejuvenating it. I saw Funk's point, but his committee didn't. They seemed to view Funk's candidacy as a game — though it was no game to my family. When Funk won, he'd not only inherit the astronomical city debt that Mayor Barnes had left behind, but he'd also have to shore up the city's finances during a recession he knew was coming. That'd be a ball of fun. Citizens wanted the purse strings tightened, but who actually liked it when that happened? Oh, shit. Maybe Andrew was right. Maybe Funk *would* be busier after he won.

By the time I'd worked through those thoughts, the committee had moved on to the next fault: "Funk doesn't work the room." True. But how would doing that help when voters were seeking non-politicians? Then, "He has no political machine." Uh, hello, that was the hugest reason why voters *would* elect him mayor.

I didn't know how Funk could take all the criticism. His committee hadn't said one nice thing about him. The negativity didn't seem to bother him, but it made me cranky. It's why I hadn't countered with anything. When my feelings are hurt, I come across as angry. I wished I could be more like him, confident down to his very core. When he knew something, he didn't need anyone to agree with him.

The litany of Funk's weaknesses finally ended. But really, what more could they have said other than Funk was still living and breathing? Joe took the opening to stick his unconfident toe in the water. I blanched when he mentioned the yard signs, as I didn't feel like having another discussion about race, but Joe's problem was only about the color of the sign. He said red, white, and blue was just too conventional for this unconventional candidate. He wanted to change the color to orange, to mimic the Orange Revolution that had taken place in the Ukraine, where the citizens had fought to gain back control of their government. Joe said Funk was trying to do the same thing in Kansas City, on a smaller scale.

I'd never heard of the Orange Revolution, but I could tell Funk was considering the idea as he rubbed his beard and gnawed on his thumb. He finally came up for air with a grin and told the group he liked the idea. Joe was visibly relieved, and I was happy for him, even if I was waiting for everyone else in the room to shit a brick over it. But to my surprise they were just as pleased with Joe's inspiration as Funk. Go figure.

I couldn't imagine orange being Funk's color. That said, I hated the traditional color scheme we had been using. Unlike Joe, I hadn't been able to come up with a color I liked more. I take that back. I did. But Funk would've never gone along with pink. Color aside, I liked the symbolism Joe had suggested. Once again, his ideas were the best in the room.

The meeting adjourned after ten p.m., and the group exited together into the brisk night air. I walked arm in arm with Ruth, talking and laughing the whole way to her car about penises, of all things. I don't remember whose we were discussing. All I know is that when we realized Dan Ryan was eavesdropping, we laughed even harder. I said goodnight and headed for my van.

I had my car key out the way I always do — just in case some rapist snuck up behind me and I had to poke his eyes out to get away — and was fumbling with the lock when I sensed a person behind me. I spun around. Seeing it was only Joe, I blurted out, "Jesus, you scared the shit out of me!"

"I'm sorry," he said, looking uncomfortable.

"Why are you still here?"

"I wanted to ask you something. Away from the others."

"What's up?" I said, the warmth of my car beckoning me inside.

"Can I come to your house on Christmas?"

That was so not what I was expecting to hear that I burst out laughing. I always did that whenever people were in pain. It was a really bad habit.

He turned bashful, so I quieted my laughter and said, "Of course you can come for Christmas, Joe. We'd love to have you!"

Man was I ever racking up lies with this campaign.

My family was known for taking in strays during the holidays, but not at Christmas. That was the one day we preferred that dinner be just the four of us. Yet how could I refuse an outright request like this? I asked about his girlfriend. "What about Allie?"

"She's going home to be with her parents, and I don't want to be alone."

I told Joe I'd let him know what time he should arrive on Christmas.

Minutes later I was climbing up the steps of my front porch, feeling surprisingly unspent. Spring, my acupuncturist, had been right: our trip to Europe did wonders for my health. I had an energy reserve that I'd never experienced before.

As soon as I opened the door I saw my son in his typical pose, sprawled out in the living room, so I gave him my usual exuberant greeting. "Hey, Ange!"

I got back a grim "You're late."

Even as the knife he had thrown so fiercely at my heart still quivered, I managed to say, "I'm sorry, Ange."

He inserted a footnote. "Again."

"I know, Andrew. I'm really sorry!"

Trying to infuse some joy into the little time we had together, I tried changing the subject.

"So, babe, what did you do after I brought you home from school?"

"You mean dumped me off?"

"Jesus, Andrew, I said I was sorry! And I told you I'd stop helping Dad if you want me to."

"I don't want you here."

"Uhhhh! Ange, c'mon!"

"Why are you helping him? You never helped at the city auditor's office."

"Why would I have helped him there?"

"I don't know, Mom, you tell me. You will anyway."

"Andrew, I've helped Dad with a million things. Christ, I practically wrote his dissertation for him."

"Mom, all you did was call cities for him."

"Yeah, but there were hundreds and hundreds of them."

"There were two, Mom. Two hundred. You're always exaggerating."

I responded with one of those typical refrains that families invent, even if no one remembers how they came into existence, "Playfully, Ange, playfully," and then "I love you." After which I paused for a second or two before adding "That's an exaggeration too, Ange."

"You're not funny, Mom."

"Yes, I am, Andrew, and I can see you trying to hide your smile."

He didn't say another thing, lest his smile broke through.

"You know I'll toss Dad aside for you in a heartbeat."

"I don't want to talk."

"Oh Lord."

And that was the end of it. My son wouldn't say anything more. Just sat staring at the TV, so I set my purse on the bench and sat next to him, but not too next, because I knew he'd jump up and go upstairs.

But I did I risk a little nudge, "Andrew?"

"I said I don't want to talk."

"Joe just asked if he could come for Christmas. I said yes, but I shouldn't have, not without asking you first. I'm sorry. What do you want me to do?"

"It's fine. I like Joe. But you better ask Tara because I don't think she likes him."

I stayed with my son until he went upstairs to bed. Then I locked the doors, turned off lights, and checked to make sure the gas stoves were off before blessedly sinking into bed to read for a few minutes.

Soon, Funk soon came upstairs, and I put my book aside so I could get the committee meeting off my chest. But when I started whining about how the group had been dissing him, Funk told me to get over it. Of course, he didn't say precisely that — he hadn't completely lost his mind — but he did start lecturing me about the way it is, being in the limelight, and how I should expect more negative talk like that in the future. He added that the talk would be about the two of us, not just him. I said that was the most ignorant reply he'd given me in his entire sorry-assed life and asked why I'd be included when this was his deal, not mine. He just stared at me as if my IQ had just dropped to seventy. Seeing that he was serious, my throat closed up and I couldn't talk, yet he acted like me choking to death right in front of him wasn't that big a deal. He just kept on, in professor mode.

"Gloria, of course you're going to be thrust into the limelight. And of course it won't be all roses. It'll be fifty-fifty. Some people will agree with us and others won't. We think outside the box. If everyone saw things the way we do, you wouldn't be seen as a renegade in the birthing industry — and citizens wouldn't be excited that I'm running for mayor."

I shivered with disgust.

Funk *always* responded to the literal instead of the emotional. What the hell was wrong with him? He had been just as cruel when our children were little. In response to my tears he'd said, "Gloria, of course your mother doesn't compliment your parenting style, nor would you want her to. If she thought you were doing a good job, that would mean you were raising our kids the way you were raised — and you didn't like the way you were raised."

When my mind began spinning out I needed a confidence boost from my husband, not a sermon. If Funk couldn't comfort me, where did that leave me? I'll tell you where: all alone, struggling in that black sea of muck.

22 DECEMBER 2006

I WOKE UP FEELING EATEN ALIVE BY GUILT.

It took everything in me not to roll toward Funk and scream, "Fuck you and your stupid-ass dream!" And I would've been right to say that too — well, not the 'fuck you' part — because what kind of a dream was this anyway? Thank God, I acted like an adult for once and decided to buy Andrew a puppy for Christmas instead.

Ginny-dog was going on twenty years old. And even though Andrew loved her, Ginny wasn't his favorite dog. My sister killed his favorite dog. At least that's what Andrew says. Akina had gotten herself run over a few years earlier. When word came from the vet of her passing, Andrew and I were the only ones at home. We went out into the freezing-cold night and dug her grave. Her new home was just under the bump-out of our dining room, sheltered from the elements.

Oddly enough, the vet had placed Akina's body in a box and stuck her in a freezer. I can't tell you how weird it was to take my son's Shiba Inu from that box and have the dog remain curled up as if she was just taking a little snooze under a tree on a sunny summer afternoon. Seeing her frozen form, my son screamed, "What the fuck!" I had no idea how to reply because the situation was indeed fucked up.

I tried to distract Andrew with a science project.

I brought Ginny-dog outside and put Akina under her nose, just to see if she'd go mad from seeing the animal she considered her offspring lying dead in my hands. But she just sniffed the balled-up mess with indifference.

The diversion had calmed Andrew. We wrapped Akina in a piece of silk that Funk had received as a gift and set her shrouded body gently in the grave. After reciting a few prayers, we threw rose petals on top of her and sealed her in with handfuls of dirt. At which time I wiped my hands, finished with the chore.

My son cried all night. Which meant, I was up all night too.

Andrew rarely showed affection, but it was there just the same. Like me, the kid felt things deeply, but unlike me, he wouldn't let his feelings out. Our dog Akina was just like him. She was always in your face demanding love, yet the minute you started giving her any she turned aloof. Reading between dog-lines, I think she was embarrassed to appear needy. That was probably why she pulled back when you went to pet her, to make it seem as if you were the one who had come to her for love.

It took Andrew a long time to stop grieving Akina, but ever since then he'd been after me to get him a puppy. I always replied, "No fucking way." Yet here I was, about to give him the best Christmas present of his life, if only to assuage my guilt over leaving him alone so often.

Good God, what kind of animal was I becoming?

I didn't believe in daycare for babies, yet I was about to lower my standards by looking for Akina's replacement on the internet. The holidays being hours away, work at the campaign had finally slowed, so I had an unencumbered window of time to devote to finding my son's gift. After ringing up a few breeders, I set up a time to visit the best puppy I could find that wasn't already claimed to go under some other guilt-ridden mother's Christmas tree. The breeder lived fifty miles away. Since it was snowing like mad, I made Funk and

Tara accompany me to the rendezvous point — the parking lot of a concession area, just beyond the tollbooth in Lawrence, Kansas.

I felt as if I was commencing a drug deal, climbing into the back of the breeder's utility van. But the feeling left as soon as Tara began oohing and aahing over the miniature poodles surrounding her. I like animals too. I just don't like them inside my home. The thought of adding another member to our family, a smelly creature that would be at my feet for the next fifteen years, had me groaning — not moaning in pleasure like Tara.

Of course Tara chose the littlest one, even though the lady told her the puppy was so fragile that if Tara dropped it by accident all its legs would break. I didn't know if the woman said that because she was a nut-case dog-lover like my daughter or if she noticed the guilt written all over my face and decided that now was the perfect time to rid her litter of the runt. But no matter, Tara wanted the cutest puppy, and I went into purchasing-my-children's-happiness mode.

Then the lady told my daughter the puppy would have a better chance of surviving if it had a companion. I thought Tara's face would explode in joy when the greedy bitch said that. And since Tara was just as gullible as her father, she reached for her second choice.

"Put it down, Tara," came Funk's quiet but firm command.

"But Daddy, you heard the lady — "

"Put it down."

As much as I hated the breeder for putting my family in this predicament, I kind of saw her point. I said, "Funk, perhaps it would be easier with two — "

Interrupting me, he said, "Gloria, Tara, let's go." He then turned to the breeder and bluntly asked, "How much?"

With relief in her eyes, she said, "For both, it'll be — "

"For one," came his sharp response.

"I would give you a discount if you took two."

"How much for one?"

Hope diminished, she answered, "Four hundred dollars."

Funk looked at me aghast. "Is that the price you agreed to?"

I gave him a look that said *pony up, buddy*. And he decided to stay married and peeled $400 from his wallet.

Exiting the woman's icy van, the four of us drove the fifty miles back to Kansas City. I dropped Funk at the double-wide. Tara, the puppy, and I headed home. I left them at the curb with instructions to my daughter to find a hiding place for the dog until Christmas morning and then I hightailed it over to the school to pick up Andrew, because I'd risk a speeding ticket rather than hear that kid complain one more time about me being late.

Home again, I snuck upstairs to my daughter's third-floor bedroom to see how she was faring with the puppy before heading back to the trailer to tie up a few bits of work. She was on the floor wrapping Christmas presents, her legs splayed apart, the poodle tucked inside her crotch. Seeing that, I wondered how many guys would like to trade places with that dog right about now, but I didn't mention it, because high emotion took over.

"Tara! What the hell are you doing?"

"What do you mean what am I doing? I'm wrapping presents for you."

"I meant, what are you doing with that dog?"

"You mean puppy?"

"Tara, it's a dog, you can't spoil her like that. She'll be hard enough for me to deal with, and right in the middle of the campaign. I don't need you making her into a bigger nightmare before you go back to college."

"Mama, she's a baby. You always say it's impossible to spoil a baby."

"Tara, don't be stupid! Put her in the kennel like the breeder said."

"If I do that, Andrew will hear her whining and your big surprise will be ruined."

"Stop toying with my emotions, Tara. You can't make this dog into a maniac just because you're in love with her.

"Every time I put her in there she whines. It'll be all right, Mama. Go back to the headquarters and finish up so we can have a nice holiday."

"Whatever. Are you still going to help me collect petition signatures later?"

"If you need me to."

"That would be good, because getting that over with will go a long way toward me, us, having a nice holiday. I'll honk for you at seven."

I rushed back to the trailer and ripped into my chores.

In walked Ruth.

I liked Ruth, but she wasn't coming by to help, only to chitchat, and I had no time for that. I sensed that Ruth would get her feelings out of whack if I ushered her to the door before she was ready to go. Not wanting trouble, I'd been putting my work aside and indulging her whenever she stopped in to talk. That normally took thirty minutes or so, but on this day, of all days, she stayed for a really long time. I berated myself as I finally drove home, my work unfinished. I should've never gone back to the office. I got nothing done. I wished so hard I had given that time to my kids.

23 DECEMBER 2006

THE DAMN PUPPY whined all night. I don't know how Andrew didn't hear it. Tara finally had to take it into bed just so she could get some sleep. In the morning, up in my daughter's room discussing the situation, we decided to surprise Andrew early.

I shouted down the steps for my son to come up to the third floor.

He shouted back from the living room in his moody teenage voice, "What do you want?"

"Andrew, just come up here. I have a surprise for you."

He groaned histrionically and stomped up the stairs, shouting halfway up, "I like it better when you're not home."

I responded with a playful, "Yeah, uh-huh Ange, sure you do," even though the bastard had almost ruined the moment.

Stepping only to the landing of the third floor, Andrew said again, "What do you want?"

Tara and I didn't say anything — she just held a box out to her brother.

"What's that?" he asked, a little interested.

"It's a surprise, Ange, from Mama and me, and Dad too."

"Is it a Christmas present?" he asked, looking confused.

"Yes," his sister and I both said in unison, brimming with anticipation and crazed smiles.

He responded, "You know I don't like opening presents early. I want to be surprised on Christmas, like I'm supposed to be."

I couldn't believe he was making us force a present on him. I was on the verge of getting grumpy when the box started moving, igniting Andrew's curiosity.

"What's in there?"

"You'll have to open it to find out, Ange," said my daughter cajolingly, practically dying of joy.

"I'm not opening that. It's a trick."

Tara intervened before things got messy. She opened the lid and lifted the puppy up slightly.

Trying to make sense of what appeared to be a stuffed animal, yet on some level knowing it was a living being, Andrew backed away.

Just then, the puppy made a little puppy sound and Andrew walked right up to the box.

"Is that real?" he asked, a little frightened.

The animal gently cradled in her hands, Tara set it inside her brother's waiting arms, telling him to be very careful, that the puppy was extremely delicate.

Andrew's whole body curled protectively around that dog, falling in love before the next beat of his heart. Yet instead of admitting that truth, he responded just the way our dead dog Akina would've, pretending he didn't already have a vise grip of love for this newest member of our family.

"Why'd you get me a dog — if you can call this thing a dog — right before I'm leaving for college?"

Yep. There it went.

Killed it.

Tara defused the situation by asking Andrew what he was going to call her.

"She looks Spanish. Her name is Maria."

25 DECEMBER 2006

ANDREW WAS UP AT DAWN because of his excitement over the puppy. And just like every morning since this kid was born, if Andrew was awake, then everyone else had to be awake too. Thus, we started Christmas at dawn that year. We all took our usual places downstairs. So began our long holiday ritual. Andrew's body curled around the puppy.

An hour into the morning, all was well. I'd hit the bull's-eye with the gifts I had asked Tara to purchase for me. Calling intermission, I heaved my tired body out of the recliner and went to the kitchen to whip up our crêpes. Three hours later — breakfast served and consumed, the gifts under the tree opened and admired — we cut the Christmas stockings down and moved the celebration upstairs, all of us piling on my bed with the stockings at our sides. Well, everyone's but mine. Santa always forgot that I lived there too.

Every year there is always that one present that I'm really excited about giving. Other than the dog, I was most excited about the one I'd placed at the bottom of Andrew's stocking. I had been waiting for months for him to open it.

It was a rare gift indeed.

Ever since Andrew had joined us on Earth, I'd been collecting penises for his Coming-of-Age Ritual. I'd found the current specimen at an Asian store few years earlier, when Tara and I were window-shopping in New York City. I never would've noticed it glistening inside the display window if it hadn't been for her. We were walking and talking when my daughter came to an abrupt halt and pointed at something, with the most scandalized expression on her face. When I turned to look, my jaw fell open as wide as hers.

Mother and daughter stayed glued to that window, gazing at hundreds of what were perhaps the most sexually detailed figurines ever made. When I wondered out loud whether the artist was reminiscing or he'd had real-life models to work from, my daughter said, "That's gross, Mama," so I shut up. For a little while. I couldn't keep my next thought inside my head.

"Tara, have you ever noticed how Asians usually come off so prim and proper, yet they make such graphic art? I mean, look at that thing, it's so — "

My daughter screamed, "Mama, enough!" so I really did shut up that time.

Now, finally, my son was about to pull the last present of the season from the stocking he'd had since birth. I could barely suppress my laughter thinking about him unwrapping that rock-hard, solid piece of glass. As soon as he pulled the wrapping off, it sparkled in the sunshine that poured through the window.

Andrew shouted in disappointment, "Oh my God, Mom, you got me another penis!"

"Not me, Ange. Santa."

My son threw it to the side.

I said, "Wait a minute, Ange. This doesn't look like the others. This one looks like a lollipop."

Andrew picked it up and started examining it.

"Taste it, why don't you? What flavor did Santa bring?"

A lover of candy, my son turned the figurine this way and that.

"C'mon, Ange, we don't have all day. Give it a lick already."

It was almost to his tongue when I couldn't contain myself any longer. Just fell over in a fit of laughter, ruining my own joke. Damn! I was so looking forward to telling my grandchildren about the time I caught their father sucking a penis. And not just any old penis, one with a hard-on.

To my hysterical joy, Andrew ripped the pretend-sucker away from his mouth, trying to be angry. But my kids love it when I laugh, and he was unable to hold back his merriment over mine.

Later that day, I was in the kitchen when I heard Joe ring the doorbell earlier than I'd told him to arrive. We had finished our family's private festivities, so it was okay with me. After rinsing bread dough off my hands, I welcomed him inside. And then I noticed my son's collection of penises lined up like little soldiers on the coffee table.

"What's all this?" Joe asked, unable to make sense of what he was seeing.

"Oh, it's just one of Andrew's many collections," I said and then shouted up the stairs for Andrew to come down and pick up his mess.

"He collects penises?"

"No. I collect them for him."

The look on Joe's face was what I had been after when I imagined Andrew licking the fake lollipop, which set me to laughing like a madwoman again. Seeing me trying to stop laughing made Joe start laughing. Turns out, Joe shared my sense of humor.

27 DECEMBER 2006

AN EMAIL ARRIVED TODAY:

> **From:** Someone on Funk's team
>
> **To:** Mr. Blankety-Blank
>
> **Subject:** Re: Contribution
>
> You should be hearing from Mark soon, but he says, according to the rules of the Missouri Ethics Commission, your contribution cannot remain anonymous and therefore he is returning your check to you.
>
> I cannot thank you enough for your moral support, and in the many other things you are doing for Mark. You are terrific.

That email made my entire day go wrong. Not because we were returning much-needed cash, but because there were people who wanted Funk to be mayor enough to write him a check yet were afraid to be seen backing their choice for mayor. The long-term ramifications of that scared me. What the hell was our family getting ourselves into?

I started obsessing about how Mr. Blankety-Blank was a grown-ass man with a high profile in the community. What kind of cowardly bullshit was that? And someone from Funk's campaign had replied to the man that he was "terrific." *Terrific*? I was the biggest chickenshit alive, yet I'd never pretend to be something I'm not.

How do people get away with this?

If I behaved like Mr. Blankety-Blank, all hell would break loose from above.

In a snap of a finger — bam! — I'd be punished by the universe. Why isn't this happening to everybody else? Like, people from above, please single me out for the lottery, why don't you!

28 DECEMBER 2006
My sister Jane's birthday

I OPENED MY INBOX to find that twenty-six requests for buttons and just as many for yard signs had come in overnight. Everyone wanted the items delivered. The buttons were cheap but they were a hot commodity, and I couldn't keep them in stock. Overriding that concern, though, Funk still hadn't brought in enough donations for us to have yard signs made.

What was I supposed to tell these people? It didn't seem like a good idea to go public with our budget constraints.

The next day Dottie stepped inside my office with the biggest smile on her face, the local newspaper hugged to her chest.

"Have you read the paper today, Gloria?"

"Not really. What's in it this time?"

"You'll have to see for yourself."

I leaned back in my chair, my smile matching hers, because can you see what I was seeing? Dottie had gotten so bold! She was totally different from the woman who had sat beside me during our "Deep Throat" meeting.

I singsonged, "Is my Little Dotsie-Whotsie playing hard to get?"

"Gloria! Please don't let anyone hear you call me that!" she screeched, letting her delighted laugh escape.

I took the newspaper from her outstretched hand. She had folded it in such a way that it displayed a column by *The Kansas City Star*'s editorial writer, Yael Abouhalkah, predicting that Funk would be the city's next mayor.

"Oh my God! Holy shit, Dottie, this is big!"

"I thought you'd like that," Dottie said over her shoulder as she ran back to her desk to pick up the ringing phone. I marveled at her ability to run, because the room suddenly felt holy and I was unable to move. I remained planted in the chair and read the article again and again.

I'd never met Yael, but Funk had talked about him so often that I felt as though I knew the man. The two of them had a close working relationship, which is why my husband had me add his name to our Christmas newsletter roster way back when. Over the years I'd often heard Funk tell someone that Yael had saved his job. That grace came by way of a column titled "Waves at City Hall," its first few words being "Good job, Mark Funkhouser." The *Star* published the column shortly after our family moved from Nashville to Kansas City. To be more precise, it was published soon after Funk, the newly installed city auditor, had not only reviewed the city's budget — a budget that had never been eyeballed by an objective third party before — but had been crazy enough to release the findings publicly.

The report was typical Funk-the-auditor stuff: an honest analysis of the city's financial status — or, should I say, of the city council's highly fudged budget. The ripple effect was that the council wanted off with the auditor's head. Mind you, this was the same city council who had hired him because he was a nationally recognized go-get-'em auditor.

The scuttlebutt around city hall — that Funk would be fired — died on the vine when Yael's editorial piece went to press. Ever since then, Yael had Funk's back. The pair hashed through the city's problems over lunch. Funk had lunch with journalists, and with concerned citizens as well, but those associations were not quite the same as the mutual admiration society to which he and Yael subscribed. I believe their fondness for one another derived from the fact that they shared an uncommon commonality: they really got on the nerves of people in high places because they pointed to problems administrators had previously swept under the rug. Both men believed that problems, unaddressed, only became greater problems. That the practical solutions were also usually ethical solutions. They said the only way to deal with social injustices was to own up to the facts and get beyond "happy talk." People had a moral imperative to address injustices, even ones that didn't impact them directly.

Turns out, those hours that Funk had spent lunching with Yael had paid off big-time. So why was I sitting inside my dilapidated office biting my nails over the good news? Searching for the answer, I realized that what gave me pause was that I'd always believed newsmen were supposed to be impartial. If I was unnerved by this turn of events, imagine what the other candidates must be feeling. Man, if I were in their shoes, I'd be raging to the gods about the unfairness of it.

Ultimately, I decided to stick to the good thoughts — wasn't it about time Funk was rewarded for having been a Goody Two-shoes for all those years? The other candidates would just have to suck it up. It wasn't as if they'd have to clench their butt cheeks too tight. Most had endless pots of money on offer by the establishment, while we still couldn't afford to have the damn yard signs printed. But with free advertising like this, who needed the establishment? Thank you, Mr. Abouhalkah, for extolling my virtuous husband! Funk was now an absolute shoo-in.

As I sat there coming to terms with the news, I was simultaneously trying to identify the noise I registered in the back of my mind. It was the sound of the campaign's PayPal account *ka-chinging* away. Thank you again, Mr. Abouhalkah. Now I don't have to wory about paying the bills this week.

Any election messages sent out from the headquarters had to first come to me for final approval. Joe had probably instigated that practice, since he hated the way Britt phrased things. Now, if something wasn't classy enough or wasn't written in Funk's voice, instead of wringing my hands wondering how I could sweetly ask that the problem be resolved, I simply sent it back for corrections. Poof, just like that. No apology, even! I suddenly had a backbone. I didn't know where that came from. Either the New and Better Me had continued to advance or the campaign had created a bigger animal of me than I realized.

I did something else that topped that. I went home from work in the middle of the day to prepare for a fundraiser we were going to host at a venue called Knuckleheads a few weeks later. Slick was headlining, and in anticipation of the event I had decided I would learn how to dance as well as my daughter. I had hired a dance instructor to come to my house to teach me some moves.

In the middle of my very first lesson, through the doorway walked the kids. They were supposed to be on the Plaza watching a movie. You should've seen the looks on their faces when they opened the door to a house that was blasting Slick's *Juke House Blues*, the instructor and me moving to the beat! If I hadn't been so embarrassed, I would've died right there on the spot. As it was, I just ran to flick off the music, shouting at them to get their asses upstairs so I could finish my lesson in peace. It didn't help. I had to listen to peals of hysteria filtering down from Andrew's bedroom. Nothing blocked the sound except the slam of the front door as I raced back to the headquarters to finish the newsletter.

29 DECEMBER 2006

IN BED, at the end of another hellishly long day, Funk told me about a big decision he had made: he was going to trash the fundraising mandate from his committee. He and I had been referring to it as "Dialing for Dollars," which was code for him telephoning the elites, the movers and shakers, to beg donations.

That was enough information for me that night, but Funk continued, despite my glazed eyes. He said he was surprised so many people had accepted his phone calls, even if the outcome was fruitless. But what he said next about how they framed their refusal interested me, as it mirrored the message in Mr. Blankety-Blank's email.

From the other end of the phone line, Funk would receive a heartfelt, "I think you would be a good mayor — no, a really great mayor. The city won't turn around without someone like you leading the recovery. I'm voting for you, don't worry about that. I just can't make a public donation. Bye." *Click.* Dead-air dial tone in Funk's ear.

Funk said the establishment refused him because its members feared they would be ostracized for supporting a candidate who was not "in the club." I was so tired that I had to ask Funk to explain the concept a few times before I finally got it. Call me naïve, ignorant, idealistic, or apolitical — I'm likely all of it. Still, I couldn't wrap my head around the idea that some adults are afraid to show their peers what they're made of. How bad could it be to voice their support for the candidate they believed was going to save their beloved city? And what would be the consequences if they did? Like, is everyone in that privileged class wearing Salvatore Oxfords without socks? Once I get past the image of slimy feet resting in there, how boring would that be?

If they'd hung up on me like that, I would've cosmically told them to fuck themselves sideways. But Funk wouldn't give up on the elites. He said he was in the mayoral race for everyone, that he was just having better luck with private sit-down meetings than with phone calls. I'd been wondering what he did all day while I was slaving away at his headquarters.

"Gloria, once they meet me in person, they're sold on my candidacy."

To which, I responded, "So? What good does that do?"

"It will pay off in the voting booth."

"C'mon Funk, seriously? If those guys can't say what they think to their friends, what makes you think they're telling *you* the truth?"

At which time his bottom lip took a side trip to China, and he phoned me from there with his answer.

"Gloria, the elite couldn't care less what I think. They're only concerned what their own kind thinks of them. They'll follow through. And I need every vote I can get."

I was too tired to carry on, so all I said was, "Well, I guess we'll see about that." But Christ, can you imagine? After an eighteen-hour day, this is what I had to go to sleep thinking about? Slimy feet?

The Little Campaign That Could

IT WAS THE TWENTY-FIRST ANNIVERSARY of our New Year's Day party. Tara and I had been preparing for three days. We had all four burners going with big pots of chili and the sideboard was sitting pretty with the cakes we'd baked. Before we even sat down for morning coffee, we kneaded six loaves of Betty's Bread. They went in a steady production line in and out of the oven, filling the house with a delectable scent.

For the previous five years or so, I'd become nervous about hosting this party. It was just too long a sprint from Thanksgiving to this day. I continued the tradition because everyone, including our guests, didn't want me to stop — especially not my husband and son. But why would they? While I'd circuited the house at least fifty billion times, where had they been? Well, Mr. Feminist's big-ass feet hadn't left the coffee table except for the times he got up to piss out the two pots of coffee he'd ingested while making love to *The Kansas City Star*. And his son, Mr. Gender Equality? That kid hadn't left his bedroom except for the ninety thousand times he'd wandered into the kitchen to say he was hungry.

I'm telling you, there was nothing different going on inside my unconventional house that wasn't going on in conventional households across the country. Women were slaving away while the men sat back in comfort.

It wasn't as though just anyone could attend. If you were one of our favorites, you received our Christmas newsletter, which included the invitation to the open house. There were 375 people on our mailing list. Since I didn't require an RSVP, I never knew how much food to make, and something told me attendance would be up this time.

I was right. Twice as many people as usual showed up, and most stayed far longer than they normally do. It took a ton of energy to be *on* for that long. By the time I fell into bed, after midnight, I was fried beyond belief.

3 JANUARY 2007

TARA HAD RETURNED TO COLLEGE and Andrew had begun his last semester of high school, so can you guess who was minding the puppy? The person who didn't want one more soul to care for. The one who didn't like animals inside her home.

Whatever. I'd promised Tara that I'd look after Maria, Andrew's "baby." So there I was, standing in my driveway on my way to the trailer. My arms were loaded down with briefcase and purse, a basket of buttons, bumper stickers, donation envelopes, puppy food, a puppy toy, a Tara-scented t-shirt, a stack of old newspapers, and the whining puppy inside her kennel.

I came banging into the double-wide, balancing my bundles over the buckled-up carpet, heading for Dottie's desk. She relieved me of the kennel, took the scared-stiff puppy out, and placed her between her breasts, murmuring words of adoration in Maria's ear. I hadn't known Dottie was a dog-nutcase like my kids, so I left her and Maria to their lovefest and took the remaining bundles into my office.

Before I started on my work, I set up a second home for the dog. I designated one corner of my office for her to sleep and the other for paper training. Once everything was in place, Dottie brought the now-sleeping Maria into my office and snuggled her inside the open kennel beside Tara's t-shirt.

A few hours later Betty Lou came prancing into my office and made a beeline to Maria's den.

"Dottie said you brought the puppy in."

"Yes, but thank God, she's sleeping now."

She got on her knees, peeked inside the cage, and squealed, "She's sooo cute!"

"Not when you get to know her, she isn't. My daughter has made her into an animal. When that puppy is awake, she doesn't stop whining until she's in someone's lap."

"Of course she doesn't. She's just a baby, Gloria," she reprimanded me.

Oh, brother, I thought, *not another one.*

Easing Maria out of the kennel, Betty Lou said, "Let me take her to my desk. You've got enough to do."

"Have at it," I said, before remembering my manners, "and thank you, Betty Lou."

With Maria cradled in her ample bosom, Betty Lou walked back to the reception room, whereupon I heard more squeals of joy from other volunteers. I wondered what was wrong with me for not feeling the same. I was taking proper care of the puppy. I would have, even if I wasn't afraid that God, Tara, and Andrew would punish me if I didn't. But I would've preferred that I was nurturing Maria because I was a good person instead of just dutiful.

I was in the middle of beating myself up for that when a little square on my office phone lit up.

"Hey, Mama. How goes it with the baby?"

Weary, I said, "You mean Maria."

"Yes, Mama."

My daughter is the child in our relationship, yet she always makes me feel like I am.

"She's fine, Tara. You can relax. Everyone here is loving her up. But I can't talk. I've been dealing with the damn dog all morning and I have to get some work done."

"Okay, Mama, I'll let you go."

"No, wait! Are you okay?"

"I'm fine, Mama. I was just checking on the puppy. Don't worry."

"Okay. I'll try to call later. I love you."

"I love you too, Mama."

4 JANUARY 2007

A PRINTED COPY of the earned-media schedule sat on my desk. It outlined Joe's brilliant plan to publicize Funk's election campaign. He had presented it the previous night to the group I called the Inner Circle. The Inner Circle, culled from the large committee, were the people doing the work decided on in the large group. Well, not really. The Inner Circle mainly consisted of Britt and me working like dogs and Joe helping out where he could.

Reading through Joe's timetable, I felt a sense of relief. I felt more peaceful when things were organized, especially things that had many moving parts, like the campaign.

You could have knocked me out of my chair when the Inner Circle rubber-stamped Joe's plan. Thanks to Funk's "groupthink" way of doing things, it usually took the committee forever to arrive at decisions. But in an exceptionally short period of time the Inner Circle had coalesced into a working unit, despite the fact that we were an unlikely lot thrown into a pot together. We'd evolved as naturally as everything else in this campaign. Somehow, we had come to a clear division of labor that harnessed each person's strengths. The press releases had Britt's, Joe's, and my hands all over them. By the time you viewed the final draft, you couldn't tell who had written which part. I could hardly believe that little, nothing me was writing press releases. Well, not exactly writing them — I was mostly sticking Funk's weird little phrases in whenever I saw an opportunity and then editing the piece in his voice. But still, my name and "press release" were being used in the same sentence — *waaah!*

The press events worried me, though, because they were kind of out of my control. Each event had been assigned to a member of the large committee. What if someone didn't follow through? Ed took responsibility for several public works–related events, and I was certain he'd do a fine job. Jeff signed up for a public safety press event. Since he was on the Police Board, I was sure he'd come up with something that rocked. The problem was, I didn't know what the other committee members brought to the table, and I hated leaving something as significant as earned media to chance.

Oh well. I could continue worrying, but it wouldn't change anything. Since I was on a never-ending quest to evolve, I resolved to place my worries off to the side.

Here's a peek of our plan of attack: But shush, please don't tell anyone. I don't want the other candidates to steal our stuff.

PRESS RELEASES AND EVENTS

Overall theme: A City That Works. Emphasize Mark's accountability.

Dates and details

- January 5 — Commitment to Kansas City
- January 8 — Housing
- January 9 — Infrastructure, housing, transportation
- January 15 — TIF and incentive plan . . . propose a moratorium on all TIFs until the new council adopts a policy; city council is rushing to get a wave of TIF packages passed. . . . Call for self-restraint
- Housing plan
- January 29 — Openness/transparency thru citizen survey, town hall, talk-back, live call-in
- February 6 — Focused plan for downtown; press conference and then a walking tour
- February ? — Public safety
- February 19 — Economic development plan; attract and retain 50,000 residents over the next decade, the majority of whom live in the urban core

- Floater date — Schools plan; cooperate with and assist the school district, support accountable "parental choice"

I was bushed when I left the double-wide, so I asked my husband to stop at the supermarket for me. Good guy that he is, he readily agreed.

In the most serendipitous way, while Funk was walking into the store he collected the last petition signature we needed. A passing driver spotted Funk, rolled down his car window, and shouted to him, "Hold up!" The guy made a U-turn and signed the petition. It was one of maybe a dozen signatures Funk brought in, and it came from a guy named Clinton Adams. As I recall, Adams was on the city's school board and had gotten down on his hands and knees and barked like a dog when he didn't like what his white colleagues said about our mainly black public school district.

This was good news for the campaign, given Clinton is black, has a huge voice and isn't afraid of showing his support for Funk.

5 JANUARY 2007

OH LORD, THE NERVES!

Our second press event was scheduled to begin at the City Clerk's office, with Funk filing his petitions to run for mayor. He'd then make a short speech in the lobby highlighting his platform. The grand finale had him signing his name with a flourish to a posterboard that proclaimed his "Commitment to Kansas City." Joe and I were banking on all the news cameras rolling during that last part. The "flourish" part wasn't scripted. I hoped my husband would do it. Hey, you have to visualize the things you want in life, you know.

Joe didn't know that he should also hope that Funk doesn't get so overcome with emotion when reciting his oath of fealty that he dropped a tear over it. But I was praying like a madwoman that it wouldn't happen, because that would be so embarrassing, and right on TV!

As usual, we arrived way too early. Funk liked to be on time, but we couldn't execute the plan until the reporters arrived — *if* they arrived — because what would be the point? The extra minutes were killing Funk, giving him just enough time to work up a good sweat. He was so edgy that he was making me edgy. I wasn't anxious for him; I just couldn't stand seeing his bottom lip protruding so far into the world. As his dutiful wife, I was trying to be pleasant. Honestly, though, I didn't know why *he* was so nervous. Joe and I had done all the work. All Funk had to do was slip the petitions into the clerk's waiting hands, make his little speech, and sign the poster in blood.

Of course he denied that he was nervous, but I could tell he was. When I stepped off the elevator, Funk didn't give me his normal "Hey, beautiful" and nor did he bend down to give me a kiss. He scowled at me for picking a piece of lint off his suit and licking down a flyaway hair, so I left him standing alone and went to the ladies' room to make sure that nothing crude was hanging from any of my orifices. If he wanted the world to know that he was a hick with a PhD, so be it.

As I exited the restroom I suddenly felt sorry for him, so I went back to his side to offer comfort. At which time I told him to calm the fuck down and shoved him into a corner so he could get ahold of himself, ignoring his protests that I leave him be.

It was almost showtime. The media had finally arrived. They trained their cameras on Funk. My mouth had that saliva going, like when you're about to puke, yet Funk had somehow gotten himself all poised-looking. He turned the petitions in and walked to the lobby to give his little speech. And Jesus, if he didn't deliver it like a natural! It was heartfelt, confident and, thank God, not the least bit sappy:

In a city that works, elected officials hold themselves accountable to their constituents. . . . I will make it my top goal to increase satisfaction with city services . . . conduct the city's business in an open and honest manner. . . . make it a priority that city workers be well trained, well equipped, and competitively compensated . . . support an effective regional transportation system . . . establish a policy for economic development that is for the benefit of our city as a whole . . . be a cooperative partner with the . . . school district.

Halfway through, having heard the speech a million times before, a memory revisited me. When Funk had become the Kansas City Auditor, my father was visiting and congratulated him, and then asked Funk whether the new job put him in a position of taking bribes. My father's eyes rang with dollar signs when Funk said yes but quickly turned to darts of poison when Funk added that he'd never consider screwing the people he had been hired to serve. The aftermath of that conversation was tough: the two men remained incredulous with each other for years, each stewing over the other's obscene principles.

Right or wrong, my line of thinking was more in line with my dad's. Not that I'd accept a bribe. I'd die of guilt, not to mention that God would put me in the gutter in less than a heartbeat. But I didn't subscribe to doing everything by the book, the way Funk did. As long as I didn't hurt anyone, I didn't see anything wrong with scheming things into reality.

I came back from my reminiscence just as Funk began stating his vow, looking straight into the camera as if he were speaking directly to the people in Kansas City. As expected, he was so sincere that I had to keep myself from gagging. Thank God my father was dead, or I never would've heard the end of it. In my dad's world it was a no-no to work as hard as Funk had just promised to, for people who weren't family.

As Joe had predicted, the press event earned the campaign tons of free advertising. Watching it on TV later that night, I said a prayer of gratitude that the cameras didn't show Funk's bottom lip glistening with passion.

Turned out, Funk was the last candidate to turn in his petitions. If I had known ahead of time that he was filing on the last possible day, I would've shit a brick.

7 JANUARY 2007

JOE WAS A FRIGGING GENIUS. Each day the campaign got more and more free "earned-media" advertising. I was humbled to think that I had looked at him so dubiously the first time he showed up on my porch. Here are a few examples of the earned media that had come our way:

> Funkhouser put on an orange tie, saying, "I've chosen orange as my official campaign color because it is fast becoming a symbol for change in politics — a shift away from back-room deal-making and toward an open style of governance that respects and listens to citizens." He pointed out spending by Mayor Barnes's administration, saying, "We've been buying stuff, but what we don't know is whether what we bought is what is worth what we paid for it." And, hooray, citizens of Kansas City were getting to know their former city auditor as "The Funk."

8 JANUARY 2007

MY GOD, I was supposed to begin teaching my new birth class. I'd signed up the students light years before I realized I'd still be helping Funk with his campaign. I couldn't fathom how I was going to focus my mind on all those rightfully needy parents-to-be.

My students were a mixed bunch, ranging from conservatives who lived in the Northland district to Jehovah's Witnesses who lived down south to born-agains, mostly military people, who drove forty miles from Fort Leavenworth, Kansas, to attend my class.

Being a childbirth instructor wasn't easy. I poured all my energy into my students, just as I did with my children. It was the only way I could get them to understand that childbirth was safe, since the medical industry had brainwashed them into thinking it was the most dangerous thing women could do.

As I began making introductions at the first meeting, a bizarre thing happened. It echoed what had been happening on the streets of Kansas City. Funk dropped by the house to replenish his basket of buttons. The moment he stepped through the doorway, my students stared at him in utter astonishment.

In previous class sessions my students had recognized Funk, the city auditor, when he arrived at home with our kids and got them ready for bed. Normally, it was easy for me to regain their attention and resume the lesson. Not this time. Upon seeing Funk's six-foot-eight frame entering our door, they erupted with questions — and not about birth. Most said they'd already decided to vote for him, so that was good. The problem was, I could barely bring the discussion back to my lesson.

Prior to the campaign, it hadn't been uncommon for one of my former students — whom Funk referred to as "the fellowship of the womb" — to stop Funk and me on the street. They typically wanted to catch me up with their lives or tell me what a difference I'd made for their family. They hardly gave Funk a glance. To be polite, I'd have to gently interrupt the conversation to pull him in.

The opposite was happening now. Now, when my former students approached us, they only had time for my candidate-husband. Other than a nod hello to me, they couldn't pull their eyes away from him. I didn't miss their attention; the exchanges were just an extension of my work. But their behavior was hard to assimilate. People treated Funk like some sort of celebrity or, worse, as if he walked on water.

9 JANUARY 2007

REMEMBER HOW NERVOUS FUNK HAD BEEN before his "Commitment to Kansas City" press event? Well, I was just as nervous on the night of Funk's first public debate, at a high school gym way up north. I called the area no-man's-land because it was far removed from the urban core. It was the community where people lived if they wanted a Kansas City address yet wanted to be as far removed from blacks as they could get. And from Jews, too. And from Hispanics. And from anyone else who wasn't plain, old Anglo-white. The concept might be most easily explained if I just said the Northland was where the Republicans lived.

I worried about how Mr. Honesty would stack up against the seasoned candidates, quite a few of whom sat on the city council or had in the past. My husband's jobs had also been highly political, but a councilmember was an entirely different beast. Funk wasn't willing to distort the truth, a habit that was second nature for many of them. I feared they would run rings around my fiscally conservative, socially liberal hick. More precisely, I was afraid my husband was screwed.

His competitors had big money, and it showed. They had heaped their tables in the gym lobby to overflowing with campaign paraphernalia — water bottles, buttons and stickers, glossy brochures, and paper fans. Like, who uses a paper fan anymore? At each table, three or four volunteers greeted passersby with smiles as big as Vanna White's.

Guess what Funk's table held? Oogotz. A basket of buttons, a stack of donation envelopes, and a lonely little volunteer sign-up sheet. And no one was womaning the table but me. All I can say is that I hoped with all my heart that when attendees strolled past Funk's table they'd think, *My, my, this guy must really be popular! All his stuff is already gone!*

Funk's competitors had dozens of people milling about sporting their candidate's button — or three or four buttons. I suspected they had been summoned to the event to make it appear as if their candidate had tons of support. My guy's turnout? The Inner Circle had drawn straws to see which of us had to cover the night's event. I won — or lost, depending on how you looked at it.

Funk and I drove to the debate together, and the ride went surprisingly well. That was a victory all by itself, because we could just as easily have gotten into the hugest fight, me being reluctant to leave my son at home alone yet again. But the peace didn't last. Before I let Funk find his seat up on the dais, I went about my wifely duty of picking lint from his suit and checking to be sure no indescribable horrors hung from his nostrils. But he became just as edgy as he had on the day of his speech at city hall, so I let him go unexamined and went back to our table to see if anyone was taking up the paltry offerings. The buttons were completely gone. Those things were like collector's items, maybe because we had recently redesigned them. The new version sported a baby blue background and navy blue "Funk for Mayor" lettering sitting inside an orange star that appeared to be shooting across the button. They were pretty snazzy and definitely original.

Unfortunately, the donation envelopes weren't viewed as collector's items. My stack still had the same knife edge it had when I first set it down. A few people had written their names on the volunteer sign-up sheet — not that the campaign needed more. Funk's supporters loved being in the headquarters, but most of them didn't like going to events, which was why I was at the gym rather than at home with Ange. All the same, knowing that more people wanted to volunteer told me that support for Funk was growing.

A few of my former students wandered over to the table. Instead of telling me how big "my babies" had gotten or what their teenagers were up to, they talked about how excited they were that my husband was running. Soon I excused myself and I found a seat in the audience, sitting off to the side so Funk wouldn't see me and get off stride. Of course we had arrived fifty hours early, so there I sat, antsy and bored, growing more anxious by the second.

Right on time, a schoolmarm-type in high heels clomped across the stage in the most unwomanly way possible, pausing at the microphone the way an elementary teacher does to strike fear into the hearts of her students if they don't quiet down. Had she been auditioning for the title, she would've run away with being the next Mrs. Midwest. The woman had beige down to an art. To complement her mousy blond hair, she wore a cream-colored blouse buttoned to the neck and tucked inside a shapeless khaki skirt. Nude-colored stockings covering what little leg was showing. She was Kansas City to the core, right down to the repressed emotions that displayed themselves most unexpectedly. Taking the microphone out of its holster, she caressed it as if it were a lover and assumed a fearsome stance. Lord! Not one part of this lady went with the other. I felt as though I was viewing her through a kaleidoscope. I was scared. And you better believe I looked alert as she spoke from that fractured posture.

I straightened in my seat and listened intently as she recited the directions for the debate. I hadn't realized we needed directions. Just as I was thinking that, she dropped her hammer: the audience would receive scorecards so they could grade each candidate's performances, ranging from zero for those who sucked balls, up to five for those who resembled Christ on the cross. Hearing that the debate would be graded, my throat closed. I remembered the button-wearers I had witnessed in the lobby.

Being Italian and my father's daughter, I toyed with the idea of sneaking two handfuls of scorecards from the pile being passed down my aisle and filling them in with zeros for the other candidates and fives for mine. But I knew Funk would kill me if I did that, even when you could bet your ass the other campaign managers had instructed their plants to do exactly that. In this early stage of the active campaign, I didn't yet know who those other managers were. But I had eyes. I'd been watching scruffy-looking folks covered with stickers walk up to people wearing high-end suits, and you didn't need psychic abilities to understand what was going on there.

The schoolmarm said that because twelve candidates were running, each would not be called on to answer every question. To ensure enough topics were covered, each candidate's response was limited to two minutes. She then turned the event over to the moderator, *Kansas City Star* reporter Steve Kraske.

As it turned out, only Funk followed the two-minute rule. As the night dragged on, all of them — except Funk — got wordier. They droned on for twice their allotted time, their responses the typical political non-answer or a gross distortion of facts. Funk responded to each question honestly and in about thirty seconds.

After an hour of listening to the bullshit pouring from the mouths of his running mates I could see that Funk was beginning to get perturbed. It wasn't hard to notice. He perched at the edge of his chair and leaned forward, his elbows stabbing the tabletop, shaking his head over every response, blackness oozing from every extremity. He clearly hoped to be called on so he could refute what his opponents had just said. I tried catching his eye to tell him to knock it off, but the fucker wouldn't look my way. So I just sat there worrying that the people in the audience noticed his behavior too and were giving him big fat zeros for it.

Funk eventually calmed down without my help. Resigning himself to the situation, he leaned back and slouched low in his chair — and out popped his size-fifteen feet from beneath the dais skirt. I thought I'd shit myself right then and there. Now the whole world knew I was married to a hick. I sat in the audience fuming, wondering how in the world he could think it was okay to sit up there all droopy looking, a grimace plastered to his face, and expect to win the debate, not to mention the race.

The next question regarded Tax Increment Financing, a.k.a. TIF — the torment of my husband's soul when he was the city auditor. As mentioned earlier, TIF was designed to lift the economically disadvantaged areas of Kansas City out of poverty. The city council had instead used the TIF money as a political wand, dispersing funds to the wealthiest sections of town while much of the urban core remained boarded up. Countless times I had listened to Funk rant about how misusing those funds wouldn't produce a desirable outcome. He said that urban blight encouraged crime, which, left unchecked, would eventually find the people who had escaped to the Northland. To which I always responded, "Yes, I know, Funk, I fucking know. Still don't care."

I blanched when the moderator asked the panel, "Do you support the Briarcliff TIF?" Up to that point, he had asked conventional questions, such as "Will you get along with the city council?" and "Will you create jobs?" Every candidate, except for Funk, of course, had ardently proclaimed they'd be the first mayor to stand *with* the people and then exaggerated the times they had already done so. It had been a complete gag-fest. And then this technical question about TIF came out of left field.

No matter, around the dais we went. The candidates who were asked to respond were all in agreement that — yes! — the wealthy Northland, where *this* roomful of attendees just happened to reside and where *this* TIF was currently being considered, needed TIF money. They assured the audience that if they were elected to be the next mayor, they would vote the project in.

And then the question reached my candidate.

By this time, Funk was so appalled by the candidates' responses that he didn't realize he'd been called to answer. The whole audience sat in silence, waiting for his response. They got nothing. He just remained slumped in his chair, his big-ass feet still poking out, an even bigger grimace on his face. I was practically doing cartwheels in the aisle trying to get his attention. To get him to say something. Do something. Finally, the moderator asked him the question a second time.

With an emphasis on "mister," he said, "*Mr.* Funkhouser," *smirk, pause, pause, pause,* "do *you* support the Briarcliff TIF?"

Hearing his name blasted over the loudspeaker caught my husband's attention all right. I could see by the look on his face that never in a hundred million years had he expected to be called on to answer a question that was clearly in his wheelhouse. He shot out of his chair and squealed with the passion of a teenage girl in love with her first crush, "*Me?* You're asking *me* if I support the Briarcliff TIF? Hell, no, I don't support it!" after which he sat back down in a huff.

In all honestly, if I were the type to get backed up, I would have shit myself right there in the middle of the auditorium in front of everyone. Like, my ass would have just exploded. All this frigging work, and my husband had just blown it, lost the election, just like that. Tunnel vision pinpricked my view, and I blasted out of my body and splashed into the black sea of muck. There I stayed, drowning . . . until I heard the round of applause.

The *first* applause of the evening. As it turned out, the other candidates said what they thought the Northlanders wanted to hear, but their answers had fallen on the wrong side of the fence.

Despite that unexpected pleasantry, Funk was on my nerves. During the whole drive home I sat in his uncomfortable Corolla and critiqued his debate performance. He had sort of asked me to.

With a self-satisfied look, he asked a question that wasn't really a question, just him looking for strokes — as if his head needed to be any bigger.

"How'd I do, babe?"

"*Me?* You're asking *me?*" I shouted, mimicking his outburst in the high school auditorium.

He wasn't expecting my wrath, so his bottom lip took an express jet to Hawaii.

"You fucking sucked, Funk, that's how you did. You just lost the election. Lost before you even got started."

"Gloria —"

"All that work, down the fucking drain!"

"Gloria —"

"And the time! Think of the time I've wasted!"

"Glor, calm —"

"You sat there like a moody teenager, looking bored and pissed off. When you weren't doing that, you gave patronizing answers, as if it was your job to keep those ridiculous children in check."

"Children?"

"You know what I mean. The councilmembers. Your opponents."

"Gloria —"

"Do you realize you were slouched so low in your chair that your fucking feet were sticking out from under the table?"

He let out a big breath of incredibly stale air and waited for me to finish.

"Are you nuts? Everyone got a good look at your shoes. Shoes that I *told* you to have polished for the occasion! Jesus, Funk, really? Who the hell is going to elect a hick to the office of mayor? Not even fucking beige people would do that!"

"Gloria —"

"Would you stop saying my name?"

My husband knows that when I'm cursing like a banshee it has more to do with me being nervous than upset with him, so he shrugged off my tirade.

"Babe, what I meant was, how did I do with my responses?"

"I already told you, your answers were condescending, and when they weren't, they were filled with passion over nothing. The other candidates spoke breathlessly about shiny new buildings, and you talked fervently about *sewers*!"

"Gloria, the audience nodded when I said the city council was out of control, using tax dollars for glitzy projects the city doesn't need. And they practically rose from their seats when I said that was like spending money on big-screen TVs when the toilets need fixing."

"C'mon Funk. You think your sewers and metal plates stack up over Glazer's ferris wheel? I was counting on your smarts tonight to bring in donations. Now what are we going to do? We'll never be able to have the yard signs made after *that* performance."

"The Northland isn't excited about the other candidates. They want someone to be in charge of their money."

"Well, maybe sewers will go over well with the conservatives, but you'd better come up with something more exciting in the districts where the people aren't like you."

"You have it wrong, darling. The Northland doesn't need sewers. But they understand what I'm talking about."

"Whatever, Funk. But you need to do a better job describing what 'A City That Works for Regular Folks' means."

"Okay."

"I'm serious, Funk! You've got to start connecting the dots. You're good at spelling out the problems, but you have to be less technical with the solutions."

"Okay."

"Paint them a picture of unflooded basements, quality schools, and communities patrolled by Officer Friendly–type cops. Show how that would lead people to move back to the urban core. If you don't, you'll not only lose this debate, but you'll also lose all the others."

Funk drew a calm breath and said, "Is that all?"

"No. Stop making faces at the other candidates. It's very unbecoming."

"You're getting to be quite the campaign manager."

"Don't annoy me, Funk. And polish your fucking shoes!"

10 JANUARY 2007

MY NEW NORM: I arrived home after eleven o'clock and didn't fall asleep until after one a.m. Most times, I still got to the trailer by seven-thirty. On this day, though, it was nearly ten a.m. by the time I tinkled Spring's doorbells.

"Good morning, Dottie!" I said with a more energy than I felt. I extended Betty Lou a chipper, "Hey, Betty Lou, Eyes-Of-Blue." Betty Lou beamed.

"It looks like you already know the results of the debate," Dottie said with a good-natured grin.

Recalling Funk's performance, my face turned hot with shame. Because here these women were, giving up their time for my husband, and now it had been all for nothing.

"Yes, I know. I was there."

Betty Lou said, "Then why so glum?"

"I'm really sorry Funk didn't do well. It was his first debate. I'm sure he'll do better next — "

"Gloria," they shrieked in unison, "he won!"

"What?"

Seeing my confusion, Dottie repeated, more quietly, "Gloria, Mark won last night's debate."

"No, Dottie, that's not true. It's a mistake."

Betty Lou couldn't contain herself. She overrode Dottie's calmness and ex- claimed, "It's no mistake, Gloria. The results were faxed to us this morning."

"Are you kidding me?"

"Look," Dottie said, as if I were elderly and needed to be spoken to slowly. I accepted the press release she handed me.

The citizens have spoken, and the results are in after the debate in the Northland featuring ten of the twelve candidates for mayor of Kansas City, Missouri.

Citizens rated the candidates with a point system between 0 (low) and 5 (high) on the following areas: Opening Statement, Vision, Integrity,

Leadership, Communication Style, Northland Issues, and Closing Question.

1. Mark Funkhouser 2,438
2. Henry Klein 2,062
3. Becky Nace 2,056
4. Alvin Brooks 1,990
5. John Fairfield 1,785
6. Chuck Eddy 1,733
7. Jim Glover 1,707
8. Janice Ellis 1,683
9. Stan Glazer 1,591
10. Katheryn Shields 1,420

Perplexed, I asked, "Does this mean Funk won?"

"No, Gloria," Betty Lou said boisterously, "it means he blew it away!"

Saying to them, "I'm sorry, I have to go make sense of this, okay?" I walked the fifteen paces to my office and steadied myself at my desk, rereading the press release, wondering what my fucking problem was.

"Take your time, Gloria," came Dottie's tender voice behind me, her words met by Betty Lou's shocked incomprehension over my response to good news. How could I have been so wrong?

It was bad enough that Funk's committee didn't think he was electable. They had no ties to him. But I was his wife. Keeping his spirits up was my number one job. I didn't have to feel the same passion he felt for his cause, but a good wife, a loyal one, shouldn't erode her husband's confidence. With that thought, a wonderful thing happened. The New and Better Me rose up strong. Putting away my cosmic whip, I picked up the phone and rang my husband.

"Congratulations, baby!"

"What did I tell you, honeybunch?"

"I know. It's amazing. I'm sorry for the way I acted."

"There's nothing to be sorry for. You were worried. But Glor, even if this campaign doesn't go as we planned, we'll be fine. Remember, winning won't be a prize."

"Yeah, I'm sure it will be more work than we can imagine, just like having kids was. But Jesus, Funk. Why do I care all of a sudden?"

"I don't know. What do you think?"

"I guess it's because I've never lost anything I've set my mind to."

"We're not going to lose."

"I know. So why am I worrying this to death?"

"Because that's what you do."

"Maybe," I acknowledged. "Next time I'm afraid about the shitty job you're doing, I'm going to send good energy to bolster you instead."

"Let's go back to having fun with this, okay? It's a once-in-a-lifetime experience that most people wouldn't think of taking on."

Feeling less ashamed, I told Funk I had to get back to work and hung up. Opening my laptop, I clicked on my inbox. Lord Almighty, if it didn't have double the emails than I had the day before. After opening the first few, I realized they were mostly receipts from PayPal for campaign donations. And with that, my dilapidated office filled with holiness.

I didn't waste time getting out of my chair to make my next move. I just hollered out to the reception area, "Pull the trigger on the yard signs, Dottie!" And then, remembering my manners, I added, "Please!" And to that I added, "And tell them to put a move on!"

Later that night, in the sacred bed with my husband, both of us trying to read and calm down after the busy day, Funk tried to take advantage of my guilt from that morning.

"Are you tired?"

"Of course I'm tired, Funk, what do you think? You've got me working around the clock. But as long as I don't have to do anything, I'll let you ravish me."

Funk immediately pulled me toward him, lifting the covers from my breasts. But he didn't pause there, just continued down his path to the River of Jordan. *Hey! You! Back the fuck out of my bedroom! Did you really think I'd divulge* that! *I mean, my kids could be reading this!*

I'm sorry. That was rotten. I didn't mean to get you worked up over nothing. Let me make it up to you. Allow me to direct your attention to Jean Auel's "Earth's Children" series and Diana Gabaldon's "Outlander" books.

Man, if only Funk was half as good as Jondalar and Jamie.

11 JANUARY 2007

I ALMOST MADE THE HUGEST MISTAKE. It would've cost the campaign thousands of dollars to rectify. I hated it when I got careless. When anyone got sloppy. But as with everything else around there, it seemed as though God was watching over us, practically rooting us on.

According to campaign rules, I was supposed to have the name of Funk's treasurer printed on the bottom of the yard signs. I phoned Evert Asjes to double-check the spelling of his name.

"Good morning, Evert. This is Gloria, Funk's wife."

"I know who you are. You don't have to explain."

"Oh, so we've come this far, have we!"

"Yes. And I'd rather talk to you any day over your husband."

"That's so sweet," I laughed. As much as I loved horsing around, I had work waiting, so I got down to it, "Am I catching you at a bad time?"

"I have all the time in the world for you."

There it went. Whore for a compliment, I threw time overboard.

"Are you flirting with me, Evert? If so, I like it."

"I am, but don't tell my wife."

"I never kiss and tell. Except for Funk. I tell him everything. And believe me, I can't wait to tell him about this."

"Don't do that!"

"Don't worry, he's no fun. He never gets jealous, but a girl's got to try, doesn't she?"

"I don't know about that, but what can I help you with?"

"I need to check the spelling of your name for the yard signs."

"We're placing the order?"

"Enough donations have come in that I feel safe having them printed. Is this how you spell your name?" After enunciating each letter, I asked if I had it right.

"The third."

"What?"

"Evert Asjes, *the third*."

"Oh, so you're a fancy-schmancy type, huh?"

We kidded around for a while before I said I had to get back to my to-do list.

"Don't push yourself too hard. Your husband isn't paying you enough."

"My husband isn't paying me at all! I'll talk to you later, Mr. Asjes *the third*!"

After hanging up from my new best friend, I started on email. The most urgent was from Joe needing approval for a blog post.

Blogging seemed to me like the weirdest fad. Who ever heard of putting your innermost thoughts on the Internet, only to have people comment? Who cares what a stranger thinks? The practice smacks of self-help books, a genre I deplore. Why would I pay someone to tell me how to tackle a problem, when I can save time and money by asking myself?

12 JANUARY 2007

I ARRIVED AT THE TRAILER and tidied up the campaign materials in the lobby before navigating the buckled-up carpet to the reception desk. Dots and Blue Eyes started right in complaining about Curly. Lord, even when Britt was trying to be nice, he came across as patronizing and superior. They wanted me to do something about it, but how do you tell someone, "Hey, I don't like your personality"? Other than agreeing that yes, Britt *was* a boor, the only comfort I could offer was to say I'd let Funk know, even though I was pretty sure he wouldn't do anything about it. Funk had no time to sort out staff conflicts.

More people than ever were signing up to volunteer, but part of that phenomenon tugged at my soul. The kind of trust that some people had in cops and doctors was now being directed toward my husband. I'd known Funk for decades, so my faith in him was well grounded, but these folks didn't know him. Not *know* him know him. The scary part was, they thought they did. Seeing someone on TV didn't mean you knew a person. Who was to say that Funk wasn't the usual sleaze running for office? I worried that such kindhearted souls might be easily conned by the media. My husband could never pull off a con, even if I helped him.

Volunteer support multiplied. We were still attracting many helpers who didn't have a nickel to spare. Yet some hailed from the creative class, and their talent was worth far more than what our biggest donors had given in dollars. For the rest, well, some were way out there. Like, woo-woo out there. A few of the newcomers told me they'd had a prophesy about the outcome of the election that dated back to when they were in grade school.

The woo-woos weren't just our volunteers. One day a random dude flagged me down at the supermarket to say that he had it on good word that Funk would win. I didn't know how he knew I was connected to Funk, but to be nice, I said, "Yeah, I've heard that, too."

The guy turned belligerent. He said I couldn't possibly know, as he was the only person who had received that information. When he said that, my New Yorker poked through, but at the last minute I saw his hand twitching and in a way that told me what I was dealing with. I tamped myself down, thanked him for the reassurance, and rolled my shopping cart to another aisle.

Some volunteers couldn't grasp that Funk couldn't be the pied piper just for the voters who lived on the fringe. By "fringe," I meant unconventional in any way, including unrefined, low-income, or rainbow-haired. Funk wanted to set a place at the table for everyone. You'd have thought the fringes would be deliriously happy knowing their new mayor had their backs. But they weren't.

They wanted it all. Well, so did I. But you have to use your wits to get what you want from life, especially when what you want is everything. Some of the fringes said that providing for everyone's needs was a sell-out.

Our volunteers wanted to try their hand at designing our direct-mail pieces. The one I loved most played on Funk's name: "Kansas City Funkadelic." When they presented their work to me, the volunteers' faces shone the way a child's does when bringing artwork home from school. Sometimes I had to struggle to maintain a sober countenance. I hated crushing anyone's soul. I loved humor, but what Northlander would vote for a man whose brochure proclaimed, "This City Is Funked Without the Funk"?

Some of the inspirations that crossed my desk were beyond wonderful. I loved the suggestion that we use the Parliament Funkadelic song "We Want the Funk." It was a catchy tune that would go a long way toward softening Funk's image, yet even the Northlanders wouldn't find it too outlandish. I was sure Joe would think of a way to incorporate it into the campaign.

Many volunteers liked to hang out at the double-wide and not do anything, not even a task as simple as licking envelopes. Yet there were a few workhorses among them. Dottie and I put a lot of effort into nurturing those volunteers.

Rhonda was one such person.

Rhonda was a tall, thin woman who didn't seem to have a care in the world for fashion. She wore jeans that my children would call mom-pants. I can say with utmost certainty that this mom wouldn't be caught dead wearing what Rhonda had on. If I had her figure, I'd be like a caged animal come loose. I'd have strutted and flashed to such a degree that my children would flinch when they saw me rocking the planet like that. Rhonda was different. A bookkeeper by profession, she had a precise and orderly way about her. I'm sure her ledgers were 100 percent accurate. She masked who she really was, albeit unsuccessfully. Her black hair hid most of her ghostly white face, but you could still catch the fright trapped there.

I liked most volunteers, but I really liked Rhonda.

"Hey, Rhondie, off work early today?"

"No, this is the usual time I get out," came her always-defensive reply.

I glanced at the clock. It was hours before what she's said in the past was her usual quitting time.

"What's shaking, woman?"

Taking the question as an invitation for a personal chat, she pulled up a chair beside mine and proceeded to tell me again how "Mr. Funkhouser" was going to "save her." How, once he was mayor, she'd never spend another night flattened to the living room floor, dodging bullets from the war zone in which she lived.

Her neighborhood, Westport, was a problem, but Christ, I hoped it wasn't as dangerous as she said. What miracle could Funk pull off, with only eight years to do it? For the zillionth time, I listened to her woes and her solutions. And then I listened again to how we *first* had to get Mr. Funkhouser elected.

Then, out of nowhere, Rhonda added something new and different to her story. She revealed her latest vision for getting Funk elected. It was a vision I could run with.

"Imagine," she said, "people waking up to find the whole town had been painted orange overnight."

I asked, "What do you mean, Rhonda?"

"Dottie said you *finally* approved the order for yard signs," she replied in a dramatic tone.

I nodded yes.

"Here's what I need you to do. Hide the signs when they arrive. *Do not* let the first one out the door. I want them placed all at once, after dark one night, so that when the city wakes up in the morning, everyone will wonder what that orange glow is."

"Oh my God, Rhonda, that's a really great idea!"

"You like it?" she said.

"I love it!"

"I like it too," she said, pinched-faced happy. "When people see our signs appear overnight, it will show just how much support there really is for Mr. Funkhouser."

"That's tremendous!"

Rhonda went mute, probably savoring the rare scrap of praise.

"Your plan is brilliant. It will build on the enthusiasm that's already out there. I'll run it by Funk as soon as he gets in — or you can, if you'd prefer."

"Don't call him that."

"Excuse me?"

"Don't call him that. He's Mr. Funkhouser."

I didn't respond to Rhonda's last command because my mind was already spinning with her inspiration, running through the logistics. Bumping against a possible glitch, I said, "Wait a minute. Are you aware of how many people want a yard sign?"

"Yes," she said, as if she were tasting bitterness on her tongue. She probably expected me to hold things up again.

"Last time I checked, there were almost five hundred households on the waiting list. Do we have enough volunteers to pull this off in one night?"

"We do. And if you'll allow me, I'll take over from here."

"I'd love for you to head this up. Thank you. You're a doll, Rhonda, as always."

She bypassed the compliment. "I've already organized requests by geographical areas of the city, and I've coordinated them to the locations where our yard-sign volunteers live."

"Wow, that's really smart!"

"Once the signs are in my physical presence, I'll let you know the date they'll be planted. You'll need to send a press release directly afterward."

"Good work, Rhonda. Thank you again." I stood up and walked her to the reception area, asking her to repeat her idea to everyone congregated there, winking at Dottie that she should make a big deal of it. I didn't stay to listen to the banter. I scooted back to my office to continue working. Finding my place and rhythm again, I blew out a sigh of relief. And then in sauntered Ruth Bates.

This was becoming a major problem. How was I supposed to get anything done when the volunteers needed my attention? Rhonda and Ruth weren't the first to seek my private time that day. My pile of work that absolutely had to be completed by the end of day remained undone, and I was a nervous wreck because of it.

I hadn't let my distress over the interruptions show, and I certainly wouldn't with Ruth. Ruth was a friend of the family. Like the trained magician I'd become, I corralled my emotions and went into playful mode, just as Ruth expected.

"Hey, ugly!"

This was our little joke. Ruth was so knockout gorgeous that I acknowledged her beauty in the most ridiculous way. She responded by giving me her shy-but-loving-the-outrageous-thing-I'd-just-said chuckle.

"Have you ever thought of becoming a model?" I asked.

"I already am."

"You are? I thought only your kids were."

"I just did a swimming ad," she said, to prove her point.

And since I'm always taking stock of people, I said, "You look like you've lost weight."

"Really?" she said, turning her body, looking at herself from all angles, and then added, "How so?"

"Ruth, you know you're tiny. Stop begging for more compliments. Are you on a diet or something?"

"No, just eating less and running more. You should try it."

Her comment hit me like a ton of bricks — the ton I'd just gone back to weighing. Did she know that just that morning I'd forced myself to step on the scale? I'd gained back all the weight I had shed in Europe the previous summer. I knew that I had, but it was miserable having it confirmed by something as undeniable as that ice-cold number.

I was obsessing about it when Ruth's voice broke into my thoughts.

"I need you to type something."

"Type what?"

"A note to leave in people's doors."

"I'm sorry Ruth, but Funk isn't into canvassing."

"I'll do it."

"Really?" I squealed before I could catch myself, since the only thing Ruth had done up to that point for the campaign was interrupt my work.

"Don't sound so shocked. Just open your computer and start typing."

I did, and she dictated:

Hi. My name is Ruth Bates, and I am your neighbor. I support Mark Funkhouser's candidacy for mayor and I hope that you will too. Mark's website is www.markfunkhouser.com. My phone number is . . . if you have questions for me.

I edited the piece and printed out a copy, but she said she wanted a hundred copies. I ran back to the printer and ran off twenty. She left the double-wide with the canvassing papers protruding from her purse.

13 JANUARY 2007

I WOKE UP AND ROLLED TOWARD FUNK, but he wasn't there.

"Funk!" I shouted, loud enough to reach the couch downstairs.

"Yes, Glor?"

"C'm'ere!"

Slowly, slowly, ever so slowly — *Why was this man so slow?* — my husband lugged himself upstairs, sounding like he was arriving back at base camp after having spent a long day doing battle on the Normandy shore.

"Yes, darling," came his always delighted-to-be-in-my-presence reply.

"Have you heard from UMKC?"

"Not since last time."

"So . . . no contract?"

"Not in hand. But yes, Glor, we have a contract."

"If it's not in your hand, then you don't have one."

"Whatever you say, darling."

"Don't 'darling' me!"

"Okay," came his passive-aggressive reply.

"Have you been looking for a backup?"

"No. Glor, you know there's no time to look for another position. I can give the mayor thing up or trust that UMKC will follow through, just as they've done on numerous occasions."

"The wait makes it seem like the deal is going south. How sure are you that it's not?"

"I'm 99.9 percent certain."

"You'd better be right."

15 JANUARY 2007

THE MINUTE SHE HEARD ME tinkle Spring's doorbells, Betty Lou rushed to the lobby to meet me, burning with news. She found me squatting on the floor in a posture that's similar to a woman pushing a baby out. I groaned like a woman in labor, cursing the buckled-up carpet for tripping me and causing my boxful of just-recorded receipts to fly all over the room. I'd done the bookkeeping work at home in order to spend some time there with my son. Besides, it was next to impossible to enter data accurately with all the distractions around the headquarters. It had felt so good to slash that item off my to-do list, and now I had to reorganize all the receipts before I could hand them off to the CPA.

Hearing me curse our ghetto headquarters, Betty Lou said, "What are you doing?"

I thought it was obvious what I was doing, so I didn't say anything. I just continued fuming, gathering up the scattered receipts. But once I looked up and saw her eyes sparking like mad, curiosity overtook my dark mood.

"What up?"

"Britt just caught Maria piddling."

"What do you mean?"

"You know those stacks of papers piled on the floor behind his desk?"

"Yeah."

"Well, Maria just used one for an outhouse."

"Oh, shit," I whispered, horrified by the image.

"No, it was number one."

Startled by the miscommunication, I said, "Betty Lou, what I meant was, that's a problem."

"Not really. Although Britt's damn mad about it."

"Mad? Really? Oh my God, that's too funny," I said laughing, matching the glee gushing from her.

"I know. He's been raging about it all morning.

"Oh Christ."

"After he caught Maria in the act, he started checking the other papers back there. They were dry, but most were stained yellow, so apparently Maria's been using his office for a long time."

My receipts now back in my box, I picked myself up off the grimy carpet and said, "I was wondering why there hasn't been much pee on the newspapers in my office. I thought maybe she'd already trained herself."

"Well, now you know," Betty Lou said with delight.

The two of us stood close, whispering the rest of the story so Britt wouldn't overhear.

"Are you sure he's mad, or is he just using that voice he gets when he talks to women?"

"No, Gloria, he's really mad."

"Oh my God, no!" I said, upset again, Maria being my responsibility and all.

And then human nature took over. I got defensive from being in the wrong. And, worse, from thinking about the apology I would have to extend to Britt. And, worse yet, resentful about why this was my problem and not Funk's.

"Oh, whatever. Serves him right for keeping his things on the floor. This operation may be low rent, but there are plenty of cabinets in his office he could use to store his papers. There's no reason to have the place looking like a mess. It's a bad reflection on Funk."

Betty Lou replied bluntly, "I don't know about it being a bad reflection, but I love that Maria did that, to him of all people. Dogs are smart that way, you know."

"What did you say when he told you?"

"I told him to get over it."

Imagining the scene, I said, "As much as I'd love to see Maria do that again, let's try to keep her to the training papers in my office, okay? I can't have her ruining Spring's trailer."

We walked to the reception area, where I said a lengthy hello to the volunteers. After I plopped down behind my desk, instead of starting in on all the work waiting for me, my mind wandered to Britt — mainly to what a handful he was.

When we met at Funk's Coming-Out Party, he said, "Every wife is involved in her spouse's campaign." But now that he had the position he had cozied up to me for, he was singing a different tune. I was pretty sure he felt his life would improve if I vanished from Earth — maybe because he didn't have the exact title he wanted. But that couldn't have been the only reason.

He'd been a complete pain from day one. And not just for me — for all the women on the campaign. Whenever a problem arose, which was about ninety thousand times a day, from a superior stance, Britt told us how the solution we'd just arrived at wouldn't work. It seemed to be an obvious cover for his incompetence. But he turned the tables, making it seem as if the women were inept.

I'd tried befriending him, but Britt only had eyes for Simon and Funk. I couldn't stand how prickly he was, so I'd given him a wide berth. The only time I engaged was when I stepped in to keep him and Dottie from tearing one another apart. I'd never seen Dottie upset by anyone until Britt came along — and she'd worked with the city council, so that was saying a lot. Dottie was such a saint that she usually ended up giving in to Britt. Not Betty Lou, though. Hoo-boy, not Betty Lou!

When Eyes-of-Blue began working at headquarters, Britt pulled his macho crap with her, but she flung his bullshit right back in his face. Surprisingly, Britt instantly heeled. I had been under the impression he didn't bother her after that. But if that was true, why would Betty Lou be giddy that Maria had used Britt's office for the "necessary" room?

I was staring up at the water-stained ceiling, thinking about how to frame an apology to Britt, when he barged into my office. My door was open, but a knock would've been polite. And a "Hi, how are you?" would've been nice, too. What I got instead was his meaty face towering above me, his bobbing curls springing madly toward my chair.

"Maria is pissing in my office."

Shrinking, I said, "Yes, Britt, I just heard. I'm really sorry. I'll try to keep her out of there."

"I appreciate that, but you need to leave her at home. This is no place for a dog."

The guy had a way of making a person want to take back an apology.

Throwing my glamour high, I matched his bearing, "That's not going to happen, Britt. I suggest you keep your important documents inside one of the cabinets just in case she gets in there again."

Red shot up his neck, but he didn't express his mad any more than that. He just turned on his heel and stomped from my office. I tell you, the stress that came with my job was really hard to take sometimes.

Later in the day I went to Funk's office for a meeting with the Inner Circle. Funk was sitting at his desk with his feet propped up. Dottie must've gone in to prepare, as extra chairs had already been brought in and placed in a circle, the way Funk likes. I placed my folder on a chair and stepped behind my husband and hugged him, rolling my eyes when I noticed Maria cradled in his lap.

The puppy was the star of the office. Except for Britt and me, everyone adored her. Tara had been delighted to hear that everyone was loving the puppy up.

When Evert arrived, I turned my attention to the kindhearted gentleman. I'd learned from the office scuttlebutt that Evert's son was ill, and I wanted to ask after his son's condition before the other Inner Circle members arrived. It wasn't hard to draw Evert out. He was a wreck and clearly needed someone to talk to. Turns out, his son was more than ill — he was fighting for his life. It destroyed me to hear things like that because I always thought, *Jesus, what if that were happening to my family?* To me, the worst blow in life would be having something bad happen to my child. Knowing what I'd need if I were Evert, I listened with my whole being as he told me about his son, and I pretended not to see the tears welling in his eyes as he spoke.

After giving me a full account of his son's diagnosis, Evert leaned back in his chair and stared at the floor. By this time, I had positioned myself around to where our knees were touching. I was rubbing his arm and murmuring words of sorrow intermingled with words of hope, when out of the corner of my eye I saw Maria fidgeting on Funk's lap. I wanted to shout over to Funk to hurry and put the fucking puppy on the newspaper in my office because I knew what her circling his balls meant. But I couldn't disrespect Evert that way. I bit back my warning and stayed intent on my new friend, while half-watching the dog.

Evert was lost in himself. Before long, Maria jumped from Mr. Oblivious's lap and trotted over to the latest edition of *The Kansas City Star*, which was lying on the floor behind his chair, Funk having missed the recycling bin with his toss that morning. Worried about what the dog was about to do but still feeling that it wouldn't be right to turn away from Evert, I again withheld my warning. Didn't say nary a word. Not even when I saw Maria sniff the newspaper, circle it a few times, assume the stance, and daintily raise her back leg so as not to soil herself as she plopped a tidy load of shit into the center of it. And because I wanted with my whole heart to give deference to the grieving man before me, I didn't speak up about what the dog had just done, not even after shit fumes reached my nostrils and I wanted so badly to run from the room in search of fresh air. Nor did I move a muscle as I witnessed with peripheral vision that steaming pile of shit begin to spread from the center of the newspaper toward its outer edge. Nope, I didn't do it. I just stayed present with Evert. It was only after the other committee members began filtering into the room that my soul faded from his. When half the committee were present in his office, Funk stepped out for a bathroom break and Evert followed him out the door.

Just then, Joe stepped into the room. I patted the empty seat beside me. Joe smiled, slumped down in the chair, and then, like a dog, made a great show of sniffing the air. In a loud voice and with a disagreeable look on his face, he said, "What's that smell?"

Since everybody but Joe was pretending they hadn't smelled something dreadful, with a deadpan expression I said, "Funk farted."

Joe's eyes shot wide with horror and the rest of the room began laughing hysterically.

Well, except for Dottie.

Accustomed to having Funk's back, her face truly was deadpan. She was almost yelling when she said, "Gloria! No one would have ever known it was him if you didn't say anything." It seemed beyond apparent to me that what I'd said was meant to be a joke, but the look on her face told me otherwise.

"I'm just kidding, Dottie! Funk is the biggest hick alive, but even he wouldn't do that in a roomful of people. Maria is just up to her old tricks. Funk missed the trash can with his newspaper, and Maria went on it. I just haven't had a moment to clean it up."

Dottie ran from her seat and began rolling up the soiled paper before I could say I'd take care of it. And since it was clear that her cleaning frenzy was her way of dispelling her deep-seated embarrassment over the situation, I left her to it and got up to open the windows instead. They were weathered shut. As I struggled to free them, in walked Funk, back from the bathroom. The roomful of eyes went to him.

Funk felt the questioning gazes.

"What?" he shouted, taking a step back, a smidgen of guilt in his voice, the way one does when accused of something, whether guilty or not.

And putting to bed what I hadn't mean to start, I said, "Funk, Maria just shit on *The Kansas City Star*, is all. Don't worry about it."

He didn't. He took his place at the head of the circle and called the meeting to order. He gave a rundown of the meet-and-greets and modestly summarized his performance at the most recent debate.

Joe expanded on how well the debates had been going, noting a positive trend. Joe hadn't attended many of the events, but because he was a debate coach and had written a book about his experience coaching inner-city youths, he knew what he was talking about. Joe said the audience was glued to Funk's every word — at the most recent forum they had practically stood on their chairs giving him applause. Funk was winning over the nameless faces at the forums.

Next, Joe gave a rundown on how well the campaign was doing thanks to earned media. The large committee and the Inner Circle were still under the impression that Joe and I know nothing much about election campaigns. To make himself appear credible, Joe went into reporter mode. Bringing his hand up to his chest level, he held it in his usual bizarre way, bent at the weirdest angles. Grabbing one finger at a time, he bullet-pointed our successes:

- Funk was frequently mentioned on television and radio reports.
- The newspaper reported on Funk regularly.
- The *Star* blogged about our candidate more than the others.
- The previous fact meant the *Star* was backing Funk.

I gulped when Joe made that last point. Unexpectedly, everyone present agreed with him, even if they did launch into their usual lecture about how Funk had to do things differently or he couldn't win the election. I'd recently concluded that the committee either didn't comprehend or weren't aware of the new politics that were rising in America, so their disheartening words didn't throw me off kilter.

I didn't stay steady for very long, though. I'd been privy to what Joe had just reported, yet when he listed them, it somehow made the victories seem bigger. I was as psyched as everyone else about the wins — amazed, more like it — but since I already knew Funk would be the next mayor, seeing everyone else realizing that too gave me a chill.

This was happening. Did I really want it to?

When Guilt Gets in Your Eyes

MY HUSBAND WAS LYING ON HIS BACK with his arms behind his head when I awoke. I didn't say anything, just brushed the back of my fingers across his cheek to let him know I was conscious.

"Good morning, beautiful!"

I rubbed his cheek again in acknowledgment.

"I'm a lucky man to wake up next to you each day."

I didn't know what this guy saw in me.

I lingered until my excitement over beginning another new day drove me from bed. Before long Andrew and I were out the door. We had a good ride in to school. That said, I suspect he was gonna take after his father because he either talked or he didn't. I was always looking for conversation or to play around, but no, I had to be on this kid's wavelength. Oh well, like I said, it was a good ride in today.

After saying my hellos to everyone in the trailer, I went to my office. I believed it was good business practice to respond to emails promptly. The missives of late had contained money, which, I'm happy to say, was trickling in at greater quantities. Unfortunately, there was still not enough to do much more than keep the lights blazing. But there was progress. I was able to pay Britt half his salary for the first time ever! It was the next thing on my to-do list, even though Funk didn't want me to write the check. The way he moaned about it you would've thought he was having a baby. I wish he were. Can you imagine how rich we'd be if he was the first male to do that? But no, he only whined like he was having one. As if hearing that out of a grown-ass man wasn't bad enough, I had to crick my neck to look up at him while he argued that the agreement had been to pay Britt *if* and *when* expenses were met and that advertising was part of those expenses. I listened impatiently, shaking my foot and tapping my fingers on the desk, before telling him his argument was bullshit and that I was paying the man. Funk eventually acquiesced. Begrudgingly. He got in a parting shot about how it would be better for Britt in the long run if we used the money for media buys. I held my ground but, softie that I am, threw him a crumb. I told him Dottie wouldn't accept her paycheck until every expense had been met, and like him, she thought expenses included advertising. Thanks to her generosity we had enough funds left for the direct-mail piece to go out. Okay, so maybe there was only enough money to have the brochure printed in black and white. And so what if it could only be sent by bulk mail?

When I saw our slightly bulging balance sheet, I shitcanned the rest of the items on my list and readied the piece for its debut into the world. Funk still liked to utilize groupthink for major campaign pushes, so I asked the committee and the Inner Circle for feedback, even though I knew it'd be mostly me, Joe, and Britt doing the work. Shockingly, the three of us made a good team. This was true for many reasons, but the most significant was that the mayor's race was nonpartisan. Joe and I shared similar viewpoints, and Britt's perspective helped round things out. We passed text between us, with Britt working up the first draft, as usual. Also as usual, I invariably gasped when I saw his initial attempt, as it was his typical in-your-face prose. Seeing it, I wondered what he was like in bed — those bobbing curls, the unnecessary decibels.

Thank God, my mind allowed me to continue toning down his words instead of running with that image.

Of course, there was one little glitch. We planned to send the brochure to targeted constituents by bulk mail, and Britt said there was no guarantee when it would land in their mailboxes. To make his point, he told me a couple of horror stories about campaign materials arriving weeks *after* the day of the election. When I replied, "Man, that would suck so bad," he argued that we needed to spend the extra for first-class mail. I told him that I'd love a guarantee of prompt delivery, but we didn't have the money for that. He wouldn't let it go. Finally, I said, "Okay, Britt. That's fine. We can send the piece first class *if* you hand me back the paycheck I just gave you." Guess what? We sent the brochure by bulk mail.

It was time for the Inner Circle meeting in Funk's office.

Giving my ass a break, I stood behind my chair and told the group that donations had been picking up steam. To highlight the good turn of events, I added that I had finally been able to pay Britt part of his salary. I was a bit mean, though. I overemphasized that Dottie wouldn't accept her check until after the bills had been paid *and* we'd purchased advertising. I know, very unbecoming. Worse, no one even thanked Dottie for her altruism.

Sometimes I could barely contain all the love I had for our volunteers. It blew my mind that strangers were throwing it all in to help Funk get elected. But ugh, how would it be possible to pay everyone back for believing in his dream? When I shared this angst with my husband, he said, "Gloria, we haven't forced anyone to help. They trust I'll make good on my word — that I'll put policies in place that will enhance the city — and the 'city' is them." That was true. People like Betty Lou and a new volunteer named Bev from the Northland seemed like they could get by with no wages. But other volunteers looked as if they could have used a hand, and I felt bad that we couldn't pay them.

Imani was one such volunteer who seemed to have fallen on hard times. She had only given the campaign a few hours here and there, yet a few days earlier she had asked me whether the campaign could loan her $600. I had a feeling that volunteers presumed Funk was rich. When I told her we had only two people on the payroll and one of them hadn't even been paid yet, she looked so deflated that I loaned her the money from my personal account. Since Funk was still without a job, the loan came by way of another cash advance from our credit card. I was pretty sure my family would never see that money again, but what could I do? We were in this deep, so what was $600 more?

I mentally rejoined the Inner Circle's meeting when I heard someone mention that Councilmember Deb Hermann, Funk's former boss, would lend her support to the campaign by January 31st. Funk had always said most councilmembers were afraid of their own shadows. Few of them took a public stance. If Hermann really had the tits to support Funk, it'd be big I tell you! It would go a long way toward getting other powerful supporters to come out of the closet, and a few of them might even open their padlocked wallets.

The last item on the agenda was choosing someone to attend the Northland Democratic Club's debate scheduled for that evening. Jeff Simon said he'd cover it because he had ties to the club. I hoped he followed through. Lord knows I had to *try* to be a mother again.

After we adjourned the meeting I went back to my office and started gathering my things to get out of there. Just as I was grabbing my car keys, in walked Ruth.

"Where are *you* going?" she said as if she'd caught me doing something wrong.

"Home, for a change," I responded almost defiantly, as if I *had* been caught.

"Don't act like you're working so hard. Everyone is helping your husband, but you're the one who will be living on easy street after he's elected."

I thought to myself, *Everyone is helping? Easy street?* But I didn't say that. I just went to my usual go-to with Ruth and started playing around.

"What's up with the Peter Pan boots?"

Twisting her ankle to view her footwear, she asked, "What's wrong with them?"

"Nothing, Ruth. If you like them, then you just go right ahead and keep wearing them. Be beige, like everyone else around here."

"Awww," she said with a laugh, before explaining what she'd come in for.

"I need more things to stick in mailboxes."

"What things?"

"You know, those slips you typed."

"You're out of them already?"

"I walked all over my neighborhood canvassing for you."

"Wow, Ruth, that's great! Thank you."

"Don't act surprised. I told you I would."

Working with friends was nerve-racking sometimes. I changed the subject and asked whether she and Mike were going to the fundraiser at Knuckleheads the next month.

"I've been waiting for you give me tickets."

"Oh. Why didn't you tell me you wanted to buy some?"

"I don't pay for tickets; I get them given to me."

Feeling even more awkward, I didn't voice that the Wolfs had purchased their tickets — and only *after* I tried stopping them from writing another check, for they'd already given the campaign more time and money than I felt comfortable with. Instead of wading through those muddy waters, I took out the pack of tickets and peeled off two.

"That's all?"

"How many do you want?"

"More than this."

I handed her two more and said I had to pick up Andrew.

When my son and I were halfway home from his school, Funk rang my cell phone to say I had to attend the debate because Jeff couldn't make it.

"Can't someone else cover it? You know I want to stay home with Andrew."

Andrew sing-songed, "I don't want you to stay home," but I ignored him.

"Everyone else has plans."

"Christ, Funk, you're not a novice anymore. Do you really need each debate critiqued?"

"Glor — "

"No, really, Funk. I've told you a hundred times to sit up tall, wipe that petulant look off your face, stop looking at the floor when you're talking, and provide more details about your plan to fix the city, which includes painting a picture of the afterglow. But you don't listen, so why should I bother coming?"

"Gloria, my performance is fine. I'm winning the debates. I don't need to be critiqued. I need someone to set up our table and answer voters' questions."

"*Our* table! Are you frigging kidding me? Oh, whatever. I'm only coming if Andrew says it's okay. If you don't see me, it means it's not."

If I could have, I would have smashed the receiver into the cradle. Someone really needed to change the way cell phones worked. There was no gratification in just clicking the red button to end a cantankerous call. To make up for the lack in technology, I threw the phone on the back seat, more to show Andrew how much I cared than to relieve my anger.

Looking at my son, I guiltily asked what his plans were for the evening. He must have sensed my torment because he got gentle. He said he was going out as soon as we got home and that I shouldn't worry about going to the debate.

Dropping him off at the curb in front of the house, I headed back to the trailer. I was so filled with shame that I overshot the exit and had to make a U-turn. Fuming, I started thinking bad thoughts about Funk. Damn that guy. No, damn myself. Why was I allowing my duty to be tilted more to him than to my children?

18 JANUARY 2007

WALKING UP THE PATH TO OUR HOME after ten p.m., I recalled what I'd said to Andrew: "I promise I won't be late. For sure this time."

Another broken promise from this deadbeat mother.

And for whom did I forsake my child? For the man who absofuckinglutely bombed the debate.

The other candidates droned on and on about nothing, yet the moderator had done nothing to stop them. Aggravating as that was, it was Funk's presentation that was for shit. He spoke about things I'd heard fifty times, "For years, Kansas City has been doing business the same way, yet we keep asking ourselves why we're in such desperate financial straits," *blah, blah, blah*. And the attendees' demeanor was the opposite of what you'd call excited.

From the moment I arrived at the trailer the next morning, one thing after another came up and I forgot all about my miseries. I went around on automatic pilot greeting volunteers, answering voters' questions, and dousing smoldering embers before they grew to be forest fires.

No one noticed my foul mood except for Dottie, and thankfully, I could be myself with her.

"You look terrible, Gloria. Why don't you go home and rest?"

"Believe me, Dots, I'd love to," came my pouty reply.

"Well, go on, I can take care of things."

"I can't, Dottie. We're both running as fast as we can, and we're still behind."

"Well, I know I won't change your mind," she said, giving up the idea, and then asked, "How'd Mark do last night?"

Looking around the room, I noticed that several new volunteers had come in. I didn't want anyone to overhear me dissing my husband, so I leaned over Dottie's desk, happy for a chance to unburden.

"Funk tanked."

"You always say that, Gloria, but Mark does just fine."

"No, Dots, I mean it this time."

We could sense the volunteers getting curious about why we were speaking softly, so I winked at her and went to my office.

I had barely sat down when Joe came in.

"Hey, Giuseppe. I'm glad to see you."

He brightened. "So, we defended our record," Joe said.

"Probably not, Joe. Funk did terrible."

"No, he didn't. It was an audience-scored debate. He placed first again."

What the hell?

In walked Dottie. "I'm sorry to bother you, Gloria," she said, "but there's—"

I interrupted her to ask if whatever it was could wait.

"No, there's a man on the phone who says he needs to speak to you," she said, while Joe simultaneously said, "I have to leave anyway."

I hugged Joe goodbye and turned to Dottie, my dark mood roaring back, "What's the rush?"

"I was trying to place an order for buttons, but the man said he needed your approval or he wouldn't ship them out tomorrow."

"Did you tell him you were the office manager?"

"Yes."

"Unbelievable. Maybe I'll look for another company, see how he likes that."

I dealt with that situation and stomped out a few more fires, but a blaze took hold when Britt came barging into my office.

"The first filing is due."

"What filing?"

"For the report."

"What report?"

"For the campaign."

If you knew how much I hated going around in circles, you'd have felt sorry for me.

"Please, Britt. Can you be more specific?"

"The first campaign finance report is due today."

Wow. A full sentence. Imagine that.

"And?"

"Are we filed?"

"How would I know? Evert and John Meara, the CPA, are in charge of things like that. I'm just tracking income and expenses."

"Are they aware?

"Are they aware of what, Britt?"

He responded as if he were speaking to a woman, "Of the Ethics Commission, *of course*."

That was the way it went with me and Britt. We went on these fantastically long journeys that took us right back to the street we started on. It was like there was a stream of consciousness inside his brain, and when he wanted to say something to the outside world, he just went in and grabbed something from the middle of the torrent and tossed a few words onto the floor for the listener to piece together. I'm sure he was smart as all get-out, but I'd never liked riddles. If my father hadn't worked the Jumble word puzzle every day of his life, I'd have had no way of understanding what Britt was saying half the time. But man, it pissed me off when Britt looked at me as if I was slow for not getting him.

"Are they aware of the Ethics Commission?" I repeated, hoping he'd see it was impossible to know *what specifically* about the Ethics Commission he was referring to. But he didn't respond. Just kept staring at me with those bulging eyes peeking out from beneath his bobbing curls.

"Britt, I don't understand. I'm not aware of every rule. That's why Funk placed people to cover those areas. But, piecing together what you've just said, are you asking whether Evert and John know to file whatever report is due today?"

"Yes, that's what I just asked you, Gloria."

"Okay. Well, to answer your question, I have no idea."

He stared me down again. I felt like a schoolgirl who had been called out for not paying attention. Throwing my glamour high, I responded on more surefooted ground.

"Look, Britt, this is the way the process goes. After I record the most recent donations and expenses, I email the updated spreadsheet to John and then make sure the receipts are dropped off at his office. I don't know what John and Evert are aware of. But what's left for them to do but to understand the rules and file whatever report is required?"

"I just called the CPA's office, and they don't know anything about that arrangement."

"What do you mean?"

"The receptionist doesn't know about the filing, and neither does John's personal secretary."

"What did John say?"

"He's out of town."

"Well, call him!"

"His secretary wouldn't give me his number. Do you have it?"

"No, but I'm sure Funk does."

Britt didn't leave to get the number. He just said menacingly, "Gloria, if we don't file today, Mark will be disqualified from the race."

I felt as if the epicenter of an earthquake had just opened beneath my chair, my body started shaking that badly. Jumping from my seat, I squeezed past Britt and ran to Funk's office. I should've known he wasn't there, otherwise Britt wouldn't have brought this situation to me. I ran back to my office and dialed Funk's cell, but the bastard didn't pick up. So, I texted him, but he didn't respond to that either. Like a lunatic, I rang his number again and again, not stopping until he picked up.

"What?" came his testy greeting.

"Funk! What the hell are you doing not answering my calls?"

"Gloria. I'm in the middle of a meet-and-greet. I only picked up because the phone kept ringing."

"Where are you now?"

"In the bathroom."

"Oh, thank God! Funk, we have the hugest problem, and I can't field this one for you."

I told him everything as I understood it, ordering him to cut the meet-and-greet short and call John Meara as soon as he got in his car.

"Okay, babe, but try to calm down. Everything's fine. John is a CPA. He has this under control."

"Calm down? Britt said you'll be disqualified if we don't file by three o'clock or five o'clock, he doesn't remember which. Have you looked at the fucking time, Funk?"

"Gloria —"

"It's almost noon!"

"We're not going to be disqualified. The Ethics Commission isn't exactly on top of these things. They get to it when they get to it, and that's only *if* they decide to get to it. If I've done something in error, I'll just ask for an extension."

"Britt says there'll be no getting around it."

"That's nonsense, Gloria."

"Nonsense!" I gasped. "You know what, Funk? I don't even know why I care. Just hurry up and call and take care of this. And don't forget to call me back. I don't want to sit here all day worrying. But leave Evert out of this. He can't handle anything, with his son being ill."

"Okay."

"Oh, and Funk, get your ass back to the trailer as soon as you can."

"I'm not coming back. My schedule has me running until late tonight."

"Jesus Christ! You're never here!"

"Glor, it'll be okay."

John was indeed out of town. And while there *was* someone in his office who was aware of his arrangement with Funk, no, they hadn't prepared the report, because they didn't know a report had to be filed. As soon as that information filtered back to us, Britt rang the Ethics Commission. No answer.

Everyone was in a tizzy, but I had tunnel vision so bad I could hardly see. At one point, Dottie slipped into my office to say that from what she could gather from the commission's website, income and expenses had to be recorded, which, of course, I'd done. So, no sweat there. Unfortunately, I had entered the data onto a spreadsheet, not the required form. And I didn't include the addresses of the stores where we had made the purchases, even when that information was right there on the receipt, because I didn't know I had to.

I wanted to ask Britt and Dottie why this important report hadn't been on our calendar, but I didn't dare. We needed to focus on the enormous task of making things right.

Britt spent the rest of the day copying my entries onto the correct form and supplementing it with the contact information for each store. That went past the maybe-three-o'clock deadline as well as the maybe-five-o'clock deadline. But Britt kept at it because somewhere in the middle of the day he decided a midnight deadline made more sense. I didn't know if he said that to calm me down, to calm himself down, or he was just saying something to say something. It didn't matter. Nothing would soothe my nerves until we had filed that damn report. Besides, without hard facts from the commission, what else was there to do?

I sat inside my office most of the day, unable to focus on anything important except getting that damn report out the door. Every twenty minutes or so I went to Britt's office asking for an update, asking if I could be of help. I can't remember much of that afternoon, but I hope to God I didn't lose my manners. I hope I offered the man a coffee or a bite to eat. I recall that amid all the fretting I forced myself to do mundane things, such as address a bunch of envelopes for thank-you notes. To blow off steam, "I penned a letter to Catherine Shaw, the author of *The Campaign Manager*." There was nothing in there about financial filings, and I needed to tell her that she had missed something important. Something *really* important.

Every now and again, Dottie, Betty Lou, Bev, Joe, and even the new volunteer tiptoed into my office to see if there was anything they could do for me or to encourage me to go home. But there was nothing anyone could do, and I wasn't going home. Not until we filed that fucking report.

With each hour that ticked by, Britt said he was almost done. First at four o'clock, then at seven, and then at nine. By ten I was so beside myself that I couldn't do anything except wring my hands. Funk eventually made it back to the trailer, and when the eleven o'clock hour neared and we still hadn't filed, he came into my office and demanded that I go home. I put up a fuss, saying I wouldn't sleep, so why go home? But he packed up my bags and stood in front of my desk with a stern look on his face until I got up from my chair.

"I can wait it out like everyone else, Funk."

"Gloria, there's no one else here but you, me, and Britt. You've been at this all day. You might as well wait at home and put your feet up."

"I'm fine."

"Gloria, you're going home. Let's go."

"No. I'm fine," I said, sitting back down.

The bastard didn't say anything, nor did he budge. Just stood there staring at me with my bags in his hands, waiting for me to obey. When Funk gets like this, there's no backing him down. Aggravated beyond words, I got up and wrestled myself into my coat and then ripped my belongings from his hands. He tried grabbing them back, but I wanted none of his help. I flew from my office like a wet cat, my bags in hand, my husband in my wake. When I was almost to the lobby, Funk shouted for me to stop. I don't know why, but I did.

"Babe, c'mon, we'll be okay. Go home. I'll call when we're filed." He looked so pathetic that I just stood there looking up at him, trying not to cry. Because . . . all this work. For nothing. Seeing my tortured state, my husband grabbed me in an embrace and I melted, a rag doll in his arms. Then, as if I were his child — the nine years between us does make it seem that way sometimes — he said it was cold outside and to put my hat on, handing it to me.

The punch gone from me, I took it. And with my briefcase in one hand, I slung my purse over my shoulder and shoved the hat on, opened the door, and stepped into the freezing night air.

On the landing, Funk tried taking my bags, but I held them tight. Placing his hand at the small of my back, he began to escort me down the trailer's creaky wooden steps. Just as we started down, my bags suddenly went flying and I was on the ground, one leg splayed out in front of me, the other behind. I had no idea what had happened; all I knew was that I was on the ground crying. Actually, I think you'd call it wailing. Not just from the pain, but from being at the limit of what I could take.

Funk dropped to my side in a heartbeat.

"I'm so sorry, Glor. I tried to catch you, but you went down fast."

"What happened?" I asked, screaming and crying.

"It's black ice. It must have sleeted while we were inside."

I just kept wailing and wailing, "Oh my God, Funk, oh my God."

"Are you hurt?"

"I don't know."

"Can you move your legs?"

Without my bags encumbering me, I tipped to one side, gripped the leg that was behind me, and tugged it forward. My legs righted, I sat on the ground leaning slightly to my left, dissolving into my husband's chest.

My weeping finally slowed and I said, "I can't take this anymore, Funk. It's too much. Tara. Andrew. I'm gone all the time. All this work, and for what? We didn't file on time."

"I'm so sorry, babe. Come on, it's cold. Let me help you up. Do you think you broke anything?"

I got up slowly. My knee was killing me. I must have landed on it. Afraid that I'd slip again, I clutched Funk's arm and together we half slid, half inched our way over to the van.

"I'm driving you home."

"No, you're not. You have to make sure the report gets filed!"

"Gloria, it doesn't matter."

"Don't be stupid, Funk."

"Britt has it."

"I know Britt has it. He's been working on it all fucking day. I'm serious, Funk, one of us has to stay with him. This is our mess, not his. I'm going. Let me know as soon as it's filed. I won't sleep until I know it's done."

My husband looked nervous and guilt ridden as he watched me pull away. My heart ached seeing him so, but there was nothing to do about it until we were together again.

I turned my attention to the icy road and drove slowly, my knee hurting more with each mile. Finally parked in our driveway, I turned in the seat, slid down, planted my feet firmly, and then stood up carefully. But I couldn't walk. I perched on the icy driveway until I thought to phone Andrew. Thank God I hadn't gotten rid of my crutches after spraining my ankle. He was outside in a flash, circling like a nervous hen as I crutched my way up the path and into the house. I hobbled to the stairs and sat on the first step, bumping up them backward until I reached the landing. I don't recall how I stood up. All I know is that when I reached my bed, I slithered onto it and collapsed.

It was almost midnight when Funk called to say that Britt had just hit Send and our first campaign report was on its way to the Missouri Ethics Commission. Thirty minutes later he was standing beside me. He gingerly placed a bag of ice on top of my swollen knee, shucked off his clothes, and lay down lightly beside me. We were both asleep within seconds.

Along about four a.m., my throbbing leg woke me from a dream-filled sleep. I was relieved to be awake, as in my dream Britt had forgotten to hit Send, and just like that, Funk had become a candidate who would've made a great mayor. I was about to elbow Funk to ask him to bring me two aspirin, but he was passed out, and I had to get up to pee anyway.

It was tricky. After several tries, I lifted my body out of the bed as if I were in a séance, grabbed the crutches, and rattled down the hallway to the bathroom. I washed two pills down with water I drank directly from the spigot. Next, I looked over at the toilet. That made me weary. How would I get back up if I sat down? The simple answer was that I wouldn't. Opening the cabinet beneath the sink, I dumped the rags from my cleaning bucket, shoved the pail between my knees, and peed in there, leaving the whole sordid mess on the floor beside the toilet.

Depending on how you view the world, I left everything in plain sight either to get Funk's help in disposing of it or to punish him when he saw what he'd reduced me to. I didn't know which, and maybe for the first time ever I didn't care to examine my motive.

Was I being a nasty, hurtful bitch? Who the fuck knew? And who the fuck cared anymore?

19 JANUARY 2007

I DIDN'T WAKE UP until after Funk returned from taking Andrew to school. I couldn't bend my leg. Funk brought breakfast upstairs and then put everything I'd need within easy reach before leaving to make it to what was left of his morning meetings. As soon as heard his muffler fade away in the distance, my phone began ringing.

I didn't pick up unless the caller ID showed it was Funk, Tara, or Andrew. It was obvious that God had stopped me in my tracks and I thought I'd better find out the reason why. I sat icing my knee, waiting impatiently for my message from above. I received oogots.

For months I'd been standing in front of a virtual pitching machine returning balls, never once missing a swing, yet the previous night one of those balls had smashed me in the knee. Knowing it was a sign, I grasped for what it meant.

The situation reminded me of the day I received the message to scale back my BirthWays business — to focus the majority of my attention on the children I'd been privileged to care for rather than on my clients. My thoughts drifted to how I shouldn't forsake my children for a grown-ass man. My next consideration was kinder. I hadn't heeded the urge to spend a weekend at our cabin for a much-needed rest. Perhaps this was just some angel's way of making me do what I couldn't to do for myself.

I called out in prayer, but I got no clear answer. Pain and guilt coursed throughout my body but I got zilch from the universe to help me interpret what it meant. I was forced to decode things for myself. By midday I had decided Funk had to fend for himself for the duration of the campaign. But as soon as I made that decision, tunnel vision overcame me, which was a sure sign that I hadn't translated correctly. Utterly confused, I answered the next phone call, just to get away from myself.

"Hey, Joe, how goes it?" I said, sounding pitiful, even to my own ears.

"Noooo, Gloria, how goes it with you?" he said, drawing each word out in his Midwestern twang, his question suffused with an apology that he was living and breathing.

"I'm sorry I left everyone alone with all that work."

"Yeah, Dottie is a little frantic. But don't be sorry. Everyone here is just sorry you got hurt. When do you think you'll make it back?"

"I don't know, Joe. I'm thinking maybe I should quit."

"You can't quit, Gloria. You're the heart and soul of the campaign!"

That took me aback. Me, the heart and soul of the campaign?

"Joe, everything is organized now. The campaign will be fine without me."

"That's not true. We need you here."

"No, I can't take the guilt anymore."

"What guilt?"

"Leaving Andrew alone all the time. Constantly rushing Tara off the phone. I've never parented this way before."

"Your kids are kind of old."

"I know it seems that way, but I think my accident was God's way of keeping me from ruining my family."

"It wasn't a sign, Gloria, you just fell. You can't quit. You're integral to the campaign."

"Funk might be disqualified for how integral I am! I'm working around the clock, and things are still slipping through the cracks. Important things. Tracking dollars to the penny was supposed to symbolize the importance Funk would place on Kansas City's finances. And I failed!"

A lump formed in my throat and I couldn't say more.

"Gloria, the campaign finances *are* spot on — you're all over them! Maybe we filed late, but we don't even know that yet."

Tears escaping, I remained silent. Joe got the message and couldn't say goodbye fast enough.

"Well, hang in there. See you Monday." *Click.*

Geez. I guess I was going back to work after the weekend.

I was too choked up to answer more phone calls, so I checked my emails instead. The most important came from Britt. "We are filed," he wrote, adding that no other candidate's website mentioned they had filed the report. "It was a doozy of a night that none of us want to repeat!"

I was filled with gratitude that Britt had updated Dottie and the other full-timers about the near-disaster. Because the biggest calamities arise from keeping people in the dark. That's when rumors fly, and gossip makes the world spin in the most hateful ways. Why do we push blackness forward instead of blue skies? And why did I think about this shit anyway? Like, what the fuck could I do about it?

I flitted through emotions as I read the next email. Our CPA, John Meara, wrote that he took "full responsibility for the filing mess-up." His message began with a confession that he had been unable to personally handle our account. Okay, I got that. Life happened. He went on to say he had underestimated the number of expenses the campaign would incur. That was a little harder to understand, but I was still with him at that point, because if you've never been part of a campaign, it's impossible to fathom the workload. Where he lost me was when he started a tirade over the chaos that we — *we!* — had created by not keeping a check register. That's when I officially flung his ass over to the "I'll-never-be-able-to-see-the-good-in-you" side of the fence. And, knowing myself, I was pretty sure that was where he'd stay for all eternity. He wrapped up his email with the words to his staff "Thanks for your incredible effort to save ME!!!!!!!!!!!!!!!!!!!!!! I am GRATEFUL!!!!!!!"

My spent knee was nothing compared with the whiplash I felt from reading his email. A check register caused all *this* heartache? Really? I still didn't know whether God gave me a sign with my knee or if it was just random, as Joe said, but I had my own sign. I needed to put my computer away and stop thinking for a while.

Hours passed. Funk brought Andrew home from school, stopping to pick up Chinese takeout. On my bed, the three of us shared an early dinner together. Halfway in, I told them I was quitting the campaign. Andrew almost suffocated on his moo-shu vegetables when I said that. Coughed up a bean thread before restating that he neither wanted nor needed me to stay home after lugging him back from school. Since he was still being all soft because of my fall, he expressed that as nicely as it gets for a teenage male.

"Mom, I love you, but you want to *think* I need you, and I'm sorry, but I don't. This is the funnest year I've ever had in school, and it's better because you're not here all the time."

"But, Ange, you're alone too much. You don't even have Nick to keep you company anymore."

"Nick is going through something, and I'm with a different set of friends now anyway. It doesn't — "

Andrew rarely participates in a conversation, yet Funk thought it was a *great* idea to interrupt him.

"Glor, Andrew's fine!" he boomed, as if Andrew wasn't in the room. "He can take care of himself. Besides, you've made plenty of provisions for him."

I looked at Funk with total disgust and said, "Would somebody please call in the trumpets? The king has spoken!"

Funk blinked.

"Jesus, you're always saying everything is fine. *This* is not fine! I was home with Tara until she left for college, and I need to be here for Andrew. Not being home is like quitting raising our children with the finish line in sight. I'm not doing that. Not anymore."

"Mom, the only reason I need you here is to push me with scholarship and college applications. But you know I'd only get mad at you if you tried to help. We'd be fighting all the time, and without Dad here that wouldn't be good."

"Andrew, it's my job to push you. Whether you're an asshole to me or not."

"Mom!" and "Gloria!" they both shouted in shocked horror.

"Whatever, guys. It's the truth, isn't it? C'mon, Andrew, you know you're an asshole. You used to like me so much. I don't know what happened."

"Now do you see why I like it better when you're not around?" he said as he flew from the bed.

"Andrew!" I screeched at the top of my lungs. "Sit your fucking ass down. I'm tired. I'm stressed to the max. I'm confused. My knee is killing me. Give me a fucking break. I can't choose my words as carefully as I should right now."

The room stilled, all of us — even Andrew — waiting to see what Andrew would do.

He came back to the bed but sat as far away from me as he could. Like, one of his butt cheeks was hanging over the edge just in case he had to make a hastier exit next time. But he didn't add anything more to the conversation. Funk had killed that, which is why I wanted to kill my husband. For that, and for the next little bit.

"Gloria," he said, before starting Paternalistic Lecture #5042, "the only reason to quit is if *you* no longer want to be part of the campaign, not from some *duty* you think you owe your son."

"That's the most ridiculous thing I've ever heard you say. Duty? If duty weren't important, you wouldn't have a campaign headquarters. Or any chairs in there. Or phones. Computers. You probably wouldn't even have the first volunteer. Your dream wouldn't be organized. Or planned out to the bitter bloody end. This isn't about duty? Good Lord, Funk, that's *all* this is about. I parent from a sense of duty. I wife from duty too, though that may change at any second. What a stupid thing to say. Duty? I'd call it loyalty."

The three of us sat in silence again.

With that out of my system, what I'd been trying to figure out all day finally came to me. It wasn't as though I hadn't lighted on it a hundred times. It's just that it hadn't filtered down from my head to my heart until just that second.

"Would one of you please kill me? I can't take the guilt anymore."

"Mom, stop being so emotional. After your leg is better you need to go back to the trailer. Dad needs you, not me."

Well, fuck. My son took after his father, even though I had thought for a while that he was more like me. After making that pronouncement, he up and left. Didn't even ask if he could be excused. I let him go, but how sad was this turn of events? Sadder yet, as much as I hated Funk, he'd be leaving the house soon too to get to a campaign event.

"Am I asking too much?" he asked.

"The situation is fine for me, Funk, but what about the kids?"

"They're fine."

"Would you stop saying that? It's like you're stuck on repeat."

"But they are fine. And it's not much longer until the primary. Besides, this is good for them. It'll make them more appreciative of you."

"Oh, like you are?"

"I appreciate everything you do for me. And not just for the campaign. I'm even more grateful that you always insist on us being a family. I hope you can hear me this time."

"That was a backhanded compliment, but whatever. I hate you so much. Do you know that? Please know that."

"I know."

More silence.

"Outside of the work, are you still having fun?"

"How would I know? I don't know anything anymore."

Funk just stared at me.

I continued, even if that's the rudest thing in the world, to not respond.

Finally, I said, "The campaign is more exciting than all the mundane tasks I do at home and less responsibility than catching babies. But this isn't something I ever wanted, and it's not what I expected to be doing. I never agreed to run your campaign, at least not on the front end. And I never agreed that you wouldn't look for another job."

"I'm sorry, Glor."

"We're eating through your retirement savings — our future. We're thousands into the credit cards."

"We can back out."

"Oh my God! You can't back out now! It's too far gone. The only way to get our money back is by getting yourself elected and securing a second job. I don't know where we are with the finances, but I'm guessing it will take the eight years you're in office to catch us back to even, and there goes my fucking dream of starting a business."

He looked miserable when I said that. But after glancing at the clock and knowing he had to go, I let him off the hook.

"But it's done, and the only thing to do is move forward. So, to answer your question, being part of the campaign isn't what I planned, but it is something different, and you know how much I love doing things out of the ordinary. So yes, I'm still having fun."

I cringed to say the next part — I can't accept a compliment, even from myself — but I said it anyway. "I think it's fun because I'm good at it, even if I didn't know the first thing about campaigns a few months ago. But do you want to know the real reason I'm staying?"

"Of course."

"I feel safer knowing someone has your back. Because, Lord knows, your back needs covered. You're so gullible."

"I like you having my back. And my front. I like you all over me."

"Go away."

Never before would my husband have left me in this condition. That was not the kind of family we were. There had been exceptions, such as when my father died and Funk didn't come immediately home from his business trip. *No! Please God, don't let me think about that.* But as a rule, when someone in our family was down, we circled them until they were up again.

Funk kissed me goodbye and headed out with Andrew. I sat inside my beautiful home feeling empty inside. It wasn't from being alone in a big old house or that I'd have to fend for myself when I could barely move. I felt like I would be missing out on something by not attending that evening's debate.

Christ Almighty, if that wasn't a sign!

For some reason I felt compelled to work on the campaign, though I didn't have the slightest hint why. The only thing I knew for sure was that it wasn't me who was behind the wheel.

So, what the fuck does that mean?

20 JANUARY 2007

IT WAS SATURDAY MORNING. It was also the first time that Evert had ever phoned me.

"Well, if it isn't Mr. Evert Asjes *the third*!"

"How are you?"

"Humbled, not being able to walk and all, but much better than yesterday."

"Get well soon. We need you. You're the heart and soul of the campaign."

What the hell? That was the second time I'd heard that in as many days.

"Thank you, Evert. How is your boy?"

"I think he might be doing better."

"That's so great! See? What did I tell you? Never give up."

He didn't respond. Midwesterners aren't used to such enthusiastic talk, though it lifts their spirits all the same.

"Please tell your son I'm rooting for him."

"Thank you. That means a lot to me, Gloria."

"Take good care of yourself, Evert."

Just as I was about to hang up, I screamed, "Wait! Are you still there?"

"Yes?"

"I forgot to say thank you for calling!"

Funk took me to see my beloved chiropractor Eric, who reassured me that I hadn't broken any bones. Following Eric's advice, I elevated my leg and worked from bed. The emails gracing my inbox doubled. I could barely keep up.

Funk planned to govern transparently, so in the newsletter I confessed about the snafu with the Ethics Commission report. I'd gone back and forth a million times, wondering how smart it was to be brutally honest, finally deciding on the total honesty route. After hitting Send, I steeled myself for a good ribbing about how the former city auditor had almost missed a financial deadline. In an unexpected twist, it was my accident that interested readers. It seemed as though they really cared. No one said a word about the filing screwup!

People emailed to say they were sorry about my knee and they'd been praying for me because I didn't deserve to get hurt. I had sensed those prayers and had even seen the results. I was healing more quickly than I ever thought possible. Their words were comforting, but they got me wondering. How would people who had never met me know whether I deserved something? Most knew me only through my candid words in a newsletter.

Fortunately, real talk came naturally to me.

When my kids first became aware of the world outside of themselves, they were stunned that I would talk to a stranger as I stood in a grocery checkout line.

"Why were you talking to them if you don't know them?"

"Uh, because we're both humans and we were in line together."

"But you asked that lady how her birth went."

"So?"

"That's personal!"

"Good Lord, guys. You know I'm fascinated with birth. Besides, that lady was dying to spill. Otherwise she wouldn't have gone on like she did."

"Who cares? It's embarrassing!"

"Don't be so frigging Midwest. Relationships bring color to our lives. Everyone in New York talks to strangers."

"Here we go again. Everything is better in New York."

"You've been there. It's true, isn't it? The people are friendlier. They say what they mean. The food is miles better. And so are the sidewalks."

"If it's so great, why don't we live there?"

"Because we have roots here. And I don't want to rip you out of school the way my parents did to me. That really sucked, I'm telling you."

"We know, we know!"

I had no patience for superficial talk. Funk loved my style of relating to others. He had a deep love of people, but he was a periphery type of guy. It wasn't his fault. Growing up in West Vagina, who was there to converse with other than the beautiful green mountains? The yin and yang of our union had served us well. We'd accomplished a lot because of it. I didn't have the first clue about running a city, and Funk couldn't speak from his heart. Through his campaign newsletters, I offered his readers what he couldn't provide.

That we even *sent* a newsletter, much less one crazy enough to include his position on issues, was something other campaign managers thought was sheer madness. And because we took it a step further by sharing our private lives, they disregarded Funk's campaign. They weren't aware of the major political shift happening in Kansas City. It wasn't the life-altering revolution of the sixties, but the air was pregnant with potential.

I was beginning to see the entire package that my husband offered. It was more than pulling the city back from bankruptcy and starting a revival through innovative economic measures. Funk was providing a meaningful connection, one that made people feel valued and safe.

Later in the day I opened an email about the day's filming of a video of well-known personalities who were endorsing Funk. This was another one of Joe's brilliant ideas on how the campaign could keep up with the Big Boys. Every candidate except ours had been endorsed by at least one highfalutin organization or individual.

Joe's video addressed assertions that Funk wasn't a viable contender because he didn't have anyone distinguished backing him, meaning none of the usual suspects supported him. Well, he did have notable people in his corner; they were just too chickenshit to say it out loud.

Sure, the Big Boys might say our endorsers were peanuts compared with theirs — but Funk's endorsers wouldn't have strings attached. He wouldn't owe them any favors. Therefore, they wouldn't dictate Funk's agenda once he was mayor.

But fuck if the committee didn't hate the video idea.

They didn't want to emphasize that we were running a grassroots campaign. It was weird. This far down the road, they were still pushing Funk to appeal to the elites, when it was the elites who had brought the city to its knees.

Funk wasn't helping. Sometimes I had to drag his ass over to Joe's way of thinking. Although he loved Joe's out-of-the-box ideas, the press events were just a little too showy for his sensibilities. Since Funk had the final say on how the campaign was run, I asked Joe to tone things down so we could move forward. Thank God he did, because if there was anything I hated more than Funk, it was inertia.

Think about it: Joe's video would cost next to nothing to produce. Besides, what harm could come of it? I suppose it could have backfired if it didn't include enough bigshots backing Funk. But as far as I knew, everyone Joe asked had agreed to participate. Until Gwen Wolf sent an email begging out of it.

I usually got miffed when people canceled at the last second, especially when it was as plain as day that they were afraid to take a stand. But Gwen's response to my email had redeeming qualities — and I tried to always look for the silver lining, lest I be friendless.

To: Ed & Gwen Wolf

Sent: Saturday, January 20, 2007 11:18 AM

Subject: Funkhouser—You're going to be famous!

Hello Mr. & Mrs. Wolf,

How are you this morning?

Joe wants to make a homemade commercial with famous people endorsing Funk, which he'll upload to our website and to YouTube.

He wants to capture everyone on Funk's committees, and that means you, too, my little Gwennie-poo, yes, you're important too.

This is the scenario.

One-minute testimony where you'll both say how you're just regular folks, not politicos, who care about the city. State why you care and why you're supporting Funk. Make sure to include that you're generous contributors.

I think Joe wants to show that, while we haven't raised as much money as the other candidates, most of their money has gone towards consultants who are trying to buy the title of Mayor.

If you're agreeable, can you set up a time with Joe?

Deeply in your debt,

Gloria

From: G Wolf

Subject: Re: Funkhouser—You're going to be famous!

To: BirthWays

Our roadrunner has been out since last night, so all the messages came in just now. Joe is coming by about 3:30.

Gloria, Gloria . . . little Gwennie-poo looks just that . . . like POOOOOO. The doctor took 7 big old places off my face the other day and I look like I have the chicken pox . . . . so Gwennie-poo will not be on film.

Eddie is preparing his statement and raring to go.

How are you doing with your knee—thank goodness it wasn't your hands . . . at least you can still type. Anyway, it will be fun to see where all this filming goes.

xo Gwen

I adored the Wolfs, especially Gwen, even if she was a little too tied to the establishment for my taste — or, I should say, she desperately wanted to be. I assumed that's why she canceled. I was pretty understanding when it came to weaknesses, probably because I have so many of my own.

The Wolfs were about twenty years my senior, and they were Republicans. But what did it matter? If you don't cause others harm and you have conversations that matter, that was good enough for me. One of the greatest joys of the campaign was the opportunity to meet the craziest assortment of the nicest people. And some, like Gwen, were becoming fast friends.

No Endorsements, No Problem —
Maria the Poodle, Take One

"YOU'RE BACK!" came Dottie's cheery welcome.

I had fallen late on Thursday night and was back at work on Monday morning, hobbling but no longer in need of crutches.

"Yes, for better or worse, I'm here."

"It's definitely better having you here!"

"Thank you for liking me, Dottie."

She tipped her head into her shoulder and smiled her blushing smile. *Oh boy, a few days away and we were back to this.*

"Excuse me, Dots, but I have to go talk with you-know-who."

She gave a knowing smile.

I knocked at Britt's open door and waited to be invited in.

"Good to have you back, Gloria."

"Thank you, Britt. I just want to say how grateful I am to you for throwing it all in the other night. I really appreciate what you did, and so does Funk."

"You already thanked me, Gloria." After he said that, he turned his eyes back to the papers on his desk, but I think it was only because he was embarrassed by the compliment.

"Yes, but I didn't thank you in person. You really saved the day, Britt. I don't know what I would have done without you."

It was true. Without Britt's perseverance, we would never have filed the report.

"You're quite welcome," he said, smiling up at me with those bulging eyes, only this time they had a small twinkle in them. For me!

I left our progress at that and went to my office, preparing myself for how high the pile of work on my desk would be. I had just sat down when Joe rushed in.

"Gloria! We just scored the hugest win!"

I wrenched myself out of my chair and excitedly asked, "What happened?"

"Tony will be here any minute to film Funk!"

I was expecting a major endorsement or tons of cash. Getting it up, I asked, "Who's Tony?"

"He's a friend. Well, more like a colleague. He's a blogger who is very influential in Kansas City politics!"

"A blogger is a big deal in local politics?"

"Yes! I had to convince him to interview Funk. If everything goes well, the Hispanic votes will be in our pocket."

Just then Spring's doorbells tinkled and I thought Joe would start tinkling too, right there on the floor next to where Maria went, that's how starstruck he was about Tony What's-His-Name gracing the trailer. When the guy walked past my door Joe flew from my office to greet him.

"Thanks so much for coming, Tony!" Joe squealed.

The guy didn't respond in kind. He just stood in the doorway, peering in at me.

"Come on, Tony, it's this way."

As Joe led him to Funk's office I thought, *This is who Joe practically pissed himself over? The guy looks like an engorged tick.*

That afternoon, we had a committee meeting at Evert's place. It had been a long time since we'd met. Joe was bursting with nerves and excitement, waiting to tell everyone about his latest inspiration. Guess who was to star in our next campaign commercial. No, not me. It was Joe's mistress. The puppy, Maria.

To execute it, Joe and I had set up a scene in my living room one night, trying to get Maria to burst through a newspaper. She couldn't do it, but we about died laughing watching her try. I didn't tell Funk, but I *really* was having a ball with the campaign! Everything was so new and different, and I loved spending time with Joe. It had been a long time since I had a guy friend — maybe not since my first year at college.

The video opened with Maria saying the crumbling sidewalks were hurting her paws, and that was why she was endorsing Funk for mayor. He was the only candidate who promised to provide clean, safe neighborhoods for everyone, including dogs! Our seven-year-old neighbor did the voice-over for Maria. Funk's only appearance came in the last few seconds, where he poked fun at the need to legitimize all things related to campaigns, saying, "Hi! I'm Mark Funkhouser and I approve this poodle." This video did exactly what I'd been telling my husband he needed to do: paint a *picture* of what his administration would provide.

To me, this was Joe's best idea to date. And that was saying a lot. But the group was worried. They wanted Funk to work harder at bringing in donations so a professional commercial could be made. And they wanted the "staff" — those of us slaving away at the headquarters — to make better use of our time.

I understood that Funk's supporters might be the only ones to view the commercial. But wasn't feeding supporters better than waiting and hoping more money would pour in to create a "real" commercial for the masses? Besides, what if Joe was right? If the internet really was the wave of the future for campaigns, this quirky video would be yet one more symbol of Funk's cutting-edge, thrifty leadership style. Midwesterners valued frugality, and our home-made commercial spoke to that.

The longer the committee spoke against it, the deeper Joe sank in his chair. I adored him, but he sure gave up easily. I caught his eye to beam a message to say we would follow through with or without the committees' approval — but since we weren't married, I don't think he got it. All I could do was pray that he'd buck the fuck up.

I had confidence issues like Joe's. In the rare instances that I got emotional support, nothing could stop me from powering forward. Yet even when I stood alone, not a cell in my body would consider giving up, even as I made myself miserable with self-doubt. Since I was standing with Joe, he needed to stop with his doom-and-gloom attitude.

Because if he didn't believe in himself, why would anyone else?

22 JANUARY 2007

A DAY IN THE LIFE of a campaign manager:

1. Responded to a million emails, including one from Simon-the-chairman, about the upcoming fundraiser and another about t-shirts.
2. Recorded purchases and donations.
3. Listened to Joe worry. Again.
4. Wrote thank-you notes to the newest volunteers and to those who were kicking ass.
5. Introduced myself to the new volunteers.
6. Spent time nurturing Dots, Betty Lou, and Bev.
7. Ran to bring lunch in for the volunteers.
8. Scheduled more meet-and-greets. Nope, Aggie hadn't scheduled the first one.
9. Took time away from the pile on my desk to chat with Gwen. I had no idea why she stopped by, but it was the funnest part of my day!
10. Restocked the table with brochures, buttons, and bumper stickers. Twice.
11. Tidied the double-wide, three times.
12. Started on the newsletter.
13. Discussed the next press event with Joe. It's a biggie, about the sidewalks.

14. Edited a press release.
15. Wrote Dottie a personal check to have someone clean the trailer. Tried not to think about my filthy house.
16. Attended a meet-and-greet with Funk.
17. Researched the cost of television and radio airtime. Hey, you gotta be ready to pull the trigger at a moment's notice!
18. Ran to pick up Andrew from school.
19. Drove back to the double-wide feeling guilty as hell for not paying attention to my son and for leaving him home alone again. Trust me, it was bullshit that he didn't want me to be there.
20. Answered fifty thousand calls from Funk. Yelled at him for not taking his schedule. Like, I'm *not* his personal secretary.
21. Listened to Britt tell us girls, again, how we couldn't do something, instead of finding a way that we could.
22. Dealt with the impact Britt had on the girls. Not Bev, because she speaks Britt's language.
23. Cleaned Maria's papers. When was this dog going to train herself?
24. Spoke to Tara twice, hung up early both times to stamp out fires.
25. Doubled-checked that Betty Lou was entering all contacts into the database because a name I was looking for wasn't there.
26. Rearranged Funk's calendar so he could stop by an absolutely "must-attend" event that Simon said he had to attend. Simon Says?
27. Went to say goodbye to everyone. But everyone except Britt had gone home already.
28. Chatted with my son until he kicked me out of his bedroom.

Is your head whirling? If it is, then I'll know you've read today's entry.

24 JANUARY 2007

LUCKY ME! I pulled the short straw!

I got to attend the forum at Southwest High School. The Ward Parkway Corridor, located in the old-money part of town, was filled with bleeding-heart liberals, many of whom also happened to be Catholic. My exchange student from Italy said the Catholic religion in Kansas City bore no resemblance to the one in her country. I was baptized Catholic, so I understood what Anna was talking about. Ward Parkway people worried excessively about what others thought of them and were cinched tighter than a chastity belt because of it — the exception being when they partied. Once they'd had a couple — or six or eight — they tossed their repressed desires to the wind and all hell broke loose. It was kind of embarrassing to watch.

At the high school, I set up our campaign table with its usual paltry offerings and then found a seat in the packed audience. Sitting off to the side, I was leery about how Funk would do, but his message seemed to resonate with the attendees. No matter which part of town hosted the debate, it seemed clear that the race had narrowed down to one issue: TIF.

An audience member asked, "Why can we build stadiums and office buildings and not maintain our schools?" Funk said, "As mayor, I will make sure Kansas City's tax-incentive program works, so that schools won't continue to be shortchanged."

Residents raged about TIF. Based on what I'd heard at the forums, they were tired of their taxes going to line developers' pockets instead of to basic services. They were pissed that the streets were covered in metal plates instead of pavement. They said their schools were for shit. They were concerned about the crime rate. And, in this part of town, they were fed up with the sewers backing up into the basements of their turn-of-the-century homes. That happened to me once, and let me tell you, it was fucking gross.

The other candidates weren't reading the room. Voters were talking about TIF, but the other candidates responded with messaging geared to the elites.

25 JANUARY 2007

TURNS OUT, Funk sucked balls at the Southwest High School forum.

He just wasn't suave enough for that part of town. Jeff, our committee chairman, phoned me to say he had attended the debate and was worried. That was chilling to hear because Jeff and I never agreed on anything.

When I hung up from Mr. Chairman, Pat Gallagher peered nervously inside my office. This was typical behavior for most new volunteers. They were highly interested in meeting Funk's wife but felt intimidated all the same. Although we were acquainted, Pat and I had never met in person. I invited her into my office and she flung a giant bag of M&Ms across my desk, saying, "I know how hard it is to get food in when you're running a campaign."

Without my invitation, she took a seat across from me and divulged personal and professional secrets from the mayor that I had no business knowing. During the telling, she rose from her chair several times to poke her head outside my door, anxiously scanning the trailer to see if anyone had come in who would report her being there.

Funk was no longer employed at city hall, but Mayor Barnes would *still* have liked to see him burned at the stake. She hated him with unbridled passion. I take that back. Her passion was unrestrained behind closed doors. Publicly she sang a different tune, with that good old Kansas City Two-Step.

The mayor had caused my family heartache and lost pay raises. Yet I felt sorry for her because Pat, one of her staff members, was sitting inside enemy headquarters talking behind her back.

As I listened to Pat, the breadth of her disloyalty sank in. It bothered me. It wasn't right to work against the woman from whom she drew her paycheck. But why did I give a shit about Barnes? Probably because, based on my experience in running a business, I could relate to the difficulties Barnes endured just for being female. Yet BirthWays was nothing compared with the mayor's job. Barnes deserved better than what she was getting from this employee.

Landing a position in the mayor's office was a privilege, and Pat was shitting in the nest. I thought, *If she has this much disdain for her boss, she should transfer to a department where she can openly express her sentiments.*

What a relief it would have been to just hate the mayor through and through, to wring as much ammunition as I could from her unfaithful servant. But no, I felt sorry for the loose-ass bitch. Christ! I can't believe I said such a hateful thing about another woman. I'll bet you anything those descriptive words were inspired by something I read in the newspaper, likely from someone who had betrayed the mayor, just as Pat was doing in my office.

But then I got ahold of myself. No way was I going to feel sorry for Barnes, who had treated my husband like scum. Unlike her unwise hiring choices, I was loyal to the bone. No way would I let her get away with what she had done to my husband. With that thought I came crashing back to Earth, focusing my Italian back on the woman sitting across from me.

"I'm sorry, Pat, could you repeat that, please? What did Barnes do next?"

Pat repeated herself, but it was nothing. The mayor had spent $20,000 for a talent show. Big deal. That wasn't what toppled Kansas City. I had the feeling the mayor was hiding something big, but Pat hadn't said boo about what that might be. Either she didn't know, or she was playing both sides of the fence. No matter. I didn't trust the woman anyway. Besides, now that I recalled how Barnes had screwed Funk, I was psyched about something: when Funk was mayor, he'd finally have the power to search for whatever was hiding in the anus of city hall. And picturing him going in after it, the music to *Jaws* started playing in the background of my mind. *Da-da-hump. Da-da-hump. Da-da-hump, da-da-hump, danta, danta, danta, danta, danta. . . .* Yeah, that's right, Barnes. Better hide the keys, girls. My man was coming to find you.

At that precise moment, Dottie transferred a call into my office. Excusing myself to Pat, I picked up the phone.

"Have you heard?"

"Oh, hey, Jeff," I replied. "How are you?"

"Hi again! Did you hear?"

"I've heard a lot of things today. Which thing are you referring to?"

"The debate."

"Nope, I haven't heard a word."

"I don't know how he did it, but Funk scored the highest."

"Nooooooo!"

"Yes! He pulled it out of his ass again!"

"Jesus, Jeff, how can that be? Funk was drier than a bone that's been laying in the desert for a hundred years."

"I know," he said with a laugh. "I was there."

"I don't know how I didn't see you."

"I was standing in the shadows of the stage, sweating bullets, listening. But Gloria, it's true. Funk won!"

We'd been told many times that it wasn't possible for Funk to woo the Southwest Corridor, even though he lived there. Yet he had. I was delighted, even if it didn't make sense.

As promised, our volunteer Rhonda had "pulled the trigger" and turned the city orange overnight. Most of the yard signs went up north, down south, or east of Redbridge. There was only a smattering in our neighborhood.

Another weird thing: since the mayor's race was nonpartisan, no one was privy to Funk's political leanings. Yet both Republicans and Democrats had claimed him as their own. Funk, a Republican? He was socially liberal and fiscally conservative. That was probably why people were confused. Funk crossed lines with ease, whether they were generational, professional, economic, or now, it seemed, party lines.

28 JANUARY 2007

THE INNER CIRCLE had begun to meet more frequently. Joe sat in the reception area waiting for the group to arrive. I could hear him talking on his cell phone to a colleague from his reporter days. With all the noise in the trailer, I'd gotten pretty good at tuning out conversations. But my ears perked up when I heard Joe mention my name. What he said next just about blew me out of my chair.

"Gloria? Oh, she's going to make a great First Lady!"

Me, a First Lady?

Holy shit. I'd never considered that before. How would my duty to Funk end once he won? Would I be able to start back at BirthWays or try my hand at building little houses for just-dumped women?

To head off dancing with that idea, I went out to schmooze with the staff and volunteers. Joe had drifted to the snack room, so I leaned over the reception cage and greeted the girls playfully.

"Hey, Dotsie-Whotsie."

"Gloria! Stop!" Dottie screeched and blushed.

"How goes it, Eyes-of-Blue?"

"I'm fine, Gloria," Betty Lou said abruptly, which was the way she talked when she was annoyed with Britt — which was all the time.

Britt and Funk were out at an event together, and I said, "Oh, Lord, what's he done now?"

"Britt's just being Britt. Ordering us around as if we are his servants."

"Should I have Funk speak with him again?"

"No, it won't do any good. It's just who Britt is."

I was about to offer another solution when I saw Maria circling the room. The dog *still* wasn't trained. I screamed, "Oh, no, Maria has to shit!" And thinking about what Betty Lou had just said, I grabbed the dog, guided her inside Britt's office, and closed the door.

I came back to an explosion of laugher.

"Gloria, you shouldn't have!" Dottie exclaimed delightedly.

"Oh yes, she should have. Serves Britt right," said Betty Lou.

That sordid little affair was exactly what I needed to take my mind off what Joe had said two minutes earlier. A moment later, Evert arrived and motioned with his head for me to join him in Funk's office.

He closed the door behind us and said, "I want to show you something."

He looked like a proud little boy. Intrigued beyond all get out, I said, "What is it, Evert?"

He didn't respond. Just began rolling up one of his shirtsleeves.

When he started doing that, I became so curious I thought I'd burst. I had no clue what he was about to show me, and I about died laughing when I saw the rose.

"A tattoo! Oh my G — "

"Shhh!" came Evert's fearful interruption.

But I couldn't stop laughing. Man, we had come a long way in our relationship in a short amount of time.

When I finally got ahold of myself, I said, "What's the big secret?"

"I don't want anyone to know. My wife doesn't even know."

"You didn't tell your wife?" I whispered incredulously.

He looked at me as if I was dense and began rolling his sleeve back down.

"What's wrong with having a tattoo?"

"It's not what my peers do," he said matter-of-factly.

"Well, isn't your wife going to see it?"

"Not if I can help it."

I wondered how that could be, but I didn't say anything.

"What made you get it?"

"I've always wanted one, and today just happened to be the day."

"*Today?* You had this done today?"

"Yes, just before I came here."

"Oh my God. That's wild, Evert!"

Again, he didn't respond. He seemed excited, but now that we were actually discussing the thing, he looked like a deer in the headlights.

"If you've always wanted a tattoo, why today?"

"I don't know. I think it's because of what my son is going through."

"Ah, that makes sense."

Evert's rose tattoo honored his family's business, Rosehill Gardens. I wanted to know more about his desire to get inked, but the minute he heard Funk's car rattle into the parking lot, Evert clammed up about it.

For the duration of the meeting, my eyes kept going to Evert, and mostly because he kept rubbing his sore arm.

30 JANUARY 2007

READING AND REPLYING TO EMAILS consumed a large chunk of my days. With the team members running in different directions, online communications had become a necessity, and messages zigzagged through the trailer.

From: FUNKHOUSER FOR MAYOR!

Subject: Thoughts from the field

Dottie: You might put this on the calendar:

Ed Ford said something to Evert about it being very good if Mark can stop by Cascone's on Thursday from 5 to 7 for a Ford Victory function and fundraiser.

Also, Evert is getting some feedback on Mark's need to work the room a little more at events.

Britt

A few thoughts swirled in my head after I read the email. First, poor Councilman Ford was not getting his wish. No one was running against him. Where would he turn now to earn the esteem he craved from his father? Second, who would I have to throw off Funk's calendar to make room for his impromptu event? Third, enough with working the room already! Funk wasn't doing it. Last, please stop wasting my time making me read unnecessary emails!

31 JANUARY 2007

THE DIRT circulating in some media outlets was scaring me. They were just rumors, but you know how shit can stick like glue. A few of the other candidates were referring to Funk as "Dr. No." They probably thought it was an ingenious play on the name Funk's supporters had begun calling him: "Dr. Funk."

By using their version of his name, Funk's opponents were trying to instill fear. They were suggesting that because Funk was against TIFs in wealthy neighborhoods, he was against economic development. That if he was elected, Dr. No would reject any plan that crossed his desk — and poof! — there'd go jobs for blue-collar workers. Of course Funk wasn't against economic development, and of course the establishment wasn't the least bit worried about regular folks. On the bright side, because his opponents were publicly attacking him, Funk's campaign was getting more earned media.

I wondered how much the other candidates were paying their staff. They sure didn't seem to be getting much for their money. Joe could have made a fortune if he had switched camps.

We Want the Funk,
Gotta Have That Funk

OH MY GOD! We were in the election month — at least, in the first go-round, the primary.

"Hey, Dots."

"Good morning, Gloria! How are you today?"

"Not so good. I feel like I never went to bed last night. I woke up as tired as when I laid down.

"I know what you mean," Dottie said with a laugh.

"This is crazy. Was it like this in the auditor's office?"

"No! Not even when we were pushing a report out."

"Oh, well. It's just a little longer. We're women enough to handle it."

As I started for my office, Dottie said, "Would you mind taking the mail with you?"

"Yezzz, ma'am," I said, pretending to be a business professional.

4 FEBRUARY 2007

FUNK AND I ATTENDED a Superbowl party at Hearne Christopher's house. Hearne was a reporter friend of Joe's. We knew him from his society column in *The Kansas City Star*, even if neither of us read it. I didn't know why we were invited and not Joe.

The committee said the invitation was a major coup, so instead of staying home to watch the game with our son, off to Johnson County we went. Forty minutes later we pulled into Hearne's housing development. His house seemed like a twentieth-century take on a *Sears & Roebuck Catalogue* home. I must've missed the news that Sears merged with McDonald's. Hearne's home presented like a supersize order of fries: it was a house built for the nouveau riche.

As we walked through the door, there stood Councilmember Becky Nace, who was running for mayor too. I'd attended enough forums by now that I could recognize all the candidates, but seeing one at an intimate house party felt different. She had an air about her that said she was already the mayor. I felt sorry for the woman. She really believed she would win. Thinking about how crushed she'd be when she lost, I removed myself from her presence.

Most of the partyers stood packed together in Hearne's "great room." It was a weird crowd in a weird space. I always got a sick, depressed feeling in my stomach when I was inside this type of home. I'd choose my family's tiny cabin in the Ozarks over this six thousand square foot place any day.

I walked about, but no *real* conversations were happening. Everyone just stood like mice in an overcrowded cage. All pretending not to be angling for the perfect place to stand, that place being where the best gossip was going down. I tried striking up a conversation with several people, but they had one ear turned to me and the other eavesdropping on conversations nearby.

The only person who wasn't excruciatingly boring was Nick Haines, a local television personality who hailed from England. I loved foreigners, so it was nice spending a few minutes with this smiley, affable guy. His love for life lit up his entire being. With that going on, you didn't notice how short he was.

Or that the few hairs remaining on his head were flaming red. Of course, him being a TV star, everyone sought his attention. When the conversation went from titillating to stale, I moved to a quiet room with walls lined with bookshelves. And there I stayed for the duration of the party, browsing the library.

I wasn't alone for long. Soon, Councilwoman Nace's husband, also looking for an escape, wandered in. We commiserated about being married to a mayoral candidate, of all things. Who knew this would be my life.

5 FEBRUARY 2007

WHEN JOE RELEASED THE MARIA THE POODLE VIDEO it went viral, getting fifteen thousand hits within twenty-four hours! I was so excited that I could barely stand living inside myself. Imagine, little nothing me had been part of something that created a national sensation. I couldn't work for thinking about it. Our quirky little campaign got oodles of earned media. It seemed as if we could do no wrong.

6 FEBRUARY 2007

THANKS TO JOE'S VIDEO, what had been a drip in donations soon became a steady trickle. And that's when the other campaigns took notice of us. Of course, they did it in the slyest of ways.

Puzzled beyond all get-out, I rose from the chair in my office and knocked on Britt's open door.

"I'm sorry to bother you, but can you come take a look at something please?"

Britt was extraordinarily difficult to deal with, but the man *was* a workhorse. He immediately got up and followed me to the problem.

"Look at this," I said, pointing to my laptop, on which a window displayed my email inbox.

Britt clicked everywhere but met my same problem. My computer was completely frozen because of all the emails pouring into my inbox. Looking intensely at my screen, his face got beet red and he spat, "They're trying to shut us down."

Britt was pissed, even if he did make that remark with sort of a laugh.

"Who's trying to shut us down?"

"Another campaign, of course."

"I don't understand. Which campaign? And what exactly are they doing?"

"I don't know whose campaign it is, but they've found a way to halt work at ours by bombarding your computer with bogus emails."

"Jesus, I didn't know you could do that!"

"Do you see the red bubble next to your inbox? What's the number?"

"I don't know. It's moving too fast. At the moment, it's 8600-something. Now it's 8800."

"Those aren't real emails, Gloria. They're empty."

Britt kept speaking in a way that told me he was steaming mad, yet something was off about his emotion because he also seemed happy. Well, happy isn't the right word. Charged was more like it, as if he was in the middle of a good fight, enjoying the hell out of the competition.

He remained staring at my laptop while he spoke, but his talk was mostly to himself.

"They've found a way to generate enough emails to disable your computer. See?" he said, clicking the keys on my beautiful machine way too roughly. "You won't be able to use your laptop with this is going on. They've very effectively ground us to a stop."

Britt was right. Emails were dumping into my BirthWays account at such a terrific speed that nothing else functioned on my laptop.

"Those bastards! That's so dirty! Is this happening to yours?"

"Let's find out."

Britt's computer was fine, as was everyone else's. We tried to get mine working, but it was no use, it was locked up. The only thing we could do was deactivate my email address and wait a few days for the ruthless assholes to have their fill of fucking with us before authorizing it again.

I wasn't too distraught about it because it seemed to indicate that our little campaign *was* relevant after all. Later in the day we got another sign that the movers and shakers were taking Funk seriously. Mayor Barnes was overheard saying, "Mark's campaign has legs."

Things moved fast from that point on. Before long, our campaign finances were so far in the black that I felt safe making our first media buy. Donations weren't prolific enough to hire a professional to engineer a commercial, but that was fine by me. Joe already had another homemade video in the works, and this time it was going on television! It would capture Funk's supporters singing that catchy Parliament tune:

> You've got a real type of thing goin' down, gettin' down
> There's a whole lot of rhythm goin' 'round
> Oww, we want the funk, give up the funk
> Oww, we need the funk, we gotta have that funk

After Joe received my typical, over-the-top, I'm-so-amazed-at-your-creativity reaction, he laid it on me that he wouldn't be in town to produce the commercial. He explained he would be getting married soon and would take a leave for his honeymoon. I was stunned to hear that he was getting married because I barely knew he had a girlfriend, much less a fiancé. When my thrill changed to, "What the fuck, Joe!" he quickly added that he'd made contingencies for his absence. A reporter colleague, Kendrick Blackwood, would take up his slack — unfortunately, not in time to film the commercial. He would leave the production to me.

Okay, first I was born. Then I endured my childhood. After that, I became a wife. A mother. A small-business owner. A sometimes unintentional baby-catcher. Just recently, I'd begrudgingly become a campaign manager. And now I was going to be the producer of a television commercial? Like really, what did I know about making a commercial?

Funk would be out of town on a consulting gig, so it would be just me, a cameraperson, and a group of Funk's supporters, dancing on a hilltop overlooking Kansas City. I'd direct them. So, no biggie.

8 FEBRUARY 2007

I WAS STANDING AT THE BACK OF A CHURCH in the Old Northeast district, attending yet another forum. It was one of the first Joe had attended, which was weird, given that he was a debate coach. I loved Joe to pieces, but I really wished he wasn't standing so close. The man was an emotional wreck, and I didn't want to catch whatever he had. Each time a candidate spoke, Joe was certain that person would be the next mayor.

He frantically whispered in my ear, "This isn't good, Gloria."

Joe was referring to Henry Klein, who was *still* in the middle of his opening speech — a speech I'd heard a hundred times.

"I've been *waaaaalking* the neighborhood . . . " said Henry in his phony we're-all-brothers-and-sisters voice.

"It's fine, Joe. Klein's a millionaire."

"So?"

"Do you really think he's walked *every* neighborhood in Kansas City? How many square miles would that be?"

"I don't know. It's poss — "

I stopped Joe before he spiraled into the pit of hell and took me with him. "C'mon, Joe. Does the guy look like someone who's concerned about the needs of ordinary folks?"

"I don't know, Gloria. He seems sincere."

"Joe, stop! The guy doesn't give one small fuck, and you know it!"

"Yeah, maybe you're right. But the audience doesn't know that. He's good. They might believe him, just like I did."

"Giuseppe, listen to me. You gotta stop with this. Funk needs your positive energy right now."

I was worried that Joe's negativity would affect Funk's performance. My husband needed to do well that night, at the first debate in one of the Hispanic parts of town.

To counteract Joe's negative influence, I focused every ounce of my being onto my husband. I penetrated his soul with my life force, prayed that God

311

would help the crowd see Funk for who he really was: honest, smart, and dedicated. The opposite of the same old, same old, Funk would be the candidate who had their back. I was so absorbed in my task that I must've looked like a little fool — so intent, so innocent, so concentrating on my man. To stop from feeling embarrassed, I told myself that at least I was in a church, where people appeared this way at times.

I had just moved on to picturing a white light surrounding my husband when something weird happened. I noticed a light was already there. Not just any light. The brightest shaft of light illuminated his entire body. Funk was so engulfed in its radiance that the other candidates looked as if they were sitting in the dark. I looked around for a spotlight, thinking someone was filming the event, but no, the cone of light originated from above the ceiling.

I don't know how I didn't notice it before. But man, how humiliated I felt seeing it now. Here I was, thinking I *had* to influence something, *could* influence something, when the heavens already had it covered.

Suddenly everything made sense. No wonder we'd been so sure Funk would win. He was supposed to be doing this.

Joe's breath was in my ear again, and I came back from those musings.

"Gloria, this guy is so good! He's going to destroy us!"

"This guy" was Al Riederer. To my knowledge, he was the last candidate to enter the race. He stood out for being incredibly short and bald, and he boomed a big persona. The man was running back and forth across the stage, broadcasting his platform with all the reverence in the world. Funny thing was, he was booming Funk's talking points on TIF. He had my husband's lines down so well that you would've thought the man had been sitting around our dining room table for the past twenty years.

Al was just one more lawyer running for mayor. The guy did give me pause, though. Because, just as Joe had anxiously asked a few minutes earlier, how would the audience know Riederer was a fake?

In a moment of clarity, I remembered that I was a New and Better Me and consoled myself: *Don't worry, Gloria. This guy's gonna be seen for who he really is. Remember the Wizard of Oz? The man who tortured poor Dorothy when her only crime was that she wanted to go home? Well, before this election is over, it'll be revealed that Riederer is nothing more than a tiny little man blustering behind a curtain trying to scare the hell out of everyone.*

With that, I turned to Joe and gently said, "Don't worry. Funk is going to win. You know that."

Looking pained, Joe said, "I wish I had your confidence."

"Listen, Joe, that little wizard has nothing on Funk."

"Little wizard!" Joe belly-laughed, coming out of his agony.

The next question addressed the way the city's sewers kept backing up into people's homes. The candidates had been asked to provide a solution. They gave the easy answer: they'd go to Washington and demand money to rebuild the system. When the debate convener asked Funk where he would find the money to solve the problem, Funk answered, "From the citizens' back pocket, of course. It would be naïve to think the fix wouldn't come from rate increases, *big* rate increases."

When Funk said that, I thought, *Why can't he learn the Kansas City Two-Step?* It wasn't hard. All you had to do was slap a big smile on your face and sidestep an answer. Everyone would believe you. Because a friend would never fuck you over, would they?

9 FEBRUARY 2007

KENDRICK BLACKWOOD helped out at headquarters during Joe's honeymoon. One morning he waltzed into my office, acting as if he'd been there a million times, and exclaimed in the most flirtatious way you can imagine, "Would you *look* at those sex-me-up red toes!"

I think he even made a *whew* sound for emphasis after he said that.

I was stunned. It was the weirdest way to introduce himself, but I took an instant shine to the guy. Because who in the Midwest plays around or flirts as much as I do?

I had been composing the week's newsletter, but I put it aside and Kendrick and I began talking as if we'd known each other forever. Taking a seat before it was offered, he continued feeding my soul. We went straight from sex talk to how Mayor Barnes was getting more hysterical the longer the election ground on. When I asked how so, he told me the latest: Barnes had called an emergency press conference to dispel the notion going around town that Funk would be a good mayor. Barnes was usually all smiles with the media, but her real self popped out when a reporter asked her to comment on what Funk had said at a recent debate: that Barnes's administration had tripled the city's debt.

Man, did it suck to be that reporter. After he posed the question, the mayor let out a screaming tirade directed at him, saying her administration hadn't tripled anything, and asked how he dared repeat such a thing. Before the guy had a chance to wipe the spit from his eye, she said if Funkhouser was saying things like that, she wouldn't *allow* him to take office.

As soon as we stopped laughing, I told Kendrick we shouldn't have laughed. That it wasn't nice. I felt sorry for Mayor Barnes because of what had happened next. Apparently, Barnes was so furious that her fake-flower boutonniere flew from her deflated breast and hit the floor. Yet no one picked it up and dusted it off for her. And that wouldn't be the worst of it. Once citizens saw her performance on the news, the town would chew her up. Her accomplishments would be out the window, forgotten in a flash. That's how much Kansas City demanded its people to hide behind nice. How sad was that?

Back to Kendrick: I loved a guy who told a story solely for the joy of the telling. This man could throw juicy bits of gossip around just like a girl.

All Right, Already — I Get the Message

10 FEBRUARY 2007

MY CONVERSION OCCURRED in the basement of a church in a rundown part of town, at a debate between mayoral candidates. There, my role as a supportive wife drastically changed. Instead of helping my husband run for office, my heart shifted to all-out believing in his cause.

The venue wasn't far from our Brookside home, but man, what a difference a few miles made once you crossed that dividing line called Troost Avenue. Most of the street signs had gone missing, so Funk and I had to drive through block upon block of what appeared to be a war-torn landscape to locate the venue.

Seeing the area in such ruins, I turned in my seat and said to my husband, "Funk, where the fuck are we?"

He looked just as quizzical, but it was me who had befuddled him, not the surroundings.

"We're in the East Side, Glor. Haven't you been this way before?"

Our kids' elementary school had been in the East Side, as was Andrew's high school.

"Don't be stupid, Funk. I've driven east a hundred million times."

Out popped my husband's bottom lip, but just a smidge.

"This looks like bombed-out Beirut. Have you driven us off the continent or something?"

"No, Glor, we're definitely still in Kansas City."

"This is awful. How do people live here?"

Kansas City had many rundown areas, but this was entirely different. An entire swath of the city was filled with boarded-up buildings. If a building wasn't boarded up, then every window was busted out, the interior exposed to the weather. Some potholes were so enormous they could swallow your car if you weren't paying attention to the road. There were neighborhoods with steps leading up to nowhere, though you could tell a house had once stood there. Flanking those used-to-be homes were empty lots filled with dried weeds reaching ten feet high.

Anything you could expect from a city — name one single amenity — you couldn't find it here. We never passed a grocery store, which made me wonder where in the world people shopped. Then again, I didn't see any people.

Due to the lack of street signs, we were taking way too long to find the place. Just as Funk was beginning to get edgy, we happened upon the church. He skirted a massive hole in the road to park at the curb, and he rushed me along the crumbling sidewalk so as not to be late. When I say crumbling, I don't mean the sidewalk was cracked in a few places like every other sidewalk in Kansas City. This sidewalk had lost whatever ingredient holds those things together. It was a mass of loose gravel, and you had to watch your footing lest you slip. And Lord knows, I couldn't handle another fall.

I was expecting the church to be in a shambles too. It was threadbare but sparkling clean. A committee of little old black ladies greeted us at the door. From the sight of them, it was clear how the place had survived in the midst of its circumstances. Funk and I said our hellos and then beat it on down to the basement meeting room.

The hall was small, and almost every seat was taken. The audience of old women and dozens of children paid rapt attention to the goings-on. I was still setting up our table when I heard the debate called to order. I rushed to finish and found an empty seat. Christ, did I ever cringe when the other candidates began their opening remarks, particularly the ones who were sitting councilmembers.

They said what they always say, including boasting about their many accomplishments. I couldn't believe they would do that here, in this brokedown place — that they didn't think to edit that part of their spiel out. What balls it took to feed these worn-out women a line of bullshit about all they'd done to help their community, the ordinances they'd personally drafted to fix the conditions in the East Side, the way they'd stuck their neck on the line for the residents. It was awful to hear. Hadn't they walked on the same sidewalk that I'd just skidded in on?

The audience was unmoved by the candidates' babblings. I was embarrassed by their cold stares. Embarrassed and afraid. What if they perceived Funk to be of the same cloth as the others on the dais? How would they know he was the exact opposite? What would make them trust that he had spent his career trying to right the wrongs for regular folks and that he decided to run for mayor to get the job done? How would they have had the time to parse that out when they were working numerous jobs just to survive?

The other candidates had been long-winded for the entire campaign, but on this morning they were even more verbose than usual. I guess they figured if they just kept talking, they'd win the crowd over. If I were being kind, I'd say most of Funk's running mates had been true to their ideals when they started out. Those ideals probably flew out the window when they encountered the first pressures of a city councilmember's office. It wasn't long before campaign favors came due and outside interests cozied up, hoping to gain something, anything, from the newly empowered.

The establishment's tactics were simple: they stroked the councilmembers' egos until the councilmembers believed themselves superior to the people they'd just been voted in to serve. And the establishment leeches wouldn't stop fondling the councilmembers' balls until the officials became addicts, begging for the next helping of flattery. You could tell when the strings had attached, as the newbies suddenly displayed a narcissistic view of themselves that far surpassed their abilities. Once that dynamic took hold, they treated constituents and staff — my husband included, back when he was the city auditor — like gum stuck to their heels.

Halfway through the debate, my skin was crawling from having to listen to them.

Each time the moderator called on a candidate, they'd shoot up from their seat and bellow their response like some kind of preacher man. I wanted to peer around the room to see how the audience was taking it, but I didn't want to make a spectacle of myself. So I walked to the ladies' room, and on my way back I perched against a wall at the back of the hall and watched the proceedings from there.

And then something changed.

My embarrassment turned into pride for being the same gender as most of the adults in the hall. This debate was living proof that women really were the civilizers of the world. If it weren't for these ladies, many of the children in the room wouldn't have a chance of succeeding. By the time the event ended I was overcome with emotion, so much that when I buckled myself back inside Funk's little red Corolla, my usual critique of his performance was stilled.

And that's when it happened.

As we rushed to the next debate of the day, something so powerful filled the car that I felt crushed by its presence. I had no idea what it was, only that I hadn't felt anything as encompassing since I was a little girl seeing a ghost in my bedroom. Whatever was inside my husband's car wasn't a ghost, but it was of spirit, and its sheer power made me want to escape it. I hunkered low in my seat and tried not to be noticed. Pretended I was engrossed in the sights passing by my window. But the more I ignored it, the more it filled the space, saturating my mind with words. When I finally got up the courage to listen, I turned to my husband in stunned amazement and repeated the message I'd heard, as if it were my own.

"Oh my God, Funk. Do you realize that you have an opportunity to do a whole lot of good for a whole lot of people?"

He stared at me, equally stunned — even a bit disgusted, and definitely irritated — as if he couldn't quite believe I was just now getting it.

"Glor, what the hell do you think I've been doing this for?"

As always, he killed it. Spirit vacated the car.

It took me a while to stop being repulsed, but after my awe returned, I committed to Funk's campaign. For real. I jumped in with my whole heart to ensure the bastard succeeded.

I was wrung out from the day's happenings. When the second debate concluded, I wanted badly to just go home and rest, but nothing doing. Funk and I had a wedding to attend, Joe's! My new best friend was getting married.

We arrived at the venue minutes before the service began. As soon as we strode in the door all eyes turned to me and Funk. It was my long-standing habit to give Funk a once-over before entering any public place, but I had been so rattled by the day's events that I'd forgotten to perform my wifely duties. Seeing the looks he was getting, I nudged Funk into a corner and assessed him. Nothing was out of the ordinary, just him looking like the hick that he is. Concerned that it was me, I tilted my head back and flared my nostrils at him, and Funk nodded, letting me know all was good up in there too. Since we both presented well, I didn't know the reason for all the stares, just that they were totally rude.

The minister opened the ceremony by passing Joe and Allie's wedding rings around, asking that each attendee hold them and bless the union. I should have known something hokey would go down, as Joe and his bride-to-be seemed to be new age types.

When their rings reached us, Funk bent his head down and began to pray. I leaned in and whispered in his good ear, "Forget that, Funk. Let's show Joe and Allie how it's done."

My husband needed no further instruction. We removed our wedding rings and intertwined ours with theirs. The four rings now tucked safely in his palm, I placed my hand over his, and we prayed for Joe and Allie's union all right. We prayed that some of our mojo would rub off on them. I was sure they would need it.

11 FEBRUARY 2007

IT WAS EARLY MORNING when the news was delivered.

There I was, innocently staring out at the neighbor's mustard-colored house, folding laundry in my dining room, when Funk came up behind me and shoved the *Star*'s editorial page between my face and the sock I was turning right-side out.

The news?

The Kansas City Star had endorsed my husband for mayor.

"Holy fucking shit, Funk, this is *fucking huge!*" I whispered reverently, barely able to breathe.

"Pretty good, huh?" came my husband's way-too-sedate response.

"Oh my God, this is amazing," I said in disbelief before screaming up the stairs for my son.

"What now?" came Andrew's bitter acknowledgment.

"Quick! Come down!" I panted.

My son came loping down the stairs and stood before me. Noticing it was his sock I was struggling with, he steadied himself for a lecture.

"Ange, you are *never* gonna believe this!"

"What?"

"The *Star* just endorsed Dad!"

"So?"

"So?" I screeched.

"C'mon, Mom, just say it."

"Andrew, this means Dad is guaranteed to win!"

"Great, Mom. Can I go now?"

That's the way it went around this joint. No one got as excited as I did. Just as I was having those dispiriting thoughts, *ring-ring* went my phone and my men scattered like ants, thankful to be free.

"Gloria?" came Jeff Simon's dazed but dazzle-filled voice.

"Hey, Jeff," I said, still panting.

"Did you see?"

"Yes Jeff, I saw. Can you please teach me how to breathe again?"

Jeff laughed. A real laugh! Finally, I had someone to share the excitement with!

"Yeah, it's pretty unbelievable."

"Honestly Jeff, I can't catch my breath."

He gave another big belly laugh and said he understood.

"Did you know this was coming?"

"I had no clue."

"How am I going to get any work done today?"

"I know. Me too."

Jeff and I spoke for twenty minutes, rejoicing in the news. As soon as we hung up, I rang Joe.

"Joe!" I squealed. "Can you fucking believe it?"

"Yes, Gloria, it's great!"

"Were you surprised?" I asked, busting with ecstasy.

"Yes, I was!"

Such a strange, short response from Joe. He was usually just as astounded by the campaign's good fortune as I was.

"That's it? That's all you're going to say?"

"No, no. We love it. It's bougie, but we love it."

"Bougie?" I said, confused.

"You know, bourgeois. It must have cost a fortune! Is it from the campaign or your family?"

"Um, Joe, are we talking about the same thing?"

"Allie and I just now opened it."

"Oh my God, you mean your wedding present!"

"Isn't that what you're talking about?"

"No, I forgot about that, but I'm glad you like the cooking pots. And of course it's from our family. Do you think Funk would let me spend campaign money?"

Now Joe sounded confused, "Well, what were you calling about?"

"The *Star* endorsed Funk."

"Oh, that. Yes, I heard. That's really great too! But I gotta go. Everyone is waiting on me to open the rest of the presents." *Click.* He hung up.

If that wasn't the craziest thing ever!

Joe had been a wreck about Funk winning, and yet his wedding gifts were more enthralling to him than the endorsement. Oh, well. I was glad he liked our present. I had bought it at Williams Sonoma because I wanted him to have something really nice. I didn't tell Funk I'd spent $500 on it, because he would've thrown a fit. But hey, you had to do what it took to keep good workers happy. The way I saw it, Funk was the product, but Joe was the genius who was making voters discover that product.

And besides, what harm could another couple of hundred . . . or three . . . or four . . . or five do to our credit card balance anyway?

12 FEBRUARY 2007

WHEN MY EYES POPPED OPEN IN THE MORNING, the view that filled them was my husband's gangly frame towering above our bed.

"Glor, what's the date of the Public Safety press event?"

"Jesus, Funk, really?"

"Gloria, it's the most important event."

Sitting up, I said, "Yes, I'm aware of that, Funk. People are dying right and left in this godforsaken city."

He stood mute, impatiently waiting for the answer so he could bolt out the door.

Seeing that I couldn't pull the date out of my ass, he inquired, "Who has the event?"

"Uh, that would be your man Jeff Simon. Ask him. He's got that and the GOTV — Get Out the Vote."

"I'm gonna be late, Mom," came my son's you're-a-terrible-mother voice from down the hall.

Was God mad at me or something?

No time to ponder, I shouted back, "I'm getting ready."

"No, you aren't. You're talking to Dad."

"Out of my way, Funk," I said, swinging my legs out from the covers.

"I'm sorry for waking you."

Ring-ring went the phone. I looked at the caller ID and, seeing it was my daughter, I gleefully answered. "Hey, baby!"

"Hey, Mama. I got your voice mail. That's really great about the *Star*!"

Finally, a normal response from another person in this family.

13 FEBRUARY 2007

PEOPLE SEEMED LIKE FAMILY at the campaign headquarters.

I was sitting inside my office justifying the previous month's checkbook when I overheard someone blurt, "Maria has to go!"

Those panicked words were quickly followed by, "Well, go put her on Britt's chair!"

I about laughed myself into a stupor.

Later on, after ten million interruptions, I was still justifying the checkbook when in walked Britt, talking his usual Britt.

"I can't tell you how much I hate this, Gloria."

I was saved from having to apologize for Maria pissing on his newspaper again because in strode Funk, seeking my advice on what to say to the woman who was waiting on the phone for him. I'd made arrangements for that call after I struck out trying to buy the rights to the Parliament tune "We Want the Funk" that we were going to use for Joe's latest commercial.

The woman was calling from Switzerland, and it seemed like they had a unique way of doing business there. Even though I was the person who knew how the campaign planned to use the Parliament tune, she would talk price only with Funk, the candidate. The problem was, Funk wasn't good at negotiating. In addition, I'd had no chance to bring him up to speed on the situation. Hence, he was standing in front of my desk asking what he should say.

Agitated by the constant interruptions and my husband's lack of street smarts, I rolled my eyes and said, "Funk, tell the lady that you're part Swiss and that you'll fuck her mother if she wants you to. Just get me the damn rights to that song."

14 FEBRUARY 2007

JOE ARRIVED AT THE TRAILER EARLY. He was worried. Again. He said Funk had to change the phrase he used at debates to describe his vision for transit because "multi-modal" sounded too wonkish. I told Joe I'd take care of it.

Later that day, having drawn the short straw again, I left the trailer with just enough time to set up our table at the next debate. These forums had grown tiresome. The same people attended, no matter the part of town. Given that, you'd think the candidates would've jazzed up their talking points, but no one said anything new except for Funk. Every time, my husband's running mates said the same things with the same overzealousness and made the same fuck-ups.

Take Janice Ellis, for instance: "Hello, I'm Janis Ellis. And I just want to say that one's life journey is important. Fundamentally important. And in becoming mayor, it's even more fundamentally so."

And Alvin Brooks: "It was the worst of times — no, I mean, it was the best of times, and it was the worst of times. Well, if I'm your next mayor, I want it to be the worst — no! — the best of times. All of the times."

On the good news front, Funk was still winning most of the debates, and they weren't lasting as long.

Reentering our home after a long day, Funk and I chatted with Andrew before we headed upstairs to bed. As we were falling asleep, Funk whispered a groggy, "We're kicking their asses, baby."

15 FEBRUARY 2007

WAITING FOR ANDREW TO GET READY FOR SCHOOL, I told Funk about Joe's concerns with the term *multi-modal*, which Funk used in part to describe his transit plan. Joe thought that the phrase was way too wonkish.

Funk agreed to change it up.

Eight hours later, during a meeting of the Inner Circle, Funk talked through his transit plan, explaining, "We need a comprehensive, coordinated, and connected transit system."

Joe's eyes flew open and he stared at my husband. He was waiting for Funk to say he was kidding — but Funk wasn't kidding.

16 FEBRUARY 2007

AS SOON AS BETTY LOU TINKLED THE DOORBELLS, she made a beeline for my office. "Look," she said, thrusting a baseball cap across my desk.

Many items had been crafted for the campaign, and most had been outstanding, but this one topped them all. The hat's logo replicated our buttons: a baby blue background featuring an orange star, and "Funk for Mayor" lettering in navy blue.

"Geez, Betty Lou, this is so professional!"

"Why, thank you, ma'am. My husband made it. He can make a bunch more if you'd like."

A worried look must have crossed my face because Betty Lou quickly added, "To donate, of course."

"Jesus, that's so nice! But you've already given Funk way too much. You're here almost as much as I am."

"The hours are fine by me."

Ever since my "baptism" into the campaign after the debate in the East Side church basement, I'd become even more obsessed about getting my work done. Betty Lou returned to her desk, and I went back to composing the next newsletter.

There was so much to tell! Happy things. Wonderful surprises just kept happening. I began with the biggest news:

The hot topic this week was the *Star*'s endorsement of Funk for Mayor! It came earlier than usual, and with only one candidate endorsed as opposed to the usual two.

The next paragraph made hay on that:

We hit the big-time! Because of the endorsement, there's been an uptick in donations. We've ordered ad time for network TV. Not too many spots. Enough to get the word out before the Primary, yet not enough to make the audience groan from seeing my guy's sweet little face too much.

We'd love for you to star in our next homemade commercial that will be featured in those ads. If interested, please meet us at Penn Valley Park on Sunday at 3:30.

After which I inserted a titillating piece of gossip:

A little bird told us that a poll was conducted and they slipped us the results: Nace placed 3rd, Brooks 2nd, and 1st place, yes folks, went to our very own Funk. It won't be too much longer before the only poll that matters comes back in our favor too. Sucks to be the candidate who paid for that information.

The newsletter ended with something Britt asked me to include:

The DoubleWide was hopping last Saturday — we had at least 30 volunteers show up. We will repeat the performance each Saturday until the Primary. COME BE A PART OF IT!!!

Of course, I used lowercase letters for the last sentence.

Moments after I hit Send, Joe came into my office. His question was interrupted by a commotion outside my doorway.

A voice said, "Maria has to shit!"

"Put her in Britt's office!" replied a chorus of voices accompanied by women's laughter.

Joe asked, "What's that about?"

"Nothing. Just the women getting even."

"Nice!"

"Not really, Joe. Maria will never be housetrained if we keep this up."

17 FEBRUARY 2007

THE FUNKY BLUES FUNDRAISER was just a week away! Slick was performing, so not only would the music be fabulous, but Tara was flying home and staying through the primary election. I was excited. It had been six long weeks since I had seen my daughter's beautiful face.

The owner of Knuckleheads, the host venue, was selling general admission tickets and donating the proceeds to the campaign. I'd been to that bar many times, but I'd never met Frank, the owner, until I arranged the event. He was gracious and I felt an instant connection, as if we'd known one another for years.

The campaign planned to beef up proceeds by selling limited-edition "Funk for Mayor" t-shirts. I'd kidded around with readers in a past newsletter, saying if they came to the fundraiser *and* bought a t-shirt, Funk would autograph it for them. I extended the fun by saying I knew they'd rather have my signature on their shirt. The joke could've easily tanked, but people responded all the next day, saying they'd be seeking my autograph, not Funk's.

It surprised me how much Funk's supporters loved *Notes from the Double-Wide*, especially the snippets about our family. Funk was right; the intimacy of the newsletter seemed to fulfill readers' need for a greater connection.

It got me thinking about how intense it would be to run a world-class city without the foundation of your family to support you.

18 FEBRUARY 2007

I RACED FROM THE TRAILER to the Dime Store before it closed to buy sheets of posterboard and a fat-tipped marker. Then I sped home and grabbed an armload of tomato stakes from my garage. It skived me to be in the garage. No one put anything back properly except for me. Bicycles dumped on the floor mingled with mouse droppings. I quickly found what I needed and beat it the hell out of there — but not before walking into a big-ass cobweb. I screamed so loudly that I startled my next-door neighbor. Betty was in her garden doing God knows what. It was wintertime. What was there to tend?

I said to her, "Hey, Mrs. Musser," hightailed it into the house, and called Andrew downstairs to help me.

I piled the supplies on top of a table in our basement. Andrew had shitty handwriting, so I did the lettering and he stapled the posters to the stakes. After a couple of hours of work we had put together a few dozen "We Want the Funk" signs.

Our handiwork was totally grassroots, but we needed the signs. In a few days we were going to make another commercial, and this one would be broadcast on TV!

19 FEBRUARY 2007

THE INNER CIRCLE was meeting almost every day. Late afternoons usually found Jeff, Britt, Joe, Evert, and little ol' me gathered in Funk's office.

Even after all this time, the handwringers remained the handwringers.

My husband always started off the meetings with news from the debates. The Inner Circle had given up on getting him to tailor his message to reach movers and shakers, but Funk offered them information to steady their nerves. He continued to win any debate that was judged by an outside source. He ticked off the wins on his fingertips: he won the Northland debate, which most members of this group had said he couldn't do; he won the Southwest debate, something else that was never supposed to happen. He placed second in other candidates' polls and in a poll by television Channel 5.

Instead of getting an "Oh, hell yeah!" for those victories, he got more pessimist talk.

One member of the Inner Circle muttered, "We can't get excited about winning. The race is a longshot. We can't let up."

I listened politely but about lost it when someone else said, "It's bad to win this early. We're going to fade if we keep coming out of the box in first place this soon."

Half the Inner Circle acted as if females were beneath them, yet they were talking like a bunch of teenage girls.

21 FEBRUARY 2007

JEFF SIMON TELEPHONED an hour before we were to begin filming the commercial to say he had a bad feeling about it. This was the fifth or sixth time he'd mentioned it.

Funk and Joe were both out of town, so Britt and I were the only ones Jeff could really spill to. It was crazy how fast and deep relationships went in campaigns. By now, I could spit back Jeff's catchphrases as well as I could Funk's.

In this case, Jeff didn't like that we were making another *homemade* commercial. He was afraid that we'd be the laughingstock of the city if we put it on TV. Never mind that the Maria the Poodle commercial had been a tremendous success. If we went through with this video, Jeff predicted it'd be the end of Funk's campaign.

That last part was new, so it unnerved me — but just for a bit.

We didn't have bushels of money to work with. "Isn't doing something better than diddling ourselves on the bench?" I asked Jeff. Again. He responded that doing nothing was better than broadcasting a tactless video. I agreed. Here's where we differed: Jeff equated low-budget with classless, but to me it simply meant we had to work harder to create something compelling from nothing. That was exactly what I planned to do, with or without Jeff's support. Just as soon as he let me off the phone.

His phone call put me way behind schedule. I drove around for an eternity trying to find the filming location, getting more panicked with each loop I made around the park. Finally I thought to phone my son.

"Andrew! How the hell do I get up to the scout statue?"

"Mom, calm down!"

"Never tell a woman to calm down, Andrew!" I screamed into the phone.

"Mom!"

"C'mon, Andrew, there are five thousand people waiting for me!"

"There are not five thousand people. You're always exaggerating!"

"Jesus! Now is not the time to be analyzing my personality. Just tell me how the fuck I get up there. I can see the statue. I just don't see how to get to it!"

"Are you driving, Mom?"

"Of course I'm driving! Just tell me how to go!"

"How would I know? Why don't you call Dad?"

"Dad? Dad is on a fucking plane!"

"Geez, don't get mad at me. How am I supposed to know?"

"Perhaps when he kissed you goodbye this morning you might have heard him tell you?"

"I didn't hear — "

"Oh, never mind! Bye." *Click.* I hung up on my uncaring son.

I circled around a few more times but kept coming back to where I had started. But then I noticed a line of cars driving up what appeared to be a dirt road for utility trucks. I decided to follow them to see where it led. Yup, straight to the statue.

Dottie's husband noticed my van and directed me to an out-of-the-way parking spot. I squeezed the van into it, grabbed the stack of tomato-stake signs, and huffed and puffed up to the filming location. When I reached the top of the hill I could hardly believe my eyes. At least 150 supporters milled about. I had prayed for more than two, but I never expected such a group. My throat closed. How would I get all of them under control, all by myself?

Angels must have been watching over me that day. First the line of cars had shown me the way to the statue. Then I got the last parking space. And now Tina, my personal trainer — well, she had been until I started helping Funk — noticed my stricken expression and took over. Tina had formerly been a gymnast, so to grab everyone's attention she began doing gymnastic moves. I didn't know a body could bend like that or change positions with such speed. She looked like one of those inflatable characters used to attract attention at a secondhand car lot.

Tina got the crowd's attention, all right. In fact, glimpsing her gyrations I think some folks were looking for a way to bolt.

Then another angel came to my rescue: Dottie's daughter, Wendy. Wendy directed the choir at her church. Cranking the music as high as it would go, she got everyone singing the Parliament hit that I had just paid the lady from Switzerland $250 for the rights to use. Wendy led supporters through the lyrics a few times and I took over from there. I described to them how the commercial would go. To open, a few supporters would hold signs high in the air and sing, "We want the Funk, gotta have that Funk." More supporters would step into the scene as the song progressed. Everyone seemed to get it, so I handed out the signs, nodded to Laz, a volunteer who was a professional cameraman, and let it rip.

In a blink, I was walking back to the van. It had been a successful wrap. All that anxiety, for nothing!

Going home to my son, I thanked God the shoot had gone well and then spent the rest of the day wondering how much money producers made — thinking maybe I should get into the business.

22 FEBRUARY 2007

JEFF'S ANXIETY had been all for nothing.

Our "We Want the Funk" commercial was a huge hit, a tipping point for the campaign. "Funk" became a household word in Kansas City, and the former city auditor was suddenly seen as hip and cool. Finally, others saw the win coming that Funk and I had known about all along.

23 FEBRUARY 2007

IT WAS FUNKY BLUES FUNDRAISER NIGHT. Just like old times, the entire family cruised to the airport to pick up Tara, and then we drove straight to Knuckleheads for the show. I let my hair down for the first time in ages and danced the night away with my family. Tara was the only one of us who could *really* dance, but the rest of us had moves too!

The night ended way too soon. As we were walking out the door Frank, the owner, asked me to wait for a moment. He handed me a wad of cash wrapped in a rubber band. I felt like a big-deal concert promoter. My gut feeling had been right about Frank: he was a delight. I thanked him profusely for everything he'd done.

The next morning I tallied the proceeds. Ticket sales totaled $600, and the t-shirts brought in a hundred more. Not too shabby for a fun night's work!

26 FEBRUARY 2007

AFTER ALL THE PLANNING, all the doing, and all the waiting, the day was almost upon us. Tomorrow was the primary election!

Tara and I rose at dawn, walked to the Plaza for exercise, grabbed a coffee from Latteland, and sipped it in front of the windows of Anthropologie. When we returned back home I took a quick shower, kissed everyone goodbye, and drove like a maniac to the trailer.

The day passed in a blur. In what felt like just a few minutes I was pulling back into the driveway, honking for Tara to come out so we could race to the last debate of this election cycle.

The forum was a first for her. Per usual, we chatted nonstop on the drive to the venue, though the talk stopped abruptly when the van crested a hill. For there in the sky was *the* most gigantic, *the* most colorful, *the* most showstopping rainbow I'd ever seen in my life. I was stunned into silence by its magnificence. My daughter was oblivious. Good mother that I am, I slowed the van so Tara could take it in, which is when the rainbow became a double rainbow!

I'm sure you know what happened after that.

I screeched the van to a halt — hey, no one was on those roads anyway — and squealed, "Jesus, Tara, are you seeing this?"

My daughter smiled and replied with a limp-dick, "Yes, Mama, I see the rainbow."

I screamed, "Christ, Tara, that's not just any old rainbow. It's a double rainbow!"

She smiled again, but I could tell she wasn't entranced. Her smile was the type she gave when she's making fun of my enthusiasm.

I was beyond thrilled. Couldn't get enough of the thing. The rainbow was so holy that I idled the van in the middle of the road, absorbing it. After another few moments I turned to my daughter and whispered reverently, "Tara, I've never seen a double rainbow before."

"Neither have I, Mama, but you better start driving. There are cars behind you."

I peered into the rearview mirror and saw she was right, so I gave it some gas. Which is when I drove directly *under* the rainbow — like, who the hell drives *under* rainbows? Then, after driving a bit farther, we came to the *end* of the rainbow — who the fuck sees the *end* of a rainbow? I stomped on the brakes. The van was completely awash in color, and I started looking around for the pot of gold.

And then it hit me.

I said in awe, "Oh my God, Tara, this is a sign. Dad really is going to win!"

My daughter takes after her father, though not as bad. She didn't exactly kill it, not until she said, "But I thought you already knew Dad was going to win."

How is it that no one in my family knew that I spoke my gut to the world with certainty, but I never believed it myself?

The hour getting late, I ripped myself away from the sacredness and made a left turn into the venue parking lot.

Compared with earlier ones, this forum was scantily attended. Also, for the first time, most of the candidates were not present. I was beginning to ask myself what that meant when Alvin Brooks — who was still the expected winner — stood up as if he owned the place, walked to the front of the stage, and asked the crowd if they'd noticed the rainbow on their way in. Most shook their heads no. Some murmured what a shame it was that they'd missed it. Apparently, no one but Tara, Mr. Brooks, and I had witnessed the beauty.

Brooks said he took the rainbow as a sign that he'd be the next mayor of Kansas City. The handful of attendees burst into applause. I gave Tara two looks: first a knowing one, because Brooks also understood the rainbow was a sign. Next a pitying one, because no way would Brooks be the next mayor. But by now my daughter had her fill of my emoting. She shot me a look that said, *Mama, don't start.*

With opening remarks behind us, a young black woman in the audience rose from her chair, pointed at the dais, and proceeded to yell at the candidates, saying they were frauds, every one of them. She screamed that no one on the city council had done a damn thing for her people, so why should she believe the promises they were making? She said that everyone on the panel had abandoned the area and left it to the women to deal with, and damned if she'd vote for them.

I thought she'd take a seat after saying all that, but she was just gearing up.

Screaming louder, spit flying, she said her children were forced to live like animals in a war zone. Her voice cracked and quivered as she described how she feared for their lives, sending them out the door for school. How they had to dodge bullets just to get educated. She said she felt like an abusive mother for making her terrified children attend school. Yet if she didn't send them into the firestorm, if they weren't educated, they'd never make it out of their hellhole, so what choice did she have?

The whole time she ranted the candidates sat quietly, saying nothing. My husband would never dream of interrupting a woman in the middle of a tirade, but I couldn't understand why the others said nothing. The woman asked if they understood the predicament they'd put her in. She didn't wait for a response, just sat her violently shaking body down.

I was impressed.

She was damned gutsy. Her situation was horrible.

As moved as I was, I didn't like that she'd lumped the candidates together. Funk had never been on the city council. And it was clear that she didn't know the first thing about him or the things he'd done in her community. Funk had advocated for streetlights to be installed throughout the city, including her neighborhood. It was something her councilwoman should've done, yet it was Funk who'd pushed the bill through, a bill that played a role in reducing the crime rate.

Noticing tears in Tara's eyes, I murmured to her how awful it was for the woman and her children. I gently added that I didn't like what the woman had insinuated about Funk, and I certainly didn't like her yelling at him.

Tara whispered back a stern, "Mama, she's upset! Her babies are being shot at. If those were your kids, you'd be doing the same thing. No, you'd be worse."

It was true. But I still didn't like it when someone talked shit on my family.

On the ride home, Tara and I talked over the events. The highlight had been not the magnificent rainbow but the gutsy woman. Just as I had become a believer in Funk's cause after the debate in the East Side, my daughter became a believer that night.

Um, Scusi. *Didn't I Hear You Say We Couldn't Win the Election?*

27 FEBRUARY 2007

FUNK USED TO TAKE OUR CHILDREN TO the Westport Flea Market on Tuesday evenings for the weekly chess club gathering. It was wonderful. I got a reprieve from making dinner and my children got to eat junk food, free of reproach. The place was nothing fancy, just an ordinary working-class bar and grill, but it reminded me of the taverns in England where friends and neighbors gathered, where everyone was welcome, including children. Sometimes I'd join them at the Flea. Joe Zwillenberg, the owner, had the personality of a New Yorker, so I felt at home in his joint.

The bar screamed Funk's platform in every way imaginable, which is why I suggested the iconic Flea to host our election night watch party instead of booking one of the swanky hotel ballrooms where Funk's competitors would be living it up. In *Notes from the DoubleWide* I had invited everyone to join us.

Primary Election Day had arrived.

That morning the Inner-*Inner* Circle — Funk, Joe, and I — drove around visiting schools, churches, and nursing homes. At midday, when the three of us were standing on the sidewalk wondering where to go next, I told them we should give it up already. I said there was nothing more we could do, that whatever would come of our efforts had already been done. That the best use of our time was to go home and rest up for the evening.

I didn't have to twist anyone's arm. They knew it too.

At home I couldn't concentrate on anything. I couldn't even have fun with the kids. All I could do was wait.

And grow antsier by the second.

And wait some more.

And do nothing.

There was nothing to do.

But wait.

And wait some more.

Finally, somewhere along seven p.m., it was time to drive to the watch party. The family piled into the van and headed to Funk's destiny. Ten minutes later we walked in the back entrance of the Flea. The joint was filled over capacity with people wearing all kinds of Funk gear.

The instant I saw how crowded and loud it was and how everyone wanted our attention, my throat closed and I wanted to go home. But I couldn't run. I was expected to be there, so there I stayed.

We squeezed through the crowd, most of whom we didn't know. Strangers smiled, cheered, stared, grabbed at our arms, called out well wishes, stared some more, started conversations, offered drinks, and stared even more. Every soul there behaved as if they knew us. When we had made our way to the center of the room, I saw Gwen waving her arms, so I blocked everything else out and paced steadily toward my beacon. She was standing beside a corner table with Ed, ex-councilwoman Aggie, and others. Gwen had saved me a seat, but I couldn't sit. I was too hyped. Too filled with tunnel vision. Too in need of nourishment. I stood there, just as I had at home, not knowing what to do but wait.

Before long, the owner of the Flea was standing at my side, shoving a beer into one of my hands and a burger into the other, asking if I was okay, saying it must be nerve-racking to have all these people wanting our attention, telling me it was okay *not* to talk if I didn't feel like talking.

I don't know how Zwillenberg knew what I was feeling, but I recall my immense relief that he did. Somehow, it made what I was experiencing seem normal. Even so, my throat constricted more and my tunnel vision became a pinpricked view.

The revelers were having a high time, wanting to talk, joke around, drink to excess, and eat to excess. Meantime, all I wanted to do was grab Funk and go hide in a corner. But there I stayed, pretending to be okay, smiling and nodding as if I was paying attention. I can't count how many times Gwen started a conversation with me, yet I couldn't concentrate on her words to respond. Or how often I startled to Aggie's shrill voice — ten thousand octaves too high for my nerves — as she spat a piece of gossip into my ear. A steady stream of acquaintances approached me all night long, wanting to engage in deep conversations. The problem was, I just wanted to be. I just wanted to stand quietly to the side and see what happened.

I wasn't afraid Funk wouldn't win. I knew he would. But I always doubted myself. Plus, now that I'd been converted, been shown that Funk would make life in the city better — especially for the types who frequented this establishment — there was more to lose. For the most part, though, the raucous goings-on were just too much for this homebody to take.

Anytime I wasn't engaged with people I knew, strangers advanced, telling me about how they'd been volunteering from the very beginning, had made several large donations, or had been talking Funk's name up all over town.

I had tunnel vision, but it's not like I didn't have my wits about me. I was familiar with Funk's supporters. I'd tracked every volunteer, every donor, yet I'd never met most of these people before, had never even heard their names mentioned around the trailer. Like, who in God's name were the two older gentlemen, Barnett and his sidekick Stanley? They kept taking my hand, holding it, caressing it, wanting me to chitchat with them as if we were the only people in the room. They said the only reason they'd ventured out was because they were "taken with me." They didn't know me. How could they be taken with me? Besides, wasn't Funk the one they should be taken with? He was the one who was going to fix the city.

As I felt myself spiraling downward, I noticed the hamburger clutched in my hand. I forced myself to take a tiny bite, then another, and another until I had consumed a quarter of it. I started feeling better. I dropped back into my body. I could look around the room with a full view again. I began to do what people wanted me to do, instead of what I wanted to do. I had placed myself in diplomat mode before leaving home. Now I threw my glamour high and stepped into the New and Better Me. I slapped my game face on and assumed the authoritative stance that everyone seemed to expect of me.

Grounded on the earth once more, I got my first indication of what was happening. I finally understood the reason for the big crowd of supporters, acquaintances, complete strangers, and news teams: the media must've polled for expected election results. Why else would every heavy hitter in town — all the big television anchors — be at *our* watch party instead of the ritzy ballrooms where the other candidates were holding court?

No wonder there was such a buzz going on! And I do mean a buzz. Everyone was so jazzed that when the first numbers rolled across the television screen showing Funk way out in the lead — miles ahead of everyone except Mr. Brooks — the room erupted in hysterical applause.

Do you think that calmed my nerves? Nope.

I nervously watched the TV for the rest of the night, unable turn my gaze away. I felt as if I had to *will* the numbers to stay in place, to use all my energy to keep Funk in front.

Funk placed second in the Primary! He had made it into the playoffs.

By the time his win was certified, I was so fried that I couldn't wait to go home and crawl under my covers and hide. But it was hours before I could leave because that was how long it took the media to wrap up their interviews with Funk. The job would've taken ten minutes if not for the reporters' lame questions: "Are you surprised you won?" "Do you think you have a chance of beating Brooks in the general election?" "If that occurs, what do you hope to accomplish in office?"

The only blessing of the seemingly endless questions was that the crowd grew bored with them too and began to disperse. Which is when I found a table in the shadows and finally sat my ass down. I wasn't alone for long. Barnett and Stanley came trotting over. I stood up to be polite, and they grabbed me in a circle embrace and whispered in my ear how they'd just made a firm decision to support Funk in the general. They stated it like it was a big, thrilling secret. Like their support was the be-all, end-all. Like they were doing Funk a favor.

As soon as they left, Kendrick and Joe filled their places, and finally I had some fun! Like a protective shield they flanked me, one on either side, until the news reporters were through with my husband.

And when Funk finally said we could go home, I was outta there.

28 FEBRUARY 2007

I WAS BAKED. I rested. Alone. Just for the morning.

Funk and I had returned home after two a.m., after the watch party and his media interviews had wrapped up. Dottie had seemed disappointed that I didn't arrive at the trailer at my usual early hour. She wanted to hash through Funk's win with me. I understood that, and I felt so bad for not being able to get there any earlier.

I didn't think it possible, but the demands of the campaign ramped even higher after the primary. Dottie and I could barely handle the goings-on, not with the constant ringing of the phone and new folks visiting the trailer. Everyone wanted to discuss the "surprise" win and sign up to volunteer, grabbing a handful of buttons — and anything else we had on hand — on their way back out the door. On top of that, Funk's committee members were calling and emailing more than ever, and new supporters blitzed my inbox asking to host meet-and-greets.

There was barely time to breathe, much less revel in the joy of primary night. I didn't leave the trailer until after ten p.m., yet I never had a minute to touch my work.

1 MARCH 2007

I WOKE UP with a terrible head cold.

Fuck. I should've seen it coming. I'd been running way too hard for way too long. Now what was I going to do? I couldn't stop. It was only a month until the general election. One thing was for sure, I couldn't go into the trailer like that. I felt like shit. And I couldn't bring myself to look in the mirror.

I got scared whenever I was sick. Actually, that was a grave understatement. I got terrified whenever I was sick. The grave part alluded to the way my mother had reacted whenever I had the slightest sniffle. To her, it was only a matter of time before I'd be suffering on some hospital bed with a ventilator slapped to my face, waiting to die. Funk usually worked from home when I wasn't feeling well — to help me keep the monsters at bay — but of course, nothing was normal anymore.

Before he left the house, I asked him to bring me a pitcher of water, some tissues, and my cell phone and computer. I didn't freak when I heard the sound of his car muffler pulling away. I just rang Dottie to tell her I wouldn't be coming in.

"Donths?" I said, breathing heavily into the phone.

"Is that you, Gloria?"

"Yeth."

"You sound terrible."

"I feel terrible."

"Oh, no! Well, you just rest up today. Don't worry about anything here."

"I can't rest. There's too much to do. It's less than a month to the general."

"Gloria," she scolded, "you can take one day off when you're sick."

"Listen, Donths, I'm only calling to let you know I'll be working from bed. I'll see you in the morning, okay?"

"I know I won't change your mind, but try to rest a little, okay?"

I passed the morning hours writing thank-you notes. I could barely keep up with how many needed to be written now and I didn't know what to do about it. Everything with the campaign was high priority, but there was too much to do in a day. When I told Funk my worry, his solution was that I should type the letters rather than writing them by hand. That wasn't the point. They *had* to be handwritten. How else could we show supporters how thankful we were?

Once the notes were in the mail, I began making phone calls.

"Hey, lady, you have some head cold."

"Yeth, I know, I'm sorry." *Pant, pant, pant,* gulp some air before adding, "Hey, I need a double order of buttons this time. . . ."

After making the phone calls I started on email. That task was intermingled with a thousand brief calls to and from Dottie, Britt, Betty Lou, Joe, Jeff, and Bev, ad infinitum. Bev Sims had taken on the role of volunteer coordinator, and she had been doing a bang-up job. Bev was from the Northland and married to a former judge. I was so lucky.

I rounded out the workday by entering data into my Excel spreadsheet. That was fun. Our campaign PayPal account was on *fire*! My inbox blew up with money every few minutes. Man, if only some of those donations had arrived in the previous months, we wouldn't have sweated it so much every time a bill came due.

2 MARCH 2007

WHEN I ARRIVED AT SEVEN-THIRTY, the trailer was already hopping. It remained packed to the rafters until long past sundown.

The influx of new volunteers was wonderful, but it did bring agita with it. I seemed to have become the darling of the trailer overnight. Most of the new volunteers wanted private time with me, which was not so good. They always begin their conversations by saying they'd supported Funk from day one, either financially or through hands-on work. I didn't know why they felt they had to say that, since it wasn't true. Plus, they were on his bandwagon now, so it was all good!

A kid came to the trailer, the youngest person yet to tinkle Spring's doorbells. Crispin Rea was a sweet little guy, and I do mean little. Turn him sideways and he'd disappear. He told me he was a college student and that he'd *continue* to devote his free time to the campaign. I always asked new volunteers why they were supporting my husband. Crispin said it was because Funk was the best professor he'd ever had and was brilliant, gutsy, walked his talk, and dedicated to the working class. Lots of folks said this about my husband, but the way Crispin so earnestly described his feelings toward my man — well, he kind of stole my heart.

Whenever I'm around young people I like to buff them up, so I said, "Hear me out, Crispin Rea, you're going to be the first Hispanic mayor of this town."

He wasn't bedazzled by my statement, which made me think I wasn't telling him anything he hadn't already thought of. I realized that on top of being sweet, he was cocky as all get out. Crispin was in his early twenties. But if you don't dream big, who the hell will do it for you?

Just as the kid was about to exit my office, someone hollered, "Maria has to shit!" That was quickly followed by the glory-filled response that had become commonplace: "Quick, put her in Britt's office!"

Crispin stopped dead in his tracks and said, "What's going on?" I dismissed what he'd overheard with a wave of my hand, "Pay it no mind. It's just a bit of bathroom humor."

The next person to shadow my threshold was a middle-aged woman who was a friend of Dottie's. The minute Frances Semler introduced herself, I recalled that I had recently scheduled Funk's visit to her garden.

He had been bowled over by her creation.

Wouldn't shut up about it the next morning. How filled with blooms her yard was . . . how artsy it was, without feeling contrived . . . how serene. After he said all that, I looked out my kitchen window to my once-beautiful garden, which was still bristling with weeds from the previous fall. So prolific were they that they were crowding out my daffodils, innocent little flowers who only wanted to sing their hearts out.

One of my greatest joys had been my garden, and this is what Funk's dream had done to it. He had some nerve to rave about some other women's yard. Since there was no time to hate him, I just responded, "Yeah, yeah. Whatever, Funk. I have to take your son to school." I didn't even kiss him goodbye.

Do you think the bastard noticed?

Two months ago, never in a million years would he have not noticed, but on that day, he didn't notice. Once the election was over, I was gonna have to take that guy in to be neutered — his balls had grown that big.

Frances took her leave when Dottie came into my office with another request. Dottie and I saw each other twenty thousand times a day, but we had no time for tête-à-têtes anymore. We just said what needed to be said, as quickly as we could, or we handed the other something that should have been done the previous week.

"Gloria, can you — ?"

"Yez, ma'am. Thank you, Dottie."

I had phones to answer. Calls to return. Emails to sort. Thank-you letters to write. Funk's calendar to keep up. Bills to pay. Receipts to bring to that freaky CPA dude. Meet-and-greet and forum tables to arrange. Critiques to give my husband. Fires to put out. More fires to put out. Andrew to retrieve from school, to arrange dinner for, to say I'm sorry to. Tara's calls to answer, to apologize to for not being able to talk. Same with my newly widowed mother. Speaking of her, there was that *other* thing — my father's death — to grieve. Good Lord, my father was dead, and I had missed his fucking funeral last summer when I was on the boat to Europe. But who had time to mourn when there was another newsletter to write? Press releases to compose. A million things to do, especially those that got my husband off my back, such as when the hell the Public Safety press event was to take place.

Jeff was responsible for two events: Public Safety and Get Out the Vote (GOTV). Public Safety hadn't happened yet, and Jeff never got around to doing the GOTV for the primary. Would he get to it before the general election?

"Gloria, we need a GOTV!" said Britt, annoyed, as if I had something to do with it.

I had barely time to breathe. I was in the middle of juggling the hyped-up demands when who should wander into my office but Gwen and Ed Wolf. I had no idea what I was about to say until I heard the words spill from my tongue.

"Hey! Nice to see you! Boy, am I glad you came in. I have to ask you something. But I gotta make it quick because the general election is a whole new thing. I'm drowning here. There are way too many volunteers who are looking to me to play hostess, and I can't keep up with my work because of it. Would it be possible for you to be here full-time? I know it's asking a lot. I can't even believe I'm asking. It's just that we're only a month out and — "

"Gloria, darling," Gwen interrupted, "of course we can be here full-time. Can't we, Eddie?"

"If you say so, Gwen, of course we can!"

"We can start now. What will you have us do?"

"Jesus! Thank you so much! What a relief. I can't believe what a hussy I am for asking."

"You're not a hussy, Gloria. You just need more help. And this is help worth giving, right Eddie?"

Hussy that I am, I didn't linger with my gratitude, just got down to business. "I would never trust this to anyone else — it's that important — but would you mind taking over writing the thank-you notes, Gwen?" Before she could answer, I added, "They have to be handwritten."

"Of course they have to be handwritten! Consider it done!" she exclaimed, slapping her hand on my desk for emphasis.

My demure little self didn't even thank her. I just turned to her husband and said, "Ed, since you were a director at city hall you must know how to deal with employees. I know these folks aren't employees — they're volunteers — but they need to be organized, nurtured, and have their work double-checked. Is that job beneath you?"

"Just show me what you need and how you want it done."

"Geez, Ed. That is so gracious!"

Everything settled, I sat back in my chair and sighed deeply. Finally I remembered my manners. "I know how much I've just asked of you. And to think we barely know each other! I owe you big. Somehow, I'll pay you back."

"You don't owe us a thing, Gloria. We all have to do our part in getting your husband elected. The city needs him. That's all the repayment we need."

The Wolfs left, but instead of getting back to work straightaway, I stared up at the water-stained ceiling, contemplating what a whore I'd become. I had hardly blinked when I made that ask of the Wolfs. I didn't agonize for weeks, wondering what to say and how to say it. I just blurted it out. I couldn't have pulled that off if I hadn't become a New and Better Me.

My family's nine-week trip to Europe the previous summer had been a time of soul growth. I had faced my fears to live out a dream. I returned to the US a different person, filled with tons more energy to get through my days with. I don't know how it happened, only that it did.

Never before would I have been able to handle all the work or had the energy to keep going.

3 MARCH 2007

THE DOUBLE-WIDE was running more smoothly with Gwen and Ed on the premises. The workload hadn't lightened up, though. As we approached the general election, each day brought more work than the day before.

And then unwelcome news arrived.

The cruelest was that Evert's son wasn't expected to make it through the day. I didn't know how Evert was coping. He must have been dying a thousand deaths. He was at his son's bedside, and I called his cell phone to try to shore him up. I said all the trite things people say, like "Don't lose faith — where there's life, there's hope." I reminded him that the body is designed to heal, that it *wants* to heal. That even if he didn't believe it, he should pretend he did, so his son didn't give up. I said his son needed to hear those words, because it was probably easier for his son to give in than to keep fighting.

I don't think the conversation made Evert feel better. It surely wouldn't have helped me, had I been in his situation. But I had to try to offer him something to hold onto.

Next came Joe's horrific tale. More awful things were going down in the East Side. The murder rate continued its upward trend. And just that morning a rat had climbed into a crib and bit a baby's nose right off its sweet little face.

Did you hear what I said?

A rat bit a baby's nose off!

The poor baby and its parents! Funk couldn't get elected fast enough.

After that came another request from the *Star*, addressing their growing fascination with me. Their asks had been unsettling, but this one included my children. What the hell? Who was the candidate for office, Funk or his family? Worse, they were pitching a story that placed me side-by-side with Brooks's wife. They wanted to differentiate between our two families and compare how each woman would do as First Lady.

First Lady? Was this the White House or something? I wouldn't have minded the request so much if Mrs. Brooks hadn't been a lot older than me. But she was, and it seemed disrespectful to compare us. I thought the *Star* should focus on one of us at a time.

Joe said I *had* to grant the interview or they'd find a way to screw Funk up the ass. But they wanted intimate things! Photos of our family. Private thoughts. Somehow, they'd gotten wind that I had asked Funk to sign a list of demands, and they wanted to see the document. Most of the demands applied to me — for example, that when Funk was done with his eight years in office, we would work on achievement of my dreams. Others were personal to our family — for example, Funk wouldn't become something he wasn't, wouldn't make promises he had no intention of keeping, and wouldn't scheme to get elected. That list was *super*-personal! I didn't care what Joe said, the *Star* wasn't touching it. It was hidden away in the safe in our hall closet. No one would ever find it.

The final upsetting thing was a message the fax machine spat out just as I was closing the trailer down for the night: yet one more request from the *Star*.

As Pipo, our exchange student from Austria, used to say, "Things are getting *pret-ty* serious around here, Glor!" Pipo was right. Things had gotten mighty strange. The general election was an entirely different animal from the primary. It was down and dirty, and I didn't like that one bit.

The *Star* preached like a holy roller in its opinion column, saying campaigns should play nice, but they seemed to be stooping low in their ethics.

Reading between the lines of the fax message, the *Star* was trying to pit Brooks and Funk against each other. On the surface, the *Star* wanted Funk to comment on how his campaign's yard signs had been stolen from homes lining Ward Parkway, the area where the well-to-do people lived. One day that road had been awash in orange signs, and then it was back to plain old normal.

My gut said the *Star* was hoping Funk would accuse Brooks's campaign of the crime. *Like, who the hell else would have done it?* But the *Star* didn't really care who had pilfered them. They were just stirring shit, trying to sell more newspapers. I was not going to help them sell newspapers. They had more than enough money; TIF had provided for that. Besides, now that I understood campaigns better, I realized that Brooks might not be aware if someone from his campaign *had* done such a thing. Plenty of times one of our volunteers showed me a nasty blog comment, and I could tell right away that someone from our campaign had anonymously posted it. That sort of underhanded behavior was a big no-no with Funk and me. I was willing to bet it was a no-no with Brooks too.

In my world, even lower than someone stealing our signs was the *Star*'s attempt to turn Brooks and Funk against one another. Why couldn't the newspaper just do what it was supposed to do — stick to the facts? I was seeing a side of the media I had never known existed. The reporting wasn't about which candidate was more capable of turning the city around. The *Star* centered their coverage on race. They were pitting black people against white people. Wasn't there already enough racial tension in town?

4 MARCH 2007

THE CAMPAIGN RECEIVED AN ANONYMOUS TIP that Funk was about to be endorsed by a major organization. It would be his first such endorsement.

Amid that celebratory call and ticking other items off my to-do list were a million interruptions from Dottie, and from me to her. We'd worn a path on the carpet between our desks. I tried to be pleasant in our interactions. Better to be playful than get grouchy from overwork. Better to be respectful than get no help.

To Dottie's latest request — which she always prefaced with an apology, as if the additional burden was her fault — I replied with a lighthearted, "*Yez*, ma'am-ie. I'll get right on it!"

"Gloria," she hollered, "not *another* name!"

"It's not another name, Dots. I've been 'yez, ma'am-ing' you for a long time now. This is just a variation on the theme."

"Oh, Gloria, you're too much," she said, laughing, as she raced from my office to answer the phone.

5 MARCH 2007

TODAY WAS AN ABSOLUTELY HORRIBLE DAY.

Poor fucking Evert. His son passed. Evert phoned me at home before the sun came up to say that we shouldn't attend his son's wake that evening. He said that a forum hosted by ACORN, an advocacy group, was scheduled at practically the same time and there'd be hell to pay if Funk missed it.

I told Evert that I knew exactly what events were on Funk's calendar and that I didn't give two shits about any of them except for the wake. Evert started to say there'd be enough people supporting him, that I shouldn't be concerned, but I hushed him up. I told him there was no fucking way we weren't coming. That he was like family now, and this took precedence. Evert didn't argue further. He just asked if this was Funk's decision too. I crossed my fingers when I said, "Yes, Funk knows, and he feels the same."

As we said goodbye, I could sense that Evert was touched that we'd chosen him over the campaign.

There was no way that I could fall back to sleep, so I headed into the trailer before the volunteers slammed into the joint. The second I tinkled the door-bells I could see the place had been vandalized. *Vandalized!*

I was so scared.

The walls of the lobby were covered with spray paint, though I couldn't make sense of any of it. I wanted to check to see whether anything else at headquarters was awry, but I was afraid to go deeper into the trailer. What if the vandal was still on the premises?

The only thing I could think to do was to shout that I was there and that if *they* were there, now would be a good time to get the hell out, as I was dialing 911.

That was another lie, but how would they know?

I couldn't call the cops. This crime had to stay under the radar. We needed to keep the focus on Funk's message of clean, safe neighborhoods for regular folks, not shine a light on slimy campaign cutthroat tactics. I assumed this was the handiwork of Alvin's campaign, because who else would ruin an already brokedown trailer?

I didn't hear a thing after I shouted my instructions to the perpetrators. No running footsteps. No window being pried open to climb the hell out. I shouted again that they'd better be gone because the police were almost there. After that, I made a bunch of noise — which wasn't hard to do, walk a few steps and the whole trailer shakes — and peered into the reception area. I didn't see a soul, but damn if there wasn't writing on every wall in there. I didn't bother looking around to check if anything was missing, because seeing the walls with paint dripping down to the floor was already too much to take. Our beautiful trailer!

My heart was pounding, but luckily I didn't get tunnel vision. That would come later, after I had everything put back to rights. That was the way things worked with me. When everyone else breathed a sigh of relief — that's when my mind decided to torture me.

I telephoned Funk.

Standing with one foot inside the door and the other one out just in case I had to run screaming from the place, I cried into the phone, "Funk! Someone broke into the trailer!"

"Where are you?"

"I'm here, where do you think?"

"Have the police arrived?"

"Are you kidding me? I didn't call the cops."

"Gloria, hang up the phone and call the police."

"Did you not hear me? We can't call the cops. It would send the wrong message."

"I don't give a fuck about the message. I want you out of there and the police to take over."

"Well, if you want to be ignorant, then you call them!"

"I'm almost at the meet-and-greet."

"Jesus Christ, Funk, you can take two minutes to call them!"

"What would I say? I'm not there. I don't have the information they'll need."

"Oh my God! Why do I have to handle this?"

"It'll be fine, Glor. Just hang up and call 911."

"Christ, Funk! Goodbye! I hate your stupid fucking guts!"

The police came speeding to the scene a *mere* forty minutes later. So there I waited by the lobby door with my thumb up my ass, knowing I had a million things to do but afraid to go into my office to start.

Things didn't get better when the cops showed up. They grilled me as if *I* had spray-painted the walls. I was expecting them to storm the place, hug me, encourage me to let it all out, have a good cry. But no. They just asked a hundred questions without the slightest hint of compassion.

Was anything missing? Did I know who did it? Did we have any enemies?

I told them a million times I had been too afraid to go past the lobby, so how would I know if anything was missing? Besides, if I had known who did it, I'd be calling that person and asking them what the fuck, not calling the cops! And what's with "Did we have enemies?" Gag me! Didn't they hear me say the trailer was being used for a campaign?

I must have been getting fat.

It was the only thing that explained their horrid behavior. Society discriminates against fat people.

Turns out, nothing was taken. The computers, phones, printer, even the soap in the bathrooms were exactly where they belonged. The only thing the vandal did was scribble unintelligible thoughts on our walls. How weird was that?

Britt arrived shortly after the police pulled away, by which time I was a complete wreck. When I told him all that had happened, he looked nervous. He seemed afraid, as if he was hiding something. His only question was to ask if anything was missing. When I said no, he turned on his heels, went inside his office, and closed the door. Without even a goodbye!

When Dottie came in, she of course gave me the opportunity to let loose. I didn't let myself cry. I just railed about how horrible it was, how scary it was to walk in on something like that. Then I started thinking about the volunteers. I wondered whether they'd bolt when they saw the condition the trailer was in. I'm telling you, the place felt eerie. Whoever wrecked the place had left their bad energy behind.

Funk walked in while I was still unloading to Dots. Man, if he hadn't, I don't know what would've happened. We went inside his office, and for the first time ever I closed the door behind me. I couldn't help it. I needed to sit on his lap and reexperience everything. Cry a little. I wasn't far into the story when Britt opened Funk's door and closed it behind him.

I mean, really! Husband and wife were having a moment. Now was not the time for this guy to be inserting himself.

"Mark, I need to speak to you."

"Britt, can it wait?" I said. "Funk doesn't have much time, and we're talking here."

Britt looked at me stone-faced, as if he was angry with me, then said as condescendingly as possible, "No, Gloria, *this* cannot wait."

The nerve! I was not his underling. He couldn't talk to me like that! First the police, and now this asshole was using the same tone?

"Mark," Britt said, "I believe I know who did this."

"You know who did this?" I repeated, horrified. "Why didn't you tell me?"

"Gloria," he spat back impatiently, "I'm talking to Mark, not you."

Well, you can imagine what that did. Sent me right through the roof.

Funk said, "No, Britt, you're talking to both of us."

And I said, "Who did it, Britt?"

Looking only at Funk, Britt said, "A friend of mine who recently started volunteering for the campaign."

I said, "Your friend did this? Why would your friend break into the trailer and do this?"

"He didn't break in. He has a key."

"He has a key? How'd he get a key?"

Britt didn't answer, so I asked again, "How'd he get a key, Britt?"

Britt said nothing.

Funk said, "Britt?"

Britt said, "I gave it to him."

I said, "You gave your friend a key?"

Britt said nothing.

My voice rose and I said, "Let me get this straight, Britt. You gave someone a key without asking our permission first?"

Britt said, "Mark, control your wife."

"Control your wife!" I shrieked, absolutely shocked.

"Mark!" came Britt's call for Funk to handle me again, furiously enough that his curls were springing madly around the room, his body saturating a deep, dark red.

Funk said, "Answer her question."

Speaking directly to Funk again, Britt said, "Yes, he had nowhere else to stay. He's been a little off in the head. I was trying to lend a hand."

I said, "You gave a known lunatic a key to the headquarters?"

"That's what I said, Gloria. But I'm talking to Mark, not you."

I gasped.

Funk said nothing.

Things really dissolved after that.

I can't remember the details. It was just a lot of back and forth, with me asking Britt why he thought it was okay to give someone a key when he knew we hardly allowed anyone to have a key and Britt commanding Funk to back his wife down.

I was upset about the break-in, but my upset wouldn't have intensified had

Britt not spoken the way he did. To me, when bad things happen, it's time for people to pull together — not tear each other apart.

The three of us were standing in the center of Funk's office dancing a terrible dance. I glanced at the clock. It was time for my husband to leave for his next appointment. "Fuck this shit," I said and started for the door.

I was more stunned by what I found on the other side of Funk's door than I was by Britt's behavior. Because on the other side of that door was a room full of volunteers, their eyes filled with compassion.

Bill tilted his head up from where he was squatting to give me a smile and immediately went back to scrubbing the graffiti from the wall. It was coming off. I never thought it would! I thought we'd have to live with it since we couldn't afford to buy paint or the labor to apply it.

Next, a kindhearted volunteer — a man who *knew* what to do without being asked — bashfully came over and handed me a rose. After I admired it, he drew me into a huge embrace and said in my ear that everything would be fine.

Then Dottie brought me a bottle of water and encouraged me to sit on the futon and sip it slowly. When I did, Gwen sat down and scooched in close — like, our asses were touching, that's how close we were — and repeated what the guy with the rose had just whispered, that everything would be fine.

But everything wasn't fine. Evert's son was dead and something terrible had happened to the campaign. The boy's death was by far more tragic. Yet, the events were more than I could assimilate at one time. I strove for peace in all my relationships and hated when things went unresolved. I hated having nowhere to go with my anger. I hated wondering whether I was justified in feeling the way I did.

I was so proud of the volunteers for standing in solidarity. For offering me, of all people, comfort. As nice as that was, what I needed more than anything in the world was to be alone with my husband. A moment just to be me. To restore my balance, so I could continue giving to others the way I'm supposed to. I needed to be comforted, without feeling guilty for needing it. To express, without being worried that I did. To unabashedly rant, without fearing that

I looked unprofessional. I needed help to settle myself as quickly as possible, so that we could plan our next move. The last thing I needed was a fight that hung unsettled in the air. But that's what I got.

Suddenly I felt tired. Unbelievably tired.

The next thing I knew, Joe was standing beside me asking if I wanted to go outside and talk, and out the door to my van we went. I had almost finished regurgitating the whole wretched thing to Joe — I was lingering over the part having to do with Britt — when I realized what the hell I was doing.

"Jesus, Joe, I'm so sorry. I don't know why I'm telling you all this."

"You have to tell someone, Gloria."

"Yes, I know. But I'm the one who usually does the hand-holding."

"It's okay, Gloria. You have to let it out."

I didn't catch the last thing he said because there was something in my eye.

"Is anything wrong?"

"I'm sorry, Joe, what did you say?"

He repeated himself. Again, I didn't respond because I was distracted with my eye.

"Are you all right?" Joe asked.

"I don't know. There's something in my eye. And now it's twitching, probably from messing with it."

"Well, as I was saying . . ." and, seeing me still obsessed, Joe stopped talking and sat staring at me with a questioning look on his face.

"This is crazy. My eye is all fucked up, and now I'm seeing double."

"Do you have a migraine?"

"My head doesn't hurt."

"You can have a migraine without your head hurting."

"I don't think that's the problem."

This being too much humanness for a man to handle, Joe said, "Let me get Gwen. She'll know what to do" and fled from the van.

Minutes later, Gwen was sitting where Joe had just been sitting.

"Are you okay, huuuu-ney?" came Gwen's comforting, long southern drawl.

"I don't know. There's something in my eye and it's making me see double, but I can't seem to get it out."

Then it came to me. The bottle of water Dottie gave me. Britt's friend must've put something in there!

"Shit, Gwen, I think I've been drugged," I said, calmer than I ever thought I'd be if something like that was going down.

"Now why would you say that, honey?"

"Because . . ." and I told her what I was just thinking.

Gwen said something, but I wasn't listening. Like an animal, I was ripping through my purse looking for my homeopathic bottle of Apis, a remedy that counteracts poison. I couldn't find it, not seeing double like I was. Gwen took my purse and was soon wrapping my hand around the bottle. I popped two balls beneath my tongue, after which I heard Gwen say, "Honey, you haven't been drugged. You're just plain wore out. I'm having Eddie take you home."

"No, Gwen! I can't go home. There's too much to do!"

"Honey, you can't get anything done in the shape you're in. Eddie will take you home, and I'm calling Mark and having him meet us there."

"Oh my God, No, don't do that! It's bad enough that I'll be out of office. Funk can't be too!"

"Now, Gloria," she said, gently scolding in a maternal way, "The two of you have been burning the candle at both ends for a *long* time. I can see the tired in his eyes as well as yours. You need an afternoon off, the two of you. Just one afternoon to gather your strength back."

My eyes kept going in and out of focus, and I didn't know why. But Gwen was right. I couldn't work, not like this. And I certainly couldn't let the volunteers see me in this condition. They looked to me as a leader. They were counting on me to be their rock, and they had just witnessed more of me than they should have. They had given me more than they should have.

Embarrassed by my weakness, I acquiesced. I told Gwen I'd go home for a bit but that she needn't call Funk. I said I had no problem calling him if I needed him.

Soon I was half-sitting, half-lying on my living room couch, unable to recall how I got there. Gwen and Ed were staring at me with concern when Funk walked in.

"Christ, Funk, what the hell are you doing here?" I said.

"Gwen called and — "

"Jesus! I would've called if I needed you. Go! Whatever you were doing, go back to doing it."

All three said at the same time there was nothing doing, and then Gwen took charge, demanding that Funk and I take the afternoon off. She said she didn't want to hear another word about it. That we needed some rest or something dreadful would happen. After that she got tender. Telling us not to worry, she said she and Eddie would fetch Andrew from school and get him dinner. I was too wrung out to argue. I just told her that Andrew was staying late at school and someone else was bringing him home, so they needn't burden themselves with that. After which I went upstairs and sat on the sacred bed. I sure hope I thanked the Wolfs for carrying me home, for all their generosity. If not, they could add "classless" to my description of myself as a hussy.

Minutes later my husband was crawling under the covers naked, as if he was situating himself for a long winter's nap. I had been forced to go home, but I had never agreed to take a nap! I hated naps. I hadn't napped since my mother woke me up from one to tell me my childhood girlfriend had died in a car accident.

"I don't know what you think you're doing, Funk, but I'm not taking a nap."

"Yes, you are, Gloria."

"Funk. . . . "

I didn't finish the argument. The next thing I knew it was six p.m. I'd slept the entire afternoon away.

I groggily looked around the bedroom, remembering the events of earlier in the day: the vandalized trailer, the argument with Britt, worry about the volunteers, seeing double, yet I woke up feeling almost normal. My vision was clear. And the way Bill had been going at the walls, they were probably free of the vandal's torment by now. I still had Britt to contend with, but I'd deal with him. After all, I was a New and Better Me. Everything checked out fine except that I had a sick, depressed feeling in my gut, which meant something was still seriously off.

What was I forgetting?

Oh, yeah. Evert's son was still fucking dead!

"Funk!" I screeched.

My husband shot up from under the covers, "Christ! What!"

"Funk! Hurry! Get the fuck up!"

Glancing at the clock, he said crossly, "Gloria, there's plenty of time to get to the forum."

"No, Funk, we have to go to Evert."

"Evert?"

"His son's wake is tonight. Remember?"

"Tonight? It's not on my calendar."

"Never mind that. C'mon, Funk, we gotta go!"

"What about ACORN?"

"Fuck ACORN! Evert's son is dead. Get your suit on and let's beat it!"

I grabbed the phone and dialed my son's cell. "Ange!" I shouted into the receiver, "I'm leaving my credit card for you to get takeout, because I have to go —"

"Don't care, Mom. I'm busy. Bye." *Click.*

I stared at the handset for a while, dumbfounded. But there was no time to fret over my relationship with my son. I had someone else's son to worry about — or his father, at any rate.

We made it to the church in time. But man, what a line of family and friends waited at the entrance!

On the drive over, I had been thinking Funk could attend both the wake and the forum, but there was no way that could happen. Not with the line inching along as it was.

Resigned to the circumstances, we stood the way we always do whenever we're in line together, me in front, my hands behind me pulling Funk close. I don't know why I do that, but I do. I like us being smooched together. Since the occasion was too solemn for talk, I just stood blinking my eyes, making sure they were still fine. I noticed Mayor Barnes was only ten paces behind us, and the other people in line were pretending not to be staring at me, Funk, and Barnes.

I turned to my husband and pulled his head down to give him a heads-up about Barnes. He whispered back that he didn't give a damn. I whispered back that he was really growing some set of nuts. Which is when Evert detected us and waved us forward.

Funk started for him, but I held him back. "Funk," I whispered incredulously, "what the hell are you doing?"

"Didn't you see? Evert just motioned to us."

"Are you crazy! We're not cutting the line!"

"Glor, if the man wants us up there, we need to go to him."

"Uh, Funk, have you looked around? Do you notice anything out of the ordinary?"

He pulled a face that said no, which told me he was oblivious, as usual.

"Lord, Funk. The *entire* line is staring at us."

"And?"

"And I'm not getting out of this line, that's what."

That settled and the line at a complete standstill, Funk and I chatted quietly, going over the next day's schedule.

Finally it was our turn to pay our respects.

"Evert, love," I said, hugging him, "you're holding up better than I thought you would. I'm so relieved to see it."

"Why didn't you come up forward when I waved?"

"I didn't want to cut ahead of everyone in line."

"Your status has grown, Gloria. You don't need to wait in lines anymore."

Trying to cheer him up, I started flirting in the way we'd been doing and said, "I'm in your heart that deeply now, Mr. Evert Asjes *the third*?"

He didn't joke back. Just kind of reproached. "You and Mark are 'The Couple' around town. No one expects you to wait for anything right now."

I had no idea what Evert was trying to say. Since he was not only grieving but also had more guests to acknowledge, I stood on tiptoes and gave him a kiss on the cheek.

He held me close and said, "I'm glad you came. It means a lot to me."

Funk and I found a corner and waited until Evert had finished greeting guests. After a few more hours, Funk and I returned to his Corolla and drove home to our boy.

Said child barely glanced up from his computer, but that was fine by me. However Andrew behaved was fine just as long as he kept breathing. I went to my bedroom and got ready for bed.

The day had been intense. I couldn't settle down, so I turned to music for help. I placed my headset on, and Jerry Garcia's reassuring presence filtered through my ears. His words sparkled and danced their way down from the top of my head and all through my body, patching my brokenness together again.

> Shaking in the forest, what have you to fear?
> Here there may be tigers, to punch you in the ear.
> With gloves of stainless steel, bats carved out of bricks
> Knock you down and beat you up and give your ass a kick.
> When push comes to shove, you're afraid of love.

Whole once more, I turned to the magic to lift my spirits. Bob Weir's way of making love to an audience came in like a passion, melted into tiny particles, and restored my spunk.

> Spanish lady come to me, she lays on me this rose
> It rainbow spirals round and round
> It trembles and explodes
> It left a smoking crater of my mind
> I like to blow away
> But the heat came round and busted me
> For smilin' on a cloudy day

My oomph back in place, I changed music tracks to Slick to rock me to sleep. Because Slick always reminded me that God is, and all is well.

> Jesus will you come by here
> Oh Jesus will you come by here
> Jesus will you come by here, come by here
> Right now is the needy time
> Right now Lawd, is the needy time
> Now is the needy time

Before slipping off to sleep, grateful for the reassurance, I asked spirit to please bless Evert, his son, and my favorite musicians.

6 MARCH 2007

OH, LORD. The trailer was all a-twitter because Funk had been a no-show at the ACORN forum.

Fuck.

With everything that had gone down the day before, it had never crossed my mind to let the advocacy group know that Funk couldn't attend their forum. Sadly, no one at the double-wide had thought to inform them either.

Shit.

I'd fumbled a million balls over the past few months, but none had hit the ground like this one. Joe was quivering in his boots about how this oversight might generate the campaign's first negative media. But the way I saw it, if there was fall-out, so be it. Mistakes happened. Nothing could have kept Funk and me from that wake. If it made the news, voters would know that with Funk, family — even friends of his family — came first.

I thought Joe was fretting about nothing. This was the Midwest after all, where family values held strong. I was sure the slip-up wouldn't cause the consequences Joe feared. If it did, what could we do about it anyway? I *knew* I should've called ACORN. My ass was sore from kicking myself over it. I had screwed up. But done was done. I'd call the guy at ACORN and explain to him that our treasurer's son went kapooey and Funk had to attend the wake.

I'd ask what I could do to make it up to him, tell him that Funk was his for the asking. Surely he'd understand.

Okay, the New and Better Me was back. Everything was going to be fine.

Later in the day, Imani stepped in to say that as soon as she got paid she'd reimburse the campaign for the loan we'd extended. I didn't tell her the money had come from my family's personal credit card. What would be the point? She already looked embarrassed. We chatted a bit and then off to her job she went. I couldn't start back on my work for thinking of her. Imani reminded me of my daughter. Both looked vavoom in a dress and were super-smart.

An earlier conversation with Imani came to mind. She had wondered aloud why every neighborhood in Kansas City couldn't look like Brookside. Why shouldn't every home have window boxes filled with flowers? Why couldn't all the city's children play hopscotch on solid sidewalks, run bases in the street, and walk to school in safety? Everyone had a right to those basic services, yet providing them had gotten extremely complicated, all because of politics. This started me pondering how crime and brokedown neighborhoods seemed to go together. Could something as simple as Funk's plan for clean, safe neighborhoods for regular folks really lead to a citywide revival? Could it reduce our city's crime rate? I didn't see why not. What could be more life-generating than lifting every neighborhood from poverty?

From my perspective, Kansas City didn't have a race issue as much as it had a class issue. But race, class, what did it matter? If Funk's plan made the *entire* city whole again — if quality schools and clean, safe, beautiful neighborhoods became the norm for *all* citizens — hate would take a back seat.

7 MARCH 2007

AH HEFF, ah heff, ah heff.

I was trying to keep up with campaign work for the general election. Could hardly catch my breath.

9 MARCH 2007

EVER SINCE MY CHILDREN WERE LITTLE, I'd wished that I could place them on a shelf while I worked and at the end of the day take them down and we'd have fun together. If I could do that, I'd never have to feel guilty or worry about them. I'd know they were safe in my pantry, not longing for me.

Now my girl had gone away to college. Knowing that she was on spring break in Mexico, I was even more concerned about her well-being. What if something bad happened and I couldn't immediately get to her? I don't ride on airplanes! Sometimes I really hated being a mom. It was too much pressure.

Tara had sent me this email:

Mama,

Cozumel was FABULOUS — we went snorkeling, got tipsy at the free bar afterwards, ate guacamole at a bar that gave us free Mexican hats for being pretty young girls.

So, everything is well, I'll have to tell you about the amazing performer from New Orleans that we may want to book in the future (I got his business card).

Last night I was kind of sad about my single status, and I wrote about it for a while, and questioned what I wanted to do with my life. I'm not as sure as I was before about everything, which is upsetting but maybe good, in a way.

Sorry for the absolutely random email. Love you.

Love,
Your Baby

I'm a classless hussy, a whore, and an absentee parent, I thought. Whatthefuckever. I emailed my reply, even though I wished I could pick up the phone and soothe my daughter with loving murmurs.

Hi baby—yes, that was a random email, I can't wait to talk about everything; you know how I hate not having details.

Richard [a guy Tara had met the previous summer on the ship to Europe] triggered your sad feelings, Tara, but like you said, sometimes things like this make you want to re-evaluate where you are and where you want to go. It's your life to create, nothing is set in stone—do what you want, it's all good! We'll talk when you get back to Pitt, or in the airport in Norlins (that's short for New Orleans).

I Love you, Lover-Breath,

Your Mammy

xoxoxo

11 MARCH 2007

SHIT.

A volunteer slipped me an article from a newspaper columnist about how Funk had missed the ACORN forum. I thought I'd put the issue put to bed after I phoned the ACORN forum organizer and apologized. But it seems I had not.

From: e kc online
Publisher's Note

Subject: Mayoral forum minus one
by Bruce Rodgers

It's hard to determine if there's a turning point for a candidate in a close election. Whether Funkhouser's no-show at the ACORN forum was a turning point or not isn't clear. However, it's easy to say that for the 60 people there, the fruitless waiting guaranteed Brooks their vote.

"He even RSVPed twice!" said a frustrated ACORN member to the audience. "He chose not to be here."

A Funkhouser spokesman [that "man" was me] said he attended a funeral service for the son of campaign treasurer Evert Asjes III. One
can't fault Funkhouser for paying his respects. One can fault his
campaign for leaving ACORN hanging without a timely explanation.

The lack of follow through makes one wonder if the intense campaigning appears to have beaten Funkhouser around a little lately. His campaign office was vandalized, and his wife Gloria has been ill, which
obviously affects him. [Uh, mister, the blurred-vision-thing put me out
for part of an afternoon. And I worked from bed with my cold!]

I forwarded the columnist's article to the committee and the Inner Circle.
The campaign could have pulled together over this situation. Instead, internal
strife reared its ugly head again.

From: Joe Miller

To: BirthWays

Subject: Re: Missed ACORN forum

This was the biggest disappointment for me. I know all the circumstances involved. And I know that day was really hard for you. But it
was tough for me, too, because you both just disappeared and didn't
tell us what was going on. I would've driven there and said that you
were ill, the place had been broken into, whatever. But to just not
show, that's just not good.

I fully support putting family first. But let's communicate and get
things covered.

All best, Joe

Cry me a bucket. Joe's email mildly repulsed me, but look at how Mr.
Goody Two-shoes responded:

From: Mark Funkhouser

To: Joe Miller, BirthWays

Joe,

You're right. I dropped the ball. I should have let you know. I'm disappointed that Britt or someone didn't see it on the schedule and deal with it, but I did see it and just didn't deal with it.

As your role has evolved in the campaign, I need to think to call on you more often.

I think Rodgers' piece is fair. People will have to look at my record on poor people's issues and make up their own minds.

Chalk it up as another mistake on my part. You'll see more. And I'll try to do better.

All the best,
Mark

Since I was still gagging about what a pansy-ass Joe was, I forwarded the emails to Gwen — mostly to vent, but I also wanted her opinion on what else I could do about the situation with ACORN. The organization's name was beginning to make more sense to me, given that they were completely frigging nuts.

From: BirthWays
To: G Wolf

Is there anything else that we should or could do to deal with ACORN?

From: G Wolf
To: BirthWays

Joe is young and idealistic. He has not come up against that 'wall' that can knock us off our feet. . . . but you and I know there are moments when we have to make hard decisions . . . and we don't owe anyone an explanation.

Joe has been brought very closely into your inner circle and he doesn't quite understand the levels of privilege and responsibility that has been visited upon you in that circle.

All regrets have been extended to ACORN that can be.

NOT TO WORRY.

XO

Gwen was as comforting as ever. Too bad her words didn't soothe me for more than a few minutes.

How I longed for the sweet days of the primary. Back then, the other candidates didn't see Funk as a threat, and the establishment didn't give him a sideways glance. Things had been easier for me on a personal level. I went about my business relatively unnoticed. I worked my ass off, but I did it in relative peace and was rewarded for my efforts. I had the pleasure of seeing hope spark in the underserved population. The general election wasn't like that.

The world outside the trailer grew dark after my screw-up with ACORN. A volunteer who had connections told me Brooks was fanning the flames, was keeping my mistake alive in the media by saying that Funk didn't stand with ordinary folks.

How did our campaign respond to the allegations? We knee-jerked a response, emailing Funk's supporters. I'll give you three guesses who wrote the email.

URGENT!!!

WE NEED YOUR HELP

THE BROOKS CAMPAIGN HAS LAUNCHED THEIR MOST NEGATIVE ATTACK

THE POLITICAL INSIDE CROWD IS CLAIMING THAT MARK DOES NOT WORK WELL WITH PEOPLE

WE ALL KNOW THAT IS NOT TRUE

PLEASE HELP US "MASS RALLY" AS MANY PEOPLE AS WE CAN AT 1:15 THIS AFTERNOON AT THE DOUBLE-WIDE

Regardless of what I thought about Britt's style, his email *was* extraordinarily effective!

Within an hour of when he hit Send, a hundred supporters and a buttload of media gathered outside the trailer. The attendees included Funk's bottom lip, which was sticking out a mile, because how dare anyone say he had no friends and didn't work well with others!

Supporters circled Funk, some holding yard signs they'd unearthed from their front lawn. I expressed a hearty thank-you to them all, after which I said hey to the media and hugged that cameraman I adored — the Italian one who had kissed me full on the lips at the announcement press event. And then I shifted from diplomat mode into wife mode. I stood next to my man, trying my hardest to un-hickify him. I brushed lint from his suit and told him to calm the fuck down. Having no luck with the latter, I stood helplessly by, watching his bottom lip travel deeper into Kansas, perhaps even as far as the border of Colorado.

Funk finally told the media to roll it. The reporters tried to get Funk to play as dirty as the Brooks campaign, but Funk didn't step into that trap. He said what he needed to say. Unfortunately, he sounded as if he was lecturing our kids. That played right into what the Brooks campaign said about Funk — that he was too blunt, too forward, not the cheerleading sort normally found in these here woods.

My husband didn't see the media rolling their eyes. And since he was ignoring my beamed messages, he didn't adjust his behavior. There I stood, thinking Funk hadn't learned the campaign world as well as I had thought. And then he made things worse. He interrupted a reporter's question to say the media had all the information they needed and that he had to get back to work.

I decided right then and there that I was voting for Alvin Brooks. I mean, really, how rude! Way to blow it, Funk.

Still, Britt did a great job of organizing the event.

12 MARCH 2007

FUCK, FUCK, FUCK. ACORN simply *would not* let it go!

I admit it, I forgot to call them, and I hated myself for it! But I'd only fucking apologized ten thousand times! C'mon, ACORN, give a girl a break! What more could I do?

Or was that volunteer's hunch correct? Was this *you*, Mr. Brooks? Well, whoever was behind this, I wished they'd knock it off. They had my guy tearing his clothes. No, not Funk, who could give two shits about it. I was talking about Joe.

I had to convince the committee, especially Joe, to be done with it already.

13 MARCH 2007

WHEN WOULD THIS NIGHTMARE FUCKING END?

Why the hell was the media keeping it alive? I *knew* I should have phoned ACORN.

Contrite me, demure me, me in diplomat mode, decided to apologize publicly one more time. I asked the committee to review my words.

From: BirthWays

To: funk Funkhouser; Joe Miller; Jeff Simon; Britt Nichols; G Wolf; kendrick blackwood

Subject: ACORN

This is a letter to the editor I think we should send. What do you think?

Dear Letter to the Editor,

This letter is an open apology to ACORN for missing their forum. We had several trying events which led to us dropping the ball on a forum we did not want to miss.

While this is no excuse, we did want you to know that our absence was not ill intentioned or indicative of a change in our stance of the last 18 years to work hard for the regular folks of this city.

We will pay careful attention not to make a similar mistake in the future.

All the best, Gloria Squitiro and Mark Funkhouser

Here's how the Inner Circle reacted to my apology.

From: G Wolf
To: BirthWays

Ed and I think it is fine. You said just enough, made your apology, and did not go into a long explanation, which would have sounded contrived. This was short, sweet and to the point. . . . and should put it to an end. XO, G&E

From: Joe Miller
To: BirthWays

I agree. Send it.

From: kendrick blackwood
To: BirthWays

looks good and contrite to me

From: BirthWays
To: kendrick blackwood

Far enough up the ass?

From: kendrick blackwood
To: BirthWays

What more can you do?

From: BirthWays
To: kendrick blackwood

Put my fist down their throat?

From: kendrick blackwood
To: BirthWays

down their throat
up their ass
same diff . . .
I can't believe I just said that

Given the responses, it seemed I'd succeeded in quieting everyone's nerves.

14 MARCH 2007

CHRIST, I THOUGHT WE WERE DONE WITH IT.

According to media reports, the advocacy group ACORN had been highly affronted by Funk's no-show. But I didn't believe that for a minute. I suspected that Brooks or his highly paid campaign manager was behind the uproar.

This side of humanity depressed me. I hated when people took the easy path in dealing with challenges. However, for a leader to be spreading myths was weak. Hurtful, too.

We hadn't had a moment to savor Funk's win in the primary election. We hadn't been able raise the first toast in cheer. Not with our signs being stolen. The trailer vandalized. Evert's son dying. The *Star* pitting Funk and Brooks against each other but making it appear as if *our* family was doing it.

Strangely, the nastier things got and the more the media put me under the spotlight, the more love Funk's supporters directed my way. If a reporter said the slightest thing that wasn't over-the-top wonderful about me, it was Funk's supporters to the rescue! They stuck up for me. Prayed for me. The volunteers even dubbed me "Queen of the DoubleWide." I think the term originated with Mr. Flirtatious, a.k.a. Evert Asjes the third! Mr. Tattoo. My own personal thug. Father of a gone-too-soon son — and fucking shit to that last part.

Things were holding strong outside the trailer too. Donations arrived in a steady stream, and we had so many volunteers that we had trouble finding things for them to do. But thankfully, that job was off my plate. Ed had it handled. I just hoped he was loving them up.

I saw another change that I wasn't sure I liked: the campaign was straying from its grassroots origins. Some of the new volunteers had great talent, and the campaign had gotten upscale because of it. We'd joined the big leagues!

A volunteer named Greg Corwin, a professional graphic designer, signed on two weeks before Election Day. Greg offered to work on our print ads and mailers. I wasn't sad to improve on the eyesores we'd previously sent out. Those bordered on classless, though they were all we could afford at the time!

We replaced them with pieces that didn't give me a single item to groan over. I rubberstamped the proofs Greg designed. They got straight to the point in the most professional way. They nipped in the bud the rumors the other campaign was putting out, and nothing about them was in-your-face. Not a single word appeared in capital letters. Greg's mailers were so good that I didn't even run them by Funk. With only a few days left until the election, we had to move!

We had taken an additional step away from our grassroots beginnings — a step I was sort of okay with and sort of not. Mortgage broker Jim Nutter, the Kansas City political kingpin, was backing Funk as promised. Mr. Moneybags was with us now. He commissioned two professionally produced commercials. The problem was, he didn't discuss it with us before he did it. I was concerned that the new commercials might be so glossy that voters would think Funk had grown a fat ass — had become one of *those* politicians. On the other hand I'd seen the video script, and by the looks of it, Nutter had actually been listening to Funk's talk all those years. For that alone, Nutter should get an Academy Award, because some days listening to Funk is a small form of torture.

Still, I missed our cute, homemade campaign videos. What can I say? I was sentimental.

15 MARCH 2007

I WAS ARRANGING THE TABLE at yet another meet-and-greet. Those events didn't bring in much in the way of donations, but Funk didn't care. Even the committee members weren't as troubled about that anymore because the bucks just keep rolling in, and without us even trying.

I was arranging the table when the first question of the event dropped. It regarded the latest "scandal," a school voucher issue. I froze in place. I didn't finish setting the buttons down, just stood with my ear cocked so I could hear better.

The question was a biggie. Brooks had been claiming that Funk was just like every other politician who stuck his finger in the air to test the wind before saying what he thought.

How absurd! Funk couldn't say something untrue if he tried.

I'd learned so much about life through the campaign. Ugly things. For example, I never knew you could *create* a scandal where none existed. I thought the police would be at your door to arrest you for lying if you reported something that wasn't true.

The "scandal" began when Funk responded that he'd give school vouchers a try if they got the middle class to move back to Kansas City. He explained that a huge reason for the mass exodus was the quality of the schools. He said Kansas City could make a comeback by attracting more people to settle in the urban core. To become viable again, the city needed the tax dollars paid by those new residents.

Oh, the commotion that followed! It was as if he had said his platform included sacrificing children to achieve his goals.

Funk's phone lit up all night long with school board members chewing his ass out for considering vouchers. Funk heard them out. They convinced him that vouchers might be a bad idea, so he promised to explore other options first. The next thing you knew, the newspaper was ringing Funk to ask for comments about Brooks having just called him a flip-flopper.

Funk's campaign must have been polling well for Brooks's campaign manager to make such a claim. I felt sorry for Brooks. It was an uneven playing field, what with the *Star* pushing my man — *wink-wink*, they were only tossing a few mean things out there to make it appear as if they were not — and Brooks having a dud for a manager. *I wonder how much Brooks is paying him. Like, I'm not getting paid anything.*

In any case, I was glad Brooks wasn't there when the meet-and-greet attendees asked Funk whether he was anti-union or pro-union. Funk answered in his usual earnest way. He gave a long-winded story about how his father had organized and worked union picket lines. And that's where it should have ended. But no, Funk added that he wasn't anti-union; he was "anti-stupid." I thought I'd swallow my tongue. As you can see, Funk was *not* the type to stick his finger in the air. Up his ass, maybe, but not in the air.

At the conclusion of the event I returned to the trailer, a black cloud swirling over my head. All day long my mind drifted back to Funk's "anti-stupid" response at the meet-and-greet. I stared up at the ceiling thinking, *We're so close. Why is he messing things up when we're this close?*

Late that afternoon Kendrick came moseying into my office, all skin and bones, looking like he was walking on water. His greeting trickled over my desk. "Hey, it's the Queen of the DoubleWide!" That was all it took to dispel my bad mood. It was delightful to have friends that I could have fun with, and just by them being themselves.

Kendrick asked how the meet-and-greet had gone, and I told him about Funk's "anti-stupid" remark.

He was as shocked as I had been, which made me even more upset. Because now I had to defend my husband, when I hated him to the ends of the earth.

"He said *what?*"

"C'mon, Kendrick. You know Funk says what he thinks."

"Can't he sidestep an issue?"

"You know the answer."

"But we're so close!"

"I know. Believe me, I fucking know."

"This is — "

"Please don't be Joe. We're not going to lose because Funk was honest."

"But — "

Kendrick gave me his smile, one that contorts his face in the most bizarre way. His expression screamed, "Love me! Please love me!" When he looked at me that way, it was impossible to not love that face.

Still, a campaign manager had to do what a campaign manager had to do.

"Kendrick, stop! Voters either want a mayor who speaks the truth, or they don't. Either they want change and the trying times that come with it, or they don't. Funk's running for mayor to get things done."

"That's some righteous talk."

"So says the guy wearing the same clothes. Now, can we please get me back in a good mood?"

When Kendrick left, I sat lost in thought again. This time, about how Funk and I might not always be on the same page, yet in this instance we definitely were. Because I'm anti-stupid too.

And that being the God's honest truth, I wondered what the hell I was doing hitched to a loser.

16 MARCH 2007

YAY!

Sometimes — most times, really — the double-wide pulled together. Here's what Imani had to say:

From: imani

Subject: Re: URGENT! Mark is being attacked by the Brooks Campaign

I hope you take the high road on this. I really believe that someone "professional" is trying to bait you. Your reaction to Brooks will show how well you get along with people.

What you are for should speak louder than what negative things people are saying about you. Like it or not, you are now a politician and have to worry about how you will be perceived. Some positions you don't necessarily have to "volunteer" unless you are specifically asked or you really feel it will put you over the top. Find out how the majority of your constituents feel about an issue/position before you voice it. (I think you know this now.)

I liked Imani, even if I didn't agree with her advice. Still, she wanted to do something, not cower in a corner. I loved that!

My husband's response?

From: Mark Funkhouser

To: imani

Imani

Thanks for this note.

Mark

Now do you understand why I took over replying to his emails?

17 MARCH 2007

ST. PATRICK'S DAY. Who knew we'd be in a parade?

Funk and I met at a rendezvous point and hopped into the back seat of a volunteer's Model T Ford. Spectators were already standing ten rows deep on both sides of the street. Soon the Model T was cruising slowly down the parade route, with Funk's volunteers walking behind it. Bill Drummond was at the wheel of my daughter's little pink pickup truck. Bill had decked it out with "Funk for Mayor" yards signs taped to the doors, a sparkly green skirt encircling the lower half, and speakers tied to the roof blaring a continuous loop of the "We Want the Funk" song.

As we traveled down the road, people in the crowd danced to the music and cheered for Funk. I felt scared to be in the center of such a throng. My throat closed. I turned to Funk and said, "Don't expect me to pull a Jackie Kennedy for you."

"Don't worry. I know I'll be used as a shield if bullets start flying."

We rode a few blocks farther, but we didn't feel right just sitting there in the car and waving. So we jumped out of the Model T and walked beside our pink truck, nestled within Funk's circle of volunteers, all of us marching down the road grooving to the beat together.

Funk, feeling his oats, suddenly dipped me back in his arms and kissed me on the lips, and oh, how the crowd roared! I'd never witnessed the showman side of him, though I knew it was there. Since both of us teach, we're aware that when you're in front of a classroom full of students, you have to give the performance of your life or the material just won't stick.

Mid-parade, Funk broke free of the circle and began loping down the street, dancing to his own beat, shaking hands with people who'd extended theirs and kissing babies held up to him. I'd been with this man for more than thirty years, yet I could hardly believe my eyes.

He was catching on, and I felt new respect for him. Past mayors had been cheerleaders — but cheerleaders only. My guy would be different. He'd bring courage and smarts to the table, enough to lift Kansas City from its doldrums. On this day he showed he had the ability to be a cheerleader too. Who knew?

18 MARCH 2007

CAMPAIGN VOLUNTEER Greg Corwin began an email chain prompted by his indignance over the "when-will-it-ever-fucking-end-scandal" that Brooks was *still* milking! Greg had never been involved in government or politics prior to this election. I found it funny to see someone else get mad about injustices.

From: Greg Corwin

To: Gloria Squitiro

Cc: Joe Miller; kendrick blackwood; funk Funkhouser

Subject: Re: Permit me to vent

I just heard another negative radio ad from Brooks—talking about Funk flip-flopping on vouchers. Obviously misleading, dishonest and wrong.

. . .

And they're intentionally lying about his "flip-flopping" because they're scared witless that we're going to win. They have to lie and call it flip-flopping because they won't call it what it honestly is – "thoughtful leadership with integrity, and the courage and strong work ethic to follow the facts."

I'm proud that we're taking the high road, (but it would feel soooo good to punch back).

I agreed with Greg's assertion that negative messaging worked for the Brooks campaign and that Funk's campaign needed to respond to those falsehoods. We—Joe, Kendrick, Britt, Greg, and I—rushed to create a perfect press release retort. At the last second, I noticed that Greg hadn't included Britt in the chain, so I added his name in my reply.

From: Gloria Squitiro

Joe—if you haven't sent the latest press release yet, I think we should respond to the negative shit Brooks putting out—the blatant lies and yet his promise not to participate in dirty campaign tactics.

I'll talk to Funk when I get a chance, but Brooks really is over the top. It's almost like if we don't say something, people will believe that it's true.

Greg — thank you for fueling my decision here.

Love to all,

QDW (*that's short for Queen of the DoubleWide*)

I was editing the press release that the group was furiously volleying back and forth when in walked Kendrie (my new nickname for Kendrick). He couldn't take sitting at home what with all the big doings going on at the trailer. He had come in to see whether he could help hurry things along. Taking a seat at my desk with his back to the door, the two of us worked individually on the draft.

Funk walked in and didn't even say hi, just started giving me a rundown on where he was going and what time I should expect him home that night. Said it as if I didn't know, even though I was the one who kept his calendar. This guy annoyed me to no end when he interrupted me as if I was his personal secretary. As if I wasn't rushing to get *his* press release out the door!

I waited impatiently for him to finish saying what he thought he needed to say. But when he bent to kiss me goodbye and then started for the door — without so much as a nod in Kendrick's direction — I helped him be a human.

"Uh, Funk. Are you going to say hey to Kendrick?"

"Hello, Kendrick."

"Funk," I said, giving my husband a look that made it clear he should lose the hick. Unfortunately, Kendrick picked up on my death stare and fell all over himself about.

Squirming in his chair, Kendrick stuttered, "That's okay, Mark, I know you're — "

Funk interrupted him, running with my cue to act like a normal person, and said, "How are you, Kendrick?"

Kendrick, who seemed not quite sure if he was supposed to respond or not, said nothing.

"Funk?" I said, hoping he'd insert the social nicety that was *still* missing.

"Thanks for helping, Kendrick," Funk said. "I really appreciate it."

"Okay, Funk, now you can leave," I said, dismissing him with a wave, which happened to coincide with Kendrick finding his voice.

"Where ya headed, Funk?"

"To a debate with Brooks."

"Aren't those at night?"

"Usually, but not this time."

Kendrick, having just witnessed the interchange between husband and wife, lightened up and got in on the act. After Funk exited my office, Kendrick cupped his hands around his mouth and shouted after him, "Don't fuck up!"

Funk, used to this type of exchange, shouted back that he wouldn't.

The trailer being as cozy as it was, of course the other volunteers overheard Kendrick, though it's unlikely they understood that "Don't fuck up" meant Funk shouldn't say anything that would cause another flip-flop scandal.

As soon as Funk's Corolla pulled away, Kendrick and I went back to editing the release. Several emails came in from the Inner Circle with more edits and thoughts to consider.

From: Greg Corwin

The press release should state how the Brooks campaign is manipulating the situation so they can have the license to dishonestly represent Funk's record and attack his character, something we have never done nor will ever do.

Have we discussed getting out a viral email?

Asking our supporters to send it to everybody they know, and encouraging blogging?

Brooks has the money, but we have the people — excited, engaged people who (unlike Brooks supporters) believe their candidate is going to transform the way our city is run.

As it turned out, the Inner Circle believed our press release was too important to rush out the door, so we decided to think about it overnight. After all the staff and volunteers had left the trailer, my husband *finally* weighed in on his own damn press release.

From: Mark Funkhouser

This is a pretty good idea. I don't think we've really discussed the "viral email" of the type Greg mentions. It could energize our people and help our get out the vote (GOTV).

Late that night I tried to unwind in the sacred bed but my thoughts drifted to, what else, the campaign. It felt as if the campaign had moved on without Funk. It was like a machine rolling. Funk hardly ever spent time at headquarters. He just blew in and out, all day long. Those of us who remained in the trailer were working, with or without Funk. We were oiling that machine, whether Funk was aware of it or not. The election was in the bag, whether outsiders were aware of it or not.

Similar to the way I had dreamed about safely stowing my children on a shelf when they were young, I wished that I could put Funk on a shelf and keep him there until election night. If I could do that, there'd be no way his mouth could fuck with destiny.

19 MARCH 2007

EIGHT DAYS TO GO until the general election!

My mind was already preparing me — as usual, without consulting me first. I couldn't get the last line of Bob Dylan's "I Shall Be Released" out of my head:

> They say everything can be replaced
> Yet every distance is not near
> So I remember every face
> Of every man who put me here
> I see my light come shining
> From the west unto the east

Any day now, any day now
I shall be released

As Funk exited the trailer late that afternoon, I heard someone call out to him, "Just another week. Don't fuck up!" I laughed. We'd come so far that volunteers were treating Funk as shabbily as his family did!

20 MARCH 2007

ENDORSEMENTS had been rolling in like gunfire. A new one arrived just seven days before the election, generating a buzz in the trailer. Everyone in the double-wide was high from the news. It came from a Hispanic political action committee, La Raza. I loved cultures that had personality and spark, people who had more colors than beige.

I was thrilled . . . until I learned that La Raza expected Funk's campaign to pay them for their endorsement. I balked so loud. Said we weren't doing that. We *earned* endorsements; we didn't *buy* them.

When Nutter caught wind that we were considering turning the "honor" down, he summoned Funk to his office to say he'd cover the cost. But the money wasn't the point. A bought endorsement would be deceitful. It was a tricky situation, I tell you.

Funk and I huddled inside his office discussing what to do. We didn't want to piss Nutter off, and we certainly didn't want to override his years of experience at winning elections. In the midst of our worried discussion about that, Dottie popped her head in and whispered that a woman named Lali Garcia, with ties to La Raza, had arrived to congratulate us.

Funk and I went out to the reception area to greet her. When she congratulated us by kissing me *full* on the lips — just the way an Italian New Yorker would — my trepidation flew out the window. I tossed Funk a look that said, *Forget it, we're accepting the endorsement,* and he shot me one back that said, *You're right, this isn't worth fighting with Nutter over.*

After that exchange, Funk hurried toward the door of the trailer to get to his next appointment. A harmony of voices called after him, "Don't fuck up!" I wished they hadn't done that in front of the lady from La Raza, so I just pretended it hadn't happened.

I walked Lali out to the parking lot, where she and I shot the shit for a while longer. She told me the Hispanic vote would decide this close mayoral race. Many people had said the same to me in recent weeks, and I'd never replied with the words I was thinking: *Funk himself — the product — would win the race.* Aside from that, the longer we spoke, the more I couldn't wait for Funk to start in on the big projects needed in Lali's community. The love-in ended when Dottie shouted that I was needed inside.

Moments before I locked up the trailer for the night, a press release from Rita Valenciano at La Raza awakened the fax.

> With regard to Mr. Funkhouser's endorsement, Ms. Valenciano stated: "He (Mr. Funkhouser) inspires the confidence of our Hispanic and urban community because he provides specifics regarding his initiatives to address our city's concerns."

The sender's name sounded familiar. When I got home, Funk jogged my memory and I began connecting the dots. Remember the blogger Joe had been starstruck over early in the campaign, the one who lived in his mother's basement and wrote a blog? Well, Rita was the Little Tick's mother.

People were so intertwined in Kansas City. Sometimes it felt a little bit incestuous.

21 MARCH 2007

FUCK IT ALL.

I had to "walk the neighborhood" with Ruth — because she simply would not let it alone. She said Funk would lose the mayoral race if I didn't show my face in the East Side, that the black vote would call this close mayoral race. She said folks needed to see for themselves that I was okay, in order to chuck Mrs.

Brooks aside and vote for my husband instead of hers. I acquiesced to canvassing with her — but only to keep public relations high, not because I agreed with her logic. I knew Funk was going to win.

At the appointed hour I drove the five minutes from my house to hers. I honked to let her know I was there, but she opened the kitchen door and motioned me out of the car. I surely didn't have time for this delay. But dutiful friend that I am, I dragged my tired ass out of the van and walked to her door. I was glad I did, because she showed me the tiles that she'd installed on the risers leading into her home. It was an ingenious and beautiful design.

After admiring her handiwork I said we better get going because I couldn't be away from the trailer for very long. Ruth kicked up a small fuss and said I didn't need to be anywhere, but then she grabbed her purse, got into my car, and directed me to — yes, the very street where Funk's rival Alvin Brooks lived. Jesus! Ruth hadn't told me this was her plan! Canvassing in that location struck me as in-your-face and disrespectful. But I went along with Ruth, even though my dignity took a beating.

We roamed up and down the hilly neighborhood, knocking on doors and tucking flyers into mailboxes. Ruth made fun of me for walking slowly and being out of breath. I'd gained back all the weight I lost in Europe and then some, all because of Funk's campaign. I gasped and plodded alongside Ruth. Why was I being punished for helping my husband?

And then I understood. Karma had given me a swift kick in the ass that day for canvassing in Brooks's neighborhood. *Whatever. Go away, universe! Pick on someone your own size.*

22 MARCH 2007

"GLORIA."

"Jesus," I said, rubbing my eyes awake, "what do you want now, Funk?"

"The Public Safety press event?"

"Have I grown hair on my chest?"

Blink-blink.

That was my husband, not understanding the question.

"Let me put it to you another way. Does Jeff sleep in this bed with you?"

Blink-blink.

"Funk, how do you expect to be mayor when you can't comprehend a question?"

"Those aren't questions, Gloria, they're sarcasm."

"Same thing."

"The press event?"

"Do I look like Jeff?"

"No. You look like someone I want to ravish."

"Get lost."

"The press event?"

"Funk, your chairman was tasked with that event a million years ago. If you want to know if it's in the pipeline, call Jeff and get on his ass instead of mine."

Glimpsing the clock, I screamed from the bed, "Ange, are you up?"

"Yes, Mom," drifted his voice from down the hallway.

"Are you ready for school?"

"No, Mom."

"Well, get a move on!"

23 MARCH 2007

IT WAS THE FINAL WEEKEND before the general election.

I arrived at the trailer early. The first email I opened put the final days of the race into perspective. News columnist Bruce Rodgers wrote,

Choosing a mayor — difficult but not too messy
by Bruce Rodgers

At the forum at the All Souls Church, the moderator seemed almost giddy at the choice of picking between "the best of the best." Funk-houser and Brooks took it in with smiles, interacting with one another in a relaxing display of easygoing competitiveness.

When asked about running a clean campaign, Brooks said that he had instructed his staff not to "bring me dirt" and that "anyone who says a bad thing about Mark" would be fired.

Funkhouser said the campaign was about ideas and that if he said anything bad about "Alvin — my wife would slap me."

As far as it's known, Funkhouser's wife has not slapped him and no one on Brooks' campaign has been fired.

Brooks repeatedly says he wants to be the "People's Mayor." He likes being out in the neighborhood; he considers it his responsibility to help those people who have suffered, he wants to console crime victims and cajole those who may seek to turn their lives around.

That's not to say Funkhouser doesn't believe in people. He just tempers the belief against his 18-year experience as city auditor. What he dealt with at times as a city employee, he calls "a culture of inside dealing," and it had a lot to do with his decision to run for mayor.

"It was driving me nuts to see how badly we were misusing the people's trust, and their dollars and doing things that were just. . . ."

And then I asked Funkhouser if the word "corrupt" was one he could use to complete the sentence?

"I think I would use the word 'corrupt.'"

It's democracy time in Kansas City. No one said it was easy to choose.

I really think the author, Mr. Rogers, should change his name, I can't look at it without cracking up. When I finished reading the long-ass article, I forwarded it to the committee and started on the newsletter. My cell phone rang. Seeing it was Evert, I picked up right away.

"So good to hear from you! How are you holding up?"

"I'm well, thank you for asking. You're practically the only one who does."

What do you say to that? I asked if he had received the buttons he'd requested.

He said he was calling to thank me for getting them over to him. Knowing I was busy, he said, "Well, that's it. Tell your husband that it's just a few more days and not to fuck it up."

"Sure thing, Evert. I'll add your name to the list of people who've already called and asked me to give him that message."

As I was finishing up with Evert, Joe stepped into my office with two of his friends — Anita Dixon and Marie Young — along with his latest inspiration.

He wanted Funk and me to join him and those friends at the Green Duck, a bar located in an economically depressed part of town. No white person had set foot inside ever since its owner, civil rights leader Leon Jordan, had been killed there in 1970. Leon had co-founded the political organization called "Freedom," and his murder shepherded in the killings that were still taking place in the East Side.

Why would Joe, Funk, and I, who are white, visit the Green Duck with Anita and Marie, who are black? The plain and simple answer. To show that my husband walked his talk, that he would make good on his promise to represent everyone who called Kansas City home.

By the time Joe concluded his proposal, the plan was embedded in my soul. I wasn't one to back down in the face of fear.

Having listened to my husband's rants for eons, I'd drawn a few conclusions. How dared the establishment have others do their dirty work for them? How could they watch the people outside their wealthy circle wage violence on each other? How could they render that population hopeless and leave them with no power to change the system?

Inertia and fear had allowed the dangerous situation to fester. Kansas City, the thirtieth-largest metropolis in the US, had been ranked the third-most-violent city in the nation. The violence was concentrated in the East Side, where the Green Duck was located.

White people were responsible for the violence but so were black people. I blamed white people for the appalling crime rate. But the fault line ran through the black part of town — and that was black people's doing. Couldn't they see they were playing into the establishment's hand?

Joe and his friends didn't have to sell me on going to the Green Duck, even though I honestly didn't see what good it would do. At least, I didn't see it with my brain. My gut screamed that we had to go.

Nine hours after that conversation with Joe, man, did I ever wish that I had allowed myself to give in to fear.

When the five of us entered the Green Duck I went out of my mind with fright. Word must have spread that Funk was coming to town, because there were a million people over what the city had posted was the capacity limit for the club. I couldn't take a deep breath because of how afraid I was. And knowing that I couldn't take a deep breath was making me more afraid.

I was shoulder to shoulder with a million others, squished beyond squished. Funk was way ahead, so I couldn't tell him I was spiraling down. It seemed as though every eye was trained on Funk, Joe, and me. The staring was giving me tunnel vision, making my throat close.

Anita must have noticed the fear oozing from my body because she grabbed my hand as if I were a little baby and wound me through the crowd to an empty space against a wall. But it was when she whispered in my ear that I shouldn't worry — that she was packing, and she had plants scattered about who would drop anyone who so much as raised a hand in our direction — that I realized she'd read my fear all wrong.

It had never occurred to me to be afraid because I was one of the three white faces in the room. At least I didn't think to be afraid until I realized *she* thought I should be afraid. Until she said she'd taken *measures* for that reason.

Holy fuck. Would I ever see my children again? And was Funk righting the wrongs in this city really worth the risk of making my children orphans? If I'd known Anita thought we were risking our lives by going to the Green Duck, I would've sent Funk by himself. Like, why did I have to be there anyway?

Oh, stop trying to pretend, Gloria. It would've been one thing for Funk to go to the Green Duck with Joe, but to bring his wife along showed that his intentions were sincere. Besides, what was I saying? Nothing could've kept me away once I heard the plan. Still! C'mon, God! Why couldn't you grant me an exception just this once?

Well, you're here, Gloria, aren't you? You're not hiding like your mother used to do — running down five flights of stairs with her eyes closed because she was afraid of seeing the other people who lived in the projects with her. Fuck it all. I guess I was staying, even if my throat was choking me to death.

Lord, I implore you. Have mercy on my children. Please don't let me die. They could live without Funk, but me? They'd kill me if I got myself killed tonight.

The evening passed quickly. Funk spoke with tons of people. I spoke with tons of people. No one was shot. My breathing eventually returned to normal. My tunnel vision left me. And once all that happened, I was even more psyched that Funk was getting this opportunity to do a whole lot of good for a whole lot of good people.

Once I calmed down, I noticed the hidden fear on the other faces in the room. I wasn't the only person who was scared. Some people had to puff themselves up like fragile little birds just to stay alive. Seeing that, I vowed that Funk's first Town Hall Meeting would be there in the East Side, where it was needed the most — down at the good ol' Green Duck.

24 MARCH 2007

IT SEEMED AS IF EVERY VOLUNTEER WAS AT THE TRAILER.

With only three days left until the general election, everyone wanted to be together. I couldn't get a stitch of work done for all the people popping into my office. Bev was sitting across from me when Funk's booming voice said farewell as he ran to his next appointment. Bev and I shouted our goodbyes, but her eyes practically popped out of her head when she heard the melody of voices respond, "Bye! Don't fuck up!"

"Gloria, that's disrespectful," said the judge's wife.

"Bev, you're here all the time. Haven't you heard that before?"

"Yes, but I don't like it. Mark is going to be the mayor soon."

"It's okay, Bev. Funk could give two shits. Actually, I think he likes the attention."

25 MARCH 2007

I ARRIVED AT THE TRAILER at dawn to get some work done before I had to "walk the neighborhood." That's right. I'd suddenly become the "face" of my husband's campaign — at least that's what the committee said. They expected me to stand in for Funk when he was too busy to do things for himself, even when they knew we disagreed with the idea of canvassing.

Funk and I had been right. Knocking on doors turned out to be a total waste of time! Who the fuck was home in the morning? And who answered the door if they were? I could answer both questions with absolute certainty: No one was home, and no one answered the door except for perverts. I didn't care what the committee said; I was never doing that again.

I was frazzled upon my return. I cut my morning round of greeting volunteers short when I heard my cell phone ringing. I ran to my office, but by the time I pulled it out of my purse it had already stopped. Which is when I noticed four missed calls — three from my daughter and one from my mother.

I sat my fat ass down and rang my daughter first, begging her forgiveness.

"It's fine, Mama. I'm just making sure you're picking me up at the airport tomorrow."

In a high-octave voice I said, "Of course. What kind of mother do you think I am?"

I'd totally forgotten about the flight. Fortunately, I didn't have to give myself away by asking what time I should be at the airport because Tara ended the call by saying she'd see me the next day at 6:45. If I had still been a practicing Catholic I would have crossed myself. Instead I just sat with my head in my hands, thinking bad thoughts about myself.

Next I rang my mother, beginning the call by asking her if something was wrong. My love and respect for her were put to the test daily. She rarely called — not because she didn't want to disturb me, knowing how busy I was. As my mother, she was exercising her God-given right to be called first. This rule had never been spoken, but it had filtered into my body by way of osmosis since childhood. It partly explained my highly developed intuition and survival skills.

"Oh my God," she said, "what's all that noise? Why is it so fucking loud?"

"Mom, it's a campaign. The final days. This is the way it goes."

"Well, I can't talk if it's gonna be like this. I just called to say I'm feeling a little better about Dad. So long!" She hung up angrily.

It was a relief to hear the part about my dad, if not her hang-up.

Two seconds later Dottie was at my desk asking if I'd heard the latest robocall generated by the Brooks campaign. I hadn't. Brooks had thrown a mountain of negativity Funk's way in the previous few days. I marched into Britt's office and asked him, "What the hell?"

Britt confirmed that Brooks was robo-phoning registered voters to talk shit about Funk. Where the fuck did Brooks's promise go, that he wouldn't resort to negative campaigning? That he'd fire anyone he caught doing such a thing? Our campaign had stuck to our end of the bargain. Just as Mr. Rodgers had written, I'd have smacked Funk upside his head if he'd employed such tactics. And to date, I hadn't gotten the pleasure of doing so.

Britt and I talked the situation through and decided to alert Funk's supporters. In the middle of all the rest of the work we were sweating over, we drafted an email, written as if it had come directly from Funk — which it basically did, since I edited it in his voice.

When I left Britt's office I didn't start back on my work. I prayed that our supporters would read the email we had just sent and *not* pick up their phones.

26 MARCH 2007

I COULDN'T TAKE all the darkness that had suddenly come into my world.

Here's the latest nasty. Not the nasty-nasty. The campaign nasty.

I had hit Send on *Notes from the DoubleWide* the previous Friday, highlighting our visit to the Green Duck. The press had never mentioned our newsletters before, yet now — probably by way of Mr. Brooks's campaign — they were having a cow that I wrote that the bar was located in the "black part of town."

I wasn't concerned but good Christ, Joe went nutso. "We're going to lose," he said, "for *sure* this time!"

Nothing would calm him down, not even the news about the media visiting the Green Duck neighborhood to ask residents how they felt about my "black part of town" phraseology. I'm pretty sure their question was meant to incite a riot. Sadly for them but good for us, residents were shown on TV wearing expressions that suggested the media were crazy for asking. They said of course it was the black part of town, what else would it be called? They told reporters to take a good look around because they wouldn't see a white face there except for their own. See, I told you Italians and Blacks are practically the same.

The committee decided to respond to this latest "scandal" by calling an impromptu press event. Funk was already committed to do a talk radio interview, so the press event had to wait until after he returned.

We drove to the radio station, using the speaker on my cell phone to listen to the Inner Circle develop the script Funk would use at the press event. By the time the plan solidified, I was mad at Joe for blowing things out of proportion. At least, that's what I was telling myself. I was still asking Funk questions as we entered the radio station.

"Funk, did I really just blow the election?"

"No."

"Is 'black part of town' a bad thing to say?"

"No."

"I thought being a racist meant you hated an entire group of people and only because of the country they emigrated from."

"That's correct."

"If that's true, then why is Brooks practically calling me a racist?"

"Glor, it's the same old same old. It's just directed at you now."

"No, Funk, that can't be. You don't toss a word like that around just to win an election!"

"Obviously they do, and we shouldn't rise to the bait."

"Don't be stupid, Funk. Brooks just purchased a lot of airtime. What if his campaign keeps repeating this shit on TV?"

"Gloria, calm down. You didn't toss — "

"I can't calm down!"

"Gloria — "

"Never mind. I'll calm down. There's nothing to do about it. I can't control what others say. Besides, who's gonna believe it? What racist sends her kids to schools that are 85 percent minority? None, I tell you. Those types have long-since jumped the fence to Prairie Village. But Funk, why, why, why, why, why . . . ?"

I'd never met Darla, our host, had never even heard of her radio show. When she overheard me asking Funk all those questions, when she saw how beside myself I was, she invited me to join the two of them in the recording booth.

I took her up on the gracious offer but didn't make a sound when she and Funk were on the air. I resumed my line of questioning during the many commercial breaks, but now my comments were directed at the two of them. Both believed the dust-up wouldn't amount to anything. They said I should stop worrying, that it was just a blip on the radar. Despite their comforting words, I still wrung my hands for the duration of the hour-long program.

Well, to be honest, I worried in-between prompting my husband to mention certain details of his platform, passing him notes so Darla's listeners didn't overhear. I had to because the guy still hadn't learned to plug himself when an opportunity presented itself.

I gave Darla a big hug when the show concluded and thanked her for her compassion, after which Funk and I beat it back to the trailer and he did the press event. I didn't get to listen to what he said because of all the reporters wanting to have side conversations with me. "Why did you say that?" "What did you mean by it?" "Do you have an issue with African Americans?" "How will you feel if this costs your husband the election?" "You're his campaign manager, shouldn't you know better?" *Me, his campaign manager? C'mon, not really.*

After the press event, Funk and I jumped into the van and I drove like a nut case to pick up Tara from the airport. And that's when my distress left me. Because gathered in our van was what was *really* important — our family. And our family did right in the world, regardless of whether others tried to misconstrue that truth.

So, bah to Mr. Brooks or to whoever had created the ruckus. I would not concern myself with it a moment longer, nor would I look for ways to get even. Karma would take care of it. And *scusi*, here's some advice about karma: the opposition could keep shakin' in their boots, looking around every corner waiting for karma to catch up with them, or they could simply change their lousy ways and move over to the serene way of life.

The choice was theirs. I just hoped they chose wisely because choices are important. Look what happened to me, after choosing Funk for a husband. Silk nowhere in sight. Yet there I was, married and with children, and nothing to do about it now.

Hey, I'm just trying to help. And I don't know why, given you're the opposition. Wait, what the hell is wrong with me? That isn't very Italian.

27 MARCH 2007

I COULDN'T BELIEVE IT. Election Day!

No one in my family had slept well. Just after dawn, Tara, Funk, and I gave it up and took our coffee to the porch until it was time to make ready for the big doings.

The polling place opened at seven a.m., and we planned on being at the doorstep when it did. We'd get voting out of the way before the rest of the day's activities swallowed us up. The polling place was just around the corner from our home but, given all the places we had to go afterward, we set out in the van to cast our votes. When we pulled up to the curb a small army of television cameras swarmed the van, which, let me tell you, was most unnerving.

They trained their cameras through the car windows at us. I had planned to glance in the mirror as I always do, but a lens was just outside my window, mere inches from my face. *My God, what could they possibly want? How interesting could it be to watch Funk's family cast their votes? Well, I suppose if I left the van without performing a body-check when I should have, it would play right into their hands. But I wasn't beholden to these guys for nothing, there was no way I was going to let that happen.* As inconspicuously as I could I gave Funk a once-over and flared my nostrils at him. After getting the all-clear I said, "Let's go." And the three of us slapped on happy faces and stepped into Funk's future.

The whole way to the voting booth we pretended cameras weren't tailing us. At least, I was hoping that a camera wasn't focused on my newly oversized ass.

With no voters present at this early hour, we were inside the voting booths in no time at all. It was strange to see the words "Mark Funkhouser" on the ballot. I stared at it for a while, and then I punched his name for mayor and pulled the curtain open. I held my ballot high in the air and made a great show of kissing it before slipping it into the ballot box with a flourish. The Italian cameraman I'd met on the campaign, the only one I liked playing around with, answered me with a wink.

Tara wanted to accompany us around town. Next up, Funk would greet employees as they filtered into city hall for the workday. Funk had worked there for eighteen years, so someone on the team suggested that going there to shake hands would be a good thing to do. I thought the idea was brilliant.

We careened off Southwest Trafficway, and who should be standing in a tiny strip of median but Crispin Rea? He was the cocky little college kid who sometimes volunteered at the trailer. He looked frantic. He practically leaped off the ground when he noticed the van, waving his arms, shouting something we couldn't hear. Funk waved back and, like one of Pavlov's trained dogs, continued on his path. I shoved an elbow into his rib and told him to stop and see what the kid needed.

Boy, was I ever sorry Funk followed my instruction.

With drivers leaning on their horns, giving us the finger as they roared around us, Funk brought the car to a stop and rolled his window down. I leaned across Funk, smiled in a motherly way, and said, "Is something wrong, Crispin?"

"I need some help out here!" he screamed, his face a mishmash of anger.

That didn't sit well with me. I was his elder; where were his manners? Withdrawing my warm maternal heart, I responded bluntly, "With what, exactly?"

He didn't notice the reduced emotion, just thundered louder, brasher, "Do you want us to lose? We need extra bodies out here! I'm the only one who is doing anything to get out the vote!"

Uh-oh. I guess the GOTV went the same as our Public Safety press event. Simon must not have made the arrangements.

I didn't reveal that information, just asked, "How do you know?"

"Because I know!" he wailed, waving one of Funk's yard signs at passersby.

I'm familiar with that answer. Crispin must be my son Andrew's brother. Funny thing, I didn't remember birthing this one.

"I don't know what help I can provide, but as soon as I get to the trailer, I'll think of something."

"You better, because — "

Poor Crispin didn't get to finish his sentence. Sensing that he'd miss his chance at city hall if he didn't get rolling, Funk interrupted, saying, "She'll work it out, Crispin. See you later!" and sped off.

"Daddy, wait! He wasn't finished talking."

"It's fine, Tara."

I turned in my seat and shrugged at my daughter. "This is how it's been, sis. Your father is a hick whose head has outgrown the van."

Looking back at Crispin in distress, she said, "But he needs. . . ."

Poor Tara. She didn't get to finish her sentence either, not with me cracking up the way I was.

Funk spent thirty minutes greeting colleagues and city hall employees — most of whom were suddenly shy around him. After that, we gunned it to the headquarters. Dottie came charging out of her cage when she heard us enter. She shoved a mile-long list into my hand, asking me to return the calls pronto. I told her I had to take care of another problem first. She seemed dismayed but let me go.

The phones were ringing wildly, so I had to wait for a line to stop blinking to call to get Crispin some relief. It was useless. The other volunteers said they were too hyped up to work outside the trailer. Chucking that idea, I went to Dottie's desk with the list she'd handed me.

"Dottie, I don't recognize a single name here. What's up?"

"Voters have been calling all morning, but they'll only speak with you."

"Why?"

"They wouldn't say. Just that it's urgent."

I didn't have time to get back to my office before another constituent called to speak with me. I ran to pick up the line and there I stayed, the phone cradled in my shoulder and Dottie's list in hand, listening to one person after another say there was a problem with the voting machines.

Those who had cast their vote electronically, upon reviewing their ballot, noticed the vote meant for Funk actually went to Alvin Brooks. When they tried correcting the error by carefully selecting Funk's name, the vote again went to Brooks.

After a few more people reported the exact same thing, I determined the problem was coming from one voting site in Midtown. I asked the next set of callers if they'd alerted the staff. Those who said they did were given a number to call to report it to the election board in Jefferson City. Which is why they were calling me. They wanted *me* to call. That bowled me over. Didn't they understand that wouldn't work? Who would believe an allegation like that coming from the candidate's wife? But to get them off the phone, I said I'd call. And I did. Twice.

I played it straight the first time. I explained who I was and why I was calling, and I could almost feel the lady's eyeballs rolling out of her head.

I used my cell phone the second time and didn't offer particulars, just pretended I was a concerned citizen.

Both times I received the expected answer. Nothing could be done. Not now. A formal complaint had to be filed. I hung up the phone and blew it off. I told myself we were winning this thing with or without the Midtown vote.

I can't believe how immune I'd become to underhanded campaign shenanigans. A year earlier I would've been railing to the gods about the injustice of it all. But now I was like, *Meh, who gives a shit?* I liked this New and Better Me. Well, I liked everything about it except my larger outline in the world. Damn Funk.

We drove from one end of the city to the other. At around four in the afternoon I called it a wrap. I said we needed to go home and rest. *Rest? Yeah, right.* But we did go home for a few hours, away from all the eyes and issues that wanted our attention.

At seven on the nut my family piled into the van — me at the wheel, Tara riding shotgun, and Funk and Ange buckled into the middle row. As I backed the van out of the driveway I saw, in my rearview mirror, Funk singing quietly to himself. He always sang when he was happy. And why shouldn't he be happy? Our family was together. We were all healthy. And he'd be realizing his dream in a few short hours.

The unusual thing was *what* he was singing. Funk had a distinct repertoire, and the current tune wasn't part of it.

> Hey, boys take me back
> I wanna ride in Geronimo's Cadillac
> Hey, boys take me back
> I wanna ride in Geronimo's Cadillac

I knew I'd heard the melody before, but I couldn't place the song. And then it came to me. I slammed on the brakes and my family shot forward in their seats, their necks stretching like rubber beyond the seat belts. The kids started screaming, "What the fuck, Mom!" and Funk got the Ginny-dog look about his face. But I ignored all that because I was screaming too, "Oh my God! It's a sign. Jesus! I've been wondering if we were getting a sign this time!"

"Fuck, Mom, seriously?" came the chorus from my beloved offspring.

I skipped over that.

"Christ, guys, didn't you hear what Dad was singing?"

"Don't care, Mom," came Andrew's teenaged reply.

I overlooked that as well. Just stared at my son in the rearview mirror and said, "It's 'Geronimo's Cadillac'! Get it?"

"No, Mom, we don't get it!" he said, speaking for him and his sister.

I turned in my seat to face my family.

"Are you guys dense or something? The Wolfs said if Dad won, they'd give him the Geronimo painting he admired in their home."

"Just spit it out, Mom," said Andrew, not very nicely.

"To hang in the mayor's office?" I said with a *duh* in my voice.

"Mahmmm!"

"Oh, c'mon, stop being such Midwesterners! You guys came out of my body. Like, the lips of my vagina slapped you in the face on the way out!"

"Ewww, Mom, you're so fucking gross!" came another horrified refrain from my kids, to which Andrew added, "And we didn't come out of your vagina. You had a C-section, remember?"

"Jesus! Why would you bring that painful subject up now?"

"Mahmmm! Just tell us what you're trying to say so we can go! We're gonna be late!"

"Here, let me paint it for you. When have you ever heard Dad sing that tune? Never, I tell you. It's a sign! God just as much as whupped us upside the head and said that Dad is going to win tonight."

It still didn't compute.

"The Wolfs are giving Dad their Geronimo painting. Dad is singing about Geronimo. *Now* do you get it?"

"No."

"Well, trust me, it's a sign."

"Can we go now, Glor?" said my husband, still rubbing the back of his neck.

Since it was his night, I said, "Sure" and resumed backing out of the driveway.

Soon I pulled the van into the parking lot at the Beaumont Club — not the Westport Flea Market. The committee and the Inner Circle had argued — and my husband and I were on the losing side — that Funk needed to spread the love around. Love? They wanted us to swap a business that our family had frequented for years for a club I'd never heard of until two weeks earlier. That sounded like disloyalty, not love. Whatever. Democracy prevailed. So there we were, walking into the Beaumont Club.

Unlike the primary, my throat didn't slam shut when I saw the crowd, even thought it was a billion times larger than the first watch party. I couldn't decide whether I was composed because I was a New and Better Me or if a thousand angels had been placed on standby without my knowledge. Whatever the reason, I was grateful that I was breathing normally and tunnel vision wasn't clouding my view.

It was dazzling to see how decked out the place was. There was orange everywhere! Orange balloons, orange banners, orange streamers, and hundreds of bodies clothed in orange "Funk for Mayor" t-shirts. It was wild and thrilling.

A neighbor who had arranged the decorations came up to us to ask if we liked her handiwork. I threw my arms around her and squealed yes, and then I oohed and aahed over everything. I had to pinch Funk on the tender part of his forearm to encourage him to participate, inflict pain on him just like my kindergarten teacher used to do to me to gain my attention. Thankfully, the gesture worked. Funk started oohing and aahing too. Okay, not really. He said, "It looks nice. Thanks."

I made the rounds, greeting our guests. One by one, I thanked everyone for coming, even the people I didn't know, which was about three-quarters of the room. Friends we hadn't seen in years were there. One couple who'd moved to a different neighborhood a dozen years earlier approached and acted as if we had just shared a beer on their porch the other night. The wife said her kids referred to Funk as Uncle Mark. Uncle Mark? We hadn't seen those kids since they were toddlers.

The welcoming took over an hour. When I returned to my little family circle, I found it was no longer our little circle. All the heavy-hitters were standing in a horseshoe around my husband, and people I'd never met before had their arms draped around his shoulders, pulling him close. And where were my children? Standing off to the side. Alone. Looking uncomfortable. Funk was so caught up with the folks crowding him — and with the others who were trying to squeeze themselves into his crowd — that he didn't notice.

I bustled over and pulled his ear down, whispering that he better get ahold of himself and act like a father. Awareness taking hold, Funk removed himself and went to stand with our kids. The crowd followed him, and the same thing happened again. My children were pushed aside.

Getting it up for them, I said brightly, "Oh, well. Dad is in work mode. I guess he'll be busy the rest of the night." The three of us stood across from him, not knowing what to do with ourselves. Actually, I had plenty to do, but I wouldn't leave my children in order to do it.

A reporter for the *Star*, Jeff Spivak, spotted me. He'd recently interviewed me at home, asking about my relationship with my husband. His questions had been far more intrusive than the ones the *Star* had asked back when they were pitting my family against Brooks's. Since Spivak had been sitting in one of my dining room chairs looking completely innocent, I didn't cringe when he pried into our lives. I answered his questions the way I normally do, with honesty and forthrightness.

I had to think for a minute before answering some of his questions. I finally told him that Funk was the first person to show me who I was and that he'd helped me see the woman I aspired to be. That he stayed by my side as I not-so-gracefully sorted out the darkness in the world. That he had been with me through various body sizes, without so much as a wayward glance. When I said that last part I teared up, couldn't talk anymore, and completely embarrassed myself. Luckily, Spivak was a good man. He said he had the same kind of relationship with his wife, which made me feel better for having revealed myself in such a weak way.

Anyhow, that was a really long way of saying that Spivak sidled up next to me at the party, wanting to show me his notebook. More specifically, he wanted to show me the calculations he had written there. With those numbers, he said, it was impossible for Funk to lose. And then he glanced around the room and hightailed it away, almost as if he didn't want to be seen with me. I wasn't able to process his information because Joe came bopping over to say hey to the kids. I wanted to tell him what Spivak had said — that Funk had already won — but something more burning took precedence.

"Joe, who are all those people mobbing Funk?"

He shifted his eyes to the horseshoe circling my husband and began naming names. He pointed first to a really girly-looking, short block of a man. Like, the guy had an ice cube-shaped body, and perched above it sat an incredibly round, flat, pale face. Tucked into the middle of all that were these red, red lips. I mean this guy's lips were so tiny and so puckered and so red — I think they're what people call rosebud lips — but whatever they're called, they were really creeping me out. They reminded me of Snow White's lips, but on a guy! I was half expecting to see little red slippers sheltering his delicate feet.

"That's Mike Sanders. You know him, right?"

"No, but I've heard Funk mention his name."

"He's the county executive."

"Is that supposed to explain something?"

"It's a significant position, Gloria."

"That's not what I mean. I don't recall him being part of the campaign."

"Oh! I get it. No, he wasn't part of the campaign, but it's really good that he's here."

"Why?"

"He's an important player around town."

I took that in, and Joe pointed to another person, "That's Henry Lyons."

To my blank stare, he added, "He's the head of the NAACP in Johnson County."

"Was *he* part of the campaign?"

"No, he wasn't either. But it's *super* good that he's here."

"Why?"

"Gloria, it just is."

"Over there is Dutch Newman. Do you see her? She's talking with Rita Valenciano. You remember Rita, right?

"The Little Tick's mother?" I asked, not sure I remembered correctly.

Joe belly-laughed upon hearing my nickname for Tony's of Kansas City and then offered the next person's name. "That's Berkley, the former mayor —"

I interrupted him because he just wasn't getting it. "Joe, this isn't what I mean. What I'm asking is, what are all these people doing here if they weren't part of the campaign?"

"I guess they're excited. They probably think Funk is going to win."

"But *why* are they excited if they weren't part of the campaign? And how did they even know where to find us if they haven't so much as received one of our newsletters?"

"I don't know, Gloria. But we're supposed to be having fun, so let's have fun!"

Joe left and I skimmed the room, noticing it was becoming more crowded. I knew I should make another circuit to greet the newcomers, but I couldn't. I felt too quiet. I needed to be with my kids — for their sake, but also for mine. I needed their loving energy to shore me up.

When I returned to them I tried making small talk, but they were quiet too. It felt as if we were on the verge of something life-altering. A game changer. Something big about to happen to our little unit.

Every now and again I'd peek around the room, being sure not to catch anyone's eye, as I knew they'd take it as an invitation to come over. The next time I got up the courage to look, my eyes went straight to Britt and Jeff. They were standing as close to Funk as it was possible to get, showing him a tiny piece of paper with big, shit-eating grins on their faces. Curious, I told the kids I'd be right back and walked over to them.

Turns out, Jeff and Britt knew someone at the election board. That someone said Funk could call it.

"Call it?" I asked, having no idea what that meant.

Jeff and Britt were beyond jubilant, so they didn't even mind answering me. They bent down and whispered enthusiastically, "Funk won the election!"

"Already!" I screamed back, just as enthusiastic.

They shushed me.

Lowering my voice, I said, "Wait a minute. How can that be when the numbers have just started coming in?"

Out popped more shit-eating grins and they replied in unison, "We just told you. We have a guy in there, and he knows!"

I thought, *Man, is there no end to the corruption in this city? It touches every single measly department.* When I rejoined the conversation, I found that it had moved on without me. Jeff and Britt were pressuring Funk to call it. Soon the media advanced and began pressuring Funk to call it too. Then some of the players Joe had just named came and said the same. Funk and I looked at each other and telepathically spoke, after which Funk said to the gathering, "I'm not calling it. It's too early." I followed that up, saying, "He's right. That wouldn't be a nice thing to do to Mr. Brooks." I quickly added, "Besides, what if we're wrong? That would be so embarrassing."

But our words fell into the word gutter of the world. Next thing you know, everyone engulfing Funk insisted that he needed to call it already! Thank God, he didn't. He waited a few more hours.

And he didn't call it then, either.

Funk and I headed over to where former mayor Berkley stood, to ask his opinion. Berkley said the race was sewn up, that it was safe to call it.

Funk still didn't call it.

Not before phoning Mr. Brooks. Holding one hand in the air, he extricated himself from the crowd that shadowed him, and he and I walked over to Tara and Andrew to tell them what was happening. Then Funk pulled his phone from his suit pocket and rang up Brooks. Brooks answered on the first ring. Funk thanked him for running an upright campaign and asked for his help going forward. That out of the way, Funk was ready to go onstage and call it.

Suddenly, all mayhem broke out. Where in the room it started, I couldn't tell. Why it started, I didn't know. The crowd let out the biggest roar I'd ever heard in an enclosed space, followed by arms flying up in the air and voices shouting, "We won, we won!"

I looked at the kids in stunned amazement and said, "Dad won?"

And my daughter, always one to notice me going down but finding it funny anyway, calmly replied, "Yes, Mama. Daddy won."

My son also noticed when I crumpled, but he didn't find it funny. It made him nervous. He moved closer and put a protective arm around my shoulder. I asked my daughter, "Tara, how do you know Dad won?"

"It just came across the television screen."

Hearing that, I wobbled a little and felt myself drift into tunnel vision. My son's protective arm got stronger, and noticing that, I got hold of myself. I started behaving like a mother. I would take care of my children, not the other way around. Knowing our family needed to stay tightly together, I looked over to Funk — only he wasn't there. I looked around and caught the tail end of Jeff and Britt whisking him up to the stage. Without us.

You don't want to know the thoughts that raced through my mind as fast as light travels. You wouldn't like me if I told you.

I'll tell you anyway.

I couldn't believe Funk was allowing himself to be dragged away from his family. He hadn't so much as given us a kiss upon hearing the news. Man, I would teach him a lesson. Any second now, I would grab my children and blow the joint. Wouldn't Funk be humiliated when someone asked for our whereabouts, and it showed on his face that he hadn't a clue? What kind of mayor would that be? He might as well forfeit to Brooks when that happened.

I was in the middle of planning my dramatic exit when tunnel vision suddenly cleared and my children's worried faces came into focus. They didn't know what was happening either. Didn't know what to make of it. Didn't know what they were supposed to be doing.

Holding tight to adulthood, I plastered as pretty a smile on my face as Mayor Barnes would've done in the same situation. I hid behind nice, just the way Midwesterners had taught me to do. Instead of marching my children out the side door, I grabbed their hands and led them onstage. There, I positioned one on either side of their father, even if they didn't stay put, preferring to drift to the wings of the stage. Once I had us settled, I turned my attention to what Jeff was saying at the mic.

With great personality and commanding presence, he preached, "They *laughed* that a bean counter thought he could run. They *laughed* when he told the truth at forums. They *laughed* when he spoke of tax incentives. They *laughed* that he thought he could win. They laughed at *him*." Pausing momentarily for effect, he pointed to the audience and shouted, "And they laughed at *us* for standing with him! Well, guess who's laughing now?

"I present Mark Funkhouser, the mayor of Kansas City!"

If the crowd had roared earlier, it was nothing like what came after Jeff spoke. It was as if the entire room had been transported back to the acid tests of the sixties, everyone at an orgy tripping their frigging brains out. It was that crazy loud! There was complete anarchy inside the club.

It was hard to stay angry with a presentation like that. I looked at Jeff with wonder and admiration, swept away by his words like everyone else. His speech had incited the riot of happiness that was taking place. Even the media, who weren't supposed to get too close, were taking part in the fun.

With perfect timing, Funk switched places with Simon, and I wondered how my husband would top Jeff's presentation. But my hick surprised me again. Top it he did. I was too blown away with emotion to comprehend his words. Too pulled away from a world that I sort of understood, already zooming toward a realm I knew nothing about. Too busy checking that my kids were okay. Too occupied with thinking how to make sure Funk remembered them, included them in his speech, and pulled them close when he introduced them.

I do recall the end of his speech. I understood those words clearly. Funk quoted Abraham Lincoln.

Standing in a beam of light, he grinned as he said, "A government of the people, by the people, for the people. That's not just elegant rhetoric. It's a damn good idea!"

And, oh my God! The roaring, the cheering, the screams of delight.

When the room quieted, Funk paraphrased Theodore Roosevelt, "To work hard at work worth doing is one of life's greatest joys." He added, "We're going to work hard, but it's going to be fun! Big fun! It'll be fun uncovering everything that's been hidden inside the bowels of city hall. Big fun sending the establishment packing. And it will be even more fun giving the city back to *you*!"

His words were followed by more hysterical fits of delight. It was madness. As if the place had become an incestuous fuck-fest!

Funk couldn't continue, for all the ecstasy taking place. He waited for the room to settle down but finally had to step around the podium and stand at the edge of the stage to get everyone to simmer down. They eventually did, yet as soon as he resumed his speech his cell phone began ringing. The crowd went wild again, crying at the hilarity of it.

I couldn't believe what Funk did next.

He actually stopped what he was saying and reached into his suit pocket, taking his cell phone out with one hand and shushing the crowd with the other.

The room went pin quiet.

Everyone just stood listening to my husband take a congratulatory call. When he hung up, someone from the audience shouted, "Who was it?" When Funk said he didn't know, there we went again, the whole place dissolving into raucous laughter.

Wrapping up, Funk thanked everyone for getting us to this place and bid them goodnight.

Many hours later, after circling the joint playing hostess to the enormous group, I stepped outside to get some fresh air. I was leaning against the van not doing anything, just dazed by the whole evening, when Anita Dixon sauntered up, saying something about how our visit to the Green Duck had pushed Funk across the finish line. I don't recall what I responded, only what I thought: *How crazy to think that one small blip created this outcome.* Luckily, I'd walked out of my home in diplomat mode, so I hugged Anita and thanked her again for arranging the evening at the Duck.

Hours later, Funk and I started for home. As he stuck the key in the car ignition, Funk's phone started ringing. It had never once stopped, not since that first call on stage. He paused and answered in that blunt way of his, "Mark Funkhouser."

And there, at two-thirty in the morning, Funk received his very first call from an Associated Press reporter. It was that quick that he entered the national stage.

Funk seeing his headquarters at the DoubleWide for the first time

Gloria at Funk's Coming-Out Party, giving the speech that wrote itself in Barcelona, Spain

Funk and our offspring

Slick and his band

Dots! (on the right)

Joe (photo courtesy of Sabrina Staires)

Kendrick (photo courtesy of Sabrina Staires)

Gwen (photo courtesy of Sabrina Staires)

Bill driving the little pink truck at the Saint Patrick's Day Parade in downtown Kansas City

The DoubleWide: Funk, Gloria, and volunteers at the "Funk Has No Friends" press event

The General Election: "Who the hell are all these people?"

The General Election: Jeff, Funk, and Britt (left to right)

What Just Happened?

FUNK AND I SLEPT until after seven. Passed out was more like it, at least for the first three hours. After that, I kept waking up every few minutes, because who could sleep? Each time I came to consciousness, a feeling came over me that something big had just happened. And then I'd remember. Oh yeah, something big *did* just happen. Majorly big! So big that I couldn't fathom the scope of it.

If those feelings hadn't roused me, the phone surely would've. Or phones, I should say: the house phone, Funk's cell phone, and my cell phone too — sometimes all three at once. It was mostly friends and family calling to congratulate us, but a lot of acquaintances were ringing us too. People from way back. Like, way, way, back. Sprinkled among them were a slew of calls from the media, many from across the United States. The reporters didn't want to speak just with Funk; some asked for me too. It was odd when Funk handed me the phone the first time. It was odder still to hear what the guy wanted to know, what all of them wanted to know: Was I really Funk's wife *and* his campaign manager? How did it feel to be responsible for winning the election?

To his first question, I said, "Yes, I'm Funk's wife, but I'm not really his campaign manager."

"I'm sorry. I was told you were. Can you give me the contact for who is?"

"Well, my husband didn't really have one."

"Oh, I thought he named you as his manager."

"I suppose I was, but only by default."

And that's when the questions really started flying.

"How did you know what to do if you didn't have experience running a campaign?" For some reason, the reporter wouldn't accept my answer — that I knew what to do because I'd read a book called *The Campaign Manager*. Like, a million times.

When I circled back to his second question — said it wasn't me who'd won the election, that my husband won it with the help of a ton of other people, including me — the reporter wouldn't accept that either. He just asked again if I was Funk's campaign manager, and we went around with that for a bit longer.

Because every phone in the house was ringing, I finally said I had to go.

The reporter signed off by giving me "a little insight." He said if I was my husband's campaign manager — even by default — I'd won the election for him.

I asked, "How so?"

He said, "Winning is always attributed to the manager. Losing is too."

"Really? I didn't know that! That's so amazing!" I replied. Because here I was, all this time, going on twelve hours now, I'd been thinking it was my husband who'd won, yet come to find, it was me and Anita Dixon all along! Oh, and La Raza. And the Ward Parkway Corridor. The Northland. Probably even the folks living in Johnson County, Kansas.

The phones blared for hours. Funk and I barely said goodbye to one person before another line was ringing. At around ten a.m. a snarling voice filtered down the hallway from my son's bedroom.

"Mom, I'm trying to sleep. Can you *please* take the phone off the hook?"

I thought to myself, *What a great idea!*

I remembered how I'd been longing for a break ever since we had returned home from Europe the previous summer. And that's when the tired crept into my bones. When the need for solitude from anyone who wasn't family became a demand from my body. When I realized, *Holy shit, we won!* I didn't have to rush into the trailer. There was nothing more to do. The campaign was finally over. I could stay right where I was. We had fucking won!

Even though I thought all that, I really couldn't process it.

I understood enough, though, to turn our cell phones off, after which I trotted downstairs to take the house phone off the hook, shoving it beneath a couch cushion so the beeping wouldn't disturb my son.

Funk followed me downstairs and got himself a bowl of cereal, and I started the coffee brewing. Once it was ready, we took everything out to the porch. As we settled into our rockers, one neighbor after the other waved and started a conversation with us from their front porch. All the while, a steady stream of cars went up and down our street, the passengers craning their necks. Once they saw Funk, they pretended they hadn't and sped away.

Finally, I couldn't take it anymore. I tilted my head at Funk, and we high-tailed it through the house and out to the back porch. Before long, the people in the houses behind ours needed to tend something in their gardens. Seeing that, I turned to my husband and said, "What the fuck?" and we retreated to the living room to talk in peace.

It had been a long time since we had sat on the couch together. Funk took his usual place in the seat nearest the front door, facing straight ahead looking at the fireplace, his feet propped on the coffee table. I sat in my usual spot, sideways, scooched down, leaning against the arm of the couch, my feet in his lap. I accidentally sat on the phone I had just placed beneath the cushion. With great effort, I crooked my tired ass to the side and took it out from under me.

Thankfully, the anger that had been smoldering inside me the previous night didn't bust loose from my body. I don't know what grace kept that awful feeling at bay — Funk being led onstage without his family, not even realizing what he was doing — to be sitting here now without scratching his eyes out.

But man, was I ever glad for it. Our family had worked so hard. We deserved this moment of happiness.

Clinging to the blessing, I said, "Well Funk, what should we talk about now that we don't have to think about the campaign anymore?"

Since the bastard was completely ignorant that he'd hurt his family's feelings, he chipperly said, "How about we talk about what a rock star you are?"

More grace. I ran with it. "Please, go on."

Before he had a chance to respond, I said, "No, wait a minute. It feels like forever since you've given me fifty-two reasons why you adore me. C'mon, big guy, let's have it."

Funk held his hand up and started ticking off the usual, "I adore you because you gave me our children. Made us a wonderful family. You make the holidays special. You always turn a simple sandwich into a magnificent meal . . ." and then he ended with something he'd never said before, "You helped me win the election."

That realization hitting me all over again, I said, "Oh my God, Funk, can you fucking believe it? We won! It's too much! I don't know what to do with myself."

"Yes, I can believe it. We worked our asses off."

"Jesus, we really did! But it was a lot of fun too. Honestly, I can hardly believe it!"

Both of us stupefied, Funk said, "Yes, it's quite amazing, darling."

We stayed quiet for a while, sipping our coffee, trying to soak everything in. I took a deep breath in and let it back out. The work was done. There was time to breathe again. It was finally over. We won. We actually fucking won!

I interrupted the stillness to say what popped into my head.

"Do you want to know something crazy, Funk? Last night Anita Dixon told me that she'd won the election for you."

"How?"

"By taking you to the Green Duck. She said that's what pushed you over the finish line. She said the East Siders had changed their votes from Alvin

Brooks to you after that visit. That the black vote that won the election. Weird, huh?"

"Yes. Very weird."

"And that reporter, the first guy I spoke with? He said it was me who'd won the election for you. Is that fucking crazy, or what? I guess you owe me bigtime, buddy!"

"It's true, Glor. In many ways, you won the election."

"That's ridiculous! Like, how? By reading a book and doing what it said? Any mom could've done that."

"No, it was the newsletter. You were the conduit from me to supporters."

"Yeah, and that's insane too. If I got a newsletter from someone I didn't know it would go straight in the trash. I would never read boring shit like that."

"The newsletters weren't boring, Glor. They were the same as our holiday newsletters — honest, intimate, and fun to read. People ate them up. I want you to keep writing them."

"Are you out of your mind?"

"No. I need to preserve the connection with constituents."

"Funk, I can't write the newsletters anymore. How would I know what to say?"

"You'd know what to say if you came up there."

"Up where?"

"To the twenty-ninth floor."

"What? I'm not fucking going up there!" *Uh-oh. Did I mention what happens when I make proclamations?*

"I know you're raring to get back to your own thing, but maybe just a couple of days a week? You said the campaign was fun. The mayor's office would be fun too."

"I don't know, Funk. It's too weird to even think about."

"Hey," screamed my son from his bedroom, "would you guys *please* be quiet?"

I hushed my voice and added, "I can't come up there, Funk. What would people say?"

My husband didn't whisper back, just spoke normally, not giving a small shit about our son's request.

"They'd say my campaign manager transitioned to the mayor's office, which usually happens."

"Are you shitting me?"

"No."

"Jesus! I didn't know I was so important."

Imagining the implications, I said, "Oh, no you don't, you're just saying that to get what you want again."

"No, Glor. It's a given that the campaign manager becomes the chief of staff."

"No way am I becoming your chief of staff, whatever that is."

"It's someone who tells the guy at city hall what to do."

"Oh, well, that's easy, I tell you what to do every day. But I'm not doing that up there."

"Okay. But what about part-time?"

"I don't know. Maybe. How about I try it, see if I like it?"

"Sounds good."

"Hey, I'm not promising anything. I said I'd try it. Don't pen me in."

"It will be a hoot. You'll want to stay."

Christ. That head. The first thing I needed to do was chisel it back down to size, not write another frigging newsletter.

My husband grabbed my foot and started rubbing it, the way he used to do before all the campaign business started.

"Would I need to tone the newsletters down?"

"No. I want them to stay the same."

We sipped our coffee, thinking solitary thoughts.

I don't know how much time passed before Funk turned in his seat and looked at me with the weirdest smirk on his face before letting out a laugh. His phony laugh. The short, forced one that sounds like "Hah!"

"What?" I asked, surprised by his sudden amusement.

I could see him imagining a scene I couldn't see. Tickled, he shook his head and smiled more broadly — maybe even a little mischievously, almost like he couldn't wait for something — and laughed again. For real this time.

"*What?*" I said.

"Oh, baby, they ain't *never* seen nothin' like you."

AUTHOR NOTES

JUNE 2022

IT'S BEEN SUCH STRANGE TIMES, for a long time now.

Politically, our country is deeply divided, and the pandemic has furthered that gulf. Both situations have contributed to the epidemic of loneliness that plagues our country. People are anxious, and some have gotten really mean.

Like many other people, I've experienced complete destruction in certain areas of my life — the parts that I've always considered the most important. As far as I can tell, the pandemic is a forced shift away from the way we've been doing things, and toward a New and Better Way of Existing. And not just in how we connect with each other, but with the Earth, spirit, and our ancestors.

I have the blessing of a barter. Except for travel expenses, I get to stay in a very remote location in Hawaii any time I want to go. In March 2022, I decided to isolate myself there for three months. It was the only way I could think of to try to comprehend the incomprehensible.

It was a self-imposed walk through the fire.

Each day, I found myself doing things and I had no idea why I was doing them. Fear intensified to crazy proportions. But soon, the ancestors came. And insights and messages filtered in. When I felt most alone, help arrived. Not the people I wanted the most, but still, I understood I wasn't alone. Turns out, the ones who came lit the way towards clarity and healing.

It was scary to dig that deep.

To be without human contact for most of every day. To learn how to cope with scorpions, gigantic spiders, poisonous centipedes — creatures come to test my mettle. Halfway through my visit, and without even noticing at first, I began finding my ground. Saw a glimmer of the best parts of my core personality returning.

At sixty-four years old, in many ways I still behave like a child. Each day my eyes blink awake feels like Christmas morning. I can't wait to see what the new day will bring. In this case, I can't wait to see if this book provided a laugh or two—more than anything else, that's what I'm hoping it will do. Offer a bit of relief at the end of your day.

A close second, I can't wait to see whether I've inspired anyone who is like me—afraid of their own shadow, or, as Funk says, is "a skydiver afraid of heights" — to reach for brave and grab the brass ring *despite* their throat-clenching fear. Through this book, have I encouraged you to dream big and go tits-to-the-world pursuing that dream, never allowing logistics to get in the way of seeing it through?

I'm beside myself to know if I've extended my reach beyond my childbirth classes. Have I inspired any women to claim their power? Have I helped to make the word *family* an important part of America's vocabulary again?

I'd love to know if I've motivated anyone to help finish the revolution that we started in the '60s. To try their hand at running a grassroots campaign, despite inexperience. Because, Lord knows, we really need that right now. Who among us wants the 1 percent to continue running our country?

Here's to you for not backing down in the face of all things incomprehensible. Giving up is easy. Toughing it out is by far the hardest.

ACKNOWLEDGMENTS

WTF IS WITH THIS PANDEMIC?

I wrote the last line of this book at 6:24 p.m. on June 24, 2016, in Long Beach, New York. The manuscript weighed in at a whopping 1,102 pages. I expected to publish it in the spring of 2020. I'm late getting it out the door because, for me, the pandemic began in 2016 with the unexpected passing of my beautiful sister Jane. That's when my world came crashing down.

Next went my brother Robert, also unexpectedly, in 2018.

In August 2019, Funk's magazine supposedly closed its doors, and he was unemployed for the first time in his life. To manage, he went into business for himself. For the first time. Ever. At sixty-nine years old. Without an entrepreneurial bone in his body.

Later that year, my mother died.

Then the Covid-19 pandemic came, in early 2020.

I picked myself up from each of those blows, until the Big Blow that came during the summer of 2020. I've been trying to lift my wobbling-ass up ever since.

Luckily, I've learned something in my sixty-four years on Earth: from out of the most horrible things, beautiful things arise.

When the Big Blow came, a few handfuls of people unexpectedly stepped up to help. I have an idealistic view of family, and they not only met that ideal, but they also made it impossible for me to keep to the notion that I am alone. If they hadn't circled the wagons, I don't know how I would have found my ground. May they never have need of the favor returned.

There are many in this category to thank.

First and foremost is Dennis Ryan, who has been my friend since I was twelve years old. When I was drowning, he reminded me of who I am. "Oh no, you don't. You're not going to second-guess yourself." Just typing his name chokes me up with love and gratitude. He is as good a brother as any.

Donna Gorman. "Gloria, you're crazy, but you're not that kind of crazy." Only a girl who I've known since I was five could say something like that and need say no more. My sister, forever.

Philipp Aichhorn, my exchange student from Austria. Pipo's concept of family is so closely aligned to mine that I don't know how he didn't come from my womb. His love and humor have been among my greatest joys. He is a good son.

Elvira Stalteri Noufal. I owe her so much. She put me back in the game of life, helping me believe I was more youthful and beautiful than I felt. A daughter of immigrant Italians, her perspective, humor, and knowing saved me on many occasions. I have no idea why she isn't my daughter.

Doug Brooks embodies the term *family doctor*, treating the mind, body, spirit, and emotion with competence, compassion, and love. He remains the only orthodox physician I trust.

My spiritual coming out began with Toby Evans in 1994. She's been friend, sister, and guide ever since. We are waaay out there. I hope everyone catches up to us soon.

Shelley Stelmach. If not for Shells, I'd be leading a greatly diminished life, and what a horror that would be. I have no adequate words to thank her for helping me become the woman I am today. That she found humor in my ungraceful journey has been a saving grace.

Sabin Bailey. Just saying her name brings a smile to my face. During my walk through the fire, each time I thought I'd turn to ashes or feared that I wasn't making progress getting a toehold back, there Sabin would be. Her love propelled me forward, and her words made sense of the inexplicable. "What happened shredded you, and you're trying to figure out how to put yourself back together." When I expressed my guilt over our lopsided relationship, she replied, "I'm attending a funeral with you. This is how it works." I can't imagine not having her in my life.

Ian Koviak is more than just the cover artist for my books. A man who "gets it" is a rarity. "I would gladly sit in prison so they could not benefit from a single penny from me. That is some low-ass shit." Ian has my heart.

Sue Norris. My college roommate. She knows me. The incredulous look on her face to my personality-in-action makes me laugh, and laughter is the thing I love most in the world.

Doug Mitchell. A man I've never met, yet without him I don't know how I would've unraveled from a fetal position. "Why isn't anyone white-knuckling this for you?" The question, exactly. More, he is the only Italian male who has ever treated me as an equal. I owe him an expensive-ass plane.

Angela Blueskies. I never heard of lineage healing before 2018, but once I did, I knew I had to do it. Angela helped me elevate my lines and kept me from thinking I was completely full of shit when relaying the images that came from our work together. More, she responded as a sister would to the Big Blow—and thank God for that.

My Italian ancestors. Great Ancestor, Lenora, Paulo, Serena, Belladonna. I can't believe I'm letting you out of the bag! Thank you for answering my call. For healing our lines. For keeping your promise to help me on the plane. For letting me know the healing is trickling down to this time. I don't know how I survived without being consciously aware of you.

Grandma Fucci. WTF was that crazy little dance? No matter. You made me laugh when I thought I'd die of heartbreak. Thank you for coming in so strong that I was able to see you. For birthing my mother. But honestly, what a handful she was!

Hawaii. Thank you for the womb tug. For the beauty and awe. The meaning of *aina*. For Pele. The ancestors who revealed themselves to me on this last trip. For letting me be on your island. For the deep healing you've brought me on each visit. You have my aloha forever, even if I don't fully understand the term.

I didn't have the first clue how to go about healing, and without a doubt, Candida DeLuise set me on the path. Feeling my sister's hands on my back is a wonder I'll never forget. And then, there's Pompei.

Reiko Mizutani is one of the few people I follow. She continues to teach me how to climb the wellness path. Long ago, she expanded my viewpoint of loyalty. "Gladia. They gave you life. Be grateful. Give, and don't expect anything back." Her words kept me from feeling like a chump, and now that my parents are gone, I have not a shred of regret for what I did or didn't do. That's a nice place to be. Reiko is family.

The Grateful Dead. I was only fourteen years old when I saw my first show at Watkins Glen. I still cannot believe my mother let me go! Their music delights me, and in dark moments, it helps advance my soul. Thank you for keeping yourselves healthy, for still walking the Earth.

Tina Sprinkle. Teense witnessed with love and compassion the tears that I rarely shed. I often wonder what lifetimes we've have had together, but I'm pretty sure one involved a machete.

Maria Charres. To borrow an expression, thank you for listening to my heart. You have mine.

Rosa Rodriguez. Thank you for being a loving friend.

I thank many others for their love, support, and for the production of this book.

Mom. In your last few years on Earth, you finally opened up! Expressed your heart. "I've been afraid all my life. It's time to grow up." You were ninety-three when you said that. You can't imagine how those words hit me. Another time, overhearing me not back down to the idiot in the hallway, you threw me one of your few crumbs. "Don't ever change." But first I had to endure, "Please shut your mouth, Gloria. He could have a gun and kill you." I smile on these small agonies now that you are gone. Thank you for waiting for me as you transitioned, for allowing me to witness your final breath. I'd midwifed many humans into this world, but I'd never midwifed any out. The wonder and beauty are the same.

Kevin Gorman. Somewhere in the middle of my "real family's" deaths, you also left us. I've never seen anyone so close to death have as much energy and zest for life as you did. The gift you gave me at the end is a marvel. "Gloria, you're the whackiest person I've ever known. Don't ever change." If you were trying to make me love you, you needn't have bothered. You had me with our frolics on your second-floor landing, even with your grandmother shaming me for participating. You will always be a brother to me.

To the volunteers, supporters, and donors of the Funk for Mayor Campaign. We won! We fucking won! We moved the Earth and made a difference. Thank you for letting me dance this dance with you.

Facebook friends and readers. Thank you for experiencing my heart on paper. There are many times that I've wished you couldn't resonate with heartbreaking scenes. All love to you.

Lisen Twigg-Smith. A large part of this book was written in Lisen and Des's home. Lisen didn't realize that lending me her home meant she'd get up-to-the minute reports on my ventures into the world "all by myself." Thank you for not letting me hear your eyes roll as I described my encounters with the creatures and the earthquake. For allowing me to experience paradise on Earth.

The Writers Room. During the pandemic, I joined a virtual writer's group. I stayed until the end of the first meeting because I didn't want to hurt anyone's feelings by leaving early. What trash! Until that night, I had no idea how talented the four women in my original group were. Candida DeLuise, Lisa Thompson, Sophy Burnham, and Frances Toler are some of the finest writers around, and though we are all past sixty, we remain sensual as all get-out. Thank you for resurrecting our group, for loving me, and for making me a better writer.

Catherine Shaw, author of the Campaign Manager (Campaign Manager needs italics). Without my campaign bible, aka, your book, there is no way I could've helped my husband become the mayor of Kansas City. My hope is that my work inspires others to run for office, using your work as the pathway to the win.

Tom Gray. Thank you for your outstanding professionalism. Most of all, thank you for your beautiful laugh.

Kansas City. Thank you again for allowing me to make a home in your home. As the years roll by, I feel your embrace more and more. This book wouldn't exist without you. And it certainly wouldn't be in print without Rush Rankin showing me that I was a writer or Sherry Sparks encouraging me with her stories about reading my words.

My birth students and doula clients. My God, the beauty you allowed me to witness! The holiness you allowed me to be immersed in. The body and soul you bared. Those experiences are an immense privilege that I still think of on most days. They pushed me toward the spiritual path I'm walking today, and that is a gift beyond measure.

The Ceil Place Gang. Dennis and Donald Ryan, Maria Charres, Donna Gorman, Kevin Fowler, Jim and Ann Marie Pumo, Alice and Shawn Gorman, Angela Ingoglia, Trudy Gorman, Hun Bun, Gene and Shari Caiola, Laura Mondeau, Brian Maginn, Frank Thomas. You have always been, and you will always be, family. A big thank-you goes to Gene for helping Funk start his new business. Funk wouldn't have gotten so far so fast without your guidance and support. And to those who have already left us. Kevin Gorman, Laurie Rooney, Fred Spinosa, Bill Elliot, and Judy Mezeul. My heart hurts that you're not here, and I'm still mad at you about it.

Andy Reed. My first-phase editor. Thank you for being gentle when taking a scalpel to my manuscript. For your friendship.

Jean Zimmer. My second-phase editor. Thank you for calming my nerves with the suggestion of weekly calls. I cannot wait to see how we do!

Denai Fuller. What crazy-ass experiences we've had! Thank you for believing, without me asking.

Darla Jaye. Thank you for the laughter, for sisterhood, and for continuing to walk the Earth.

Doug Carter. We've been in more jams together! Thank you for seeing them through.

To all the females in America who are trying to move us past the witch hunt that remains in progress. Please remember this truth: women are so sensual, so powerful, and so underrated. Eyes to the horizon until we beat this thing back.

And then there's Funk. In a category all to himself. What a ride! They tried to kill us so many times, yet here we are! Four feet, baby. We're wearing a groove into the same road, while we sometimes blessedly get to see the world. Thank you for thinking I'm all that. For your unconditional love.

BIOGRAPHY

Gloria Squitiro has a bachelor's degree in psychology. She is published in *Harper's Magazine* and is the author of the bestselling *May Cause Drowsiness and Blurred Vision: The Side Effects of Bravery*, the first in the three-book C'mon Funk memoir series. She has been married to Mark Funkhouser for forty-plus long-ass years. It seems Gloria's mission in life is to make every other man on Earth grateful he's not married to her.

Squitiro's personality type has changed! She is now an ENFJ: extroverted (not really!), iNtuitive (kind of stupid spelling), feeling, and judging. These types are idealistic and thoughtful and strive to have a positive impact on the world. They can't help but do the right thing, even when the doing is difficult.

In 2006, Gloria became Funk's campaign manager by default. She has the rare distinction of being the only First Lady to be legally banned from the city hall office where her husband was mayor. *Good Morning America*, *Fox and Friends*, *NPR*, *The Wall Street Journal*, the *New York Times*, *USA Today*, the *Washington Post* — even Great Britain's left-wing *Guardian* and — eww — America's right-wing *Rush Limbaugh* — reported stories about her.

They can throw her out, but they can't shut her up!

CONNECT

Please keep in touch
    gloriasquitiro.com
    facebook.com/gloria.squitiro
    facebook.com/gloriasquitiroauthor
    twitter.com/gloriasquitiro
    instagram.com/gloriasquitiroauthor
    linkedin.com/in/gloria-squitiro-6990aa70/

Subscribe to my newsletter
    Go to gloriasquitiro.com/subscribe for a humorous look at life, love, spirits, and politics. I offer real talk voiced through the perspective of an anxious mind.

I welcome you to post a review
    On amazon.com, search for "Gloria Squitiro"
    On goodreads.com, search for "Gloria Squitiro"

Made in the USA
Monee, IL
19 October 2025

32359573R00252